TIME-SERIES SALES
FORECASTING AND PREDICTION
USING MACHINE LEARNING
WITH TKINTER

VIVIAN SIAHAAN
RISMON HASIHOLAN SIANIPAR

Published: SEPT 2023
Production reference: 0409123
Published by BALIGE Publishing Ltd.
BALIGE, North Sumatera

ABOUT THE AUTHOR

Vivian Siahaan is a highly motivated individual with a passion for continuous learning and exploring new areas. Born and raised in Hinalang Bagasan, Balige, situated on the picturesque banks of Lake Toba, she completed her high school education at SMAN 1 Balige. Vivian's journey into the world of programming began with a deep dive into various languages such as Java, Android, JavaScript, CSS, C++, Python, R, Visual Basic, Visual C#, MATLAB, Mathematica, PHP, JSP, MySQL, SQL Server, Oracle, Access, and more. Starting from scratch, Vivian diligently studied programming, focusing on mastering the fundamental syntax and logic. She honed her skills by creating practical GUI applications, gradually building her expertise. One particular area of interest for Vivian is animation and game development, where she aspires to make significant contributions. Alongside her programming and mathematical pursuits, she also finds joy in indulging in novels, nurturing her love for literature. Vivian Siahaan's passion for programming and her extensive knowledge are reflected in the numerous ebooks she has authored. Her works, published by Sparta Publisher, cover a wide range of topics, including "Data Structure with Java," "Java Programming: Cookbook," "C++ Programming: Cookbook," "C Programming For High Schools/Vocational Schools and Students," "Java Programming for SMA/SMK," "Java Tutorial: GUI, Graphics and Animation," "Visual Basic Programming: From A to Z," "Java Programming for Animation and Games," "C# Programming for SMA/SMK and Students," "MATLAB For Students and Researchers," "Graphics in JavaScript: Quick Learning Series," "JavaScript Image Processing Methods: From A to Z," "Java GUI Case Study: AWT & Swing," "Basic CSS and JavaScript," "PHP/MySQL Programming: Cookbook," "Visual Basic: Cookbook," "C++ Programming for High Schools/Vocational Schools and Students," "Concepts and Practices of C++," "PHP/MySQL For Students," "C# Programming: From A to Z," "Visual Basic for SMA/SMK and Students," and "C# .NET and SQL Server for High School/Vocational School and Students." Furthermore, at the ANDI Yogyakarta publisher, Vivian Siahaan has contributed to several notable books, including "Python Programming Theory and Practice," "Python GUI Programming," "Python GUI and Database," "Build From Zero School Database Management System In Python/MySQL," "Database Management System in Python/MySQL," "Python/MySQL For Management Systems of Criminal Track Record Database," "Java/MySQL For Management Systems of Criminal Track Records Database," "Database and Cryptography Using Java/MySQL," and "Build From Zero School Database Management System With Java/MySQL." Vivian's diverse range of expertise in programming languages, combined with her passion for exploring new horizons, makes her a dynamic and versatile individual in the field of technology. Her dedication to learning, coupled with her strong analytical and problem-solving skills, positions her as a valuable asset in any programming endeavor. Vivian Siahaan's contributions to the world of programming and literature continue to inspire and empower aspiring programmers and readers alike.

Rismon Hasiholan Sianipar, born in Pematang Siantar in 1994, is a distinguished researcher and expert in the field of electrical engineering. After completing his education at SMAN 3 Pematang Siantar, Rismon ventured to the city of Jogjakarta to pursue his academic journey. He obtained his Bachelor of Engineering (S.T) and Master of Engineering (M.T) degrees in Electrical Engineering from Gadjah Mada University in 1998 and 2001, respectively, under the guidance of esteemed professors, Dr. Adhi Soesanto and Dr. Thomas Sri Widodo. During his studies, Rismon focused on researching non-stationary signals and their energy analysis using time-frequency maps. He explored the dynamic nature of signal energy distribution on time-frequency maps and developed innovative techniques using discrete wavelet transformations to design non-linear filters for data pattern analysis. His research showcased the application of these techniques in various fields. In recognition of his academic prowess, Rismon was awarded the prestigious Monbukagakusho scholarship by the Japanese Government in 2003. He went on to pursue his Master of Engineering (M.Eng) and Doctor of Engineering (Dr.Eng) degrees at Yamaguchi University, supervised by Prof. Dr. Hidetoshi Miike. Rismon's master's and doctoral theses revolved around combining the SR-FHN (Stochastic Resonance Fitzhugh-Nagumo) filter strength with the cryptosystem ECC (elliptic curve cryptography) 4096-bit. This innovative approach effectively suppressed noise in digital images and videos while ensuring their authenticity. Rismon's research findings have been published in renowned international scientific journals, and his patents have been officially registered in Japan. Notably, one of his patents, with registration number 2008-009549, gained recognition. He actively collaborates with several universities and research institutions in Japan, specializing in cryptography, cryptanalysis, and digital forensics, particularly in the areas of audio, image, and video analysis. With a passion for knowledge sharing, Rismon has authored numerous national and international scientific articles and authored several national books. He has also actively participated in workshops related to cryptography, cryptanalysis, digital watermarking, and digital forensics. During these workshops, Rismon has assisted Prof. Hidetoshi Miike in developing applications related to digital image and video processing, steganography, cryptography, watermarking, and more, which serve as valuable training materials. Rismon's field of interest encompasses multimedia security, signal processing, digital image and video analysis, cryptography, digital communication, digital forensics, and data compression. He continues to advance his research by developing applications using programming languages such as Python, MATLAB, C++, C, VB.NET, C#.NET, R, and Java. These applications serve both research and commercial purposes, further contributing to the advancement of signal and image analysis. Rismon Hasiholan Sianipar is a dedicated researcher and expert in the field of electrical engineering, particularly in the areas of signal processing, cryptography, and digital forensics. His academic achievements, patented inventions, and extensive publications demonstrate his commitment to advancing knowledge in these fields. Rismon's contributions to academia and his collaborations with prestigious institutions in Japan have solidified his position as a respected figure in the scientific community. Through his ongoing research and development of innovative applications, Rismon continues to make significant contributions to the field of electrical engineering.

This project leverages the power of data visualization and exploration to provide a comprehensive understanding of sales trends over time. Through an intuitive GUI built with Tkinter, users can seamlessly navigate through various aspects of their sales data.

The journey begins with a detailed visualization of the dataset. This critical step allows users to grasp the overall structure, identify trends, and spot outliers. The application provides a user-friendly interface to interact with the data, offering an informative visual representation of the sales records.

Moving forward, users can delve into the distribution of features within the dataset. This feature distribution analysis provides valuable insights into the characteristics of the sales data. It enables users to identify patterns, anomalies, and correlations among different attributes, paving the way for more accurate forecasting and prediction.

One of the central functionalities of this application lies in its ability to perform sales forecasting using machine learning regressors. By employing powerful regression models, such as Random Forest Regressor, KNN regressor, Support Vector Regressor, AdaBoost regressor, Gradient Boosting Regressor, MLP regressor, Lasso regressor, and Ridge regressor, the application assists users in predicting future sales based on historical data. This empowers businesses to make informed decisions and plan for upcoming periods with greater precision.

The application takes sales forecasting a step further by allowing users to fine-tune their models using Grid Search. This powerful optimization technique systematically explores different combinations of hyperparameters to find the optimal configuration for the machine learning models. This ensures that the models are fine-tuned for maximum accuracy in sales predictions.

In addition to sales forecasting, the application addresses the critical issue of customer churn prediction. It identifies customers who are likely to churn based on a combination of features and behaviors. By employing a selection of machine learning models and Grid Search such as Random Forest Classifier, Support Vector Classifier, and K-Nearest Neighbors Classifier, Linear Regression Classifier, AdaBoost Classifier, Support Vector Classifier, Gradient Boosting Classifier, Extreme Gradient Boosting Classifier, and Multi-Layer Perceptron Classifier, the application provides a robust framework for accurately predicting which customers are at risk of leaving.

The project doesn't just stop at prediction; it also includes functionalities for evaluating model performance. Users can assess the accuracy, precision, recall, and F1-score of their models, allowing them to gauge the effectiveness of their forecasting and customer churn predictions.

Furthermore, the application incorporates an intuitive user interface with widgets such as menus, buttons, listboxes, and comboboxes. These elements facilitate seamless interaction and navigation within the application, ensuring a user-friendly experience.

To enhance user convenience, the application also supports data loading from external sources. It enables users to import their sales datasets directly into the application, streamlining the analysis process.

The project is built on a foundation of modular and organized code. Each functionality is encapsulated within separate classes, promoting code reusability and maintainability. This ensures that the application is robust and can be easily extended or modified to accommodate future enhancements.

You can download the dataset from: http://viviansiahaan.blogspot.com/2023/09/time-series-sales-forecasting-and.html.

DESIGNING WINDOW WITH TKINTER — 1

Main Window — 1
Configuring Visual Style — 2
Creating Menu Bar — 3
Adding Button Widgets — 6
Adding Label Widgets — 7
Adding Canvas Widgets — 8
Adding Listbox Widget — 9
Adding Combobox Widgets — 10
Creating Form 1 — 12
Creating Form 2 — 13
Creating Form 3 — 14
Main Program — 15

PROCESSING DATA — 18

Reading Dataset — 18
Performing Data Transformations — 19
Creating Dummy Dataframe — 21
Normalizing Year-Wise Data — 22
Normalizing Month-Wise Data — 23
Performing RFM Analysis — 24
Identifying Churned Customers — 26
Encoding Categorical Data — 28
Feature Importance — 29
Saving Result of Model's Prediction — 31

SALES REGRESSION — 33

Splitting Data for Regression Model — 33
Loading Preprocessed Data Files — 36
Performing Regression — 37
Linear Regression — 39
Random Forest Regression — 40
Decision Tree Regression — 42
Gradient Boosting Regression — 43
Extreme Gradient Boosting Regression — 45
Multi-Layer Perceptron Regression — 47
Lasso Regression — 48

Ridge Regression	50
AdaBoost Regression	51
K-Nearest Neighbors Regression	53

PREDICTING CHURNED CUSTOMERS — **56**

Oversampling and Splitting Data for Prediction Model	56
Loading Files	59
Logistic Regression Prediction	60
Random Forest Prediction	63
K-Nearest Neighbors Prediction	65
Decision Tree Prediction	68
Gradient Boosting Prediction	70
Extreme Gradient Boosting Prediction	71
Multi-Layer Perceptron Prediction	73
Support Vector Prediction	74
AdaBoost Prediction	76

PLOTTING UTILITIES — **78**

Helper Plot Class	78
Showing Table	79
Missing Values	80
Pie Chart and Horizontal Bar Chart	82
Pie Chart and Horizontal Bar Chart of Grouped Dataframe	84
Stacked Bar Plot	85
Box Plot	87
Dataset Information	88
Statistical Description	89
The Count of Null Values	90
The Count of Null Values of Postal Code	92
Missing Values Before and After Filling	93
Case Distribution of Two Categorical Variables	94
Setting Up the Menu Options Related to Dataset Operations	95
Setting Up the Menu Options Related to Visualizing Distribution of Features	96
Window to Display Box Plot	98
Window to Display Categorized Distribution	98
Window to Visualize Grouped Distribution	99
Setting Up the Menu Options Related to Visualizing Categorized Distribution	100
Displaying Various Plots and Visualizations Based on the User's Selection	103
Line Plot of a Specific Feature	106
Line Plot of Normalized Data	108
Line Plot of Mean/EWM Data	109
Window to Display Line Plot of Feature	110
Window to Display Line Plot of Mean/EWM Data	111
Various Types of Plots	112
Window to Visualize Trends of Data	114
Setting Up the Menu Options Related to Year-Wise Analysis	115
Selecting Plotting Functions Related to Year-Wise Analysis	116

Line Plot of Month-Wise Data 117
Sales Data over the Months 118
Window to Visualize Sales Data on Month-Wise Basis 120
Monthly Sales Data for Different Regions over Time 121
Monthly Sales Quantity for Different Product Categories over Time 122
Monthly Sales Data for Different Segments over Time 123
Monthly Sales Data for Different Cities over Time 124
Monthly Sales Data for Different Shipping Modes over Time 126
Monthly Sales Data for Different Product Names over Time 127
Monthly Sales Data for Different Sub-Categories over Time 128
Windows to Visualize Monthly Sales Data of Specific Category 130
Setting Up the Menu Options Related to Month-Wise Analysis 133
Setting Up the Combobox Options Related to Month-Wise Analysis 136
Window to Visualize RFM Case Distribution 138
Window to Visualize RFM Grouped Distribution 139
Visualize Monthly Sales Based on Different Customer Segments 140
Setting Up the Menu Options Related to RFM Analysis 142
Setting Up the Combobox Options Related to RFM Analysis 143
Visualizing Random Forest Feature Importance 145
Visualizing Extra Trees Feature Importance 146
Visualizing Recursive Feature Elimination Feature Importance 147
Visualizing Correlation Coefficients 149
Visualizing Correlation Matrix 150
Setting Up the Menu Options Related to Feature Importance 152
Actual versus Predicted Values of a Regression Model 153
Regression Model's Performance 155
Performing Various Regression Models 157
Visualizing Confusion Matrix and ROC 161
Visualizing Learning Curve and True Values versus Predicted Values of a Classifier 162
Predicting Churn Customers Using Machine Learning Classifier 164

PLOTTING THE RESULTS **168**
Completing the Main Class 161
The Result of Viewing Dataset 173
The Result of Case Distribution 174
The Result of Sales Distribution 179
The Result of Year-Wise Sales Distribution 186
The Result of Month-Wise Sales Distribution 189
The Result of RFM Analysis 194
The Result of Feature Analysis 198
The Result of Regression 200
The Result of Prediction 202

Full Source Code 206

Bibliography 266

DESIGNING WINDOW
WITH TKINTER

Main Window

Open a new python file and name it as main_window.py. In it, create a class named Main_Window:

```python
#main_window.py
import tkinter as tk
from tkinter import ttk
from matplotlib.figure import Figure
from matplotlib.backends.backend_tkagg import FigureCanvasTkAgg

class Main_Window:
```

This code is the beginning of the script for creating a graphical user interface (GUI) using the Tkinter library. Tkinter is a built-in Python module that provides a set of tools for creating windows, widgets, and handling events in a graphical application. The script starts by importing the necessary modules. tkinter is imported as tk, and the ttk submodule is imported separately. tkinter is the standard Python interface to the Tk GUI toolkit, which is widely used for creating desktop applications with graphical interfaces. ttk provides themed widgets that have a more modern and consistent look across different platforms.

The script also imports components related to matplotlib, a popular Python library for creating static, animated, and interactive visualizations. Specifically, it imports the Figure class, which represents a single figure in a matplotlib plot, and FigureCanvasTkAgg, which is a Tkinter-compatible canvas for displaying Figure objects. This indicates that the GUI might include some form of graphical plotting or visualization.

The class Main_Window is defined but currently empty. It's common in object-oriented programming to define a class for the main application window. This class will contain methods and attributes to set up the GUI components, handle user interactions, and manage any backend logic associated with the application.

Configuring Visual Style

In Main_Window class, define a new method named set_style(). It is responsible for configuring the visual style of the GUI components using the ttk module from Tkinter. This method takes two arguments: self (which refers to the instance of the class) and root (presumably the main window).

```python
def set_style(self, root):
    # variables created for colors
    ebg = '#404040'
    fg = '#FFFFFF'

    style = ttk.Style()

    # Be sure to include this or style.map() won't function as expected.
    style.theme_use('alt')

    # the following alters the Listbox
    root.option_add('*TCombobox*Listbox.Background', ebg)
    root.option_add('*TCombobox*Listbox.Foreground', fg)
    root.option_add('*TCombobox*Listbox.selectBackground', fg)
    root.option_add('*TCombobox*Listbox.selectForeground', ebg)

    # the following alters the Combobox entry field
    style.map('TCombobox', fieldbackground=[('readonly', ebg)])
    style.map('TCombobox', selectbackground=[('readonly', ebg)])
    style.map('TCombobox', selectforeground=[('readonly', fg)])
    style.map('TCombobox', background=[('readonly', ebg)])
    style.map('TCombobox', foreground=[('readonly', fg)])
```

Here's a breakdown of what this method does:
1. It defines two color variables, ebg and fg, which represent background and foreground colors, respectively. These are specified as hexadecimal color codes.
2. It creates an instance of ttk.Style() which allows customization of the appearance of widgets.
3. It sets the theme to be used by calling style.theme_use('alt'). This is setting a specific theme for the widgets. The 'alt' theme is a built-in alternative theme provided by ttk.
4. Several root.option_add() calls are made to adjust the appearance of the Listbox inside the Combobox widget. These calls are using patterns to target specific elements of the Combobox.
   - *TCombobox*Listbox.Background: Sets the background color of the listbox.

- *TCombobox*Listbox.Foreground: Sets the foreground (text) color of the listbox.
- *TCombobox*Listbox.selectBackground: Sets the background color of the selected item in the listbox.
- *TCombobox*Listbox.selectForeground: Sets the foreground (text) color of the selected item in the listbox.

5. The style.map() calls customize the appearance of the Combobox entry field. They are using the fieldbackground and selectbackground options to set the background color for different states of the Combobox (in this case, when it's in a 'readonly' state, which means the user can't directly edit it).

6. Similar to step 5, style.map() is used to adjust the text and background colors for the Combobox entry field in various states (e.g., 'readonly').

Overall, this method is focused on customizing the visual style of specific components in the GUI, particularly Comboboxes, to give them a specific look and feel based on the defined color variables.

Creating Menu Bar

In Main_Window class, define a new method named add_menu(). It is responsible for creating a menu bar with various cascading menus in the GUI. This method takes two arguments: self (which refers to the instance of the class) and root (the main window).

```python
def add_menu(self, root):
    self.menu_bar = tk.Menu(root)

    #Creates a Dataset menu
    self.dataset_menu = tk.Menu(self.menu_bar, tearoff=0)
    self.dataset_menu.add_command(label="View Dataset")
    self.dataset_menu.add_command(label="Dataset Information")
    self.dataset_menu.add_command(label="Statistical Description")
    self.dataset_menu.add_command(label="Null Values")
    self.dataset_menu.add_command(label="Postal Code Null Values")
    self.menu_bar.add_cascade(label="About Dataset", menu=self.dataset_menu)

    #Creates a feature distribution menu
    self.dist_menu = tk.Menu(self.menu_bar, tearoff=0)
    self.dist_menu.add_command(label="Missing Values")
    self.dist_menu.add_command(label="Day and Month")
    self.dist_menu.add_command(label="Quarter and Year")
    self.dist_menu.add_command(label="Country and City")
    self.dist_menu.add_command(label="State and Region")
    self.dist_menu.add_command(label="Customer Name and Customer ID")
    self.dist_menu.add_command(label="Ship Mode and Segment")
    self.dist_menu.add_command(label="Product Name and Product ID")
    self.dist_menu.add_command(label="Category and Sub-Category")
    self.menu_bar.add_cascade(label="Features Distribution", menu=self.dist_menu)
```

```python
        #Creates category distribution menu
        self.dist_cat = tk.Menu(self.menu_bar, tearoff=0)
        self.dist_cat.add_command(label="Sales by Year and Quarter")
        self.dist_cat.add_command(label="Sales by Day and Month")
        self.dist_cat.add_command(label="Sales by Ship Mode and Segment")
        self.dist_cat.add_command(label="Sales by Category and Sub-Category")
        self.dist_cat.add_command(label="Sales by Product Name and Product ID")
        self.dist_cat.add_command(label="Sales by Customer Name and Customer ID")
        self.dist_cat.add_command(label="Sales by City and State")
        self.dist_cat.add_command(label="Categorized Sales")
        self.dist_cat.add_command(label="Categorized Sales by Year and Quarter")
        self.dist_cat.add_command(label="Categorized Sales by Day and Month")
        self.dist_cat.add_command(label="Categorized Sales by Segment and Sub-
Category")
        self.dist_cat.add_command(label="Categorized Sales by Region and State")
        self.dist_cat.add_command(label="Day versus Sales Per Category")
        self.dist_cat.add_command(label="Month versus Sales Per Segment")
        self.dist_cat.add_command(label="Sub-Category versus Sales Per Year")
        self.dist_cat.add_command(label="Region versus Sales Per Quarter")
        self.menu_bar.add_cascade(label="Categorized Distribution",
menu=self.dist_cat)

        #Creates year-wise distribution menu
        self.year_wise = tk.Menu(self.menu_bar, tearoff=0)
        self.year_wise.add_command(label="Year-Wise Sales Distribution 2015 and
2016")
        self.year_wise.add_command(label="Year-Wise Sales Distribution 2017 and
2018")
        self.year_wise.add_command(label="Year-Wise Sales Mean and EWM")
        self.year_wise.add_command(label="Sales by Year")
        self.year_wise.add_command(label="Sales by Quarter")
        self.year_wise.add_command(label="Sales by Month")
        self.year_wise.add_command(label="Sales by Day")
        self.year_wise.add_command(label="Sales by Week")
        self.menu_bar.add_cascade(label="Year-Wise Distribution",
menu=self.year_wise)

        #Creates month-wise distribution menu
        self.month_wise = tk.Menu(self.menu_bar, tearoff=0)
        self.month_wise.add_command(label="Sales Quarter 1 and 2 Year 2018")
        self.month_wise.add_command(label="Sales Quarter 3 and 4 Year 2018")
        self.month_wise.add_command(label="Sales Quarter 1 and 2 Year 2017")
        self.month_wise.add_command(label="Sales Quarter 3 and 4 Year 2017")
        self.month_wise.add_command(label="Sales Quarter 1 and 2 Year 2016")
        self.month_wise.add_command(label="Sales Quarter 3 and 4 Year 2016")
        self.month_wise.add_command(label="Sales Quarter 1 and 2 Year 2015")
        self.month_wise.add_command(label="Sales Quarter 3 and 4 Year 2015")
        self.month_wise.add_command(label="Sales Month 1 and 2 Year 2018")
        self.month_wise.add_command(label="Sales Month 3 and 4 Year 2017")
        self.month_wise.add_command(label="Sales Month 5 and 6 Year 2016")
        self.month_wise.add_command(label="Sales Month 7 and 8 Year 2015")
        self.month_wise.add_command(label="Month-Wise Sales Mean and EWM")
        self.month_wise.add_command(label="Sales by Month")
        self.month_wise.add_command(label="Region-Based Monthly Sales")
        self.month_wise.add_command(label="Category-Based Monthly Quantities")
        self.month_wise.add_command(label="Segment-Based Monthly Sales")
        self.month_wise.add_command(label="City-Based Monthly Sales")
```

```python
        self.month_wise.add_command(label="Ship Mode-Based Monthly Sales")
        self.month_wise.add_command(label="Product Name-Based Monthly Sales")
        self.month_wise.add_command(label="Sub-Category-Based Monthly Sales")
        self.menu_bar.add_cascade(label="Month-Wise Distribution",
menu=self.month_wise)

        #Creates RFM distribution menu
        self.rfm_analysis = tk.Menu(self.menu_bar, tearoff=0)
        self.rfm_analysis.add_command(label="Customer Segment")
        self.rfm_analysis.add_command(label="Sales by Customer Segment")
        self.rfm_analysis.add_command(label="Customer Segment by Year and Quarter")
        self.rfm_analysis.add_command(label="Customer Segment by Day and Month")
        self.rfm_analysis.add_command(label="Customer Segment by Segment and Sub-
Category")
        self.rfm_analysis.add_command(label="Customer Segment by Region and State")
        self.rfm_analysis.add_command(label="RFM-Based Monthly Sales")
        self.menu_bar.add_cascade(label="RFM and Product Analysis",
menu=self.rfm_analysis)

        #Creates feature engineering
        self.feat_eng = tk.Menu(self.menu_bar, tearoff=0)
        self.feat_eng.add_command(label="Correlation Matrix")
        self.feat_eng.add_command(label="Correlation Coefficients")
        self.feat_eng.add_command(label="Random Forest Feature Importance")
        self.feat_eng.add_command(label="Extra Trees Feature Importance")
        self.feat_eng.add_command(label="RFE Feature Importance")
        self.menu_bar.add_cascade(label="Feature Importance", menu=self.feat_eng)

        root.config(menu=self.menu_bar)
```

Here's an overview of what this method does:

1. It creates a menu bar using tk.Menu(root) and assigns it to the instance variable self.menu_bar.
2. It creates several sub-menus within the menu bar, each containing a list of commands (menu items) related to specific functionalities or categories. For example, the first sub-menu is named "About Dataset" and contains commands like "View Dataset", "Dataset Information", etc. Each sub-menu is created as an instance of tk.Menu.
3. For each sub-menu, a series of add_command() calls are made to add specific menu items to the sub-menu. These menu items are the labels of the commands that will be displayed to the user. For example, self.dataset_menu.add_command(label="View Dataset") adds an item with the label "View Dataset" to the "About Dataset" sub-menu.
4. The sub-menus are added to the main menu bar using self.menu_bar.add_cascade(label="Label", menu=sub_menu).
5. This process is repeated for several other categories of functionality, creating a hierarchical menu structure.
6. Finally, root.config(menu=self.menu_bar) is used to configure the main window root to use the created menu bar.

Overall, this method sets up an extensive menu structure with various categories and associated commands, providing the user with a range of options for interacting with the application.

Adding Button Widgets

In Main_Window class, define a new method named add_buttons(). The purpose of this method is to create and position buttons within the graphical user interface (GUI) using the Tkinter library:

```python
def add_buttons(self, root):
    #Adds button
    self.btn_load = tk.Button(root, height=2, width=35, text="LOAD DATASET")
    self.btn_load.grid(row=0, column=0, padx=5, pady=5, sticky="w")

    self.btn_reg = tk.Button(root, height=2, width=35, text="SPLIT DATA FOR
FORECASTING")
    self.btn_reg.grid(row=9, column=0, padx=5, pady=5, sticky="w")

    self.btn_pred = tk.Button(root, height=2, width=35, text="SPLIT DATA FOR
PREDICTION")
    self.btn_pred.grid(row=12, column=0, padx=5, pady=5, sticky="w")
```

Here's the explanation of what this code does:
1. Creating Buttons:
    - Three buttons are created using the tk.Button widget.
    - Each button is assigned to an instance variable (self.btn_load, self.btn_reg, and self.btn_pred) for later reference within the class.
2. Button Properties:
    - Each button is given specific properties:
        - height=2: The button has a height equivalent to two lines of text.
        - width=35: The button has a fixed width of 35 characters.
        - text="...": The text displayed on the button. This describes the action or purpose of the button.
3. Button Placement:
    - The grid() method is used to position the buttons within the window.
    - For example, self.btn_load.grid(row=0, column=0, padx=5, pady=5, sticky="w") places the "LOAD DATASET" button in the first row (row 0) and first column (column 0) of the grid layout.
    - The padx and pady arguments add padding (space) around the button to improve visual appearance.
    - sticky="w" ensures that the button sticks to the west (left) side of its cell in the grid.
4. Button Labels:

The text on each button ("LOAD DATASET", "SPLIT DATA FOR FORECASTING", "SPLIT DATA FOR PREDICTION") indicates the intended action when the button is clicked.

These buttons serve as interactive elements for the user to trigger specific actions or operations within the application. For example, "LOAD DATASET" would initiate the process of loading a dataset, and the other two buttons are involved in data splitting for forecasting and prediction tasks.

Overall, this method adds buttons to the GUI, providing a user-friendly way to interact with the application's functionalities.

Adding Label Widgets

In Main_Window class, define a new method named add_labels().

```python
def add_labels(self, root):
    #Adds labels
    self.label1 = tk.Label(root, text = "CHOOSE DISTRIBUTION")
    self.label1.grid(row=1, column=0, padx=5, pady=1, sticky="w")

    self.label2 = tk.Label(root, text = "YEAR-WISE TIME-SERIES PLOT")
    self.label2.grid(row=3, column=0, padx=5, pady=1, sticky="w")

    self.label3 = tk.Label(root, text = "MONTH-WISE TIME-SERIES PLOT")
    self.label3.grid(row=5, column=0, padx=5, pady=1, sticky="w")

    self.label4 = tk.Label(root, text = "RFM ANALYSIS")
    self.label4.grid(row=7, column=0, padx=5, pady=1, sticky="w")

    self.label5 = tk.Label(root, text = "CHOOSE FORECASTING")
    self.label5.grid(row=10, column=0, padx=5, pady=1, sticky="w")

    self.label6 = tk.Label(root, text = "CHOOSE PREDICTION")
    self.label6.grid(row=13, column=0, padx=5, pady=1, sticky="w")
```

The add_labels() method in the Main_Window class is responsible for creating and positioning labels in the graphical user interface (GUI). Labels are static elements that provide textual information or descriptions to guide users within the application.

In this method, six labels are instantiated and associated with the tk.Label widget. Each label is assigned a specific text, describing a category or action. For instance, "CHOOSE DISTRIBUTION" suggests an option for selecting a distribution-related feature. The labels are then placed within the grid layout of the window using the grid method. The parameters row and column determine the position of each label, while padx and pady add some padding around the label for better visual spacing. Additionally, sticky="w" ensures that each label adheres to the left side of its grid cell.

Overall, these labels serve as informative elements, helping users understand the purpose of associated functionalities or options in the GUI. They provide clear indications of the available choices and guide users in navigating and interacting with the application effectively. For example, labels like "YEAR-WISE TIME-SERIES PLOT" provide context for specific actions a user might take related to time-series data analysis.

Adding Canvas Widgets

In Main_Window class, define a new method named add_canvas():

```python
def add_canvas(self, root):
    #Menambahkan canvas1 widget pada root untuk menampilkan hasil
    self.figure1 = Figure(figsize=(6.2, 7.6), dpi=100)
    self.figure1.patch.set_facecolor('#F0F0F0')
    self.canvas1 = FigureCanvasTkAgg(self.figure1, master=root)
    self.canvas1.get_tk_widget().grid(row=0, column=1, columnspan=1,
        rowspan=25, padx=5, pady=5, sticky="n")

    #Menambahkan canvas2 widget pada root untuk menampilkan hasil
    self.figure2 = Figure(figsize=(6.2, 7.6), dpi=100)
    self.figure2.patch.set_facecolor('#F0F0F0')
    self.canvas2 = FigureCanvasTkAgg(self.figure2, master=root)
    self.canvas2.get_tk_widget().grid(row=0, column=2, columnspan=1,
        rowspan=25, padx=5, pady=5, sticky="n")
```

It is responsible for adding two canvas widgets to the graphical user interface (GUI) using the Tkinter library. A canvas widget provides a drawable area that can be used for rendering graphical elements like plots or charts.

Here's the explanation of what this code does:
1. Creating Figures:
   Two Figure objects (self.figure1 and self.figure2) are created. These objects represent the canvas where plots or visualizations will be drawn. Each figure has a specified size and dpi (dots per inch) for rendering.
2. Setting Figure Background Color:
   - self.figure1.patch.set_facecolor('#F0F0F0') and self.figure2.patch.set_facecolor('#F0F0F0') set the background color of the figures. The color is specified using a hexadecimal code, in this case, a light grayish color.
3. Creating Canvas Widgets:
   Two FigureCanvasTkAgg objects (self.canvas1 and self.canvas2) are created. These objects serve as the bridge between the matplotlib figures and the Tkinter GUI.

4. Placing Canvas Widgets:
   - The grid() method is used to position the canvas widgets within the window.
   - For example, self.canvas1.get_tk_widget().grid(row=0, column=1, columnspan=1, rowspan=25, padx=5, pady=5, sticky="n") places the first canvas in the first row (row 0) and second column (column 1) of the grid layout. The columnspan and rowspan parameters determine how many columns and rows the widget should span. The padx and pady arguments add padding around the canvas, and sticky="n" ensures that the canvas sticks to the north (top) side of its cell.

Overall, this method adds two canvas widgets to the GUI, providing areas where visualizations or plots can be displayed. The figures are associated with these canvas widgets, allowing for dynamic updates of the displayed content.

Adding Listbox Widgets

In Main_Window class, define a new method named add_listboxes():

```python
def add_listboxes(self, root):
    #Creates list widget
    self.listbox = tk.Listbox(root, height=15, selectmode=tk.SINGLE, width=40,
        fg ="black", bg="#F0F0F0",
        highlightcolor="black", selectbackground="red",relief="flat",
        borderwidth=5, highlightthickness=0)
    self.listbox.grid(row=2, column=0, sticky='n', padx=5, pady=1)

    self.scrollbar_v = tk.Scrollbar(root,
orient="vertical",command=self.listbox.yview)
    self.scrollbar_v.grid(row=2, column=0, sticky='nse')

    self.scrollbar_h = tk.Scrollbar(root,
orient="horizontal",command=self.listbox.xview)
    self.scrollbar_h.grid(row=2, column=0, sticky='ews')

    self.listbox.config(yscrollcommand=self.scrollbar_v.set,
xscrollcommand=self.scrollbar_h.set)

        # Menyisipkan item ke dalam list widget
    items = ["Missing Values",
            "Year", "Day",
            "Month", "Quarter",
            "Country and City",
            "State and Region",
            "Customer Name and Customer ID",
            "Ship Mode and Segment",
            "Product Name and Product ID",
            "Category and Sub-Category",
            "Sales by Year and Quarter",
```

```
                "Sales by Day and Month",
                "Sales by Ship Mode and Segment",
                "Sales by Category and Sub-Category",
                "Sales by Product Name and Product ID",
                "Sales by Customer Name and Customer ID",
                "Sales by City and State",
                "Categorized Sales by Year and Quarter",
                "Categorized Sales by Day and Month",
                "Categorized Sales by Segment and Sub-Category",
                "Categorized Sales by Region and State"]
    for item in items:
        self.listbox.insert(tk.END, item)
```

The add_listboxes() method creates a listbox widget in the graphical user interface (GUI) using Tkinter. A listbox is a UI element that allows users to select from a list of options. In this method, a listbox is created with specific attributes, including its height, width, select mode, foreground and background colors, and more. The listbox is then positioned in the GUI using the grid ()method, specifying its row and column placement. Additionally, both vertical and horizontal scrollbars are added to the listbox, allowing users to navigate through the list if the content exceeds the visible area. These scrollbars are linked to the listbox's view so that they interact together. Finally, a list of items is inserted into the listbox. Each item represents an option that a user can select, covering various data analysis categories.

Overall, this method sets up a functional listbox within the GUI, enhancing user interactivity by providing a convenient way to make selections from a predefined list of data analysis options. The inclusion of scrollbars ensures that users can explore the entire list even if it extends beyond the visible area of the listbox.

Adding Combobox Widgets

In Main_Window class, define a new method named add_comboboxes():

```
def add_comboboxes(self, root):
    # Create ComboBoxes
    self.combo_year = ttk.Combobox(root, width=38)
    self.combo_year["values"] = ["Year-Wise Sales Distribution 2017 and 2018",
        "Year-Wise Sales Distribution 2015 and 2016",
        "Year-Wise Sales Mean and EWM",
        "Normalized Year-Wise Data"]
    self.combo_year.grid(row=4, column=0, padx=5, pady=1, sticky="n")

    self.combo_month = ttk.Combobox(root, width=38, style='TCombobox')
    self.combo_month["values"] = ["Sales Quarter 1 and 2 Year 2018",
        "Sales Quarter 3 and 4 Year 2018",
        "Sales Quarter 1 and 2 Year 2017",
        "Sales Quarter 3 and 4 Year 2017",
        "Sales Quarter 1 and 2 Year 2016",
        "Sales Quarter 3 and 4 Year 2016",
```

```python
                "Sales Quarter 1 and 2 Year 2015",
                "Sales Quarter 3 and 4 Year 2015",
                "Month-Wise Sales Mean and EWM",
                "Sales by Month",
                "Region-Based Monthly Sales",
                "Category-Based Monthly Quantities",
                "Segment-Based Monthly Sales",
                "City-Based Monthly Sales",
                "Ship Mode-Based Monthly Sales",
                "Product Name-Based Monthly Sales",
                "Sub-Category-Based Monthly Sales"]
        self.combo_month.grid(row=6, column=0, padx=5, pady=1, sticky="n")

        self.combo_rfm = ttk.Combobox(root, width=38, style='TCombobox')
        self.combo_rfm["values"] = ["Customer Segment",
                "Sales by Customer Segment",
                "Customer Segment by Year and Quarter",
                "Customer Segment by Day and Month",
                "Customer Segment by Segment and Sub-Category",
                "Customer Segment by Region and State",
                "RFM-Based Monthly Sales"]
        self.combo_rfm.grid(row=8, column=0, padx=5, pady=1, sticky="n")

        self.combo_reg = ttk.Combobox(root, width=38, style='TCombobox')
        self.combo_reg["values"] = ["Linear Regression", "RF Regression",
                "Decision Trees Regression", "KNN Regression",
                "AdaBoost Regression", "Gradient Boosting Regression",
                "MLP Regression", "SVR Regression", "Lasso Regression", "Ridge
Regression"]
        self.combo_reg.grid(row=11, column=0, padx=5, pady=1, sticky="n")

        self.combo_pred = ttk.Combobox(root, width=38, style='TCombobox')
        self.combo_pred["values"] = ["Logistic Regression", "Random Forest",
                "Decision Trees", "K-Nearest Neighbors",
                "AdaBoost", "Gradient Boosting",
                "Extreme Gradient Boosting", "Light Gradient Boosting",
                "Multi-Layer Perceptron", "Support Vector Classifier"]
        self.combo_pred.grid(row=14, column=0, padx=5, pady=1, sticky="n")
```

It creates and configures five combobox widgets within the graphical user interface (GUI) of the application. Each combobox provides a dropdown menu of options for the user to select, with each option representing a specific type of data analysis or regression method.

For example, self.combo_year is the first combobox created. It is configured to have a width of 38 characters. The list of values it offers for selection includes options related to year-wise sales distribution and normalization. This combobox is placed in the fourth row and first column of the GUI grid layout. It's also set to stick to the top of its cell.

Next, self.combo_month is the second combobox. It has the same width and additional styling with a custom style ('TCombobox'). This combobox provides options for selecting various aspects of sales data, including sales by quarter, month, and region-based quantities. It is placed in the sixth row and first column of the grid layout.

The third combobox, self.combo_rfm, is similar in configuration but offers options related to customer segments and RFM-based monthly sales. It is positioned in the eighth row and first column.

Following that, self.combo_reg and self.combo_pred are the fourth and fifth comboboxes, respectively. They present options for selecting regression methods, including linear regression, decision trees regression, and various others. They are placed in the eleventh and fourteenth rows, both in the first column.

Overall, the add_comboboxes() function sets up a user-friendly interface by providing dropdown menus that allow the user to choose from a range of data analysis and regression options, enhancing the versatility and functionality of the application.

Creating Form 1

The script creates a graphical user interface (GUI) using the Tkinter library. It defines a class called Form1 that serves as the foundation for the GUI. The main application window is set to have dimensions of 1520 pixels in width and 760 pixels in height.

Within the Form1 class, there is a method named add_canvas() which is responsible for adding canvases to the GUI. It creates two frames, frame1 and frame2, which serve as containers for the canvases. These frames are configured with a border of 3 pixels and a "groove" relief style.

For each canvas, a Figure object is created from the Matplotlib library. These figures are set to be 7.4x7.4 inches in size with a resolution of 100 dots per inch (dpi). The background color of the figures is a light gray shade (#F0F0F0). The canvases themselves are instances of FigureCanvasTkAgg and are associated with the respective frames.

The script also contains a conditional block that checks if this module is being run directly. If so, it creates an instance of the Tkinter Tk class to create the main application window. It then creates an instance of the Form1 class, setting up the GUI with the defined canvases. Finally, it starts the main event loop with window.mainloop(), which keeps the GUI running and responsive to user interactions.

```python
#form1.py
import tkinter as tk
from tkinter import ttk
from matplotlib.figure import Figure
from matplotlib.backends.backend_tkagg import FigureCanvasTkAgg

class Form1:
```

```python
    def __init__(self, window):
        self.window = window
        width = 1520
        height = 760
        self.window.geometry(f"{width}x{height}")

        #Adds canvasses
        self.add_canvas(self.window)

    def add_canvas(self, master):
        # Create a frame for canvas1 with a border
        frame1 = ttk.Frame(master, borderwidth=3, relief="groove")
        frame1.grid(row=0, column=0, columnspan=1, rowspan=25, padx=5, pady=5,
sticky="n")

        # Adds canvas1 widget to frame1
        self.figure1 = Figure(figsize=(7.4, 7.4), dpi=100)
        self.figure1.patch.set_facecolor('#F0F0F0')
        self.canvas1 = FigureCanvasTkAgg(self.figure1, master=frame1)
        self.canvas1.get_tk_widget().pack(fill=tk.BOTH, expand=True)

        # Create a frame for canvas2 with a border
        frame2 = ttk.Frame(master, borderwidth=3, relief="groove")
        frame2.grid(row=0, column=1, columnspan=1, rowspan=25, padx=5, pady=5,
sticky="n")

        # Adds canvas2 widget to frame2
        self.figure2 = Figure(figsize=(7.4, 7.4), dpi=100)
        self.figure2.patch.set_facecolor('#F0F0F0')
        self.canvas2 = FigureCanvasTkAgg(self.figure2, master=frame2)
        self.canvas2.get_tk_widget().pack(fill=tk.BOTH, expand=True)

if __name__ == "__main__":
    window = tk.Tk()
    Form1(window)
    window.mainloop()
```

Creating Form 2

The Python script defines a class named Form2 that creates a graphical user interface (GUI) using the Tkinter library. Similar to Form1, it sets up a main application window with specified dimensions of 1300 pixels in width and 500 pixels in height.

Inside the Form2 class, there is an __init__() method which initializes an instance of the class. Within this method, a scrolled text widget is created using the ScrolledText class from the tkinter.scrolledtext module. This widget allows for the display of multiline text and provides a scrollbar for navigation. The wrap=tk.WORD argument ensures that text wraps at word boundaries. The background color of the text widget is set to a light gray shade (#F0F0F0).

The text widget is then packed using the pack method, allowing it to expand and fill both the horizontal and vertical directions within the main application window.

Additionally, there is a conditional block at the end of the script that checks if this module is being run directly. If so, it creates an instance of the Tkinter Tk class to create the main application window. It then creates an instance of the Form2 class, setting up the GUI with the scrolled text widget. Finally, it starts the main event loop with window.mainloop(), which keeps the GUI running and responsive to user interactions.

```python
#form2.py
import tkinter as tk
from tkinter import ttk
from matplotlib.figure import Figure
from matplotlib.backends.backend_tkagg import FigureCanvasTkAgg
from tkinter import scrolledtext

class Form2:
    def __init__(self, window):
        self.window = window
        width = 1300
        height = 500
        self.window.geometry(f"{width}x{height}")

        self.text = scrolledtext.ScrolledText(self.window, wrap=tk.WORD,
bg="#F0F0F0")
        self.text.pack(expand=True, fill='both')

if __name__ == "__main__":
    window = tk.Tk()
    Form2(window)
    window.mainloop()
```

Creating Form 3

The Python script defines a class named Form3 which sets up a graphical user interface (GUI) using the Tkinter library. This class creates a main application window with specific dimensions of 1520 pixels in width and 760 pixels in height.

Inside the Form3 class, there is an __init__() method which initializes an instance of the class. Within this method, a frame named frame1 is created using the ttk.Frame class. This frame has a border with a width of 3 pixels and a relief style set to "groove". It is then placed in the main application window using the grid method.

Inside frame1, a figure named self.figure1 is created using the Figure class from the matplotlib.figure module. This figure has a specified size of 15 inches in width and 7.4 inches in height, with a DPI (dots per inch) setting of 100. The background color of the figure is set to a light gray shade (#F0F0F0).

Next, a canvas widget (self.canvas1) is added to frame1 using FigureCanvasTkAgg. This widget embeds the figure within the frame. It is configured to fill both the horizontal and vertical directions, allowing it to expand as needed. The canvas widget is then packed.

Finally, there is a conditional block at the end of the script that checks if this module is being run directly. If so, it creates an instance of the Tkinter Tk class to create the main application window. It then creates an instance of the Form3 class, setting up the GUI with the framed canvas widget. The main event loop is started with window.mainloop(), which keeps the GUI running and responsive to user interactions.

```python
#form3.py
import tkinter as tk
from tkinter import ttk
from matplotlib.figure import Figure
from matplotlib.backends.backend_tkagg import FigureCanvasTkAgg

class Form3:
    def __init__(self, window):
        self.window = window
        width = 1520
        height = 760
        self.window.geometry(f"{width}x{height}")

        #Adds canvasses
        self.add_canvas(self.window)

    def add_canvas(self, master):
        # Create a frame for canvas1 with a border
        frame1 = ttk.Frame(master, borderwidth=3, relief="groove")
        frame1.grid(row=0, column=0, columnspan=1, rowspan=25, padx=5, pady=5,
sticky="n")

        # Adds canvas1 widget to frame1
        self.figure1 = Figure(figsize=(15, 7.4), dpi=100)
        self.figure1.patch.set_facecolor('#F0F0F0')
        self.canvas1 = FigureCanvasTkAgg(self.figure1, master=frame1)
        self.canvas1.get_tk_widget().pack(fill=tk.BOTH, expand=True)


if __name__ == "__main__":
    window = tk.Tk()
    Form3(window)
    window.mainloop()
```

Main Program

The script main_sales.py contains a class named Main_Sales and a conditional block that starts the application when the script is run directly.

The Main_Sales class is initialized with the __init__() method. Within this method, the application window's dimensions are set to a width of 1560 pixels and a height of 790 pixels using the geometry method. Additionally, the title of the window is set to "TIME-SERIES SUPERSTORE SALES FORECASTING AND PREDICTION USING MACHINE LEARNING" using the title method.

Next, an instance of the Main_Window class is created using self.obj_window = Main_Window(). This suggests that Main_Window is a separate class or module that is imported and used to manage the main window's widgets.

Finally, the add_widgets() method from Main_Window is called to place the necessary widgets in the root window. This method is presumably responsible for adding buttons, labels, and other UI elements to the application.

The conditional block at the end of the script checks if the module is being run directly (as opposed to being imported as a module in another script). If it is being run directly, it creates an instance of the Tkinter Tk class to create the main application window. It then creates an instance of the Main_Sales class, initializing the GUI. The main event loop is started with root.mainloop(), which keeps the GUI running and responsive to user interactions.

```python
#main_sales.py
import os
import pandas as pd
import tkinter as tk
from tkinter import *
from main_window import Main_Window

class Main_Sales():
    def __init__(self, root):
        #super().__init__()
        self.initialize()

    def initialize(self):
        self.root = root
        width = 1560
        height = 790
        self.root.geometry(f"{width}x{height}")
        self.root.title("TIME-SERIES SUPERSTORE SALES FORECASTING AND PREDICTION
USING MACHINE LEARNING")

        #Creates necessary objects
        self.obj_window = Main_Window()

        #Places widgets in root
        self.obj_window.add_widgets(self.root)

if __name__ == "__main__":
    root = tk.Tk()
    app = Main_Sales(root)
```

```
    root.mainloop()
```

Run main_sales.py. You will see the designed window as shown in figure 1.1.

Figure 1.1 The designed window using Tkinter

PROCESSING DATA

Open a new python file and name it as process_data.py. In it, create a class named Process_Data:

```python
#process_data.py
import os
import pandas as pd
from datetime import datetime
import numpy as np
from sklearn.preprocessing import LabelEncoder
from sklearn.ensemble import RandomForestClassifier, ExtraTreesClassifier
from sklearn.linear_model import LogisticRegression
from sklearn.feature_selection import RFE

class Process_Data:
```

The Python script process_data.py is a class for data processing and includes several libraries for this purpose. It starts by importing the necessary modules, such as os for interacting with the operating system, pandas for data manipulation, datetime for working with dates and times, numpy for numerical operations, and various components from the scikit-learn library for machine learning tasks.

Within the file, a class named Process_Data is defined. This class is responsible for encapsulating methods and operations related to data processing. The class contains functionality for handling data transformation, encoding categorical variables, and performing feature selection using machine learning algorithms.

Then, in the class, define a new method named read_dataset(). It is responsible for reading a dataset from a specified file:

```python
def read_dataset(self, filename):
    #Reads dataset
    curr_path = os.getcwd()
    path = os.path.join(curr_path, filename)
    df = pd.read_csv(path)

    return df
```

Here's the explanation of the code:

1. def read_dataset(self, filename):: This line defines a method named read_dataset() within the Process_Data class. The method takes two parameters: self (which is a reference to the current instance of the class) and filename (the name of the file to be read).
2. curr_path = os.getcwd(): This line retrieves the current working directory using the os.getcwd() function and assigns it to the variable curr_path. The current working directory is the directory from which the Python script is being executed.
3. path = os.path.join(curr_path, filename): This line uses the os.path.join() function to combine the current working directory (curr_path) with the provided filename. This creates the complete path to the dataset file.
4. df = pd.read_csv(path): This line uses the pandas library to read the dataset from the specified file path (path). It assumes that the dataset is in a CSV (Comma Separated Values) format. The resulting DataFrame is assigned to the variable df.
5. return df: Finally, the method returns the DataFrame (df) containing the dataset.

In summary, the read_dataset() method takes a filename as input, constructs the complete file path, reads the dataset from that file, and returns it as a Pandas DataFrame. This allows for further processing and analysis of the data within the Python script.

Performing Data Transformations

In the Process_Data class, define a new method named preprocess(). It performs various data transformations, including date extraction, type conversion, column removal, sorting, and filling missing values, to prepare the dataset for further analysis:

```python
def preprocess(self):
    df = self.read_dataset("train.csv")

    #Extracts day, month, week, quarter, and year from order date
    df['Date'] = pd.to_datetime(df['Order Date'], format="%d/%m/%Y")
    df['Day'] = df['Date'].dt.weekday
    df['Month'] = df['Date'].dt.month
    df['Year']  = df['Date'].dt.year
    df['Week'] = df['Date'].dt.isocalendar().week
    df['Quarter']= df['Date'].dt.quarter

    #Sets Date column as index
```

```python
df = df.set_index("Date")

#Converts data types to datetime
df['Order Date'] = pd.to_datetime(df['Order Date'], format="%d/%m/%Y")
df['Ship Date'] = pd.to_datetime(df['Ship Date'], format="%d/%m/%Y")

# Drop columns
df = df.drop(['Row ID'],axis=1)

# Sort values by order date
df.sort_values('Order Date', ascending=True, inplace=True)

# Fillna values in 'Postal Code' with correct postal code
df2 = df.copy()
df2['Postal Code'] = df['Postal Code'].fillna(5401)

return df, df2
```

Below is the explanation of each step:

1. df = self.read_dataset("train.csv"): This line calls the read_dataset() method to read a dataset from a file named "train.csv". The resulting DataFrame is stored in the variable df.

2. Date Extraction:

   - df['Date'] = pd.to_datetime(df['Order Date], format="%d/%m/%Y"): This line converts the 'Order Date' column to datetime format and creates a new column named 'Date' containing the datetime values.

   - df['Day'] = df['Date'].dt.weekday: This line extracts the day of the week (0 for Monday, 1 for Tuesday, and so on) from the 'Date' column and stores it in a new column named 'Day'.

   - df['Month'] = df['Date'].dt.month: This line extracts the month from the 'Date' column and stores it in a new column named 'Month'.

   - df['Year'] = df['Date'].dt.year: This line extracts the year from the 'Date' column and stores it in a new column named 'Year'.

   - df['Week'] = df['Date'].dt.isocalendar().week: This line extracts the week number of the year from the 'Date' column and stores it in a new column named 'Week'.

   - df['Quarter']= df['Date'].dt.quarter: This line extracts the quarter of the year from the 'Date' column and stores it in a new column named 'Quarter'.

3. df = df.set_index("Date"): This line sets the 'Date' column as the index of the DataFrame. This is often done to facilitate time-series analysis.

4. Date Data Type Conversion:

   - df['Order Date'] = pd.to_datetime(df['Order Date'], format="%d/%m/%Y"): This line converts the 'Order Date' column to datetime format using the specified date format.

   - df['Ship Date'] = pd.to_datetime(df['Ship Date'], format="%d/%m/%Y"): Similarly, this line converts the 'Ship Date' column to datetime format.

5. Column Removal and Sorting:
   - df = df.drop(['Row ID'],axis=1): This line removes the 'Row ID' column from the DataFrame.
   - df.sort_values('Order Date', ascending=True, inplace=True): This line sorts the DataFrame by the 'Order Date' column in ascending order.
6. Filling Missing Values:
   - df2 = df.copy(): This line creates a copy of the DataFrame df named df2.
   - df2['Postal Code'] = df['Postal Code'].fillna(5401): This line fills missing values in the 'Postal Code' column with the value 5401.
7. Finally, the method returns two DataFrames, df and df2.

Creating Dummy Dataframe

In the Process_Data class, define a new method named create_dummy(). It is responsible for creating a modified DataFrame df_dummy for visualization purposes:

```python
def create_dummy(self, df):
    #Creates a dummy dataframe for visualization
    df_dummy=df.copy()

    #Converts days and months from numerics to meaningful string
    days = {0:'Sunday',1:'Monday',2:'Tuesday',3:'Wednesday',
            4:'Thursday',5: 'Friday',6:'Saturday'}
    df_dummy['Day'] = df_dummy['Day'].map(days)

    months={1:'January',2:'February',3:'March',4:'April',
            5:'May',6:'June',7:'July',8:'August',9:'September',
            10:'October',11:'November',12:'December'}
    df_dummy['Month']= df_dummy['Month'].map(months)

    quarters = {1:'Jan-March', 2:'April-June',3:'July-Sept',
                4:'Oct-Dec'}
    df_dummy['Quarter'] = df_dummy['Quarter'].map(quarters)

    #Categorizes Sales feature
    labels = ['0-10', '10-20',  '20-50', '50-100', '100-150', '150-200','250-300','300-400', '>400']
    df_dummy['Cat_Sales'] = pd.cut(df_dummy['Sales'],
        [0, 10, 20, 50, 100, 150, 200, 250, 300, 400], labels=labels)

    return df_dummy
```

Here's the explanation of each step:

1. df_dummy=df.copy(): This line creates a copy of the original DataFrame df to prevent any modifications from affecting the original data.
2. Days and Months Conversion:
    - days and months are dictionaries that map numeric representations of days (0 to 6) and months (1 to 12) to their corresponding meaningful strings (e.g., Sunday, January).
    - df_dummy['Day'] = df_dummy['Day'].map(days): This line replaces the numeric representation of days in the 'Day' column with their corresponding string representation.
    - df_dummy['Month']= df_dummy['Month'].map(months): Similarly, this line replaces the numeric representation of months in the 'Month' column with their corresponding string representation.
3. Quarter Categorization:
    - quarters is a dictionary that maps numeric representations of quarters (1 to 4) to meaningful strings (e.g., Jan-March).
    - df_dummy['Quarter'] = df_dummy['Quarter'].map(quarters): This line replaces the numeric representation of quarters in the 'Quarter' column with their corresponding string representation.
4. Sales Categorization:
    - labels is a list of labels representing different sales categories based on predefined ranges (e.g., '0-10', '10-20').
    - df_dummy['Cat_Sales'] = pd.cut(df_dummy['Sales'], [0, 10, 20, 50, 100, 150, 200, 250, 300, 400], labels=labels): This line creates a new column 'Cat_Sales' in df_dummy by categorizing the 'Sales' values into predefined bins based on the specified ranges and assigning the corresponding label.
5. Finally, the modified DataFrame df_dummy is returned. This DataFrame is now ready for visualization, with certain columns transformed for easier interpretation and analysis.

Normalizing Year-Wise Data

In the Process_Data class, define a new method named normalize_year_wise_data(). It is responsible for normalizing the year-wise sales data:

```python
def normalize_year_wise_data(self, df):
    #Normalizes year-wise data
    year_data_mean = df["Sales"].resample('y').mean()
    year_data_ewm = year_data_mean.ewm(span=5).mean()
    year_norm = (year_data_mean - year_data_mean.min()) / (year_data_mean.max() - year_data_mean.min())

    return year_data_mean, year_data_ewm, year_norm
```

Here's the explanation of each step:

1. year_data_mean = df["Sales"].resample('y').mean(): This line first extracts the 'Sales' column from the DataFrame df. It then uses the resample function to group the data by year ('y') and calculates the mean sales value for each year. This results in a new time series of annual mean sales values.

2. year_data_ewm = year_data_mean.ewm(span=5).mean(): Here, the exponentially weighted moving average (EWMA) of the year-wise mean sales data is computed. The ewm function applies exponential smoothing to the time series, with a span of 5. This helps in reducing noise and emphasizing trends.

3. year_norm = (year_data_mean - year_data_mean.min()) / (year_data_mean.max() - year_data_mean.min()): This line performs min-max normalization on the year-wise mean sales data. It scales the values to fall within the range of 0 to 1, making them more comparable.

4. Finally, the method returns three pieces of information: year_data_mean (the original year-wise mean sales data), year_data_ewm (the exponentially weighted moving average), and year_norm (the normalized year-wise sales data). These values can be used for further analysis and visualization.

Normalizing Month-Wise Data

In the Process_Data class, define a new method named normalize_month_wise_data(). It performs normalization on the month-wise sales data:

```python
def normalize_month_wise_data(self, df):
    month_data_mean = df["Sales"].resample('m').mean()
    month_data_ewm = month_data_mean.ewm(span=5).mean()

    month_norm = (month_data_mean - month_data_mean.min()) / 
(month_data_mean.max() - month_data_mean.min())

    return month_data_mean, month_data_ewm, month_norm
```

Here's how it works:

1. month_data_mean = df["Sales"].resample('m').mean(): This line extracts the 'Sales' column from the DataFrame df. It then uses the resample function to group the data by month ('m') and calculates the mean sales value for each month. This results in a new time series of monthly mean sales values.

2. month_data_ewm = month_data_mean.ewm(span=5).mean(): Similar to the year-wise data, this line computes the exponentially weighted moving average (EWMA) of the month-wise mean sales data. The ewm function applies exponential smoothing with a span of 5, which helps in reducing noise and highlighting trends.

3. month_norm = (month_data_mean - month_data_mean.min()) / (month_data_mean.max() - month_data_mean.min()): This line performs min-max normalization on the month-wise mean sales data. It scales the values to fall within the range of 0 to 1, making them more comparable.

4. Finally, the method returns three pieces of information: month_data_mean (the original month-wise mean sales data), month_data_ewm (the exponentially weighted moving average), and month_norm (the normalized month-wise sales data). These values can be used for further analysis and visualization.

Performing RFM Analysis

In the Process_Data class, define a new method named calculate_RFM(). It is used to perform RFM (Recency, Frequency, Monetary) analysis on customer data.

```python
def calculate_RFM(self, df, df_dummy):
    # Calculating recency
    recency_df = df.groupby('Customer Name', as_index=False)['Order Date'].max()
    recent_date = recency_df['Order Date'].max()
    recency_df['Recency'] = recency_df['Order Date'].apply(
        lambda x: (recent_date - x).days)
    recency_df.rename(columns={'Order Date':'Last Purchase Date'}, inplace=True)

    # Calculating Frequency
    frequency_df = df.groupby('Customer Name', as_index=False)['Order
Date'].count()
    frequency_df.rename(columns={'Order Date':'Frequency'}, inplace=True)

    # Calculating monetary
    monetary_df = df.groupby('Customer Name', as_index=False)['Sales'].sum()
    monetary_df.rename(columns={'Sales':'Monetary'}, inplace=True)

    # Merging all three df in one df
    rfm_df = recency_df.merge(frequency_df, on='Customer Name')
    rfm_df = rfm_df.merge(monetary_df, on='Customer Name')
    rfm_df['Monetary'] = rfm_df['Monetary'].round(2)
    rfm_df.drop(['Last Purchase Date'], axis=1, inplace=True)

    rank_df = rfm_df.copy() # We make copy of rfm_df because we will need RFM
features later

    # Normalizing the rank of the customers
    rank_df['r_rank'] = rank_df['Recency'].rank(ascending=False)
    rank_df['f_rank'] = rank_df['Frequency'].rank(ascending=False)
    rank_df['m_rank'] = rank_df['Monetary'].rank(ascending=False)

    rank_df['r_rank_norm'] = (rank_df['r_rank'] / rank_df['r_rank'].max()) * 100
    rank_df['f_rank_norm'] = (rank_df['f_rank'] / rank_df['f_rank'].max()) * 100
    rank_df['m_rank_norm'] = (rank_df['m_rank'] / rank_df['m_rank'].max()) * 100

    rank_df.drop(['r_rank','f_rank','m_rank'], axis=1, inplace=True)
```

```python
    # Calculating RFM scores
    rank_df['rfm_score'] = (0.15*rank_df['r_rank_norm']) +
(0.28*rank_df['f_rank_norm']) + (0.57*rank_df['m_rank_norm'])
    rank_df = rank_df[['Customer Name','rfm_score']]
    rank_df['rfm_score'] = round(rank_df['rfm_score']*0.05, 2)

    # Masking all customers rfm scores by rating conditions to set customer
segments easily
    top_customer_mask = (rank_df['rfm_score'] >= 4.5)
    high_value_mask = ((rank_df['rfm_score']<4.5) & (rank_df['rfm_score']>=4))
    medium_value_mask = ((rank_df['rfm_score']<4) & (rank_df['rfm_score']>=3))
    low_value_mask = ((rank_df['rfm_score']<3) & (rank_df['rfm_score']>=1.6))
    lost_mask = (rank_df['rfm_score'] < 1.6)

    rank_df.loc[top_customer_mask, 'Customer Segment'] = 'Top Customer'
    rank_df.loc[high_value_mask, 'Customer Segment'] = 'High Value Customer'
    rank_df.loc[medium_value_mask, 'Customer Segment'] = 'Medium Value Customer'
    rank_df.loc[low_value_mask, 'Customer Segment'] = 'Low Value Customer'
    rank_df.loc[lost_mask, 'Customer Segment'] = 'Lost Customer'

    # Merge the DataFrames on 'Customer Name'
    merged_rank_dummy = rank_df.merge(df_dummy, on='Customer Name', how='inner')

    # Convert index to datetime
    merged_rank_dummy.index = pd.to_datetime(merged_rank_dummy.index)

    # Set 'Order Date' as the index
    merged_rank_dummy.set_index('Order Date', inplace=True)

    return rfm_df, rank_df, merged_rank_dummy
```

Let's break down the steps:
1. Recency Calculation:
    - The method first groups the data by customer name and finds the latest order date for each customer using df.groupby('Customer Name', as_index=False)['Order Date'].max().
    - It then calculates the recency by subtracting each customer's last purchase date from the most recent date in the dataset. This is done using a lambda function that computes the difference in days: lambda x: (recent_date - x).days.
    - The resulting DataFrame (recency_df) contains columns for 'Customer Name', 'Last Purchase Date', and 'Recency'.
2. Frequency Calculation:
    - It groups the data by customer name and counts the number of orders for each customer using df.groupby('Customer Name', as_index=False)['Order Date'].count().
    - The resulting DataFrame (frequency_df) contains columns for 'Customer Name' and 'Frequency'.
3. Monetary Calculation:

- It groups the data by customer name and calculates the total sales amount for each customer using df.groupby('Customer Name', as_index=False)['Sales'].sum().
- The resulting DataFrame (monetary_df) contains columns for 'Customer Name' and 'Monetary'.

4. Merging DataFrames:
   The three DataFrames (recency_df, frequency_df, monetary_df) are merged on the 'Customer Name' column to create the rfm_df DataFrame. This DataFrame contains columns for 'Customer Name', 'Recency', 'Frequency', and 'Monetary'.

5. Ranking and Normalization:
   The method creates a copy of rfm_df as rank_df and then ranks customers based on Recency, Frequency, and Monetary values. These ranks are normalized to a scale of 0 to 100.

6. Calculating RFM Scores:
   The RFM scores are calculated by applying weights (0.15 for Recency, 0.28 for Frequency, and 0.57 for Monetary) and summing them up.

7. Assigning Customer Segments:
   Based on the RFM scores, customers are categorized into different segments like 'Top Customer', 'High Value Customer', etc.

8. Merging with Dummy Data:
   The method then merges the rank_df with the previously created dummy DataFrame (df_dummy) on the 'Customer Name' column.

9. Setting Index:
   Finally, the index of the resulting DataFrame (merged_rank_dummy) is converted to datetime, and the 'Order Date' column is set as the index.

The method returns three DataFrames: rfm_df (with Recency, Frequency, and Monetary values), rank_df (with RFM scores and customer segments), and merged_rank_dummy (the merged DataFrame with dummy data).

Identifying Churned Customers

In the Process_Data class, define a new method named find_churn_customer(). It is responsible for identifying churned and non-churned customers based on certain criteria:

```python
def find_churn_customer(self, df, rfm_df, rank_df):
    #Find time since first purchase for every customer
    first_purchase_df = df.groupby('Customer Name', as_index=False)['Order
Date'].min()
    first_purchase_df.rename(columns={'Order Date':'First Purchase Date'},
inplace=True)
```

```python
        df_final = df.copy() # Make sure changes we will make doesn't affect original
df so we copy it
        df_final = df_final.merge(first_purchase_df, on='Customer Name',how='left')
        df_final['Time Since First Purchase'] = (df_final['Order Date'].max() -
                                                 df_final['First Purchase Date']).dt.days

        # Add recancy,frequency,monetary and segment columns to df. We found those
features in the previous section
        df_final = df_final.merge(rfm_df, on='Customer Name', how='left')
        df_final = df_final.merge(rank_df, on='Customer Name', how='left')

        # Find churned and not churned customers
        churned = (df_final['Customer Segment'] == 'Lost Customer')
        not_churned = (df_final['Customer Segment'] != 'Lost Customer')

        df_final.loc[churned, 'Churned'] = 1
        df_final.loc[not_churned, 'Churned'] = 0
        df_final['Churned'] = df_final['Churned'].astype('int64')

        #Rename Churned column to Churn
        df_final.rename(columns={'Churned':'Churn'}, inplace=True)

        # Convert index to datetime
        df_final.index = pd.to_datetime(df_final.index)

        # Set 'Order Date' as the index
        df_final.set_index('Order Date', inplace=True)

        return df_final
```

Here's what each part of the method does:

1. Finding Time Since First Purchase:
   - It starts by creating a DataFrame called first_purchase_df which contains each customer's first purchase date.
   - This is done by grouping the data by customer name and finding the minimum order date for each customer.
   - The resulting DataFrame is then merged with the original data (df) on the 'Customer Name' column.
2. Calculating Time Since First Purchase:
   - The method computes the time (in days) since the first purchase for each customer.
   - It subtracts the 'First Purchase Date' from the maximum order date in the dataset to get this information.
3. Adding RFM Features and Customer Segment:
   The method then merges the rfm_df and rank_df DataFrames, which contain Recency, Frequency, Monetary values, and customer segments, with the df_final DataFrame.
4. Identifying Churned Customers:
   It creates boolean masks for churned and non-churned customers based on the 'Customer Segment' column. Customers labeled as 'Lost Customer' are considered churned.

5. Assigning Churn Labels:
    - It assigns the value 1 to churned customers and 0 to non-churned customers in the 'Churn' column of the df_final DataFrame.
    - The column is then converted to the integer data type.
6. Renaming the 'Churned' Column:
    The column name 'Churned' is changed to 'Churn' for consistency.
7. Setting Index:
    The index of the DataFrame (df_final) is converted to datetime, and the 'Order Date' column is set as the index.

The method returns a DataFrame (df_final) with updated information, including a 'Churn' column indicating whether each customer has churned or not.

Encoding Categorical Data

In the Process_Data class, define a new method named encode_df(). It is responsible for preparing the dataset for machine learning tasks:

```python
def encode_df(self, df):
    #Drops Daily Summary column
    df.drop(['Order ID', 'Ship Date', 'Customer ID', 'Cat_Sales', 'Day', 'Month',
'Week', 'Quarter'], axis=1, inplace=True)

    #Controls the size of dataset for regression and prediction to suit your
computing power
    df=df[df["Year"] == 2018]
    #df = df[(df["Year"] == 2016) & (df["Month"] >= 3) & (df["Month"] <= 7)]
    #Selects data in year 2015-2016, because very big dataset
    #df = df[df['Year'].isin([2015, 2016])]

    # Encodes all non-numeric columns
    non_numeric_columns = df.select_dtypes(exclude=['number']).columns
    label_encoder = LabelEncoder()
    for column in non_numeric_columns:
        df[column] = label_encoder.fit_transform(df[column])

    print(df.head().to_string())

    #Extracts output and input variables for prediction
    y1 = df['Churn'] # Target for the model
    X1 = df.drop(['Churn'], axis = 1)

    y2 = df['Sales'] # Target for regression
    X2 = df.drop(['Sales'], axis = 1)

    return df, X1, y1, X2, y2
```

Here's what each part of the method does:

1. Dropping Irrelevant Columns:

   It drops several columns from the DataFrame that are not needed for the machine learning tasks. These columns include 'Order ID', 'Ship Date', 'Customer ID', 'Cat_Sales', 'Day', 'Month', 'Week', and 'Quarter'.

2. Filtering Data for Year 2018:

   It filters the dataset to include only records from the year 2018. This is done to control the size of the dataset, which can be important for computational efficiency.

3. Encoding Categorical Variables:

   - It identifies non-numeric columns in the DataFrame (columns with data types other than numbers).

   - For each non-numeric column, it uses a Label Encoder to convert categorical data into numerical form. This is important because most machine learning models require numerical input.

4. Extracting Input and Output Variables:

   - It separates the target variables (Churn and Sales) from the rest of the features (X1 and X2 respectively).

   - y1 is the target variable for classification (predicting churn), and X1 contains the features for classification.

   - y2 is the target variable for regression (predicting sales), and X2 contains the features for regression.

5. Printing the Head of the DataFrame:

   It prints the first five rows of the DataFrame after these operations for visual inspection.

6. Finally, the method returns the modified DataFrame (df) along with the input and output variables for both classification and regression tasks.

Feature Importance

In the Process_Data class, define three new method named feat_importance_rf(), feat_importance_et(), and feat_importance_rfe(). They are responsible for performing feature importance analysis using different machine learning models:

```python
def feat_importance_rf(self, X, y):
    names = X.columns
    rf = RandomForestClassifier()
    rf.fit(X, y)

    result_rf = pd.DataFrame()
    result_rf['Features'] = X.columns
    result_rf ['Values'] = rf.feature_importances_
    result_rf.sort_values('Values', inplace = True, ascending = False)
```

```python
        return result_rf

    def feat_importance_et(self, X, y):
        model = ExtraTreesClassifier()
        model.fit(X, y)

        result_et = pd.DataFrame()
        result_et['Features'] = X.columns
        result_et ['Values'] = model.feature_importances_
        result_et.sort_values('Values', inplace=True, ascending =False)

        return result_et

    def feat_importance_rfe(self, X, y):
        model = LogisticRegression()
        #Creates the RFE model
        rfe = RFE(model)
        rfe = rfe.fit(X, y)

        result_lg = pd.DataFrame()
        result_lg['Features'] = X.columns
        result_lg ['Ranking'] = rfe.ranking_
        result_lg.sort_values('Ranking', inplace=True , ascending = False)

        return result_lg
```

Here's what each method does:
1. feat_importance_rf(self, X, y):
    - This method performs feature importance analysis using a Random Forest Classifier.
    - It first fits a Random Forest Classifier on the input features (X) and target variable (y).
    - It then creates a DataFrame result_rf to store feature names and their corresponding importance scores.
    - The features are sorted based on their importance scores in descending order.
    - Finally, it returns the sorted DataFrame.
2. feat_importance_et(self, X, y):
    - This method performs feature importance analysis using an Extra Trees Classifier.
    - Similar to the previous method, it fits an Extra Trees Classifier on the input features (X) and target variable (y).
    - It creates a DataFrame result_et to store feature names and their corresponding importance scores.
    - The features are sorted based on their importance scores in descending order.
    - It then returns the sorted DataFrame.
3. feat_importance_rfe(self, X, y):

- This method performs feature importance analysis using Recursive Feature Elimination (RFE) with a Logistic Regression model.
- It first creates an instance of a Logistic Regression model.
- Then, it creates an RFE model using this logistic regression model and fits it on the input features (X) and target variable (y).
- It creates a DataFrame result_lg to store feature names and their corresponding rankings based on RFE.
- The features are sorted based on their rankings in descending order.
- Finally, it returns the sorted DataFrame.

These methods are useful for understanding which features are the most important for making accurate predictions in the respective models.

Saving Result of Model's Prediction

In the Process_Data class, define a new method named save_result(). It is responsible for saving the results of the model's predictions:

```python
def save_result(self, y_test, y_pred, fname):
    # Convert y_test and y_pred to pandas Series for easier handling
    y_test_series = pd.Series(y_test)
    y_pred_series = pd.Series(y_pred)

    # Calculate y_result_series
    y_result_series = pd.Series(y_pred - y_test == 0)
    y_result_series = y_result_series.map({True: 'True', False: 'False'})

    # Create a DataFrame to hold y_test, y_pred, and y_result
    data = pd.DataFrame({'y_test': y_test_series, 'y_pred': y_pred_series,
'result': y_result_series})

    # Save the DataFrame to a CSV file
    data.to_csv(fname, index=False)
```

Here's what this method does:
1. Input Parameters:
    - y_test: This is a pandas Series containing the true target values.
    - y_pred: This is a pandas Series containing the predicted target values.
    - fname: This is a string representing the file name where the results will be saved.
2. Conversion to Pandas Series:
    Both y_test and y_pred are converted to pandas Series. This conversion makes it easier to handle and manipulate the data.

3. Calculation of y_result_series:
   - y_result_series is calculated based on the comparison between y_pred and y_test. It checks if the predicted values are equal to the true values.
   - The result is a boolean Series (True if the prediction is correct, False otherwise).
   - Then, map is used to convert these boolean values to strings ('True' and 'False') for better readability.
4. Creating a DataFrame:
   - A DataFrame named data is created to hold three columns: y_test, y_pred, and result.
   - y_test_series contains the true values, y_pred_series contains the predicted values, and y_result_series contains the result of the comparison.
5. Saving to CSV:
   The DataFrame data is saved to a CSV file with the file name specified by fname. The index=False argument ensures that the index is not included in the saved file.

Overall, this method facilitates the process of saving the model's predictions and their corresponding true values, as well as indicating whether each prediction was correct or not. This information can be valuable for further analysis and evaluation of the model's performance.

SALES REGRESSION

Splitting Data for Regression Model

Open a new python file and name it as regression.py. In it, create a class named Regression. It designed for conducting regression analysis using various regression models:

```python
#regression.py
import pandas as pd
import numpy as np
from sklearn.preprocessing import MinMaxScaler
import joblib
from sklearn.metrics import mean_squared_error, mean_absolute_error
from sklearn.metrics import roc_auc_score,roc_curve, r2_score,
explained_variance_score
from sklearn.linear_model import LinearRegression
from sklearn.ensemble import RandomForestRegressor, GradientBoostingRegressor,
AdaBoostRegressor
from sklearn.model_selection import GridSearchCV
from sklearn.tree import DecisionTreeRegressor
from xgboost import XGBRegressor
from sklearn.neural_network import MLPRegressor
from sklearn.linear_model import LassoCV
from sklearn.linear_model import RidgeCV
from sklearn.neighbors import KNeighborsRegressor

class Regression:
```

Let's go over some of the key methods within this class:
1. Initialization:

The class is designed for regression tasks as it contains various regression models. The initialization of the class sets up the necessary attributes or configurations for performing regression analysis.

2. Method for Data Scaling:
   The class contains a method for scaling the features of the dataset. This is crucial for many machine learning models, especially those sensitive to the scale of input features. The method uses Min-Max scaling (MinMaxScaler) to normalize the feature values.
3. Model Training Methods:
   The class includes methods for training various regression models. These models may include:
   - Linear Regression (LinearRegression)
   - Random Forest Regression (RandomForestRegressor)
   - Gradient Boosting Regression (GradientBoostingRegressor)
   - AdaBoost Regression (AdaBoostRegressor)
   - Decision Tree Regression (DecisionTreeRegressor)
   - XGBoost Regression (XGBRegressor)
   - MLP Regression (MLPRegressor)
   - Lasso Regression (LassoCV)
   - Ridge Regression (RidgeCV)
   - K-Nearest Neighbors Regression (KNeighborsRegressor)

   These methods involves hyperparameter tuning using techniques like Grid Search (GridSearchCV) to find the best set of hyperparameters for each model.
4. Loading and Saving Models:
5. The class have methods for saving trained regression models to disk (joblib) and for loading pre-trained models for later use.

Overall, this class is a comprehensive tool for performing various regression tasks, including data preprocessing, model training, evaluation, and model persistence. It provides a modular and organized way to conduct regression analysis using different algorithms.

Then, in Regression class, define a new method named splitting_data_regression(). It handles the data preprocessing and splitting for a regression task:

```python
def splitting_data_regression(self, X, y_final):
    #Normalizes data
    scaler = MinMaxScaler()
    X_minmax_data = scaler.fit_transform(X)
    X_final = pd.DataFrame(columns=X.columns, data=X_minmax_data, index=X.index)
    print('Shape of features : ', X_final.shape)
    print('Shape of target : ', y_final.shape)
```

```python
#Shifts target array to predict the n + 1 samples
n=90
y_final = y_final.shift(-1)
y_val = y_final[-n:-1]
y_final = y_final[:-n]

#Takes last n rows of data to be validation set
X_val = X_final[-n:-1]
X_final = X_final[:-n]

print("\n -----After process------ \n")
print('Shape of features : ', X_final.shape)
print('Shape of target : ', y_final.shape)
print(y_final.tail().to_string())

y_final=y_final.astype('float64')

#Splits data into training and test data at 80% and 20% respectively
split_idx=round(0.8*len(X))
print("split_idx=",split_idx)
X_train_reg = X_final[:split_idx]
y_train_reg = y_final[:split_idx]
X_test_reg = X_final[split_idx:]
y_test_reg = y_final[split_idx:]

#Saves into pkl files
joblib.dump(X, 'X_Ori.pkl')
joblib.dump(X_final, 'X_final_reg.pkl')
joblib.dump(X_train_reg, 'X_train_reg.pkl')
joblib.dump(X_test_reg, 'X_test_reg.pkl')
joblib.dump(X_val, 'X_val_reg.pkl')
joblib.dump(y_final, 'y_final_reg.pkl')
joblib.dump(y_train_reg, 'y_train_reg.pkl')
joblib.dump(y_test_reg, 'y_test_reg.pkl')
joblib.dump(y_val, 'y_val_reg.pkl')
```

Let's break down the steps:

1. Data Normalization:

    The method starts by normalizing the feature data X using MinMaxScaler, which scales the features to a specified range (typically 0 to 1). The scaled data is stored in X_final.

2. Shifting the Target:

    The target variable y_final is shifted by one position (y_final = y_final.shift(-1)). This means that each value in y_final is replaced by the value that follows it. This creates a dataset for predicting the next value based on the current input.

3. Validation Set Preparation:

    A parameter n is set to 90. Then, the last n rows of the data are selected as the validation set. These rows will be used later for evaluating the model's performance.

4. Data Shape and Print Statements:

    The shapes of the feature and target datasets are printed, along with some details about their dimensions.

5. Data Type Conversion:
   The target variable y_final is explicitly converted to type 'float64'.
6. Train-Test Split:
   The data is split into training and testing sets using an 80-20 split. The training set (X_train_reg, y_train_reg) will be used to train the regression model, while the testing set (X_test_reg, y_test_reg) will be used for evaluation.
7. File Saving:
   Various datasets (X, X_final, X_train_reg, X_test_reg, X_val, y_final, y_train_reg, y_test_reg, y_val) are saved as pickle files (.pkl). These files contain the preprocessed data that can be used later for training and testing the regression models.

Overall, this method performs crucial preprocessing steps for a regression task, including normalization, target shifting, and dataset splitting. The saved files ensure that the preprocessed data can be reused in future runs without the need for reprocessing.

Loading Preprocessed Data Files

In Regression class, define a new method named load_regression_files(). It is used to load previously saved files that contain various datasets used in regression tasks:

```python
def load_regression_files(self):
    X_Ori = joblib.load('X_Ori.pkl')
    X_final_reg = joblib.load('X_final_reg.pkl')
    X_train_reg = joblib.load('X_train_reg.pkl')
    X_test_reg = joblib.load('X_test_reg.pkl')
    X_val_reg = joblib.load('X_val_reg.pkl')
    y_final_reg = joblib.load('y_final_reg.pkl')
    y_train_reg = joblib.load('y_train_reg.pkl')
    y_test_reg = joblib.load('y_test_reg.pkl')
    y_val_reg = joblib.load('y_val_reg.pkl')

    return X_Ori, X_final_reg, X_train_reg, X_test_reg, X_val_reg, y_final_reg, y_train_reg, y_test_reg, y_val_reg
```

Here's a breakdown of what this method does:
1. Loading Data:
   It loads multiple datasets from the saved pickle files. These datasets include both features and target variables.
2. Returned Values:
   The method returns all the loaded datasets in the following order:
   - X_Ori: Original feature dataset.
   - X_final_reg: Preprocessed and normalized feature dataset for regression.
   - X_train_reg: Training set features for regression.
   - X_test_reg: Testing set features for regression.

- X_val_reg: Validation set features for regression.
- y_final_reg: Preprocessed target variable for regression.
- y_train_reg: Training set target variable for regression.
- y_test_reg: Testing set target variable for regression.
- y_val_reg: Validation set target variable for regression.

3. These loaded datasets can then be used for training and evaluating regression models without the need for reprocessing the data.

Overall, this method provides a convenient way to load preprocessed data for regression tasks, allowing for easy reuse of the datasets in different parts of the program.

Performing Regression

In Regression class, define a new method named perform_regression(). It is designed to perform regression using a specified model:

```python
def perform_regression(self, model, X, y, xtrain, ytrain, xtest, ytest, xval,
yval, label):
    model.fit(xtrain, ytrain)
    predictions_test = model.predict(xtest)
    predictions_train = model.predict(xtrain)
    predictions_val = model.predict(xval)

    # Convert ytest and predictions_test to NumPy arrays
    ytest_np = ytest.to_numpy().flatten()
    predictions_test_np = predictions_test.flatten()

    str_label = 'RMSE using ' + label
    print(str_label + f': {np.sqrt(mean_squared_error(ytest_np,
predictions_test_np))}')
    print("mean square error: ", mean_squared_error(ytest_np,
predictions_test_np))
    print("variance or r-squared: ", explained_variance_score(ytest_np,
predictions_test_np))
    print("mean absolute error (MAE): ", mean_absolute_error(ytest_np,
predictions_test_np))
    print("R2 (R-squared): ", r2_score(ytest_np, predictions_test_np))
    print("Adjusted R2: ", 1 - (1-r2_score(ytest_np,
predictions_test_np))*(len(ytest_np)-1)/(len(ytest_np)-xtest.shape[1]-1))

    mean_percentage_error = np.mean((ytest_np - predictions_test_np) / ytest_np)
* 100
    print("Mean Percentage Error (MPE): ", mean_percentage_error)

    mean_absolute_percentage_error = np.mean(np.abs((ytest_np -
predictions_test_np) / ytest_np)) * 100
    print("Mean Absolute Percentage Error (MAPE): ",
mean_absolute_percentage_error)

    print('ACTUAL: Avg. ' + f': {ytest_np.mean()}')
```

```python
print('ACTUAL: Median ' + f': {np.median(ytest_np)}')
print('PREDICTED: Avg. ' + f': {predictions_test_np.mean()}')
print('PREDICTED: Median ' + f': {np.median(predictions_test_np)}')

# Evaluation of regression on all dataset
all_pred = model.predict(X)
print("mean square error (whole dataset): ", mean_squared_error(y, all_pred))
print("variance or r-squared (whole dataset): ", explained_variance_score(y,
all_pred))

return predictions_test, predictions_train, predictions_val, all_pred
```

Below is an explanation of what this method does:
1. Model Training:
   model.fit(xtrain, ytrain): This line trains the provided regression model (model) on the training data (xtrain and ytrain).
2. Predictions:
   - predictions_test: This variable stores the predictions made by the model on the test set (xtest).
   - predictions_train: Similarly, this variable stores the predictions made on the training set (xtrain).
   - predictions_val: This variable stores the predictions made on the validation set (xval).
3. Evaluation Metrics:
   The method calculates and prints several regression evaluation metrics for the test set:
   - Root Mean Squared Error (RMSE)
   - Mean Squared Error (MSE)
   - Variance or R-Squared (explained variance score)
   - Mean Absolute Error (MAE)
   - R-Squared (R2)
   - Adjusted R-Squared (Adjusted R2)
   - Mean Percentage Error (MPE)
   - Mean Absolute Percentage Error (MAPE)
   - Mean and Median values for both actual and predicted data.
4. Evaluation on Full Dataset:
   The model is also evaluated on the entire dataset (X and y), and MSE and explained variance score are printed.
5. Returned Values:
   The method returns the predictions made on the test set (predictions_test), training set (predictions_train), validation set (predictions_val), and predictions on the full dataset (all_pred).

Overall, this method is used to train a regression model, make predictions, and evaluate its performance using various regression metrics. It provides comprehensive insights into how well the model is performing on different subsets of the data.

Linear Regression

In Regression class, define a new method named linear_regression(). It performs a grid search to find the best hyperparameters for a Linear Regression model:

```python
def linear_regression(self, X_train, y_train):
    #Linear Regression
    #Creates a Linear Regression model
    lin_reg = LinearRegression()

    #Defines the hyperparameter grid to search
    param_grid = {
        'fit_intercept': [True, False],    # Try both True and False for
fit_intercept
        'normalize': [True, False]         # Try both True and False for normalize
    }

    #Creates GridSearchCV with the Linear Regression model and the hyperparameter
grid
    grid_search = GridSearchCV(lin_reg, param_grid, cv=5,
scoring='neg_mean_squared_error')

    #Fits the GridSearchCV to the training data
    grid_search.fit(X_train, y_train)

    #Gets the best Linear Regression model from the grid search
    best_lin_reg = grid_search.best_estimator_

    #Prints the best hyperparameters found
    print("Best Hyperparameters for Linear Regression:")
    print(grid_search.best_params_)

    return best_lin_reg
```

Below is an explanation of what this method does:
1. Creating a Linear Regression Model:
   lin_reg = LinearRegression(): This line creates an instance of the Linear Regression model.
2. Hyperparameter Grid:
   - param_grid: This variable defines a grid of hyperparameters to search. For Linear Regression, it explores the following hyperparameters:
   - fit_intercept: Whether or not to fit an intercept term in the model.
   - normalize: Whether or not to normalize the input variables.
3. Grid Search:

grid_search = GridSearchCV(lin_reg, param_grid, cv=5, scoring='neg_mean_squared_error'): This line sets up a GridSearchCV object. It uses 5-fold cross-validation (cv=5) and uses negative mean squared error (scoring='neg_mean_squared_error') as the evaluation metric.

4. Fitting Grid Search:

grid_search.fit(X_train, y_train): This fits the GridSearchCV object to the training data. It performs an exhaustive search over the hyperparameter grid, evaluating each combination using cross-validation.

5. Best Model:

best_lin_reg = grid_search.best_estimator_: This line retrieves the best Linear Regression model found during the grid search.

6. Printing Best Hyperparameters:

print("Best Hyperparameters for Linear Regression:") and print(grid_search.best_params_): These lines print out the best hyperparameters discovered by the grid search.

7. Returning Best Model:

The method returns the best Linear Regression model.

Overall, this method automates the process of hyperparameter tuning for the Linear Regression model, helping to find the optimal settings for better predictive performance.

Random Forest Regression

In Regression class, define a new method named rf_regression(). It performs a grid search to find the best hyperparameters for a Random Forest Regression model:

```python
def rf_regression(self, X_train, y_train):
    #Random Forest Regression
    # Create a RandomForestRegressor model
    rf_reg = RandomForestRegressor()

    # Define the hyperparameter grid to search
    param_grid = {
        'n_estimators': [50, 100, 150],          # Number of trees in the forest
        'max_depth': [None, 5, 10],              # Maximum depth of the tree
        'min_samples_split': [2, 5, 10],         # Minimum number of samples
required to split an internal node
        'min_samples_leaf': [1, 2, 4],           # Minimum number of samples
required to be at a leaf node
        'bootstrap': [True, False]               # Whether bootstrap samples
are used when building trees
    }

    # Create GridSearchCV with the RandomForestRegressor model and the
hyperparameter grid
```

```python
        grid_search = GridSearchCV(rf_reg, param_grid, cv=5,
scoring='neg_mean_squared_error')

        # Fit the GridSearchCV to the training data
        grid_search.fit(X_train, y_train)

        # Get the best RandomForestRegressor model from the grid search
        best_rf_reg = grid_search.best_estimator_

        # Print the best hyperparameters found
        print("Best Hyperparameters for RandomForestRegressor:")
        print(grid_search.best_params_)

        return best_rf_reg
```

Here's an explanation of what this method does:
1. Creating a Random Forest Regression Model:
   rf_reg = RandomForestRegressor(): This line creates an instance of the Random Forest Regression model.
2. Hyperparameter Grid:
   param_grid: This variable defines a grid of hyperparameters to search. For Random Forest Regression, it explores the following hyperparameters:
   - n_estimators: The number of trees in the forest.
   - max_depth: The maximum depth of the trees.
   - min_samples_split: The minimum number of samples required to split an internal node.
   - min_samples_leaf: The minimum number of samples required to be at a leaf node.
   - bootstrap: Whether bootstrap samples are used when building trees.
3. Grid Search:
   grid_search = GridSearchCV(rf_reg, param_grid, cv=5, scoring='neg_mean_squared_error'): This line sets up a GridSearchCV object. It uses 5-fold cross-validation (cv=5) and uses negative mean squared error (scoring='neg_mean_squared_error') as the evaluation metric.
4. Fitting Grid Search:
   grid_search.fit(X_train, y_train): This fits the GridSearchCV object to the training data. It performs an exhaustive search over the hyperparameter grid, evaluating each combination using cross-validation.
5. Best Model:
   best_rf_reg = grid_search.best_estimator_: This line retrieves the best Random Forest Regression model found during the grid search.
6. Printing Best Hyperparameters:
   print("Best Hyperparameters for RandomForestRegressor:") and print(grid_search.best_params_): These lines print out the best hyperparameters discovered by the grid search.

7. Returning Best Model:

    The method returns the best Random Forest Regression model.

Overall, this method automates the process of hyperparameter tuning for the Random Forest Regression model, helping to find the optimal settings for better predictive performance.

Decision Tree Regression

In Regression class, define a new method named dt_regression(). It performs a grid search to find the best hyperparameters for a Decision Tree Regression model:

```python
def dt_regression(self, X_train, y_train):
    #Decision Tree (DT) regression
    # Create a DecisionTreeRegressor model
    dt_reg = DecisionTreeRegressor(random_state=100)

    # Define the hyperparameter grid to search
    param_grid = {
        'max_depth': [None, 5, 10, 15],          # Maximum depth of the tree
        'min_samples_split': [2, 5, 10],         # Minimum number of samples
required to split an internal node
        'min_samples_leaf': [1, 2, 4, 6],        # Minimum number of samples
required to be at a leaf node
    }

    # Create GridSearchCV with the DecisionTreeRegressor model and the
hyperparameter grid
    grid_search = GridSearchCV(dt_reg, param_grid, cv=5,
scoring='neg_mean_squared_error')

    # Fit the GridSearchCV to the training data
    grid_search.fit(X_train, y_train)

    # Get the best DecisionTreeRegressor model from the grid search
    best_dt_reg = grid_search.best_estimator_

    # Print the best hyperparameters found
    print("Best Hyperparameters for DecisionTreeRegressor:")
    print(grid_search.best_params_)

    return best_dt_reg
```

Here's an explanation of what this method does:
1. Creating a Decision Tree Regression Model:

    dt_reg = DecisionTreeRegressor(random_state=100): This line creates an instance of the Decision Tree Regression model. random_state=100 sets a seed for the random number generator for reproducibility.
2. Hyperparameter Grid:

param_grid: This variable defines a grid of hyperparameters to search. For Decision Tree Regression, it explores the following hyperparameters:

- max_depth: The maximum depth of the tree.
- min_samples_split: The minimum number of samples required to split an internal node.
- min_samples_leaf: The minimum number of samples required to be at a leaf node.

3. Grid Search:

grid_search = GridSearchCV(dt_reg, param_grid, cv=5, scoring='neg_mean_squared_error'): This line sets up a GridSearchCV object. It uses 5-fold cross-validation (cv=5) and uses negative mean squared error (scoring='neg_mean_squared_error') as the evaluation metric.

4. Fitting Grid Search:

grid_search.fit(X_train, y_train): This fits the GridSearchCV object to the training data. It performs an exhaustive search over the hyperparameter grid, evaluating each combination using cross-validation.

5. Best Model:

best_dt_reg = grid_search.best_estimator_: This line retrieves the best Decision Tree Regression model found during the grid search.

6. Printing Best Hyperparameters:

print("Best Hyperparameters for DecisionTreeRegressor:") and print(grid_search.best_params_): These lines print out the best hyperparameters discovered by the grid search.

7. Returning Best Model:

The method returns the best Decision Tree Regression model.

This method automates the process of hyperparameter tuning for the Decision Tree Regression model, helping to find the optimal settings for better predictive performance.

Gradient Boosting Regression

In Regression class, define a new method named gb_regression(). It is responsible for performing a grid search to find the best hyperparameters for a Gradient Boosting regression model:

```python
def gb_regression(self, X_train, y_train):
    #Gradient Boosting regression
    # Create the GradientBoostingRegressor model
    gb_reg = GradientBoostingRegressor()

    # Define the hyperparameter grid to search
    param_grid = {
        'n_estimators': [50, 100, 150],            # Number of boosting
stages (trees) to build
```

```
        'learning_rate': [0.01, 0.1, 0.5],              # Step size at each
boosting iteration
        'max_depth': [3, 5, 7],                         # Maximum depth of the
individual trees
        'min_samples_split': [2, 5, 10],                # Minimum number of
samples required to split an internal node
        'min_samples_leaf': [1, 2, 4],                  # Minimum number of
samples required to be at a leaf node
    }

    # Create GridSearchCV with the GradientBoostingRegressor model and the
hyperparameter grid
    grid_search = GridSearchCV(gb_reg, param_grid, cv=5,
scoring='neg_mean_squared_error')

    # Fit the GridSearchCV to the training data
    grid_search.fit(X_train, y_train)

    # Get the best GradientBoostingRegressor model from the grid search
    best_gb_reg = grid_search.best_estimator_

    # Print the best hyperparameters found
    print("Best Hyperparameters for GradientBoostingRegressor:")
    print(grid_search.best_params_)

    return best_gb_reg
```

Here's a breakdown of what this method does:

1. Creating a Gradient Boosting Regression Model:

   gb_reg = GradientBoostingRegressor(): This line creates an instance of the Gradient Boosting regression model.

2. Hyperparameter Grid:

   param_grid: This variable defines a grid of hyperparameters to search. It explores the following hyperparameters:

   - n_estimators: The number of boosting stages (trees) to build.
   - learning_rate: The step size at each boosting iteration.
   - max_depth: The maximum depth of the individual trees.
   - min_samples_split: The minimum number of samples required to split an internal node.
   - min_samples_leaf: The minimum number of samples required to be at a leaf node.

3. Grid Search:

   grid_search = GridSearchCV(gb_reg, param_grid, cv=5, scoring='neg_mean_squared_error'): This line sets up a GridSearchCV object. It uses 5-fold cross-validation (cv=5) and uses negative mean squared error (scoring='neg_mean_squared_error') as the evaluation metric.

4. Fitting Grid Search:

grid_search.fit(X_train, y_train): This fits the GridSearchCV object to the training data. It performs an exhaustive search over the hyperparameter grid, evaluating each combination using cross-validation.

5. Best Model:
   best_gb_reg = grid_search.best_estimator_: This line retrieves the best Gradient Boosting regression model found during the grid search.

6. Printing Best Hyperparameters:
   print("Best Hyperparameters for GradientBoostingRegressor:") and print(grid_search.best_params_): These lines print out the best hyperparameters discovered by the grid search.

7. Returning Best Model:
   The method returns the best Gradient Boosting regression model.

This method automates the process of hyperparameter tuning for the Gradient Boosting regression model, helping to find the optimal settings for better predictive performance.

Extreme Gradient Boosting Regression

In Regression class, define a new method named xgb_regression(). It is responsible for performing a grid search to find the best hyperparameters for an Extreme Gradient Boosting (XGBoost) regression model:

```python
def xgb_regression(self, X_train, y_train):
    #Extreme Gradient Boosting (XGB)
    # Create the XGBRegressor model
    xgb_reg = XGBRegressor()

    # Define the hyperparameter grid to search
    param_grid = {
        'n_estimators': [50, 100, 150],            # Number of boosting stages
(trees) to build
        'learning_rate': [0.01, 0.1, 0.5],         # Step size at each boosting
iteration
        'max_depth': [3, 5, 7],                    # Maximum depth of the
individual trees
        'min_child_weight': [1, 2, 4],             # Minimum sum of instance
weight (hessian) needed in a child
        'gamma': [0, 0.1, 0.2],                    # Minimum loss reduction
required to make a further partition on a leaf node
        'subsample': [0.8, 1.0],                   # Subsample ratio of the
training instances
        'colsample_bytree': [0.8, 1.0]             # Subsample ratio of columns
when constructing each tree
    }

    # Create GridSearchCV with the XGBRegressor model and the hyperparameter grid
    grid_search = GridSearchCV(xgb_reg, param_grid, cv=5,
scoring='neg_mean_squared_error')
```

```
# Fit the GridSearchCV to the training data
grid_search.fit(X_train, y_train)

# Get the best XGBRegressor model from the grid search
best_xgb_reg = grid_search.best_estimator_

# Print the best hyperparameters found
print("Best Hyperparameters for XGBRegressor:")
print(grid_search.best_params_)

return best_xgb_reg
```

Here's a breakdown of what this method does:

1. Creating an XGBoost Regression Model:

   xgb_reg = XGBRegressor(): This line creates an instance of the XGBoost regression model.

2. Hyperparameter Grid:

   param_grid: This variable defines a grid of hyperparameters to search. It explores the following hyperparameters:

   - n_estimators: The number of boosting stages (trees) to build.
   - learning_rate: The step size at each boosting iteration.
   - max_depth: The maximum depth of the individual trees.
   - min_child_weight: The minimum sum of instance weight (hessian) needed in a child.
   - gamma: The minimum loss reduction required to make a further partition on a leaf node.
   - subsample: The subsample ratio of the training instances.
   - colsample_bytree: The subsample ratio of columns when constructing each tree.

3. Grid Search:

   grid_search = GridSearchCV(xgb_reg, param_grid, cv=5, scoring='neg_mean_squared_error'): This line sets up a GridSearchCV object. It uses 5-fold cross-validation (cv=5) and uses negative mean squared error (scoring='neg_mean_squared_error') as the evaluation metric.

4. Fitting Grid Search:

   grid_search.fit(X_train, y_train): This fits the GridSearchCV object to the training data. It performs an exhaustive search over the hyperparameter grid, evaluating each combination using cross-validation.

5. Best Model:

   best_xgb_reg = grid_search.best_estimator_: This line retrieves the best XGBoost regression model found during the grid search.

6. Printing Best Hyperparameters:

print("Best Hyperparameters for XGBRegressor:") and print(grid_search.best_params_): These lines print out the best hyperparameters discovered by the grid search.

7. Returning Best Model:
   The method returns the best XGBoost regression model.

This method automates the process of hyperparameter tuning for the XGBoost regression model, helping to find the optimal settings for better predictive performance.

Multi-Layer Perceptron Regression

In Regression class, define a new method named mlp_regression(). It is responsible for performing a grid search to find the best hyperparameters for a Multi-Layer Perceptron (MLP) regression model:

```python
def mlp_regression(self, X_train, y_train):
    #MLP regression
    # Create the MLPRegressor model
    mlp_reg = MLPRegressor()

    # Define the hyperparameter grid to search
    param_grid = {
        'hidden_layer_sizes': [(50,), (100,), (50, 50), (100, 50)],    # Number
of neurons in each hidden layer
        'activation': ['relu', 'tanh'],                               #
Activation function for the hidden layers
        'solver': ['adam', 'sgd'],                                    # Solver
for weight optimization
        'learning_rate': ['constant', 'invscaling', 'adaptive'],      # Learning
rate schedule
        'learning_rate_init': [0.01, 0.001],                         # Initial
learning rate
        'max_iter': [100, 200, 300],                                 # Maximum
number of iterations
    }

    # Create GridSearchCV with the MLPRegressor model and the hyperparameter grid
    grid_search = GridSearchCV(mlp_reg, param_grid, cv=5,
scoring='neg_mean_squared_error')

    # Fit the GridSearchCV to the training data
    grid_search.fit(X_train, y_train)

    # Get the best MLPRegressor model from the grid search
    best_mlp_reg = grid_search.best_estimator_

    # Print the best hyperparameters found
    print("Best Hyperparameters for MLPRegressor:")
    print(grid_search.best_params_)

    return best_mlp_reg
```

Here's the explanation of the steps taken in this method:

1. Creating an MLP Regression Model:

    mlp_reg = MLPRegressor(): This line creates an instance of the MLP regression model.

2. Hyperparameter Grid:

    param_grid: This variable defines a grid of hyperparameters to search. It explores the following hyperparameters:

    - hidden_layer_sizes: The number of neurons in each hidden layer.
    - activation: The activation function for the hidden layers.
    - solver: The solver for weight optimization.
    - learning_rate: The learning rate schedule.
    - learning_rate_init: The initial learning rate.
    - max_iter: The maximum number of iterations.

3. Grid Search:

    grid_search = GridSearchCV(mlp_reg, param_grid, cv=5, scoring='neg_mean_squared_error'): This line sets up a GridSearchCV object. It uses 5-fold cross-validation (cv=5) and uses negative mean squared error (scoring='neg_mean_squared_error') as the evaluation metric.

4. Fitting Grid Search:

    grid_search.fit(X_train, y_train): This fits the GridSearchCV object to the training data. It performs an exhaustive search over the hyperparameter grid, evaluating each combination using cross-validation.

5. Best Model:

    best_mlp_reg = grid_search.best_estimator_: This line retrieves the best MLP regression model found during the grid search.

6. Printing Best Hyperparameters:

    print("Best Hyperparameters for MLPRegressor:") and print(grid_search.best_params_): These lines print out the best hyperparameters discovered by the grid search.

7. Returning Best Model:

    The method returns the best MLP regression model.

This method automates the process of hyperparameter tuning for the MLP regression model, helping to find the optimal settings for better predictive performance.

Lasso Regression

In Regression class, define a new method named lasso_regression(). It is responsible for performing a grid search to find the best hyperparameters for a Lasso Regression model:

```python
def lasso_regression(self, X_train, y_train):
    # Create the LassoCV model
```

```python
    lasso_reg = LassoCV(n_alphas=1000, max_iter=3000, random_state=0)

    # Define the hyperparameter grid to search
    param_grid = {
        'normalize': [True, False],        # Whether to normalize the features
before fitting the model
        'fit_intercept': [True, False]     # Whether to calculate the intercept
for this model
    }

    # Create GridSearchCV with the LassoCV model and the hyperparameter grid
    grid_search = GridSearchCV(lasso_reg, param_grid, cv=5,
scoring='neg_mean_squared_error')

    # Fit the GridSearchCV to the training data
    grid_search.fit(X_train, y_train)

    # Get the best LassoCV model from the grid search
    best_lasso_reg = grid_search.best_estimator_

    # Print the best hyperparameters found
    print("Best Hyperparameters for Lasso Regression:")
    print(grid_search.best_params_)

    return best_lasso_reg
```

Here's an explanation of the steps taken in this method:

1. Creating a LassoCV Model:

    lasso_reg = LassoCV(n_alphas=1000, max_iter=3000, random_state=0): This line creates an instance of the LassoCV regression model. n_alphas specifies the number of alphas (regularization strengths) to try, and max_iter sets the maximum number of iterations for the solver.

2. Hyperparameter Grid:

    param_grid: This variable defines a grid of hyperparameters to search. It explores the following hyperparameters:

    - normalize: Whether to normalize the features before fitting the model.
    - fit_intercept: Whether to calculate the intercept for this model.

3. Grid Search:

    grid_search   =   GridSearchCV(lasso_reg,   param_grid,   cv=5, scoring='neg_mean_squared_error'): This line sets up a GridSearchCV object. It uses 5-fold cross-validation (cv=5) and uses negative mean squared error (scoring='neg_mean_squared_error') as the evaluation metric.

4. Fitting Grid Search:

    grid_search.fit(X_train, y_train): This fits the GridSearchCV object to the training data. It performs an exhaustive search over the hyperparameter grid, evaluating each combination using cross-validation.

5. Best Model:

best_lasso_reg = grid_search.best_estimator_: This line retrieves the best Lasso regression model found during the grid search.

6. Printing Best Hyperparameters:
   print("Best Hyperparameters for Lasso Regression:") and print(grid_search.best_params_): These lines print out the best hyperparameters discovered by the grid search.

7. Returning Best Model:
   The method returns the best Lasso regression model.

This method automates the process of hyperparameter tuning for the Lasso regression model, helping to find the optimal settings for better predictive performance.

Ridge Regression

In Regression class, define a new method named ridge_regression(). It is responsible for performing Ridge Regression along with an optional hyperparameter search:

```python
def ridge_regression(self, X_train, y_train):
    #Ridge regression
    ridge_reg = RidgeCV(gcv_mode='auto')

    # Define the hyperparameter grid to search (optional if you want to include
other hyperparameters)
    param_grid = {
        'normalize': [True, False],        # Whether to normalize the features
before fitting the model
        'fit_intercept': [True, False]     # Whether to calculate the intercept
for this model
    }

    # Create GridSearchCV with the RidgeCV model and the hyperparameter grid
(optional if you include the param_grid)
    grid_search = GridSearchCV(ridge_reg, param_grid, cv=5,
scoring='neg_mean_squared_error')

    # Fit the GridSearchCV to the training data
    grid_search.fit(X_train, y_train)

    # Get the best RidgeCV model from the grid search
    best_ridge_reg = grid_search.best_estimator_

    # Print the best hyperparameters found (optional if you included the
param_grid)
    print("Best Hyperparameters for Ridge Regression:")
    print(grid_search.best_params_)

    return best_ridge_reg
```

Here's an explanation of the steps taken in this method:

1. Creating a RidgeCV Model:

   ridge_reg = RidgeCV(gcv_mode='auto'): This line creates an instance of the RidgeCV regression model. gcv_mode='auto' enables automatic selection of the best alpha value.

2. Hyperparameter Grid (Optional):

   param_grid: This variable defines a grid of hyperparameters to search. In this case, it explores the following hyperparameters:

   - normalize: Whether to normalize the features before fitting the model.
   - fit_intercept: Whether to calculate the intercept for this model. (Note: This step is optional and can be excluded if not needed)

3. Grid Search (Optional):

   grid_search = GridSearchCV(ridge_reg, param_grid, cv=5, scoring='neg_mean_squared_error'): This line sets up a GridSearchCV object. It uses 5-fold cross-validation (cv=5) and uses negative mean squared error (scoring='neg_mean_squared_error') as the evaluation metric. (Note: This step is optional and can be excluded if not needed)

4. Fitting Grid Search (Optional):

   grid_search.fit(X_train, y_train): This fits the GridSearchCV object to the training data. It performs an exhaustive search over the hyperparameter grid, evaluating each combination using cross-validation. (Note: This step is optional and can be excluded if not needed)

5. Best Model:

   best_ridge_reg = grid_search.best_estimator_: This line retrieves the best Ridge regression model found during the grid search. (Note: If the hyperparameter search was not performed, you can simply use the ridge_reg model without grid search).

6. Printing Best Hyperparameters (Optional):

   print("Best Hyperparameters for Ridge Regression:") and print(grid_search.best_params_): These lines print out the best hyperparameters discovered by the grid search. (Note: This step is optional and can be excluded if not needed)

7. Returning Best Model:

   The method returns the best Ridge regression model.

This method allows for Ridge Regression with optional hyperparameter tuning, providing flexibility in the modeling process.

AdaBoost Regression

In Regression class, define a new method named adaboost_regression(). It is responsible for performing AdaBoost Regression along with an optional hyperparameter search:

```python
def adaboost_regression(self, X_train, y_train):
    #Adaboost regression
    # Create the AdaBoostRegressor model
    ada_reg = AdaBoostRegressor()

    # Define the hyperparameter grid to search
    param_grid = {
        'n_estimators': [50, 100, 150],             # Number of boosting stages
(trees) to build
        'learning_rate': [0.01, 0.1, 0.5],          # Step size at each boosting
iteration
        'loss': ['linear', 'square', 'exponential']  # Loss function to use when
updating weights
    }

    # Create GridSearchCV with the AdaBoostRegressor model and the hyperparameter
grid
    grid_search = GridSearchCV(ada_reg, param_grid, cv=5,
scoring='neg_mean_squared_error')

    # Fit the GridSearchCV to the training data
    grid_search.fit(X_train, y_train)

    # Get the best AdaBoostRegressor model from the grid search
    best_ada_reg = grid_search.best_estimator_

    # Print the best hyperparameters found
    print("Best Hyperparameters for AdaBoostRegressor:")
    print(grid_search.best_params_)

    return best_ada_reg
```

Here's an explanation of the steps taken in this method:

1. Creating an AdaBoostRegressor Model:

    ada_reg = AdaBoostRegressor(): This line creates an instance of the AdaBoostRegressor model.

2. Hyperparameter Grid (Optional):

    param_grid: This variable defines a grid of hyperparameters to search. In this case, it explores the following hyperparameters:

    - n_estimators: Number of boosting stages (trees) to build.
    - learning_rate: Step size at each boosting iteration.
    - loss: Loss function to use when updating weights.

3. Grid Search (Optional):

    grid_search = GridSearchCV(ada_reg, param_grid, cv=5, scoring='neg_mean_squared_error'): This line sets up a GridSearchCV object. It uses 5-fold cross-validation (cv=5) and uses negative mean squared error (scoring='neg_mean_squared_error') as the evaluation metric. (Note: This step is optional and can be excluded if not needed)

4. Fitting Grid Search (Optional):

   grid_search.fit(X_train, y_train): This fits the GridSearchCV object to the training data. It performs an exhaustive search over the hyperparameter grid, evaluating each combination using cross-validation. (Note: This step is optional and can be excluded if not needed)

5. Best Model:

   best_ada_reg = grid_search.best_estimator_: This line retrieves the best AdaBoost regression model found during the grid search. (Note: If the hyperparameter search was not performed, you can simply use the ada_reg model without grid search).

6. Printing Best Hyperparameters (Optional):

   print("Best Hyperparameters for AdaBoostRegressor:") and print(grid_search.best_params_): These lines print out the best hyperparameters discovered by the grid search. (Note: This step is optional and can be excluded if not needed)

7. Returning Best Model:

   The method returns the best AdaBoost regression model.

This method allows for AdaBoost Regression with optional hyperparameter tuning, providing flexibility in the modeling process.

K-Nearest Neighbors Regression

In Regression class, define a new method named knn_regression(). It is responsible for performing K-Nearest Neighbors (KNN) Regression along with an optional hyperparameter search:

```python
def knn_regression(self, X_train, y_train):
    #KNN regression
    # Create a KNeighborsRegressor model
    knn_reg = KNeighborsRegressor()

    # Define the hyperparameter grid to search
    param_grid = {
        'n_neighbors': [3, 5, 7, 9],                      # Number of neighbors to use for
regression
        'weights': ['uniform', 'distance'],          # Weight function used in
prediction
        'algorithm': ['auto', 'ball_tree', 'kd_tree', 'brute']  # Algorithm used
to compute the nearest neighbors
    }

    # Create GridSearchCV with the KNeighborsRegressor model and the
hyperparameter grid
    grid_search = GridSearchCV(knn_reg, param_grid, cv=5,
scoring='neg_mean_squared_error')

    # Fit the GridSearchCV to the training data
    grid_search.fit(X_train, y_train)
```

```python
# Get the best KNeighborsRegressor model from the grid search
best_knn_reg = grid_search.best_estimator_

# Print the best hyperparameters found
print("Best Hyperparameters for KNeighborsRegressor:")
print(grid_search.best_params_)

return best_knn_reg
```

Here's an explanation of the steps taken in this method:
1. Creating a KNeighborsRegressor Model:

    knn_reg = KNeighborsRegressor(): This line creates an instance of the KNeighborsRegressor model.
2. Hyperparameter Grid (Optional):

    param_grid: This variable defines a grid of hyperparameters to search. In this case, it explores the following hyperparameters:
    - n_neighbors: Number of neighbors to use for regression.
    - weights: Weight function used in prediction (uniform or distance).
    - algorithm: Algorithm used to compute the nearest neighbors (auto, ball_tree, kd_tree, or brute).
3. Grid Search (Optional):

    grid_search = GridSearchCV(knn_reg, param_grid, cv=5, scoring='neg_mean_squared_error'): This line sets up a GridSearchCV object. It uses 5-fold cross-validation (cv=5) and uses negative mean squared error (scoring='neg_mean_squared_error') as the evaluation metric. (Note: This step is optional and can be excluded if not needed)
4. Fitting Grid Search (Optional):

    grid_search.fit(X_train, y_train): This fits the GridSearchCV object to the training data. It performs an exhaustive search over the hyperparameter grid, evaluating each combination using cross-validation. (Note: This step is optional and can be excluded if not needed)
5. Best Model:

    best_knn_reg = grid_search.best_estimator_: This line retrieves the best K-Nearest Neighbors regression model found during the grid search. (Note: If the hyperparameter search was not performed, you can simply use the knn_reg model without grid search).
6. Printing Best Hyperparameters (Optional):

    print("Best Hyperparameters for KNeighborsRegressor:") and print(grid_search.best_params_): These lines print out the best hyperparameters discovered by the grid search. (Note: This step is optional and can be excluded if not needed)
7. Returning Best Model:

    The method returns the best K-Nearest Neighbors regression model.

This method allows for K-Nearest Neighbors (KNN) Regression with optional hyperparameter tuning, providing flexibility in the modeling process.

PREDICTING CHURNED CUSTOMERS

Oversampling and Splitting Data for Prediction Model

Open a new python file and name it as machine_learning.py. In it, create a class named Machine_Learning:

```python
#machine_learning.py
import numpy as np
from imblearn.over_sampling import SMOTE
from sklearn.model_selection import train_test_split, RandomizedSearchCV,
GridSearchCV, StratifiedKFold
from sklearn.preprocessing import StandardScaler
import joblib
from sklearn.linear_model import LogisticRegression
from sklearn.metrics import confusion_matrix, accuracy_score, recall_score,
precision_score
from sklearn.metrics import classification_report, f1_score, plot_confusion_matrix
from sklearn.ensemble import RandomForestClassifier
from sklearn.neighbors import KNeighborsClassifier
from sklearn.tree import DecisionTreeClassifier
from sklearn.ensemble import AdaBoostClassifier, GradientBoostingClassifier
from xgboost import XGBClassifier
from sklearn.neural_network import MLPClassifier
from sklearn.svm import SVC
import os
import joblib
import pandas as pd
```

```python
from process_data import Process_Data

class Machine_Learning:
    def __init__(self):
        self.obj_data = Process_Data()
```

This script is dedicated to machine learning tasks for predicting churned customers and includes various libraries and modules related to data processing and classification.

Here's a breakdown of the contents so far:
1. Importing Libraries:

   It imported several essential libraries for machine learning tasks. These include NumPy for numerical operations, imblearn for dealing with imbalanced datasets, train_test_split and various model evaluation metrics from sklearn, and specific classifiers from different algorithms like Logistic Regression, Random Forest, K-Nearest Neighbors, Decision Trees, AdaBoost, Gradient Boosting, XGBoost, MLP (Multi-layer Perceptron), and Support Vector Machines.
2. Importing Local Modules:

   It is importing a local module named Process_Data. This module is responsible for data preprocessing tasks.
3. Class Definition:

   It defines a class named Machine_Learning. The __init__() method initializes an instance of this class.

Then, in Machine_Learning class, define a new method named oversampling_splitting(). It is focused on handling imbalanced data by oversampling and preparing the data for training a machine learning model:

```python
def oversampling_splitting(self, df):
    #Sets target column
    y = df["Churn"]

    #Ensures y is of integer type
    y = np.array([1 if i>0 else 0 for i in y]).astype(int)

    #Drops irrelevant column
    X = df.drop(["Churn"], axis =1)

    #Checks null values because of technical indicators
    print(X.isnull().sum().to_string())
    print('Total number of null values: ', X.isnull().sum().sum())

    #Fills each null value in every column with mean value
    cols = list(X.columns)
    for n in cols:
        X[n].fillna(X[n].mean(),inplace = True)

    #Checks again null values
```

```python
print(X.isnull().sum().to_string())
print('Total number of null values: ', X.isnull().sum().sum())

# Check and convert data types
X = X.astype(float)
y = y.astype(int)

sm = SMOTE(random_state=42)
X,y = sm.fit_resample(X, y)

#Splits the data into training and testing
X_train, X_test, y_train, y_test = train_test_split(X, y, test_size = 0.2,
random_state = 2021, stratify=y)

#Use Standard Scaler
scaler = StandardScaler()
X_train_stand = scaler.fit_transform(X_train)
X_test_stand = scaler.transform(X_test)

#Saves into pkl files
joblib.dump(X_train_stand, 'X_train.pkl')
joblib.dump(X_test_stand, 'X_test.pkl')
joblib.dump(y_train, 'y_train.pkl')
joblib.dump(y_test, 'y_test.pkl')
```

Here's a breakdown of what it does:
1. Setting Up Target and Features:
   It separates the target variable y (which is "Churn") and the features X from the DataFrame df.
2. Handling Missing Values:
   It checks for and handles missing values in the features (X). It prints out the initial count of null values and then fills any null values with the mean value of the respective column.
3. Data Type Conversion:
   It ensures that the data types of features in X are converted to float and the target variable y to integer.
4. SMOTE for Oversampling:
   It applies Synthetic Minority Over-sampling Technique (SMOTE) to oversample the minority class (churned customers) in order to balance the class distribution.
5. Train-Test Split:
   It splits the data into training and testing sets (80% training, 20% testing) using stratified sampling, which is important when dealing with imbalanced classes.
6. Standardization:
   It applies standardization using StandardScaler to both the training and testing features.
7. Saving Data:
   It saves the preprocessed data and splits into separate files (X_train.pkl, X_test.pkl, y_train.pkl, y_test.pkl) using joblib.

Overall, this method is crucial for preparing the data for training a machine learning model, especially when dealing with imbalanced classes. It ensures that the data is in the right format and that any missing values are appropriately handled.

Loading Files

In Machine_Learning class, define a new method named load_files(). It is responsible for loading the preprocessed and split data (both features and target) from the saved files:

```python
def load_files(self):
    X_train = joblib.load('X_train.pkl')
    X_test = joblib.load('X_test.pkl')
    y_train = joblib.load('y_train.pkl')
    y_test = joblib.load('y_test.pkl')

    return X_train, X_test, y_train, y_test
```

Here's a brief overview of what it does:
1. Loading Data:
   It uses joblib.load to load the preprocessed and split data from the files X_train.pkl, X_test.pkl, y_train.pkl, and y_test.pkl.
2. Returning Data:
   It returns the loaded data, specifically X_train, X_test, y_train, and y_test.

This method allows you to easily retrieve the preprocessed data when needed for model training and evaluation.

Training Model and Predicting

In Machine_Learning class, define three new methods named train_model(), predict_model(), and run_model(). These methods are related to training and evaluating a classification model:

```python
def train_model(self, model, X, y):
    model.fit(X, y)
    return model

def predict_model(self, model, X, proba=False):
    if ~proba:
        y_pred = model.predict(X)
    else:
        y_pred_proba = model.predict_proba(X)
        y_pred = np.argmax(y_pred_proba, axis=1)

    return y_pred

def run_model(self, name, model, X_train, X_test, y_train, y_test, proba=False):
```

```
y_pred = self.predict_model(model, X_test, proba)

accuracy = accuracy_score(y_test, y_pred)
recall = recall_score(y_test, y_pred, average='weighted')
precision = precision_score(y_test, y_pred, average='weighted')
f1 = f1_score(y_test, y_pred, average='weighted')

print(name)
print('accuracy: ', accuracy)
print('recall: ', recall)
print('precision: ', precision)
print('f1: ', f1)
print(classification_report(y_test, y_pred))

return y_pred
```

Let's break down what each function does:
1. train_model():
    This function trains a given model (model) on a set of features (X) and their corresponding labels (y).
    It uses the fit method of the model to train it on the provided data.
    It returns the trained model.
2. predict_model():
    This function makes predictions using a trained model (model) on a set of features (X).
    If proba is False, it returns the class labels predicted by the model.
    If proba is True, it returns the class probabilities predicted by the model.
3. run_model():
    This function is used to run a trained model (model) on a test set (X_test) and evaluate its performance.
    It prints out various classification metrics including accuracy, recall, precision, and F1-score.
    It also prints a detailed classification report.
    It returns the predicted labels.

These functions allow you to efficiently train, predict, and evaluate classification models. The run_model() function in particular provides a summary of how well the model performs on the test set.

Logistic Regression Prediction

In Machine_Learning class, define a new method named logistic_regression(). It essentially automates the process of finding the best hyperparameters for the logistic regression model using grid search:

```
def logistic_regression(self, name, X_train, X_test, y_train, y_test):
```

```python
#Logistic Regression Classifier
# Define the parameter grid for the grid search
param_grid = {
    'C': [0.01, 0.1, 1, 10],
    'penalty': ['none', 'l2'],
    'solver': ['newton-cg', 'lbfgs', 'liblinear', 'saga'],
}

# Initialize the Logistic Regression model
logreg = LogisticRegression(max_iter=5000, random_state=2021)

# Create GridSearchCV with the Logistic Regression model and the parameter grid
grid_search = GridSearchCV(logreg, param_grid, cv=3, scoring='accuracy', n_jobs=-1)

# Train and perform grid search
grid_search.fit(X_train, y_train)

# Get the best Logistic Regression model from the grid search
best_model = grid_search.best_estimator_

#Saves model
joblib.dump(best_model, 'LR_Model.pkl')

# Print the best hyperparameters found
print(f"Best Hyperparameters for LR:")
print(grid_search.best_params_)

return best_model
```

It performs the following tasks:
1. Grid Search for Logistic Regression:
    - It performs a grid search to find the best hyperparameters for a logistic regression model. The hyperparameters being tuned are 'C' (inverse of regularization strength), 'penalty' (type of regularization), and 'solver' (algorithm to use for optimization).
    - The parameter grid is defined with different values for these hyperparameters.
2. Initializing Logistic Regression:
    It initializes a Logistic Regression model with a maximum number of iterations (max_iter) set to 5000 and a random seed (random_state) set to 2021.
3. Creating GridSearchCV:
    - It creates a GridSearchCV object with the initialized Logistic Regression model and the defined parameter grid.
    - The cv parameter is set to 3, indicating 3-fold cross-validation, and scoring is set to 'accuracy', indicating that accuracy will be used as the evaluation metric.
4. Training and Grid Search:
    It trains the GridSearchCV object on the training data (X_train and y_train) to perform the grid search.

5. Getting the Best Model:
   It retrieves the best Logistic Regression model from the grid search.
6. Saving the Model:
   It saves the best model using joblib.dump as 'LR_Model.pkl'.
7. Printing Best Hyperparameters:
   It prints the best hyperparameters found during the grid search.
8. Returning the Best Model:
   It returns the best trained logistic regression model.

This method essentially automates the process of finding the best hyperparameters for the logistic regression model using grid search. The best model is then saved for future use.

Then, in the same class, define a new method named implement_LR():

```python
def implement_LR(self, chosen, X_train, X_test, y_train, y_test):
    file_path = os.getcwd()+"/LR_Model.pkl"
    if os.path.exists(file_path):
        model = joblib.load('LR_Model.pkl')
        y_pred = self.run_model(chosen, model, X_train, X_test, y_train, y_test,
proba=True)
    else:
        model = self.logistic_regression(chosen, X_train, X_test, y_train,
y_test)
        y_pred = self.run_model(chosen, model, X_train, X_test, y_train, y_test,
proba=True)

        #Saves result into excel file
        self.obj_data.save_result(y_test, y_pred, "results_LR.csv")

        print("Training Logistic Regression done...")
        return model, y_pred
```

It performs the following tasks:
1. Checking for Existing Model:
   It checks if a saved Logistic Regression model (LR_Model.pkl) exists in the current working directory.
2. Loading Existing Model:
   If a saved model is found, it loads the model using joblib.load.
3. Running Model:
   - It then calls the run_model() method to make predictions using the loaded or newly trained Logistic Regression model (model).
   - The proba=True argument indicates that probabilities will be returned.
4. Saving Results:
   It saves the results (actual vs. predicted) into an Excel file named "results_LR.csv" using the save_result() method.

5. Training and Saving New Model (if needed):
   - If no saved model is found, it calls the logistic_regression() method to train a new Logistic Regression model.
   - The newly trained model is then used for predictions.
6. Printing Message:
   It prints a message indicating that the training of the Logistic Regression model is done.
7. Returning Model and Predictions:
   It returns the trained Logistic Regression model (model) and the predictions (y_pred).

This method provides an implementation of the Logistic Regression model for predicting churned customers. If a pre-trained model exists, it loads and uses that. Otherwise, it trains a new model, makes predictions, and saves the results. Finally, it returns the model and predictions.

Random Forest Prediction

In Machine_Learning class, define two new methods named random_forest() and implement_RF():

```python
def random_forest(self, name, X_train, X_test, y_train, y_test):
    #Random Forest Classifier
    # Define the parameter grid for the grid search
    param_grid = {
        'n_estimators': [100, 200, 300],
        'max_depth': [10, 20, 30, 40, 50],
        'min_samples_split': [2, 5, 10],
        'min_samples_leaf': [1, 2, 4]
    }

    # Initialize the RandomForestClassifier model
    rf = RandomForestClassifier(random_state=2021)

    # Create GridSearchCV with the RandomForestClassifier model and the parameter grid
    grid_search = GridSearchCV(rf, param_grid, cv=3, scoring='accuracy', n_jobs=-1)

    # Train and perform grid search
    grid_search.fit(X_train, y_train)

    # Get the best RandomForestClassifier model from the grid search
    best_model = grid_search.best_estimator_

    #Saves model
    joblib.dump(best_model, 'RF_Model.pkl')

    # Print the best hyperparameters found
    print(f"Best Hyperparameters for RF:")
    print(grid_search.best_params_)

    return best_model
```

```python
def implement_RF(self, chosen, X_train, X_test, y_train, y_test):
    file_path = os.getcwd()+"/RF_Model.pkl"
    if os.path.exists(file_path):
        model = joblib.load('RF_Model.pkl')
        y_pred = self.run_model(chosen, model, X_train, X_test, y_train, y_test,
proba=True)
    else:
        model = self.random_forest(chosen, X_train, X_test, y_train, y_test)
        y_pred = self.run_model(chosen, model, X_train, X_test, y_train, y_test,
proba=True)

    #Saves result into excel file
    self.obj_data.save_result(y_test, y_pred, "results_RF.csv")

    print("Training Random Forest done...")
    return model, y_pred
```

The random_forest() method is responsible for training a Random Forest Classifier. It takes in the training and testing data (X_train, X_test, y_train, y_test) along with a parameter name (though it is not utilized within the method). The method employs hyperparameter tuning using a grid search.

1. Parameter Definition:
   - name: This parameter is present in the method's signature but is not used within the method's body.
   - X_train, X_test: These are the feature sets of the training and testing data respectively.
   - y_train, y_test: These are the target labels for the training and testing data.
2. Hyperparameter Grid:
   A set of hyperparameters (n_estimators, max_depth, min_samples_split, min_samples_leaf) is defined. This grid represents different combinations of these hyperparameters that will be explored during the grid search.
3. Random Forest Initialization:
   An instance of the RandomForestClassifier is created with a specified random seed for reproducibility.
4. Grid Search Setup:
   A GridSearchCV object is instantiated. This object will perform a search over the hyperparameter grid defined earlier. It uses 3-fold cross-validation, employs accuracy as the scoring metric, and allows for parallel processing.
5. Training and Model Selection:
   The GridSearchCV object is fitted to the training data. It tries various combinations of hyperparameters to find the best performing model.
6. Best Model Extraction:
   The best Random Forest model is obtained from the grid search results.
7. Model Saving:
   The best model is saved to a file named "RF_Model.pkl" for future use.

8. Printing Best Hyperparameters:
   The hyperparameters that resulted in the best model performance are printed to the console.
9. Return Value:
   The best Random Forest model is returned.

The implement_RF() method implements the Random Forest Classifier for predicting churned customers. It checks if a pre-trained model exists and, if so, loads and uses it. Otherwise, it trains a new model.

1. Parameter Definition:
   - chosen: This parameter is included in the method signature but is not utilized within the method.
   - X_train, X_test: These are the feature sets of the training and testing data respectively.
   - y_train, y_test: These are the target labels for the training and testing data.
2. Checking for Existing Model:
   The method first checks if a pre-trained Random Forest model (RF_Model.pkl) exists in the current working directory.
3. Loading Existing Model:
   If a saved model is found, it is loaded using joblib.load('RF_Model.pkl').
4. Running Model:
   The run_model() method is called to make predictions using the loaded or newly trained Random Forest model (model). The proba=True argument indicates that probabilities will be returned.
5. Saving Results:
   The actual vs. predicted results are saved into an Excel file named "results_RF.csv" using the save_result method.
6. Training and Saving New Model (if needed):
   If no saved model is found, the random_forest() method is called to train a new Random Forest model. This newly trained model is then used for predictions.
7. Printing Message:
   A message is printed to indicate that the training of the Random Forest model is complete.
8. Return Value:
   The trained Random Forest model and the predictions are returned.

K-Nearest Neighbors Prediction

In Machine_Learning class, define two new methods named knearest_neighbors() and implement_KNN():

```python
    def knearest_neigbors(self, name, X_train, X_test, y_train, y_test):
        #KNN Classifier
        # Define the parameter grid for the grid search
        param_grid = {
            'n_neighbors': list(range(2, 10))
        }

        # Initialize the KNN Classifier
        knn = KNeighborsClassifier()

        # Create GridSearchCV with the KNN model and the parameter grid
        grid_search = GridSearchCV(knn, param_grid, cv=3, scoring='accuracy',
n_jobs=-1)

        # Train and perform grid search
        grid_search.fit(X_train, y_train)

        # Get the best KNN model from the grid search
        best_model = grid_search.best_estimator_

        #Saves model
        joblib.dump(best_model, 'KNN_Model.pkl')

        # Print the best hyperparameters found
        print(f"Best Hyperparameters for KNN:")
        print(grid_search.best_params_)

        return best_model

    def implement_KNN(self, chosen, X_train, X_test, y_train, y_test):
        file_path = os.getcwd()+"/KNN_Model.pkl"
        if os.path.exists(file_path):
            model = joblib.load('KNN_Model.pkl')
            y_pred = self.run_model(chosen, model, X_train, X_test, y_train, y_test,
proba=True)
        else:
            model = self.knearest_neigbors(chosen, X_train, X_test, y_train, y_test)
            y_pred = self.run_model(chosen, model, X_train, X_test, y_train, y_test,
proba=True)

        #Saves result into excel file
        self.obj_data.save_result(y_test, y_pred, "results_KNN.csv")

        print("Training KNN done...")
        return model, y_pred
```

The knearest_neigbors() method is responsible for training a K-Nearest Neighbors (KNN) Classifier. It takes in the training and testing data (X_train, X_test, y_train, y_test) along with a parameter name (though it is not utilized within the method). The method employs hyperparameter tuning using a grid search.

1. Parameter Definition:

  - name: This parameter is present in the method's signature but is not used within the method's body.

- X_train, X_test: These are the feature sets of the training and testing data respectively.
- y_train, y_test: These are the target labels for the training and testing data.

2. Hyperparameter Grid:

   A set of hyperparameters (n_neighbors) is defined. This grid represents different numbers of neighbors that will be explored during the grid search.

3. KNN Initialization:

   An instance of the KNeighborsClassifier is created.

4. Grid Search Setup:

   A GridSearchCV object is instantiated. This object will perform a search over the hyperparameter grid defined earlier. It uses 3-fold cross-validation, employs accuracy as the scoring metric, and allows for parallel processing.

5. Training and Model Selection:

   The GridSearchCV object is fitted to the training data. It tries various combinations of hyperparameters to find the best performing model.

6. Best Model Extraction:

   The best KNN model is obtained from the grid search results.

7. Model Saving:

   The best model is saved to a file named "KNN_Model.pkl" for future use.

8. Printing Best Hyperparameters:

   The hyperparameters that resulted in the best model performance are printed to the console.

9. Return Value:

   The best KNN model is returned.

The implement_KNN() method implements the K-Nearest Neighbors (KNN) Classifier for predicting churned customers. It checks if a pre-trained model exists and, if so, loads and uses it. Otherwise, it trains a new model.

1. Parameter Definition:
   - chosen: This parameter is included in the method signature but is not utilized within the method.
   - X_train, X_test: These are the feature sets of the training and testing data respectively.
   - y_train, y_test: These are the target labels for the training and testing data.

2. Checking for Existing Model:

   The method first checks if a pre-trained KNN model (KNN_Model.pkl) exists in the current working directory.

3. Loading Existing Model:

   If a saved model is found, it is loaded using joblib.load('KNN_Model.pkl').

4. Running Model:

The run_model() method is called to make predictions using the loaded or newly trained KNN model (model). The proba=True argument indicates that probabilities will be returned.

5. Saving Results:

The actual vs. predicted results are saved into an Excel file named "results_KNN.csv" using the save_result method.

6. Training and Saving New Model (if needed):

If no saved model is found, the knearest_neigbors method is called to train a new KNN model. This newly trained model is then used for predictions.

7. Printing Message:

A message is printed to indicate that the training of the KNN model is complete.

8. Return Value:

The trained KNN model and the predictions are returned.

Decision Tree Prediction

In Machine_Learning class, define two new methods named decision_trees() and implement_DT():

```python
def decision_trees(self, name, X_train, X_test, y_train, y_test):
    # Initialize the DecisionTreeClassifier model
    dt_clf = DecisionTreeClassifier(random_state=2021)

    # Define the parameter grid for the grid search
    param_grid = {
        'max_depth': np.arange(1, 51, 1),
        'criterion': ['gini', 'entropy'],
        'min_samples_split': [2, 5, 10],
        'min_samples_leaf': [1, 2, 4],
    }

    # Create GridSearchCV with the DecisionTreeClassifier model and the parameter grid
    grid_search = GridSearchCV(dt_clf, param_grid, cv=3, scoring='accuracy', n_jobs=-1)

    # Train and perform grid search
    grid_search.fit(X_train, y_train)

    # Get the best DecisionTreeClassifier model from the grid search
    best_model = grid_search.best_estimator_

    #Saves model
    joblib.dump(best_model, 'DT_Model.pkl')

    # Print the best hyperparameters found
    print(f"Best Hyperparameters for DT:")
    print(grid_search.best_params_)
```

```python
        return best_model

    def implement_DT(self, chosen, X_train, X_test, y_train, y_test):
        file_path = os.getcwd()+"/DT_Model.pkl"
        if os.path.exists(file_path):
            model = joblib.load('DT_Model.pkl')
            y_pred = self.run_model(chosen, model, X_train, X_test, y_train, y_test,
proba=True)
        else:
            model = self.decision_trees(chosen, X_train, X_test, y_train, y_test)
            y_pred = self.run_model(chosen, model, X_train, X_test, y_train, y_test,
proba=True)

        #Saves result into excel file
        self.obj_data.save_result(y_test, y_pred, "results_DT.csv")

        print("Training Decision Trees done...")
        return model, y_pred
```

The decision_trees() method is responsible for training a Decision Tree Classifier. It starts by initializing an instance of the DecisionTreeClassifier with a specified random state. It then defines a parameter grid, including hyperparameters like max_depth, criterion, min_samples_split, and min_samples_leaf. These parameters control the complexity of the decision tree. A grid search is performed to find the best combination of hyperparameters. The grid search uses 3-fold cross-validation and accuracy as the scoring metric. After training, the best model is saved as "DT_Model.pkl". Finally, the best hyperparameters found during the grid search are printed to the console.

The implement_DT() method implements the Decision Tree Classifier for predicting churned customers. It first checks if a pre-trained model exists. If a saved model (DT_Model.pkl) is found, it is loaded. Otherwise, a new model is trained using the decision_trees method. Next, the run_model method is called to make predictions using the loaded or newly trained Decision Tree model. The proba=True argument indicates that probabilities will be returned. The actual vs. predicted results are saved into an Excel file named "results_DT.csv" using the save_result method. If a new model was trained, it is returned along with the predictions.

In summary, the decision_trees() method trains a Decision Tree Classifier with hyperparameter tuning, while implement_DT() checks for an existing model, loads it if available, or trains a new one. It then uses the model to make predictions and saves the results in a CSV file. The training process is logged to the console for user feedback.

Gradient Boosting Prediction

In Machine_Learning class, define two new methods named gradient_boosting() and implement_GB():

```python
    def gradient_boosting(self, name, X_train, X_test, y_train, y_test):
        #Gradient Boosting Classifier
        # Initialize the GradientBoostingClassifier model
        gbt = GradientBoostingClassifier(random_state=2021)

        # Define the parameter grid for the grid search
        param_grid = {
            'n_estimators': [100, 200, 300],
            'max_depth': [10, 20, 30],
            'subsample': [0.6, 0.8, 1.0],
            'max_features': [0.2, 0.4, 0.6, 0.8, 1.0],
        }

        # Create GridSearchCV with the GradientBoostingClassifier model and the
parameter grid
        grid_search = GridSearchCV(gbt, param_grid, cv=3, scoring='accuracy',
n_jobs=-1)

        # Train and perform grid search
        grid_search.fit(X_train, y_train)

        # Get the best GradientBoostingClassifier model from the grid search
        best_model = grid_search.best_estimator_

        #Saves model
        joblib.dump(best_model, 'GB_Model.pkl')

        # Print the best hyperparameters found
        print(f"Best Hyperparameters for GB:")
        print(grid_search.best_params_)

        return best_model

    def implement_GB(self, chosen, X_train, X_test, y_train, y_test):
        file_path = os.getcwd()+"/GB_Model.pkl"
        if os.path.exists(file_path):
            model = joblib.load('GB_Model.pkl')
            y_pred = self.run_model(chosen, model, X_train, X_test, y_train, y_test,
proba=True)
        else:
            model = self.gradient_boosting(chosen, X_train, X_test, y_train, y_test)
            y_pred = self.run_model(chosen, model, X_train, X_test, y_train, y_test,
proba=True)

        #Saves result into excel file
        self.obj_data.save_result(y_test, y_pred, "results_GB.csv")

        print("Training Gradient Boosting done...")
        return model, y_pred
```

The gradient_boosting() method is responsible for training a Gradient Boosting Classifier. It starts by initializing an instance of the GradientBoostingClassifier with a specified random state. It then defines a parameter grid including hyperparameters such as n_estimators, max_depth, subsample, and max_features. These parameters control the complexity and behavior of the gradient boosting ensemble. A grid search is performed to find the best combination of hyperparameters. The grid search uses 3-fold cross-validation and accuracy as the scoring metric. After training, the best model is saved as "GB_Model.pkl". Finally, the best hyperparameters found during the grid search are printed to the console.

The implement_GB() method is responsible for implementing the Gradient Boosting Classifier for predicting churned customers. It first checks if a pre-trained model exists. If a saved model (GB_Model.pkl) is found, it is loaded. Otherwise, a new model is trained using the gradient_boosting method. Next, the run_model method is called to make predictions using the loaded or newly trained Gradient Boosting model. The proba=True argument indicates that probabilities will be returned. The actual vs. predicted results are saved into an Excel file named "results_GB.csv" using the save_result() method. If a new model was trained, it is returned along with the predictions.

In summary, the gradient_boosting() method trains a Gradient Boosting Classifier with hyperparameter tuning, while implement_GB() checks for an existing model, loads it if available, or trains a new one. It then uses the model to make predictions and saves the results in a CSV file. The training process is logged to the console for user feedback.

Extreme Gradient Boosting Prediction

In Machine_Learning class, define two new methods named extreme_gradient_boosting() and implement_XGB():

```python
def extreme_gradient_boosting(self, name, X_train, X_test, y_train, y_test):
    # Define the parameter grid for the grid search
    param_grid = {
        'n_estimators': [100, 200, 300],
        'max_depth': [10, 20, 30],
        'learning_rate': [0.01, 0.1, 0.2],
        'subsample': [0.6, 0.8, 1.0],
        'colsample_bytree': [0.6, 0.8, 1.0],
    }

    # Initialize the XGBoost classifier
    xgb = XGBClassifier(random_state=2021, use_label_encoder=False,
eval_metric='mlogloss')

    # Create GridSearchCV with the XGBoost classifier and the parameter grid
    grid_search = GridSearchCV(xgb, param_grid, cv=3, scoring='accuracy',
n_jobs=-1)
```

```python
    # Train and perform grid search
    grid_search.fit(X_train, y_train)

    # Get the best XGBoost classifier model from the grid search
    best_model = grid_search.best_estimator_

    #Saves model
    joblib.dump(best_model, 'XGB_Model.pkl')

    # Print the best hyperparameters found
    print(f"Best Hyperparameters for XGB:")
    print(grid_search.best_params_)

    return best_model

def implement_XGB(self, chosen, X_train, X_test, y_train, y_test):
    file_path = os.getcwd()+"/XGB_Model.pkl"
    if os.path.exists(file_path):
        model = joblib.load('XGB_Model.pkl')
        y_pred = self.run_model(chosen, model, X_train, X_test, y_train, y_test,
proba=True)
    else:
        model = self.extreme_gradient_boosting(chosen, X_train, X_test, y_train,
y_test)
        y_pred = self.run_model(chosen, model, X_train, X_test, y_train, y_test,
proba=True)

    #Saves result into excel file
    self.obj_data.save_result(y_test, y_pred, "results_XGB.csv")

    print("Training Extreme Gradient Boosting done...")
    return model, y_pred
```

The extreme_gradient_boosting() method is responsible for training an Extreme Gradient
Boosting (XGBoost) Classifier. It begins by defining a parameter grid containing hyperparameters
such as n_estimators, max_depth, learning_rate, subsample, and colsample_bytree. These
parameters control the complexity and behavior of the XGBoost ensemble. Next, an instance of
the XGBoost classifier is initialized with a specified random state, and certain settings like
use_label_encoder and eval_metric are configured. A GridSearchCV object is created with the
XGBoost classifier and the parameter grid. This grid search uses 3-fold cross-validation and
accuracy as the scoring metric. The model is then trained using the fit method of GridSearchCV.
After training, the best model is saved as "XGB_Model.pkl". Finally, the best hyperparameters
found during the grid search are printed to the console.

The implement_XGB() method handles the implementation of the XGBoost Classifier for
predicting churned customers. It first checks if a pre-trained model exists. If a saved model
(XGB_Model.pkl) is found, it is loaded. Otherwise, a new model is trained using the
extreme_gradient_boosting() method. Next, the run_model method is called to make predictions
using the loaded or newly trained XGBoost model. The proba=True argument indicates that

probabilities will be returned. The actual vs. predicted results are saved into an Excel file named "results_XGB.csv" using the save_result() method. If a new model was trained, it is returned along with the predictions.

In summary, the extreme_gradient_boosting() method trains an XGBoost Classifier with hyperparameter tuning, while implement_XGB checks for an existing model, loads it if available, or trains a new one. It then uses the model to make predictions and saves the results in a CSV file. The training process is logged to the console for user feedback.

Multi-Layer Perceptron Prediction

In Machine_Learning class, define two new methods named multi_layer_perceptron() and implement_MLP():

```python
def multi_layer_perceptron(self, name, X_train, X_test, y_train, y_test):
    # Define the parameter grid for the grid search
    param_grid = {
        'hidden_layer_sizes': [(50,), (100,), (50, 50), (100, 50), (100, 100)],
        'activation': ['logistic', 'relu'],
        'solver': ['adam', 'sgd'],
        'alpha': [0.0001, 0.001, 0.01],
        'learning_rate': ['constant', 'invscaling', 'adaptive'],
    }

    # Initialize the MLP Classifier
    mlp = MLPClassifier(random_state=2021)

    # Create GridSearchCV with the MLP Classifier and the parameter grid
    grid_search = GridSearchCV(mlp, param_grid, cv=3, scoring='accuracy',
n_jobs=-1)

    # Train and perform grid search
    grid_search.fit(X_train, y_train)

    # Get the best MLP Classifier model from the grid search
    best_model = grid_search.best_estimator_

    #Saves model
    joblib.dump(best_model, 'MLP_Model.pkl')

    # Print the best hyperparameters found
    print(f"Best Hyperparameters for MLP:")
    print(grid_search.best_params_)

    return best_model

def implement_MLP(self, chosen, X_train, X_test, y_train, y_test):
    file_path = os.getcwd()+"/MLP_Model.pkl"
    if os.path.exists(file_path):
        model = joblib.load('MLP_Model.pkl')
```

```python
            y_pred = self.run_model(chosen, model, X_train, X_test, y_train, y_test,
proba=True)
        else:
            model = self.multi_layer_perceptron(chosen, X_train, X_test, y_train,
y_test)
            y_pred = self.run_model(chosen, model, X_train, X_test, y_train, y_test,
proba=True)

        #Saves result into excel file
        self.obj_data.save_result(y_test, y_pred, "results_MLP.csv")

        print("Training Multi-Layer Perceptron done...")
        return model, y_pred
```

The multi_layer_perceptron() method is responsible for training a Multi-Layer Perceptron (MLP) Classifier, which is a type of artificial neural network. It starts by defining a parameter grid containing hyperparameters like hidden_layer_sizes, activation, solver, alpha, and learning_rate. These parameters control the architecture and behavior of the MLP. Next, an instance of the MLP Classifier is initialized with a specified random state. A GridSearchCV object is created with the MLP Classifier and the parameter grid. This grid search uses 3-fold cross-validation and accuracy as the scoring metric. The model is then trained using the fit method of GridSearchCV. After training, the best model is saved as "MLP_Model.pkl". Finally, the best hyperparameters found during the grid search are printed to the console.

The implement_MLP() method handles the implementation of the Multi-Layer Perceptron Classifier for predicting churned customers. It first checks if a pre-trained model exists. If a saved model (MLP_Model.pkl) is found, it is loaded. Otherwise, a new model is trained using the multi_layer_perceptron() method. Next, the run_model method is called to make predictions using the loaded or newly trained MLP model. The proba=True argument indicates that probabilities will be returned. The actual vs. predicted results are saved into an Excel file named "results_MLP.csv" using the save_result() method. If a new model was trained, it is returned along with the predictions.

In summary, the multi_layer_perceptron() method trains an MLP Classifier with hyperparameter tuning, while implement_MLP() checks for an existing model, loads it if available, or trains a new one. It then uses the model to make predictions and saves the results in a CSV file. The training process is logged to the console for user feedback.

Support Vector Prediction

In Machine_Learning class, define two new methods named support_vector() and implement_SVC():

```python
    def support_vector(self, name, X_train, X_test, y_train, y_test):
```

```python
#Support Vector Classifier
# Define the parameter grid for the grid search
param_grid = {
    'C': [0.1, 1, 10],
    'kernel': ['linear', 'poly', 'rbf'],
    'gamma': ['scale', 'auto', 0.1, 1],
}

# Initialize the SVC model
model_svc = SVC(random_state=2021, probability=True)

# Create GridSearchCV with the SVC model and the parameter grid
grid_search = GridSearchCV(model_svc, param_grid, cv=3, scoring='accuracy',
n_jobs=-1, refit=True)

# Train and perform grid search
grid_search.fit(X_train, y_train)

# Get the best MLP Classifier model from the grid search
best_model = grid_search.best_estimator_

#Saves model
joblib.dump(best_model, 'SVC_Model.pkl')

# Print the best hyperparameters found
print(f"Best Hyperparameters for SVC:")
print(grid_search.best_params_)

return best_model

def implement_SVC(self, chosen, X_train, X_test, y_train, y_test):
    file_path = os.getcwd()+"/SVC_Model.pkl"
    if os.path.exists(file_path):
        model = joblib.load('SVC_Model.pkl')
        y_pred = self.run_model(chosen, model, X_train, X_test, y_train, y_test,
proba=True)
    else:
        model = self.support_vector(chosen, X_train, X_test, y_train, y_test)
        y_pred = self.run_model(chosen, model, X_train, X_test, y_train, y_test,
proba=True)

    #Saves result into excel file
    self.obj_data.save_result(y_test, y_pred, "results_SVC.csv")

    print("Training Support Vector Classifier done...")
    return model, y_pred
```

The support_vector() method is used to train a Support Vector Classifier (SVC). It starts by defining a parameter grid containing hyperparameters like C, kernel, and gamma. These parameters control the trade-off between classification accuracy and margin width, the type of kernel function used, and the influence of data points on the decision boundary. Next, an instance of the SVC model is initialized with a specified random state, and the probability parameter is set to True to enable probability estimates. A GridSearchCV object is created with the SVC model and the parameter grid. This grid search uses 3-fold cross-validation and accuracy as the scoring metric. The model is then trained using the fit method of GridSearchCV. After training, the best model is saved as "SVC_Model.pkl". Finally, the best hyperparameters found during the grid search are printed to the console.

The implement_SVC() method handles the implementation of the Support Vector Classifier for predicting churned customers. It first checks if a pre-trained model exists. If a saved model (SVC_Model.pkl) is found, it is loaded. Otherwise, a new model is trained using the support_vector() method. Next, the run_model method is called to make predictions using the loaded or newly trained SVC model. The proba=True argument indicates that probabilities will be returned. The actual vs. predicted results are saved into an Excel file named "results_SVC.csv" using the save_result() method. If a new model was trained, it is returned along with the predictions.

In summary, the support_vector() method trains an SVC with hyperparameter tuning, while implement_SVC checks for an existing model, loads it if available, or trains a new one. It then uses the model to make predictions and saves the results in a CSV file. The training process is logged to the console for user feedback.

AdaBoost Prediction

In Machine_Learning class, define two new methods named adaboost_classifier() and implement_ADA():

```python
def adaboost_classifier(self, name, X_train, X_test, y_train, y_test):
    # Define the parameter grid for the grid search
    param_grid = {
        'n_estimators': [50, 100, 150],
        'learning_rate': [0.01, 0.1, 0.2],
    }

    # Initialize the AdaBoost classifier
    adaboost = AdaBoostClassifier(random_state=2021)

    # Create GridSearchCV with the AdaBoost classifier and the parameter grid
    grid_search = GridSearchCV(adaboost, param_grid, cv=3, scoring='accuracy',
n_jobs=-1)

    # Train and perform grid search
    grid_search.fit(X_train, y_train)

    # Get the best AdaBoost Classifier model from the grid search
    best_model = grid_search.best_estimator_

    #Saves model
    joblib.dump(best_model, 'ADA_Model.pkl')
```

```python
        # Print the best hyperparameters found
        print(f"Best Hyperparameters for AdaBoost:")
        print(grid_search.best_params_)

        return best_model

    def implement_ADA(self, chosen, X_train, X_test, y_train, y_test):
        file_path = os.getcwd()+"/ADA_Model.pkl"
        if os.path.exists(file_path):
            model = joblib.load('ADA_Model.pkl')
            y_pred = self.run_model(chosen, model, X_train, X_test, y_train, y_test,
proba=True)
        else:
            model = self.adaboost_classifier(chosen, X_train, X_test, y_train,
y_test)
            y_pred = self.run_model(chosen, model, X_train, X_test, y_train, y_test,
proba=True)

        #Saves result into excel file
        self.obj_data.save_result(y_test, y_pred, "results_ADA.csv")

        print("Training AdaBoost done...")
        return model, y_pred
```

The adaboost_classifier() method is responsible for training an AdaBoost Classifier. It starts by defining a parameter grid containing hyperparameters like n_estimators and learning_rate. These parameters control the number of weak learners (base estimators) to use in the ensemble and the contribution of each weak learner to the final prediction. Next, an instance of the AdaBoostClassifier is initialized with a specified random state. A GridSearchCV object is created with the AdaBoostClassifier model and the parameter grid. This grid search uses 3-fold cross-validation and accuracy as the scoring metric. The model is then trained using the fit method of GridSearchCV. After training, the best model is saved as "ADA_Model.pkl". Finally, the best hyperparameters found during the grid search are printed to the console.

The implement_ADA() method handles the implementation of the AdaBoost Classifier for predicting churned customers. It first checks if a pre-trained model exists. If a saved model (ADA_Model.pkl) is found, it is loaded. Otherwise, a new model is trained using the adaboost_classifier method. Next, the run_model() method is called to make predictions using the loaded or newly trained AdaBoost model. The proba=True argument indicates that probabilities will be returned. The actual vs. predicted results are saved into an Excel file named "results_ADA.csv" using the save_result method. If a new model was trained, it is returned along with the predictions.

In summary, the adaboost_classifier() method trains an AdaBoost Classifier with hyperparameter tuning, while implement_ADA() checks for an existing model, loads it if available, or trains a new one. It then uses the model to make predictions and saves the results in a CSV file. The training process is logged to the console for user feedback.

PLOTTING UTILITIES

Open a new python file and name it as helper_plot.py. In it, create a class named Helper_Plot:

```python
#helper_plot.py
import matplotlib.pyplot as plt
import tkinter as tk
from tkinter import *
import seaborn as sns
import numpy as np
import pandas as pd
import sys
from pandastable import Table
from io import StringIO
from sklearn.metrics import confusion_matrix, roc_curve, accuracy_score
from sklearn.model_selection import learning_curve
from process_data import Process_Data
from main_window import Main_Window
from form1 import Form1
from form2 import Form2
from form3 import Form3
from machine_learning import Machine_Learning
from regression import Regression

class Helper_Plot:
    def __init__(self):
        self.obj_window = Main_Window()
        self.obj_data = Process_Data()
        self.obj_reg = Regression()
```

```
self.obj_ml = Machine_Learning()
```

Here's a brief overview of the Helper_Plot class:
1. Imports: The class begins with several import statements. It brings in various libraries and modules such as matplotlib for plotting, tkinter for creating GUI components, seaborn for enhancing the style of plots, and others like numpy, pandas, sys, pandastable, and modules from your project such as Process_Data, Main_Window, Form1, Form2, Form3, Machine_Learning, and Regression.
2. Constructor: The __init__() method is the class constructor. It initializes an instance of Main_Window as self.obj_window, an instance of Process_Data as self.obj_data, an instance of Regression as self.obj_reg, and an instance of Machine_Learning as self.obj_ml. These instances serve as interfaces to various functionalities in the project.

Overall, this class appears to serve as a central utility for plotting and visualization, utilizing functionality from other parts of your project such as data processing, regression, and machine learning. If you have specific questions or if you'd like to see specific methods or functionalities within this class explained, feel free to ask!

Showing Table

In Helper_Plot class, define a new method named shows_table(). It is a function within the Helper_Plot class designed to display a table in a graphical user interface using the Tkinter library:

```
def shows_table(self, root, df, width, height, title):
    frame = Toplevel(root) #new window
    self.table = Table(frame, dataframe=df, showtoolbar=True, showstatusbar=True)

    # Sets dimension of Toplevel
    frame.geometry(f"{width}x{height}")
    frame.title(title)
    self.table.show()
```

Here's a breakdown of how it works:
1. Creating a New Window:
   frame = Toplevel(root): This line initializes a new window using Tkinter's Toplevel widget. The Toplevel widget is used to create additional windows that appear on top of the main application window (root in this case). This new window will be used to display the table.
2. Embedding the Table:
   self.table = Table(frame, dataframe=df, showtoolbar=True, showstatusbar=True): Here, a table widget is created using the pandastable library. The table is associated with the DataFrame df, meaning it will display the data contained within df. Additionally, two optional parameters, showtoolbar and showstatusbar, are set to True. This indicates that

the table will have a toolbar and a status bar, which can provide users with additional functionality.

3. Setting Window Dimensions and Title:
    - frame.geometry(f"{width}x{height}"): This line sets the dimensions of the new window created in the first step. The width and height arguments determine the size of the window. The format {width}x{height} is a string interpolation method to incorporate the specified values.
    - frame.title(title): This line sets the title of the new window. The title argument is a string provided when calling the method, and it will be displayed in the title bar of the window.

4. Displaying the Table:
    self.table.show(): This command renders and displays the table in the window. The show() method is specific to the pandastable library and is used to visualize the DataFrame data in a tabular format.

In summary, this method facilitates the creation of a separate window to display a table, allowing users to view and interact with tabular data in a graphical interface. It provides options for customizing the window's dimensions and title, as well as displaying the table with additional features like toolbars and status bars.

Missing Values

In Helper_Plot class, define a new method named plot_missing_values(). It is designed to generate a bar chart that visualizes the missing values in a given DataFrame (df):

```python
def plot_missing_values(self, df, figure, canvas, title=""):
    figure.clear()
    ax = figure.add_subplot(1,1,1)
    #Plots null values
    missing = df.isna().sum().reset_index()
    missing.columns = ['features', 'total_missing']
    missing['percent'] = (missing['total_missing'] / len(df)) * 100
    missing.index = missing['features']
    del missing['features']
    missing['total_missing'].plot(kind = 'bar', ax=ax)
    ax.set_title(title, fontsize = 12)
    ax.set_facecolor('#F0F0F0')

    # Set font for tick labels
    ax.tick_params(axis='both', which='major', labelsize=5)
    ax.tick_params(axis='both', which='minor', labelsize=5)
    figure.tight_layout()
    canvas.draw()
```

Let's break down how this method works:

1. Clearing Previous Plot:
   figure.clear(): This command ensures that any previous plot content is removed before generating a new plot. This is important to prevent overlapping plots.
2. Creating Subplot:
   ax = figure.add_subplot(1,1,1): This line creates a single subplot within the figure. The parameters (1,1,1) specify that there is only one row and one column of subplots, and this is the first (and only) subplot.
3. Calculating Missing Values:
   missing = df.isna().sum().reset_index(): This line counts the number of missing values for each feature in the DataFrame df. The result is stored in a new DataFrame called missing.
4. Formatting the Data:
   missing.columns = ['features', 'total_missing']: This line renames the columns in the missing DataFrame. The first column is renamed to 'features', and the second column is renamed to 'total_missing'.
5. Calculating Percentages:
   missing['percent'] = (missing['total_missing'] / len(df)) * 100: This line calculates the percentage of missing values for each feature by dividing the total number of missing values by the total number of rows in the DataFrame and multiplying by 100.
6. Setting Index:
   missing.index = missing['features']: This line sets the index of the missing DataFrame to be the 'features' column. This allows for more meaningful plotting.
7. Generating the Bar Chart:
   missing['total_missing'].plot(kind='bar', ax=ax): This line creates a bar chart. It uses the 'total_missing' column from the missing DataFrame as the data to be plotted, and specifies that the chart should be a bar chart. The ax=ax argument indicates that the plot should be added to the subplot created earlier.
8. Setting Title and Background Color:
   - ax.set_title(title, fontsize=12): This line sets the title of the subplot. The title argument can be provided when calling this method.
   - ax.set_facecolor('#F0F0F0'): This sets the background color of the subplot to a light grey shade.
9. Adjusting Tick Label Font Size:
   ax.tick_params(axis='both', which='major', labelsize=5): This command adjusts the font size of the tick labels on both the x-axis and y-axis.
10. Optimizing Layout and Redrawing Canvas:
    - figure.tight_layout(): This command ensures that the plot elements are properly spaced for a clean presentation.
    - canvas.draw(): Finally, this command redraws the canvas to display the updated plot.

In summary, this method efficiently visualizes the missing values in a DataFrame by employing a bar chart. The customization options include providing a title for the plot, making it versatile for different datasets.

Pie Chart and Horizontal Bar Chart

In Helper_Plot class, define a new method named plot_piechart(). It creates a figure with two subplots, where the top subplot is a pie chart and the bottom subplot is a horizontal bar plot:

```python
# Defines function to create pie chart and bar plot as subplots
def plot_piechart(self, df, var, figure, canvas, title='', top_ten=False):
    figure.clear()

    # Optionally filter the DataFrame to consider only the top ten values
    if top_ten:
        value_counts = df[var].value_counts().nlargest(10)
    else:
        value_counts = df[var].value_counts()

    # Pie Chart (top subplot)
    ax1 = figure.add_subplot(2,1,1)
    label_list = list(value_counts.index)
    colors = sns.color_palette("Set1", len(label_list))
    _, _, autopcts = ax1.pie(value_counts, autopct="%1.1f%%", colors=colors,
        startangle=30, labels=label_list,
        wedgeprops={"linewidth": 2, "edgecolor": "white"},  # Add white edge
        shadow=True, textprops={'fontsize': 7})
    ax1.set_title(title, weight="bold", fontsize=12)

    # Bar Plot (bottom subplot)
    ax2 = figure.add_subplot(2,1,2)
    ax = value_counts.plot(kind="barh", color=colors, alpha=0.8, ax = ax2)
    for i, j in enumerate(value_counts.values):
        ax.text(.7, i, j, weight="bold", fontsize=7)

    ax2.set_title(title, weight="bold", fontsize=12)
    ax2.set_xlabel("Count")
    ax2.set_facecolor('#F0F0F0')
    figure.tight_layout()

    # Autoscale the subplots
    ax1.autoscale()
    ax2.autoscale()

    canvas.draw()
```

Let's break down how this method works:
1. Clearing Previous Plot:
    figure.clear(): This command ensures that any previous plot content is removed before generating a new plot. This is crucial to prevent overlapping plots.

2. Filtering Data (Optional):
   If top_ten is set to True, the method will consider only the top ten values in the specified variable var from the DataFrame df.
3. Creating Top Subplot for Pie Chart:
   ax1 = figure.add_subplot(2, 1, 1): This creates the top subplot, specifying a 2-row grid and 1 column. This means that the top subplot will span the entire width, while the bottom subplot will be placed below it.
4. Generating Pie Chart:
   ax1.pie(): This generates the pie chart. It uses the value counts from the filtered data. The autopct="%1.1f%%" argument adds the percentage labels to the pie slices. The colors parameter sets the colors of the pie slices. Labels, colors, and other properties are configured here.
5. Creating Bottom Subplot for Bar Plot:
   ax2 = figure.add_subplot(2, 1, 2): This creates the bottom subplot, which will display the bar plot.
6. Generating Bar Plot:
   value_counts.plot(kind="barh", ...): This creates a horizontal bar plot from the filtered value counts. It uses the same color palette as the pie chart.
7. Adding Value Labels to Bar Plot:
   for i, j in enumerate(value_counts.values): ax.text(.7, i, j, weight="bold", fontsize=7): This loop adds the count values as labels to the bars.
8. Setting Titles and Labels:
   Both subplots are given the same title specified in the title argument. The bottom subplot is labeled on the x-axis with "Count".
9. Setting Background Color:
   ax2.set_facecolor('#F0F0F0'): This sets the background color of the bottom subplot to a light grey shade.
10. Tightening Layout:
    figure.tight_layout(): This command ensures that the plot elements are properly spaced for a clean presentation.
11. Autoscaling Subplots:
    - ax1.autoscale(): This command adjusts the scale of the top subplot to fit the contents.
    - ax2.autoscale(): This does the same for the bottom subplot.
12. Drawing Canvas:
    canvas.draw(): Finally, this command redraws the canvas to display the updated plot.

In summary, this method efficiently generates a figure with two subplots containing a pie chart and a bar plot. It provides an option to filter the data for the top values and allows for customization of colors, labels, and titles. The method ensures that the subplots are appropriately spaced and scaled for a visually appealing presentation.

Pie Chart and Horizontal Bar Chart of Grouped Dataframe

In Helper_Plot class, define a new method named plot_piechart_group(). It generates a figure with two subplots, similar to the previous method. It combines a pie chart in the top subplot and a horizontal bar plot in the bottom subplot.

```python
def plot_piechart_group(self, df, figure, canvas, title="", label=""):
    figure.clear()

    # Pie Chart (top subplot)
    ax1 = figure.add_subplot(2,1,1)
    label_list = list(df.index)
    print(label_list)
    colors = sns.color_palette("Set1", len(label_list))
    _, _, autopcts = ax1.pie(df.values, autopct="%1.1f%%", colors=colors,
        startangle=30, labels=label_list,
        wedgeprops={"linewidth": 2, "edgecolor": "white"},  # Add white edge
        shadow=True, textprops={'fontsize': 7})
    ax1.set_title(title, fontsize=10)

    # Bar Plot (bottom subplot)
    ax2 = figure.add_subplot(2,1,2)
    ax = df.plot(kind="barh", color=colors, alpha=0.8, ax = ax2)
    for i, j in enumerate(df.values):
        ax.text(.7, i, j, weight="bold", fontsize=7)

    ax2.set_title(title, fontsize=10)
    ax2.set_xlabel("Count")
    ax2.set_facecolor('#F0F0F0')

    # Set font for tick labels
    ax.tick_params(axis='both', which='major', labelsize=6)
    ax.tick_params(axis='both', which='minor', labelsize=6)
    figure.tight_layout()
    canvas.draw()
```

The plot_piechart_group() function is designed to create a figure with two subplots. This method is well-suited for visualizing categorical data, providing insights into the distribution of different categories. Here's how it operates:

1. Pie Chart Subplot:

   In the first subplot (ax1), a pie chart is created to represent the distribution of categorical variables. Each slice of the pie corresponds to a category, and its size is proportional to the frequency of that category in the dataset. The labels are set to the index of the DataFrame, which represent the category names.

2. Color Palette and Aesthetics:

   The colors for the pie chart are obtained from a color palette called "Set1". This palette is a set of visually distinct colors, ensuring that each category is easily distinguishable. Additionally, autopct="%1.1f%%" formats the autopct (autopct stands for auto percentage) parameter, displaying percentages with one decimal place.

3. Bar Plot Subplot:

   In the second subplot (ax2), a horizontal bar plot is created using the DataFrame df. This bar plot represents the count of occurrences of each category. Each bar corresponds to a category, and its length is proportional to the count of that category. Labels representing the counts are added to each bar for clarity.

4. Styling and Titles:

   Both subplots are assigned the same title specified in the title argument. The second subplot has the x-axis labeled as "Count". The background color of the second subplot is set to a light grey shade for a consistent aesthetic.

5. Tick Label Font Size:

   The tick labels on both subplots are adjusted to have a font size of 6. This ensures that the labels are legible and appropriately sized.

6. Tightening Layout:

   The layout of the figure is adjusted using figure.tight_layout() to ensure that all elements are properly spaced and displayed without overlapping.

7. Canvas Update:

   Finally, canvas.draw() is called to update the canvas and display the newly created plot.

In summary, the plot_piechart_group() function is a versatile tool for visualizing categorical data. It provides an effective way to compare the distribution of different categories, making it a valuable asset for exploratory data analysis. The method's use of color, labels, and layout adjustments ensures that the resulting plot is informative and visually appealing.

Stacked Bar Plot

In Helper_Plot class, define two new methods named put_label_stacked_bar() and dist_one_vs_another_plot():

```python
#Puts label inside stacked bar
def put_label_stacked_bar(self, ax,fontsize):
    #patches is everything inside of the chart
    for rect in ax.patches:
        # Find where everything is located
        height = rect.get_height()
        width = rect.get_width()
        x = rect.get_x()
        y = rect.get_y()
```

```python
        # The height of the bar is the data value and can be used as the label
        label_text = f'{width:.0f}'

        # ax.text(x, y, text)
        label_x = x + width / 2
        label_y = y + height / 2

        # plots only when height is greater than specified value
        if width > 0:
            ax.text(label_x, label_y, label_text, \
                ha='center', va='center', \
                weight = "bold",fontsize=fontsize)

#Plots one variable against another variable
def dist_one_vs_another_plot(self, df, cat1, cat2, figure, canvas, title):
    figure.clear()
    ax1 = figure.add_subplot(1,1,1)

    group_by_stat = df.groupby([cat1, cat2]).size()
    colors = sns.color_palette("Set1", len(df[cat1].unique()))
    group_by_stat.unstack().plot(kind='barh', stacked=True, ax=ax1,color=colors)
    ax1.set_title(title, fontsize=12)
    ax1.set_xlabel('Number of Cases', fontsize=10)
    ax1.set_ylabel(cat1, fontsize=10)
    self.put_label_stacked_bar(ax1,7)

    # Set font for tick labels
    ax1.tick_params(axis='both', which='major', labelsize=8)
    ax1.tick_params(axis='both', which='minor', labelsize=8)
    ax1.legend(facecolor='#E6E6FA', edgecolor='black', fontsize=8)
    ax1.set_facecolor('#F0F0F0')
    figure.tight_layout()
    canvas.draw()
```

The put_label_stacked_bar() method is used to place labels inside a stacked bar chart. This function iterates through each bar (rect) in the chart and extracts information about its position, size, and value. It then calculates the position at which the label should be placed (at the center of the bar). If the width of the bar (which represents the data value) is greater than zero, it adds a label to the bar. The label is positioned at the calculated coordinates and contains the width value formatted as an integer. The label is centered both horizontally and vertically within the bar. This ensures that labels are placed inside the bars appropriately.

The dist_one_vs_another_plot() function is designed to create a horizontal stacked bar plot to compare the distribution of one categorical variable (cat1) against another categorical variable (cat2). This method first groups the data by the combination of cat1 and cat2 using groupby, and then calculates the size of each group. The colors for the bars are obtained from a color palette called "Set1", ensuring that each category in cat1 has a distinct color. The unstack method is used to pivot the grouped data to create a table where cat2 values become columns. This allows for easy plotting of the stacked bars. The stacked bar plot is then created using plot with the stacked=True parameter, resulting in bars stacked on top of each other. The plot is drawn on the first subplot (ax1) of the figure.

The title of the plot is set using set_title(), and labels for the x-axis and y-axis are added with set_xlabel() and set_ylabel(), respectively. The put_label_stacked_bar() method is called to put labels inside the bars. The tick_params() method is used to set the font size of tick labels on both the x-axis and y-axis. The legend, which represents the categories in cat2, is displayed with a specified font size, face color, and edge color. The background color of the subplot is set to a light grey shade (#F0F0F0) for a consistent aesthetic. Finally, tight_layout() is called to adjust the layout of the figure, ensuring that all elements are properly spaced and displayed without overlapping.

Overall, the dist_one_vs_another_plot() function is a powerful tool for visualizing the relationship between two categorical variables. The stacked bar plot provides a clear view of how the distribution of cat1 varies with different categories of cat2. Labels inside the bars enhance the interpretability of the plot, and careful attention to aesthetics ensures that the plot is informative and visually appealing.

Box Plot

In Helper_Plot class, define a new method named box_plot(). It is designed to create a box plot, a statistical visualization that provides a summary of a dataset's distribution:

```python
def box_plot(self, df, x, y, hue, figure, canvas, title):
    figure.clear()
    ax1 = figure.add_subplot(1,1,1)

    sns.boxplot(data = df, x = x, y = y, hue = hue, ax=ax1)
    ax1.set_title(title, fontsize=14)
    ax1.set_xlabel(x, fontsize=10)
    ax1.set_ylabel(y, fontsize=10)
    ax1.set_facecolor('#F0F0F0')
    ax1.legend(facecolor='#E6E6FA', edgecolor='black')
    figure.tight_layout()
    canvas.draw()
```

Here's how the function works:
1. Clearing the Figure and Adding a Subplot: The method starts by clearing any existing content from the figure to ensure a clean slate. Then, it adds a single subplot (ax1) to the figure using add_subplot. This subplot will be used to display the box plot.
2. Creating the Box Plot: The box plot itself is generated using sns.boxplot, a function from the Seaborn library. It takes several parameters:
    - data: The DataFrame (df) containing the data to be plotted.

- x: The variable that will be displayed on the x-axis.
- y: The variable that will be displayed on the y-axis.
- hue: An optional parameter that allows for additional grouping based on a categorical variable. This can be useful for comparing multiple groups within the same box plot.
- ax: The axes where the box plot will be drawn (in this case, ax1).

3. Setting Titles and Labels: The method sets the title of the plot using set_title. The titles for the x-axis and y-axis are set using set_xlabel() and set_ylabel(), respectively.
4. Setting Aesthetics and Legend: The background color of the subplot is set to a light grey shade (#F0F0F0) for a consistent aesthetic. Additionally, a legend is added to the plot using legend. The legend displays the categories represented by the hue parameter. The face color of the legend is set to a pale lavender shade (#E6E6FA) and the edge color to black.
5. Tightening Layout and Drawing the Figure: tight_layout is called to adjust the layout of the figure, ensuring that all elements are properly spaced and displayed without overlapping.
6. Drawing the Canvas: Finally, canvas.draw() is used to update the canvas and display the newly created box plot.

Overall, this method provides a convenient way to generate box plots for visualizing the distribution of variables in a dataset, and it offers options for grouping data by a categorical variable (hue). The method's parameters (df, x, y, hue, figure, canvas, and title) allow for customization of the plot based on the specific data and variables of interest.

Dataset Information

In Helper_Plot class, define a new method named dataset_info(). It is designed to display information about a DataFrame in window.

```python
def dataset_info(self, df):
    win = tk.Toplevel()
    form2 = Form2(win)
    win.title("Dataset Information")

    # Capture sys.stdout
    original_stdout = sys.stdout
    sys.stdout = StringIO()

    # Get df.info() output
    df.info()

    # Get the string value
    info_string = sys.stdout.getvalue()

    # Reset sys.stdout
```

```
sys.stdout = original_stdout

# Insert the info string into the Text widget
form2.text.insert(tk.END, info_string)
```

Here's how it works:
1. Creating a New Window (Toplevel): The method starts by creating a new top-level window (win) using the tk.Toplevel() function. This window will serve as the container for displaying the dataset information.
2. Initializing Form2: An instance of the Form2 class (presumably a GUI form or widget) is created within the win window. This form (form2) is designed to display text or information.
3. Setting Window Title: The title of the win window is set to "Dataset Information" using win.title().
4. Capturing Standard Output (sys.stdout): The method captures the standard output using the sys.stdout object. This is typically the stream to which the print function writes. By redirecting it to a StringIO object, any printed content will be stored as a string.
5. Getting df.info() Output: The df.info() method is called. This provides concise summary information about the DataFrame, including data types, non-null counts, and memory usage.
6. Storing Output as a String: The output that would have been printed to the console is stored as a string in the variable info_string.
7. Resetting sys.stdout: The standard output is reset back to its original value to ensure that future print statements go to the console as expected.
8. Inserting Info String into Text Widget: The info_string is inserted into the text widget of form2. This involves using the insert() method of the text widget to display the dataset information.

Overall, this method effectively captures and displays the output of df.info() in a GUI window using the Form2 widget. It provides a user-friendly way to view important information about the dataset.

Statistical Description

In Helper_Plot class, define a new method named dataset_describe(). It is designed to display the statistical description of a DataFrame in a window:

```
def dataset_describe(self, df):
    win = tk.Toplevel()
    form2 = Form2(win)
    win.title("Statistical Description")

    # Capture df.describe() output as a string
```

```python
describe_string_io = StringIO()
df.describe().to_string(buf=describe_string_io)

# Get the string value
describe_string = describe_string_io.getvalue()

# Insert the info string into the Text widget
form2.text.insert(tk.END, describe_string)
```

Here's how it works:

1. Creating a New Window (Toplevel): The method starts by creating a new top-level window (win) using the tk.Toplevel() function. This window will serve as the container for displaying the statistical description.

2. Initializing Form2: An instance of the Form2 class (presumably a GUI form or widget) is created within the win window. This form (form2) is designed to display text or information.

3. Setting Window Title: The title of the win window is set to "Statistical Description" using win.title().

4. Capturing df.describe() Output as a String: The describe_string_io variable is created as a StringIO object. This object is like a file that can store text in memory. The output of df.describe() is then written to this StringIO object using the to_string method.

5. Getting the String Value: The describe_string variable is created by getting the value stored in describe_string_io.

6. Inserting Describe String into Text Widget: The describe_string is inserted into the text widget of form2. This involves using the insert method of the text widget to display the statistical description.

Overall, this method effectively captures and displays the output of df.describe() in a GUI window using the Form2 widget. It provides a user-friendly way to view the statistical summary of the dataset.

The Count of Null Values

In Helper_Plot class, define a new method named display_null_counts(). It is designed to display the counts of null values in a DataFrame in a window:

```python
def display_null_counts(self, df):
    win = tk.Toplevel()
    form2 = Form2(win)
    win.title("Null Value Counts")

    # Capture sys.stdout
    original_stdout = sys.stdout
    sys.stdout = StringIO()
```

```python
# Get df.isnull().sum() output
null_counts = df.isnull().sum()

# Get the string value
null_counts_string = null_counts.to_string()

# Reset sys.stdout
sys.stdout = original_stdout

# Insert the info string into the Text widget
form2.text.insert(tk.END, null_counts_string)
```

Here's how it works:
1. Creating a New Window (Toplevel): The method starts by creating a new top-level window (win) using the tk.Toplevel() function. This window will serve as the container for displaying the null value counts.
2. Initializing Form2: An instance of the Form2 class (presumably a GUI form or widget) is created within the win window. This form (form2) is designed to display text or information.
3. Setting Window Title: The title of the win window is set to "Null Value Counts" using win.title().
4. Capturing df.isnull().sum() Output as a String: The null_counts variable is created by applying the isnull().sum() method to the DataFrame df. This gives a Series containing the counts of null values for each column.
5. Converting to String: The null_counts Series is converted to a string format using the to_string() method. This string will display the column names along with their corresponding null value counts.
6. Capturing sys.stdout: The standard output (sys.stdout) is temporarily redirected to a StringIO object to capture any printed output.
7. Inserting Null Counts String into Text Widget: The null_counts_string is inserted into the text widget of form2. This involves using the insert method of the text widget to display the null value counts.
8. Resetting sys.stdout: The standard output is reset back to its original value after capturing the null value counts string.

Overall, this method provides a user-friendly way to view the counts of null values in a DataFrame through a GUI window. It captures the output that would typically be printed in the console and displays it in the GUI.

The Count of Null Values of Postal Code

In Helper_Plot class, define a new method named display_null_postal_code_rows(). It is designed to present rows from a DataFrame where the "Postal Code" column contains null values within a window:

```python
def display_null_postal_code_rows(self, df):
    win = tk.Toplevel()
    form2 = Form2(win)
    win.title("Postal Code Null Value Counts")

    # Filter rows where "Postal Code" is null
    null_postal_code_df = df[df["Postal Code"].isnull()]

    # Convert DataFrame to string representation
    null_postal_code_str = null_postal_code_df.to_string(index=False)

    # Insert the string into the ScrolledText widget
    form2.text.insert(tk.END, null_postal_code_str)
```

It operates as follows:
1. Creating a New Window (Toplevel) and Form Instance: Initially, it creates a new top-level window (win) using the tk.Toplevel() function. This window serves as the container for displaying the null postal code rows. Subsequently, an instance of the Form2 class is initialized as form2 within this window. Form2 represents a GUI form or widget designed for displaying text or information.
2. Setting the Window Title: The title of the win window is set to "Postal Code Null Value Counts" using the win.title() method. This title provides context to the user about the content they can expect to see in the window.
3. Filtering Rows with Null Postal Codes: The method proceeds by creating a new DataFrame named null_postal_code_df. This DataFrame is derived from the original DataFrame df by applying a filter that retains only those rows where the "Postal Code" column contains null values (df["Postal Code"].isnull()).
4. Converting DataFrame to String Format: The null_postal_code_df DataFrame is then converted to a string representation using the to_string() method. By specifying index=False, the string will represent the DataFrame without including the index values.
5. Inserting String into Text Widget: The resulting string, null_postal_code_str, which contains the representation of the DataFrame with null postal codes, is inserted into the ScrolledText widget of form2. This is typically accomplished using the insert method of the text widget.

In summary, this method provides an interactive way for users to view rows from a DataFrame where the "Postal Code" column contains null values. It achieves this through a GUI window that is created, titled, and populated with the relevant data. This functionality facilitates effective data exploration and analysis.

In Helper_Plot class, define a new method named plot_missing_values_and_coeff(). It is responsible for displaying a window that presents two sets of visualizations related to missing values:

```python
def plot_missing_values_and_coeff(self, df0, df1):
    win = tk.Toplevel()
    form1 = Form1(win)
    win.title("Missing Values and Correlation Coefficients")
    self.plot_missing_values(df0, form1.figure1, form1.canvas1, "Before Filling
Null Values")
    self.plot_missing_values(df1, form1.figure2, form1.canvas2, "After Filling
Null Values")
```

Here's how it works:
1. Creating a New Window (Toplevel) and Form Instance: The method begins by creating a new top-level window (win) using the tk.Toplevel() function. This window will serve as the container for displaying the missing values. Next, an instance of the Form1 class is initialized as form1 within this window. Form1 represents a GUI form or widget designed for displaying visualizations.
2. Setting the Window Title: The title of the win window is set to "Missing Values and Correlation Coefficients" using the win.title() method. This title provides context to the user about the content they can expect to see in the window.
3. Plotting Missing Values Before and After Filling: The method calls the plot_missing_values method twice. The first call (self.plot_missing_values(df0, form1.figure1, form1.canvas1, "Before Filling Null Values")) plots missing values for a DataFrame df0 in the first subfigure of form1. This figure is labeled "Before Filling Null Values". The second call (self.plot_missing_values(df1, form1.figure2, form1.canvas2, "After Filling Null Values")) plots missing values for a DataFrame df1 in the second subfigure of form1. This figure is labeled "After Filling Null Values".
4. Displaying the Window: Once the visualizations are set up in the form, the window is displayed to the user. This will allow them to interact with and view the missing values and correlation coefficients plots.

In summary, this method provides a user-friendly interface for comparing missing values between two DataFrames. It does this by opening a new window with visualizations generated using the Form1 class. This can aid in understanding data quality and relationships between variables before and after filling missing values.

In Helper_Plot class, define a new method named plot_case_distribution(). It generates a window for visualizing the distribution of cases based on two categorical variables from a DataFrame:

```python
def plot_case_distribution(self, df, var1, var2, title="", label="",
top_ten=False):
    win = tk.Toplevel()
    form1 = Form1(win)
    win.title(title)
    self.plot_piechart(df, var1, form1.figure1, form1.canvas1, "Case Distribution
of " + label + var1, top_ten)
    self.plot_piechart(df, var2, form1.figure2, form1.canvas2, "Case Distribution
of " + label + var2, top_ten)
```

Here's a breakdown of how this method works:

1. Creating a New Window (Toplevel) and Form Instance: The method starts by creating a new top-level window (win) using tk.Toplevel(). This window will serve as the container for displaying the pie charts. An instance of the Form1 class is then initialized as form1 within this window. Form1 is a GUI form or widget designed for displaying visualizations.

2. Setting the Window Title: The title of the win window is set to the value provided in the title parameter. This title provides context to the user about the content they can expect to see in the window.

3. Plotting Pie Charts for Each Categorical Variable: The method calls the plot_piechart method twice. The first call (self.plot_piechart(df, var1, form1.figure1, form1.canvas1, "Case Distribution of " + label + var1, top_ten)) generates a pie chart for the categorical variable var1 in the first subfigure of form1. The chart is labeled with a title that combines the provided label and var1. The top_ten parameter determines whether to consider only the top ten values. The second call (self.plot_piechart(df, var2, form1.figure2, form1.canvas2, "Case Distribution of " + label + var2, top_ten)) does the same for the categorical variable var2 in the second subfigure of form1.

4. Displaying the Window: Once the pie charts are set up in the form, the window is displayed to the user. This allows them to interact with and view the distribution of cases based on the specified categorical variables.

In summary, this method provides a user-friendly interface for visualizing the distribution of cases based on two categorical variables from a DataFrame. It does this by opening a new window with pie charts generated using the Form1 class. This can be useful for understanding how cases are distributed across different categories.

Setting Up the Menu Options Related to Dataset Operations

In Helper_Plot class, define a new method named binds_menu_open_dataset(). It is responsible for configuring the options in a menu related to dataset operations:

```python
def binds_menu_open_dataset(self, df_before, df_after, root, window):
    window.dataset_menu.entryconfigure("View Dataset",
        command =lambda:self.shows_table(root, df_after, 1250, 600, "Superstore
Sales Dataset"))

    window.dataset_menu.entryconfigure("Dataset Information",
        command =lambda:self.dataset_info(df_after))

    window.dataset_menu.entryconfigure("Statistical Description",
        command =lambda:self.dataset_describe(df_after))

    window.dataset_menu.entryconfigure("Null Values",
        command =lambda:self.display_null_counts(df_before))

    window.dataset_menu.entryconfigure("Postal Code Null Values",
        command =lambda:self.display_null_postal_code_rows(df_before))
```

Here's how it works:
1. View Dataset Option: This code binds the "View Dataset" option in the dataset menu to a specific command. When selected, it will execute the shows_table() method. This method displays the dataset in a new window using a tabular format. The df_after DataFrame is used for this operation, and the dimensions of the window are set to 1250 pixels in width and 600 pixels in height. The title of the window is set to "Superstore Sales Dataset". This allows the user to view the dataset in a structured table format.
2. Dataset Information Option: This code binds the "Dataset Information" option to a command that triggers the dataset_info() method. When selected, this option opens a new window displaying information about the dataset. The df_after DataFrame is used for this operation. The information displayed typically includes data types, non-null counts, and memory usage. This can be useful for gaining a quick overview of the dataset's characteristics.
3. Statistical Description Option: This code binds the "Statistical Description" option to a command that invokes the dataset_describe() method. When selected, this option opens a new window displaying statistical summary information about the dataset. The df_after DataFrame is used for this operation. This summary includes measures like mean, standard deviation, minimum, maximum, and quartiles for each numeric column.
4. Null Values Option: This code binds the "Null Values" option to a command that triggers the display_null_counts() method. When selected, this option opens a new window showing the count of null values for each column in the dataset. The df_before DataFrame is used for this operation, indicating that this information is based on the dataset before any modifications.

5. Postal Code Null Values Option: This code binds the "Postal Code Null Values" option to a command that executes the display_null_postal_code_rows() method. When selected, this option opens a new window displaying the rows where the "Postal Code" column has null values. This is useful for identifying and handling missing or incomplete postal code information.

In summary, the binds_menu_open_dataset() method sets up the menu options related to dataset operations, providing functionality to view, explore, and analyze the dataset in various ways.

Setting Up the Menu Options Related to Visualizing Distribution of Features

In Helper_Plot class, define a new method named binds_features_distribution(). It sets up the menu options related to visualizing the distribution of features in the dataset:

```python
def binds_features_distribution(self, window, df0, df1, df2):
    window.dist_menu.entryconfigure("Missing Values",
        command = lambda:self.plot_missing_values_and_coeff(df0, df1))

    window.dist_menu.entryconfigure("Day and Month",
        command = lambda:self.plot_case_distribution(df2, "Day", "Month",
            "The Case Distribution of Day and Month"))

    window.dist_menu.entryconfigure("Quarter and Year",
        command = lambda:self.plot_case_distribution(df2, "Quarter", "Year",
            "The Case Distribution of Quarter and Year"))

    window.dist_menu.entryconfigure("Country and City",
        command = lambda:self.plot_case_distribution(df2, "Country", "City",
            "The Case Distribution of Top Ten Country and Year", " Top 10 ",
top_ten=True))

    window.dist_menu.entryconfigure("State and Region",
        command = lambda:self.plot_case_distribution(df2, "State", "Region",
            "The Case Distribution of State and Year", " Top 10 ", top_ten=True))

    window.dist_menu.entryconfigure("Customer Name and Customer ID",
        command = lambda:self.plot_case_distribution(df2, "Customer Name",
"Customer ID",
            "The Case Distribution of Customer Name and Customer ID", " Top 10 ",
top_ten=True))

    window.dist_menu.entryconfigure("Ship Mode and Segment",
        command = lambda:self.plot_case_distribution(df2, "Ship Mode", "Segment",
            "The Case Distribution of Ship Mode and Segment"))

    window.dist_menu.entryconfigure("Product Name and Product ID",
        command = lambda:self.plot_case_distribution(df2, "Product Name",
"Product ID",
            "The Case Distribution of Product Name and Product ID", " Top 10 ",
top_ten=True))
```

```
window.dist_menu.entryconfigure("Category and Sub-Category",
        command = lambda:self.plot_case_distribution(df2, "Category", "Sub-
Category",
        "The Case Distribution of Category and Sub-Category"))
```

Here's how it works:
1. Missing Values Option: This code binds the "Missing Values" option in the distribution menu to a command that triggers the plot_missing_values_and_coeff() method. When selected, this option displays a window with two plots. The first plot shows the missing values before filling, and the second plot shows the missing values after filling.
2. Day and Month Option: This code binds the "Day and Month" option to a command that triggers the plot_case_distribution() method. This option plots the distribution of cases by day and month. The title of the plot is set to "The Case Distribution of Day and Month".
3. Quarter and Year Option: This code binds the "Quarter and Year" option to a command that triggers the plot_case_distribution() method. This option plots the distribution of cases by quarter and year. The title of the plot is set to "The Case Distribution of Quarter and Year".
4. Country and City Option: This code binds the "Country and City" option to a command that triggers the plot_case_distribution() method. This option plots the distribution of cases by country and city, considering only the top ten countries. The title of the plot is set to "The Case Distribution of Top Ten Country and Year".
5. State and Region Option: This code binds the "State and Region" option to a command that triggers the plot_case_distribution() method. This option plots the distribution of cases by state and region, considering only the top ten states. The title of the plot is set to "The Case Distribution of State and Year".
6. Customer Name and Customer ID Option: This code binds the "Customer Name and Customer ID" option to a command that triggers the plot_case_distribution() method. This option plots the distribution of cases by customer name and customer ID, considering only the top ten customers. The title of the plot is set to "The Case Distribution of Customer Name and Customer ID".
7. Ship Mode and Segment Option: This code binds the "Ship Mode and Segment" option to a command that triggers the plot_case_distribution() method. This option plots the distribution of cases by ship mode and segment. The title of the plot is set to "The Case Distribution of Ship Mode and Segment".
8. Product Name and Product ID Option: This code binds the "Product Name and Product ID" option to a command that triggers the plot_case_distribution() method. This option plots the distribution of cases by product name and product ID, considering only the top ten products. The title of the plot is set to "The Case Distribution of Product Name and Product ID".

9. Category and Sub-Category Option: This code binds the "Category and Sub-Category" option to a command that triggers the plot_case_distribution() method. This option plots the distribution of cases by category and sub-category. The title of the plot is set to "The Case Distribution of Category and Sub-Category".

Window to Display Box Plot

In Helper_Plot class, define a new method named plot_box_distribution(). It creates a new window using tkinter and displays a box plot using the box_plot() method:

```python
def plot_box_distribution(self, df, var1="", var2="", var3="", title=""):
    win = tk.Toplevel()
    form3 = Form3(win)
    self.box_plot(df, var1, var2, var3, form3.figure1, form3.canvas1, title)
```

Here's how it works:
1. Creating a New Window: The method starts by creating a new tkinter Toplevel window named win. This window will be used to display the box plot.
2. Creating an Instance of Form3: It creates an instance of the Form3 class and assigns it to the variable form3. This allows access to the attributes and methods defined in Form3.
3. Calling the box_plot() Method: The box_plot() method is called with the provided arguments df, var1, var2, var3, form3.figure1, form3.canvas1, and title. This method is responsible for generating the box plot.
4. Displaying the Box Plot: The box plot is displayed in the Form3 window, utilizing the figure and canvas attributes.

Overall, this method facilitates the visualization of box plots for the specified variables in a separate window.

Window to Display Categorized Distribution

In Helper_Plot class, define a new method named plot_categorized_distribution(). It is responsible for displaying two distribution plots in a new tkinter window:

```python
def plot_categorized_distribution(self, df, var1="", var2="", var3="",
    var4="", title1="", title2=""):
    win = tk.Toplevel()
    form1 = Form1(win)

    self.dist_one_vs_another_plot(df, var1, var2, form1.figure1, form1.canvas1,
title1)
    self.dist_one_vs_another_plot(df, var3, var4, form1.figure2, form1.canvas2,
title2)
```

Here's how it works:

1. Creating a New Window: The method begins by creating a new tkinter Toplevel window named win. This window will be used to display the distribution plots.
2. Creating an Instance of Form1: It creates an instance of the Form1 class and assigns it to the variable form1. This allows access to the attributes and methods defined in Form1.
3. Calling the dist_one_vs_another_plot() Method: The dist_one_vs_another_plot() method is called twice. This method is used to generate distribution plots for different pairs of variables. The method is called with the provided arguments df, var1, var2, form1.figure1, form1.canvas1, and title1 for the first plot, and with df, var3, var4, form1.figure2, form1.canvas2, and title2 for the second plot.
4. Displaying the Distribution Plots: The distribution plots are displayed in the Form1 window, utilizing the figure and canvas attributes.

Overall, this method enables the visualization of categorized distribution plots for the specified variables in a separate window.

Window to Visualize Grouped Distribution

In Helper_Plot class, define a new method named plot_grouped_distribution(). It is responsible for displaying two grouped distribution plots in a new tkinter window:

```python
def plot_grouped_distribution(self, df, var1="", var2="", var3="",
    var4="", title1="", title2="", label="", mode=""):
    win = tk.Toplevel()
    form1 = Form1(win)
    win.title("Distribution of " + var2 + " by " + var1 + " and " + var3)
    sum_by_cat1 = df.groupby(var1)[var2].sum()
    sum_by_cat_top_ten1 = sum_by_cat1.nlargest(10)
    sum_by_cat2 = df.groupby(var3)[var4].sum()
    sum_by_cat_top_ten2 = sum_by_cat2.nlargest(10)

    if mode == "":
        self.plot_piechart_group(sum_by_cat1, form1.figure1, form1.canvas1,
title1, label)
        self.plot_piechart_group(sum_by_cat2, form1.figure2, form1.canvas2,
title2, label)
    else:
        self.plot_piechart_group(sum_by_cat_top_ten1, form1.figure1,
form1.canvas1, title1, label)
        self.plot_piechart_group(sum_by_cat_top_ten2, form1.figure2,
form1.canvas2, title2, label)
```

Here's how it works:

1. Creating a New Window: The method begins by creating a new tkinter Toplevel window named win. This window will be used to display the grouped distribution plots.

2. Creating an Instance of Form1: It creates an instance of the Form1 class and assigns it to the variable form1. This allows access to the attributes and methods defined in Form1.
3. Creating Grouped Summaries: It calculates the sum of the variable var2 grouped by the variable var1, and the sum of the variable var4 grouped by the variable var3. These summaries are stored in the variables sum_by_cat1 and sum_by_cat2, respectively.
4. Selecting Top Ten Categories: It selects the top ten categories with the highest sums from both sum_by_cat1 and sum_by_cat2. These are stored in the variables sum_by_cat_top_ten1 and sum_by_cat_top_ten2.
5. Conditionally Plotting Pie Charts: Depending on the value of mode, the method either plots pie charts for the entire dataset or only for the top ten categories. If mode is not specified, it defaults to plotting for the entire dataset.
6. Displaying the Distribution Plots: The grouped distribution plots are displayed in the Form1 window, utilizing the figure and canvas attributes.

Overall, this method enables the visualization of grouped distribution plots for the specified variables in a separate window, with the option to focus on the top ten categories if desired.

Setting Up the Menu Options Related to Visualizing Categorized Distribution

In Helper_Plot class, define a new method named binds_categories_distribution(). It sets up commands for various menu options related to displaying distribution plots and summaries for different categories in the dataset:

```python
def binds_categories_distribution(self, window, df):
    window.dist_cat.entryconfigure("Sales by Year and Quarter",
        command = lambda:self.plot_grouped_distribution(df, "Year", "Sales",
        "Quarter", "Sales", "Sales by Year", "Sales by Quarter", "Sales"))

    window.dist_cat.entryconfigure("Sales by Day and Month",
        command = lambda:self.plot_grouped_distribution(df, "Day", "Sales",
        "Month", "Sales", "Sales by Day", "Sales by Month", "Sales"))

    window.dist_cat.entryconfigure("Sales by Ship Mode and Segment",
        command = lambda:self.plot_grouped_distribution(df, "Ship Mode", "Sales",
        "Segment", "Sales", "Sales by Ship Mode", "Sales by Segment", "Sales"))

    window.dist_cat.entryconfigure("Sales by Category and Sub-Category",
        command = lambda:self.plot_grouped_distribution(df, "Category", "Sales",
        "Sub-Category", "Sales", "Sales by Category", "Sales by Sub-Category",
"Sales"))

        window.dist_cat.entryconfigure("Sales by Product Name and Product ID",
            command = lambda:self.plot_grouped_distribution(df, "Product Name",
"Sales",
            "Product ID", "Sales", "Sales by Product Name", "Sales by Product ID",
"Sales", "top-ten"))
```

```python
        window.dist_cat.entryconfigure("Sales by Customer Name and Customer ID",
            command = lambda:self.plot_grouped_distribution(df, "Customer Name",
"Sales",
            "Customer ID", "Sales", "Sales by Customer Name", "Sales by Customer ID",
"Sales", "top-ten"))

        window.dist_cat.entryconfigure("Sales by City and State",
            command = lambda:self.plot_grouped_distribution(df, "City", "Sales",
            "State", "Sales", "Sales by City", "Sales by State", "Sales", "top-ten"))

        window.dist_cat.entryconfigure("Categorized Sales",
            command = lambda:self.plot_case_distribution(df, "Cat_Sales", "Category",
            "The Case Distribution of Categorized Sales and Category"))

        window.dist_cat.entryconfigure("Categorized Sales by Year and Quarter",
            command = lambda:self.plot_categorized_distribution(df, "Year",
"Cat_Sales",
                "Quarter", "Cat_Sales",
                "The Case Distribution of Categorized Sales by Year",
                "The Case Distribution of Categorized Sales by Quarter"))

        window.dist_cat.entryconfigure("Categorized Sales by Day and Month",
            command = lambda:self.plot_categorized_distribution(df, "Day",
"Cat_Sales",
                "Month", "Cat_Sales",
                "The Case Distribution of Categorized Sales by Day",
                "The Case Distribution of Categorized Sales by Month"))

        window.dist_cat.entryconfigure("Categorized Sales by Segment and Sub-
Category",
            command = lambda:self.plot_categorized_distribution(df, "Segment",
"Cat_Sales",
                "Sub-Category", "Cat_Sales",
                "The Case Distribution of Categorized Sales by Segment",
                "The Case Distribution of Categorized Sales by Sub-Category"))

        window.dist_cat.entryconfigure("Categorized Sales by Region and State",
            command = lambda:self.plot_categorized_distribution(df, "Region",
"Cat_Sales",
                "State", "Cat_Sales",
                "The Case Distribution of Categorized Sales by Region",
                "The Case Distribution of Categorized Sales by State"))

        window.dist_cat.entryconfigure("Day versus Sales Per Category",
            command = lambda:self.plot_box_distribution(df, "Day", "Sales",
"Category",
                "Day versus Sales Per Category"))

        window.dist_cat.entryconfigure("Month versus Sales Per Segment",
            command = lambda:self.plot_box_distribution(df, "Month", "Sales",
"Segment",
                "Month versus Sales Per Segment"))

        window.dist_cat.entryconfigure("Sub-Category versus Sales Per Year",
            command = lambda:self.plot_box_distribution(df, "Sub-Category", "Sales",
"Year",
                "Sub-Category versus Sales Per Year"))
```

```
window.dist_cat.entryconfigure("Region versus Sales Per Quarter",
    command = lambda:self.plot_box_distribution(df, "Region", "Sales",
"Quarter",
        "Region versus Sales Per Quarter"))
```

Here's an explanation of each menu option:

1. Sales by Year and Quarter: This option triggers the plot_grouped_distribution() method to display sales distribution plots grouped by year and quarter.
2. Sales by Day and Month: This option triggers the plot_grouped_distribution() method to display sales distribution plots grouped by day and month.
3. Sales by Ship Mode and Segment: This option triggers the plot_grouped_distribution() method to display sales distribution plots grouped by ship mode and segment.
4. Sales by Category and Sub-Category: This option triggers the plot_grouped_distribution() method to display sales distribution plots grouped by category and sub-category.
5. Sales by Product Name and Product ID: This option triggers the plot_grouped_distribution() method to display sales distribution plots grouped by product name and product ID.
6. Sales by Customer Name and Customer ID: This option triggers the plot_grouped_distribution() method to display sales distribution plots grouped by customer name and customer ID.
7. Sales by City and State: This option triggers the plot_grouped_distribution() method to display sales distribution plots grouped by city and state.
8. Categorized Sales: This option triggers the plot_case_distribution() method to display pie charts representing the distribution of categorized sales.
9. Categorized Sales by Year and Quarter: This option triggers the plot_categorized_distribution() method to display categorized sales distribution plots grouped by year and quarter.
10. Categorized Sales by Day and Month: This option triggers the plot_categorized_distribution() method to display categorized sales distribution plots grouped by day and month.
11. Categorized Sales by Segment and Sub-Category: This option triggers the plot_categorized_distribution() method to display categorized sales distribution plots grouped by segment and sub-category.
12. Categorized Sales by Region and State: This option triggers the plot_categorized_distribution() method to display categorized sales distribution plots grouped by region and state.
13. Day versus Sales Per Category: This option triggers the plot_box_distribution() method to display box plots representing the relationship between day and sales for each category.

14. Month versus Sales Per Segment: This option triggers the plot_box_distribution() method to display box plots representing the relationship between month and sales for each segment.

15. Sub-Category versus Sales Per Year: This option triggers the plot_box_distribution() method to display box plots representing the relationship between sub-category and sales for each year.

16. Region versus Sales Per Quarter: This option triggers the plot_box_distribution() method to display box plots representing the relationship between region and sales for each quarter.

Each menu option is associated with a specific command that calls the appropriate plotting method with the relevant parameters. This allows for easy access to different visualizations of the dataset's category-related information.

Displaying Various Plots and Visualizations Based on the User's Selection

In Helper_Plot class, define a new method named choose_plot(). It is responsible for displaying various plots and visualizations based on the user's selection. It takes two dataframes (df1 and df2), the user's choice (chosen), and two figure/canvas pairs (figure1, canvas1, figure2, canvas2) for displaying the plots:

```python
def choose_plot(self, df1, df2, chosen, figure1, canvas1, figure2, canvas2):
    print(chosen)
    if chosen == "Day":
        self.plot_piechart(df2, "Day", figure1, canvas1, "Case Distribution of
Day")

    elif chosen == "Month":
        self.plot_piechart(df2, "Month", figure2, canvas2, "Case Distribution of
Month")

    elif chosen == "Quarter":
        self.plot_piechart(df2, "Quarter", figure1, canvas1, "Case Distribution
of Quarter")

    elif chosen == "Year":
        self.plot_piechart(df2, "Year", figure2, canvas2, "Case Distribution of
Year")

    elif chosen == "Missing Values":
        self.plot_missing_values(df1, figure1, canvas1)

    elif chosen == "Correlation Coefficient":
        self.plot_corr_coeffs(df1, figure2, canvas2)

    elif chosen == "Country and City":
        self.plot_piechart(df2, "Country", figure1, canvas1, "Case Distribution
of Country")
```

```python
        self.plot_piechart(df2, "City", figure2, canvas2, "Case Distribution of
City", top_ten=True)

        elif chosen == "State and Region":
            self.plot_piechart(df2, "State", figure1, canvas1, "Case Distribution of
State", top_ten=True)
            self.plot_piechart(df2, "Region", figure2, canvas2, "Case Distribution of
Region")

        elif chosen == "Customer Name and Customer ID":
            self.plot_piechart(df2, "Customer Name", figure1, canvas1, "Case
Distribution of Customer Name", top_ten=True)
            self.plot_piechart(df2, "Customer ID", figure2, canvas2, "Case
Distribution of Customer ID", top_ten=True)

        elif chosen == "Ship Mode and Segment":
            self.plot_piechart(df2, "Ship Mode", figure1, canvas1, "Case Distribution
of Ship Mode")
            self.plot_piechart(df2, "Segment", figure2, canvas2, "Case Distribution
of Segment")

        elif chosen == "Product Name and Product ID":
            self.plot_piechart(df2, "Product Name", figure1, canvas1, "Case
Distribution of Product Name", top_ten=True)
            self.plot_piechart(df2, "Product ID", figure2, canvas2, "Case
Distribution of Product ID", top_ten=True)

        elif chosen == "Category and Sub-Category":
            self.plot_piechart(df2, "Category", figure1, canvas1, "Case Distribution
of Category", top_ten=True)
            self.plot_piechart(df2, "Sub-Category", figure2, canvas2, "Case
Distribution of Sub-Category", top_ten=True)

        elif chosen == "Sales by Year and Quarter":
            self.plot_piechart_group(df2.groupby('Year')['Sales'].sum(), figure1,
canvas1, "Sales by Year")
            self.plot_piechart_group(df2.groupby('Quarter')['Sales'].sum(), figure2,
canvas2, "Sales by Quarter")

        elif chosen == "Sales by Day and Month":
            self.plot_piechart_group(df2.groupby('Day')['Sales'].sum(), figure1,
canvas1, "Sales by Day")
            self.plot_piechart_group(df2.groupby('Month')['Sales'].sum(), figure2,
canvas2, "Sales by Month")

        elif chosen == "Sales by Ship Mode and Segment":
            self.plot_piechart_group(df2.groupby('Ship Mode')['Sales'].sum(),
figure1, canvas1, "Sales by Ship Mode")
            self.plot_piechart_group(df2.groupby('Segment')['Sales'].sum(), figure2,
canvas2, "Sales by Segment")

        elif chosen == "Sales by Category and Sub-Category":
            self.plot_piechart_group(df2.groupby('Category')['Sales'].sum(), figure1,
canvas1, "Sales by Category")
            self.plot_piechart_group(df2.groupby('Sub-Category')['Sales'].sum(),
figure2, canvas2, "Sales by Sub-Category")

        elif chosen == "Sales by Product Name and Product ID":
```

```python
            self.plot_piechart_group(df2.groupby('Product
Name')['Sales'].sum().nlargest(10), figure1, canvas1, "Sales by Product Name")
            self.plot_piechart_group(df2.groupby('Product
ID')['Sales'].sum().nlargest(10), figure2, canvas2, "Sales by Product ID")

        elif chosen == "Sales by Customer Name and Customer ID":
            self.plot_piechart_group(df2.groupby('Customer
Name')['Sales'].sum().nlargest(10),
                figure1, canvas1, "Sales by Customer Name")
            self.plot_piechart_group(df2.groupby('Customer
ID')['Sales'].sum().nlargest(10),
                figure2, canvas2, "Sales by Customer ID")

        elif chosen == "Sales by City and State":
            self.plot_piechart_group(df2.groupby('City')['Sales'].sum().nlargest(10),
                figure1, canvas1, "Sales by City")

self.plot_piechart_group(df2.groupby('State')['Sales'].sum().nlargest(10),
                figure2, canvas2, "Sales by State")

        elif chosen == "Categorized Sales by Year and Quarter":
            self.dist_one_vs_another_plot(df2, "Year", "Cat_Sales", figure1, canvas1,
"Categorized Sales by Year")
            self.dist_one_vs_another_plot(df2, "Quarter", "Cat_Sales", figure2,
canvas2, "Categorized Sales by Quarter")

        elif chosen == "Categorized Sales by Day and Month":
            self.dist_one_vs_another_plot(df2, "Day", "Cat_Sales", figure1, canvas1,
"Categorized Sales by Day")
            self.dist_one_vs_another_plot(df2, "Month", "Cat_Sales", figure2,
canvas2, "Categorized Sales by Month")

        elif chosen == "Categorized Sales by Segment and Sub-Category":
            self.dist_one_vs_another_plot(df2, "Segment", "Cat_Sales", figure1,
canvas1, "Categorized Sales by Segment")
            self.dist_one_vs_another_plot(df2, "Sub-Category", "Cat_Sales", figure2,
canvas2, "Categorized Sales by Sub-Category")

        elif chosen == "Categorized Sales by Region and State":
            self.dist_one_vs_another_plot(df2, "Region", "Cat_Sales", figure1,
canvas1, "Categorized Sales by Region")
            self.dist_one_vs_another_plot(df2, "State", "Cat_Sales", figure2,
canvas2, "Categorized Sales by State")

        if chosen == "Correlation Matrix":
            self.plot_corr_mat(df1, figure1, canvas1)
```

Here's an explanation of the different cases handled by choose_plot based() on the value of chosen:

1. Day, Month, Quarter, Year: These options trigger the plot_piechart() method to display pie charts showing the case distribution of the selected time periods.

2. Missing Values: This option triggers the plot_missing_values() method to display a bar chart showing the missing values in the dataset.

3. Correlation Coefficient: This option triggers the plot_corr_coeffs() method to display a horizontal bar chart showing the correlation coefficients of features with the "Adj Close" column.

4. Country and City, State and Region, Customer Name and Customer ID, Ship Mode and Segment, Product Name and Product ID, Category and Sub-Category: These options trigger the plot_piechart_group() method to display pie charts showing the case distribution of the selected categories.

5. Sales by Year and Quarter, Day and Month, Ship Mode and Segment, Category and Sub-Category, Product Name and Product ID, Customer Name and Customer ID, City and State: These options group the data by the selected categories and use plot_piechart_group() to display pie charts of the total sales for each category.

6. Categorized Sales by Year and Quarter, Day and Month, Segment and Sub-Category, Region and State: These options use dist_one_vs_another_plot() to display stacked bar charts showing the distribution of categorized sales by the selected categories.

7. Correlation Matrix: This option triggers the plot_corr_mat() method to display a heatmap showing the correlation matrix of the features.

In summary, choose_plot() acts as a dispatcher that selects and displays the appropriate visualization method based on the user's choice.

Line Plot of a Specific Feature

In Helper_Plot class, define a new method named line_plot_year_wise(). It is responsible for creating a line plot of a specific feature (feat) for two different years (year1 and year2) using the data from the DataFrame df. The method takes a matplotlib figure (figure) and its associated canvas (canvas) as arguments for displaying the plot:

```python
def line_plot_year_wise(self, df, feat, year1, year2, figure, canvas):
    figure.clear()
    ax1 = figure.add_subplot(2, 1, 1)
    data1 = df[df["Year"]==year1]
    data2 = df[df["Year"]==year2]
    # Convert the column and index to NumPy arrays
    date_index1 = data1.index.to_numpy()
    date_index2 = data2.index.to_numpy()

    # Line plot
    ax1.plot(date_index1, data1[feat].to_numpy(),
        color="red", marker='o', linestyle='-', linewidth=2, markersize=1,
label=feat)
    ax1.set_xlabel('YEAR')
    ax1.set_title(feat + ' (YEAR = ' + str(year1) + ')', fontsize=12)
    ax1.legend(facecolor='#E6E6FA', edgecolor='black')
    ax1.set_facecolor('#F0F0F0')
    ax1.grid(True)
```

```python
        ax2 = figure.add_subplot(2, 1, 2)
        ax2.plot(date_index2, data2[feat].to_numpy(),
            color="blue", marker='o', linestyle='-', linewidth=2, markersize=1,
label=feat)
        ax2.set_xlabel('YEAR')
        ax2.set_title(feat + ' (YEAR = ' + str(year2) + ')', fontsize=12)
        ax2.legend(facecolor='#E6E6FA', edgecolor='black')
        ax2.set_facecolor('#F0F0F0')
        ax2.grid(True)

        figure.tight_layout()
        canvas.draw()
```

Here's how the method works:
1. Clear Figure: The method begins by clearing the provided figure to ensure a clean canvas for the new plot.
2. Create Subplots: The figure is divided into two subplots using add_subplot(2, 1, 1) and add_subplot(2, 1, 2). This results in a vertical arrangement of two subplots.
3. Data Filtering: The DataFrame df is filtered to obtain data for the specified years (year1 and year2). The resulting DataFrames are stored in data1 and data2, respectively.
4. Data Preparation: The index of each DataFrame (which presumably represents dates or time periods) is converted to NumPy arrays using to_numpy().
5. Line Plot: The line plot is generated using ax1.plot() and ax2.plot(). The x-axis represents the date index, and the y-axis represents the values of the specified feature (feat). The plot is styled with a red color for the first year and a blue color for the second year. Markers ('o') are added at data points, and the line style is set to solid ('-'). The line width is set to 2, and marker size is set to 1. The label of the plot is set to the feature name.
6. Axis Labels and Titles: The x-axis is labeled as 'YEAR'. The title of each subplot includes the feature name and the corresponding year.
7. Legend and Styling: A legend is added to each subplot, displaying the label of the feature. The legend is styled with a light purple face color and a black edge. The background color of the subplot is set to a light gray shade (#F0F0F0), and grid lines are enabled.
8. Tight Layout: The layout is adjusted to ensure that the subplots do not overlap.
9. Canvas Update: Finally, the canvas is redrawn to display the updated plot.

In summary, line_plot_year_wise() creates two subplots displaying line plots for a specified feature in two different years. The method provides a clear visualization of how the feature's values change over time.

Line Plot of Normalized Data

In Helper_Plot class, define a new method named line_plot_norm_data(). It is designed to generate a line plot of normalized data. This method is provided with the following arguments:

- norm_data: This parameter refers to the DataFrame or Series containing the normalized data that is to be plotted.
- figure: This is the Matplotlib figure where the plot will be displayed.
- canvas: The associated canvas for updating the figure.
- label: The label to be used for the y-axis.
- title: The title of the plot.

```python
def line_plot_norm_data(self, norm_data, figure, canvas, label, title):
    figure.clear()
    ax = figure.add_subplot(1, 1, 1)

    # Convert the column and index to NumPy arrays
    date_index = norm_data.index.to_numpy()

    values = norm_data.to_numpy()
    ax.plot(values, date_index, marker='o', linestyle='-',
                linewidth=3, markersize=2, label="SALES")

    ax.set_ylabel(label)
    ax.set_title(title, fontsize=12)
    ax.legend(fontsize=7, facecolor='#E6E6FA', edgecolor='black')
    ax.set_facecolor('#F0F0F0')
    ax.grid(True)

    figure.tight_layout()
    canvas.draw()
```

Here's a breakdown of the steps performed by the function:
1. Clear Figure: The function starts by clearing the provided figure, ensuring a clean canvas for the new plot.
2. Create Subplot: The figure is divided into a single subplot using add_subplot(1, 1, 1).
3. Data Preparation: The index of the norm_data DataFrame (which represents dates or time periods) is converted to a NumPy array using to_numpy(). The values are also extracted as a NumPy array.
4. Line Plot: The line plot is generated using ax.plot(). In this case, the x-axis represents the values of the normalized data, while the y-axis represents the date index. Markers ('o') are added at data points, and the line style is set to solid ('-'). The line width is set to 3, and marker size is set to 2. The label of the plot is set to "SALES".
5. Axis Labels and Title: The y-axis is labeled with the provided label, and the plot is given the specified title.

6. Legend and Styling: A legend is added to the plot, displaying the label "SALES". The legend is styled with a light purple face color and a black edge. The background color of the subplot is set to a light gray shade (#F0F0F0), and grid lines are enabled.
7. Tight Layout: The layout is adjusted to ensure that the plot is well-organized.
8. Canvas Update: Finally, the canvas is redrawn to display the updated plot.

In summary, line_plot_norm_data() creates a line plot of normalized data, providing a clear visualization of how the normalized values change over time. The function is flexible and can be used with different sets of normalized data by passing appropriate arguments.

Line Plot of Mean/EWM Data

In Helper_Plot class, define a new method named line_plot_data_mean_ewm(). It is designed to generate a line plot comparing the mean and exponentially weighted moving average (EWM) of a dataset. This method is provided with the following arguments:
- data_mean: A DataFrame or Series containing the mean values.
- data_ewm: A DataFrame or Series containing the exponentially weighted moving average values.
- figure: The Matplotlib figure where the plot will be displayed.
- canvas: The associated canvas for updating the figure.
- xlabel: The label for the x-axis.
- ylabel: The label for the y-axis.

```python
    def line_plot_data_mean_ewm(self, data_mean, data_ewm, figure, canvas, xlabel,
ylabel):
        figure.clear()
        ax1 = figure.add_subplot(1, 1, 1)

        # Convert the column and index to NumPy arrays
        date_index = data_mean.index.to_numpy()

        # Line plot
        ax1.plot(date_index, data_mean.to_numpy(),
            color="red", marker='o', linestyle='-', linewidth=2, markersize=1,
label="Mean")
        ax1.plot(date_index,data_ewm.to_numpy(),
            color="blue", marker='o', linestyle='-', linewidth=2, markersize=1,
label="EWM")
        ax1.set_title("Year-Wise Mean/EWM of Sales", fontsize=12)
        ax1.legend(facecolor='#E6E6FA', edgecolor='black')
        ax1.set_xlabel(xlabel)
        ax1.set_ylabel(ylabel)
        ax1.set_facecolor('#F0F0F0')
        ax1.grid(True)

        figure.tight_layout()
```

```
canvas.draw()
```

Here's a breakdown of the steps performed by the function:
1. Clear Figure: The function starts by clearing the provided figure, ensuring a clean canvas for the new plot.
2. Create Subplot: The figure is divided into a single subplot using add_subplot(1, 1, 1).
3. Data Preparation: The index of the data_mean DataFrame (which represents dates or time periods) is converted to a NumPy array using to_numpy().
4. Line Plots: Two line plots are generated using ax1.plot(). One represents the mean values (in red), and the other represents the exponentially weighted moving average (in blue). Markers ('o') are added at data points, and the line style is set to solid ('-'). The line width is set to 2, and marker size is set to 1. The legend labels for the two lines are set to "Mean" and "EWM".
5. Axis Labels and Title: The x-axis is labeled with xlabel, and the y-axis is labeled with ylabel. The plot is given the title "Year-Wise Mean/EWM of Sales".
6. Legend and Styling: A legend is added to the plot, displaying the labels "Mean" and "EWM". The legend is styled with a light purple face color and a black edge. The background color of the subplot is set to a light gray shade (#F0F0F0), and grid lines are enabled.
7. Tight Layout: The layout is adjusted to ensure that the plot is well-organized.
8. Canvas Update: Finally, the canvas is redrawn to display the updated plot.

In summary, line_plot_data_mean_ewm() creates a line plot comparing the mean and EWM of a dataset over time. This provides insights into the trend and variability of the data. The function is versatile and can be used with different sets of data by passing appropriate arguments.

Window to Display Line Plot of Feature

In Helper_Plot class, define a new method named plot_year_wise(). It is designed to create a graphical representation of a specific feature (feat) over two different years (year1 and year2):

```python
def plot_year_wise(self, df, feat, year1, year2):
    win = tk.Toplevel()
    form3 = Form3(win)
    self.line_plot_year_wise(df, feat, year1, year2, form3.figure1,
form3.canvas1)
```

This method is provided with the following arguments:
- df: The DataFrame containing the dataset.
- feat: The feature to be plotted.
- year1: The first year for comparison.
- year2: The second year for comparison.

Here's an explanation of how the function works:
1. Create a New Window: A new window (tk.Toplevel()) is created using Tkinter. This will serve as the container for displaying the plot.
2. Initialize Form3: The Form3 instance (form3) is created, which provides the Matplotlib figure and canvas needed for plotting.
3. Call line_plot_year_wise(): This function is then called with the provided arguments (df, feat, year1, year2, form3.figure1, and form3.canvas1).
4. The purpose of this call is to generate a line plot comparing the feature over the two specified years. The resulting plot will be displayed in the Form3 window.

In summary, plot_year_wise() is a higher-level function that facilitates the creation of a year-wise comparison plot for a specific feature. It leverages the line_plot_year_wise() function to achieve this. The function provides a convenient way to visualize and compare data across different years.

Window to Display Line Plot of Mean/EWM Data

In Helper_Plot class, define a new method named plot_year_wise_mean_ewm(). It is designed to create a graphical representation comparing two sets of data: the mean (data_mean) and exponentially weighted moving average (data_ewm):

```python
def plot_year_wise_mean_ewm(self, data_mean, data_ewm):
    win = tk.Toplevel()
    form3 = Form3(win)
    self.line_plot_data_mean_ewm(data_mean, data_ewm, form3.figure1,
form3.canvas1, "YEAR", "SALES")
```

This method is provided with the following arguments:
- data_mean: The dataset representing the mean values.
- data_ewm: The dataset representing exponentially weighted moving average values.

Here's an explanation of how the function works:
1. Create a New Window: A new window (tk.Toplevel()) is created using Tkinter. This will serve as the container for displaying the plot.
2. Initialize Form3: The Form3 instance (form3) is created, which provides the Matplotlib figure and canvas needed for plotting.
3. Call line_plot_data_mean_ewm(): This function is then called with the provided arguments (data_mean, data_ewm, form3.figure1, and form3.canvas1).
4. The purpose of this call is to generate a line plot comparing the mean and exponentially weighted moving average values. The resulting plot will be displayed in the Form3 window.

In summary, plot_year_wise_mean_ewm() is a higher-level function that facilitates the creation of a comparison plot for two sets of data: mean and exponentially weighted moving average. It leverages the line_plot_data_mean_ewm() function to achieve this. The function provides a convenient way to visualize and compare these two types of data.

Various Types of Plots

In Helper_Plot class, define a new method named box_violin_strip_heat(). It is designed to create a series of graphical representations for a given dataset. It uses various types of plots like box plots, violin plots, strip plots, and swarm plots to visualize the distribution of data based on specific filters:

```python
def box_violin_strip_heat(self, data, filter, feat1, figure1, canvas1, figure2,
canvas2, title):
    figure1.clear()
    ax1 = figure1.add_subplot(2, 1, 1)
    sns.boxplot(x = filter, y = feat1, data = data, ax=ax1)
    ax1.set_title("Box Plot of " + feat1 + " by " + filter, fontsize=12)
    # Set font for tick labels
    ax1.tick_params(axis='both', which='major', labelsize=6)
    ax1.tick_params(axis='both', which='minor', labelsize=6)
    ax1.grid(True)
    ax1.set_facecolor('#F0F0F0')

    ax2 = figure1.add_subplot(2, 1, 2)
    sns.violinplot(x = filter, y = feat1, data = data, ax=ax2)
    ax2.set_title("Violin Plot of " + feat1 + " by " + filter, fontsize=12)
    # Set font for tick labels
    ax2.tick_params(axis='both', which='major', labelsize=6)
    ax2.tick_params(axis='both', which='minor', labelsize=6)
    ax2.grid(True)
    ax2.set_facecolor('#F0F0F0')
    figure1.tight_layout()
    canvas1.draw()

    figure2.clear()
    ax3 = figure2.add_subplot(2, 1, 1)
    sns.stripplot(x = filter, y = feat1, data = data, ax=ax3)
    ax3.set_title("Strip Plot of " + feat1 + " by " + filter, fontsize=12)
    # Set font for tick labels
    ax3.tick_params(axis='both', which='major', labelsize=6)
    ax3.tick_params(axis='both', which='minor', labelsize=6)
    ax3.set_facecolor('#F0F0F0')
    ax3.grid(True)

    ax4 = figure2.add_subplot(2, 1, 2)
    sns.swarmplot(x = filter, y = feat1, data = data, ax=ax4)
    ax4.set_title("Swarm Plot of " + feat1 + " by " + filter, fontsize=12)
    # Set font for tick labels
    ax4.tick_params(axis='both', which='major', labelsize=6)
    ax4.tick_params(axis='both', which='minor', labelsize=6)
    ax4.grid(True)
```

```
ax4.set_facecolor('#F0F0F0')
figure2.tight_layout()
canvas2.draw()
```

Here is an explanation of how the function works:
1. Clear Existing Figures: Both figure1 and figure2 are cleared to remove any existing plots.
2. Create Subplots for Box and Violin Plots:
    - ax1 and ax2 are created for the box and violin plots, respectively, in the first figure (figure1). These subplots are arranged in a 2x1 grid.
    - sns.boxplot() is used to generate the box plot, and sns.violinplot() is used for the violin plot. These functions are provided with specific data and filtering criteria.
3. Set Titles and Aesthetics for Box and Violin Plots:
    - Titles are set for both the box and violin plots, indicating which feature is being visualized and by which filter.
    - Tick label font sizes are adjusted, and grid lines are enabled for better readability.
4. Create Subplots for Strip and Swarm Plots:
    Similarly, ax3 and ax4 are created for the strip and swarm plots in the second figure (figure2), following the same 2x1 grid arrangement.
5. Generate Strip and Swarm Plots:
    sns.stripplot() is used to create the strip plot, and sns.swarmplot() is used for the swarm plot. Again, specific data and filtering criteria are provided.
6. Set Titles and Aesthetics for Strip and Swarm Plots:
    - Titles are set for both the strip and swarm plots, indicating which feature is being visualized and by which filter.
    - Tick label font sizes are adjusted, and grid lines are enabled for better readability.
7. Adjust Figure Layout and Draw Plots:
    - figure1.tight_layout() and figure2.tight_layout() ensure that subplots are properly spaced and fit within the figure.
    - canvas1.draw() and canvas2.draw() are called to render the plots on the respective canvases.

In summary, the box_violin_strip_heat() function creates a comprehensive set of plots (box, violin, strip, and swarm plots) to visualize the distribution of a feature (feat1) based on a specified filter (filter). The function provides a detailed and varied view of the data distribution for exploratory analysis.

Window to Visualize Trends of Data

In Helper_Plot class, define a new method named plot_year_trends(). It creates a visualization of trends in the dataset by calling the box_violin_strip_heat function:

```python
def plot_year_trends(self, df, var1, var2, title=""):
    win = tk.Toplevel()
    form1 = Form1(win)
    self.box_violin_strip_heat(df, var1, var2, form1.figure1, form1.canvas1,
        form1.figure2, form1.canvas2, title)
```

Here's how it works:

1. Create a New Window:

   A new window (win) is created using Tkinter's Toplevel() method. This window serves as the container for the visualizations.

2. Initialize Form1:

   An instance of Form1 is created, which is assumed to have attributes figure1, canvas1, figure2, and canvas2 that correspond to different plotting areas.

3. Call box_violin_strip_heat():

   The box_violin_strip_heat() function is called with the following arguments:

   - df: The dataset to be visualized.
   - var1: The filter or category variable for the plots.
   - var2: The feature being visualized.
   - form1.figure1: The first figure for the box and violin plots.
   - form1.canvas1: The canvas associated with the first figure.
   - form1.figure2: The second figure for the strip and swarm plots.
   - form1.canvas2: The canvas associated with the second figure.
   - title: An optional title for the plots.

4. Display Plots:

   The box_violin_strip_heat() function generates and displays the box, violin, strip, and swarm plots based on the provided arguments.

In summary, the plot_year_trends() function opens a new window, initializes an instance of Form1 to access plotting attributes, and then calls the box_violin_strip_heat() function to create visualizations of trends in the dataset based on specified filter variables (var1 and var2). The resulting plots are displayed in the window for further analysis.

Setting Up the Menu Options Related to Year-Wise Analysis

In Helper_Plot class, define a new method named binds_year_wise(). It sets up bindings for various options related to year-wise analysis:

```python
def binds_year_wise(self, window, df, data_mean, data_ewm):
    window.year_wise.entryconfigure("Year-Wise Sales Distribution 2017 and 2018",
        command = lambda:self.plot_year_wise(df, "Sales", 2017, 2018))

    window.year_wise.entryconfigure("Year-Wise Sales Distribution 2015 and 2016",
        command = lambda:self.plot_year_wise(df, "Sales", 2015, 2016))

    window.year_wise.entryconfigure("Year-Wise Sales Mean and EWM",
        command = lambda:self.plot_year_wise_mean_ewm(data_mean, data_ewm))

    window.year_wise.entryconfigure("Sales by Year",
        command = lambda:self.plot_year_trends(df, "Year", "Sales"))

    window.year_wise.entryconfigure("Sales by Quarter",
        command = lambda:self.plot_year_trends(df, "Quarter", "Sales"))

    window.year_wise.entryconfigure("Sales by Month",
        command = lambda:self.plot_year_trends(df, "Month", "Sales"))

    window.year_wise.entryconfigure("Sales by Day",
        command = lambda:self.plot_year_trends(df, "Day", "Sales"))

    window.year_wise.entryconfigure("Sales by Week",
        command = lambda:self.plot_year_trends(df, "Week", "Sales"))
```

Here's what each option does:
1. Year-Wise Sales Distribution 2017 and 2018:
   When selected, this option calls the plot_year_wise() function with the dataset df, the feature "Sales", and the years 2017 and 2018 as arguments. This will plot the sales distribution for these specific years.
2. Year-Wise Sales Distribution 2015 and 2016:
   Similar to the first option, this one calls the plot_year_wise() function with the dataset df, the feature "Sales", and the years 2015 and 2016 as arguments. This will plot the sales distribution for these specific years.
3. Year-Wise Sales Mean and EWM:
   This option calls the plot_year_wise_mean_ewm() function with data_mean and data_ewm as arguments. This will plot the mean and exponentially weighted moving average (EWM) of sales over the years.
4. Sales by Year, Quarter, Month, Day, and Week:
   These options call the plot_year_trends() function with different filter variables ("Year", "Quarter", "Month", "Day", and "Week") and the feature "Sales". Each option visualizes the sales trends over the specified time periods.

In summary, the binds_year_wise() function sets up a menu with various options for year-wise analysis. When a specific option is selected, it triggers the corresponding plotting function with appropriate arguments, allowing for the visualization of sales trends and distributions over different time periods.

Selecting Plotting Functions Related to Year-Wise Analysis

In Helper_Plot class, define a new method named choose_year_wise(). It is responsible for selecting and executing the appropriate plotting function based on the user's choice:

```python
def choose_year_wise(self, df, data_mean, data_ewm, data_norm, chosen, figure1,
canvas1, figure2, canvas2):
    if chosen == "Year-Wise Sales Distribution 2017 and 2018":
        self.line_plot_year_wise(df, "Sales", 2017, 2018, figure1, canvas1)

    if chosen == "Year-Wise Sales Distribution 2015 and 2016":
        self.line_plot_year_wise(df, "Sales", 2015, 2016, figure2, canvas2)

    if chosen == "Year-Wise Sales Mean and EWM":
        self.line_plot_data_mean_ewm(data_mean, data_ewm, figure1, canvas1,
"YEAR", chosen)

    if chosen == "Normalized Year-Wise Data":
        self.line_plot_norm_data(data_norm, figure2, canvas2, "YEAR", chosen)
```

Here's what each condition does:
1. Year-Wise Sales Distribution 2017 and 2018:
   If the user selects this option, it calls the line_plot_year_wise() function with the dataset df, the feature "Sales", and the years 2017 and 2018 as arguments. This function plots the sales distribution for these specific years.
2. Year-Wise Sales Distribution 2015 and 2016:
   If this option is chosen, it calls the line_plot_year_wise() function with the dataset df, the feature "Sales", and the years 2015 and 2016 as arguments. This function plots the sales distribution for these specific years.
3. Year-Wise Sales Mean and EWM:
   When this option is selected, it calls the line_plot_data_mean_ewm() function with data_mean and data_ewm as arguments. This function plots the mean and exponentially weighted moving average (EWM) of sales over the years.
4. Normalized Year-Wise Data:
   If the user chooses this option, it calls the line_plot_norm_data() function with data_norm as an argument. This function plots the normalized data.

In summary, the choose_year_wise() function takes the user's choice and triggers the corresponding plotting function with the appropriate arguments, resulting in visualizations of various aspects of the data based on the chosen option.

Line Plot of Month-Wise Data

In Helper_Plot class, define a new method named line_plot_month_wise(). It is designed to create line plots for a specific feature (feat1) over a given year (year). The data is filtered based on two conditions: filter and filter1 or filter2:

```python
def line_plot_month_wise(self, df, feat1, year, filter, filter1, filter2,
figure, canvas):
    figure.clear()
    ax1 = figure.add_subplot(2, 1, 1)

    data1 = df[(df["Year"]==year)&(df[filter]==filter1)]
    data2 = df[(df["Year"]==year)&(df[filter]==filter2)]

    # Convert the column and index to NumPy arrays
    date_index1 = data1.index.to_numpy()
    date_index2 = data2.index.to_numpy()

    # Line plot
    ax1.plot(date_index1, data1[feat1].to_numpy(),
        color="red", marker='o', linestyle='-', linewidth=2, markersize=1,
label=feat1)
    ax1.set_xlabel('DATE')
    ax1.set_ylabel(feat1)
    ax1.set_title(feat1 + " " + filter + " = " + filter1 + " " + str(year),
fontsize=12)
    ax1.legend(facecolor='#E6E6FA', edgecolor='black')
    ax1.set_facecolor('#F0F0F0')
    ax1.grid(True)

    # Set font for tick labels
    ax1.tick_params(axis='both', which='major', labelsize=7)
    ax1.tick_params(axis='both', which='minor', labelsize=7)

    ax2 = figure.add_subplot(2, 1, 2)
    ax2.plot(date_index2, data2[feat1].to_numpy(),
        color="red", marker='o', linestyle='-', linewidth=2, markersize=1,
label=feat1)
    ax2.set_xlabel('DATE')
    ax2.set_ylabel(feat1)
    ax2.set_title(feat1 + " " + filter + " = " + filter2 + " " + str(year),
fontsize=12)
    ax2.legend(facecolor='#E6E6FA', edgecolor='black')
    ax2.set_facecolor('#F0F0F0')
    ax2.grid(True)

    # Set font for tick labels
    ax2.tick_params(axis='both', which='major', labelsize=7)
    ax2.tick_params(axis='both', which='minor', labelsize=7)
```

```
figure.tight_layout()
canvas.draw()
```

Here's an explanation of the function's parameters and its functionality:
- df: The DataFrame containing the dataset.
- feat1: The feature (column) that you want to plot on the y-axis.
- year: The specific year for which you want to plot the data.
- filter: The column (filter) you want to use for categorizing the data.
- filter1: The first filter value to consider for the specified column.
- filter2: The second filter value to consider for the specified column.
- figure: The Matplotlib figure object where the plots will be drawn.
- canvas: The Tkinter canvas associated with the figure for updating the display.

Here's how the function works:
1. It clears the existing content on the provided Matplotlib figure.
2. It extracts two subsets of data from the DataFrame df based on the specified year (year) and the two filter values (filter1 and filter2). These subsets will be used to create two separate line plots.
3. For each subset of data, it converts the index of the DataFrame to NumPy arrays to be used as the x-axis values.
4. It creates two line plots on separate subplots within the same figure:
   - The first subplot (ax1) represents the data where the specified filter column matches filter1. It plots the values of feat1 for the given year and filter.
   - The second subplot (ax2) represents the data where the specified filter column matches filter2. It also plots the values of feat1 for the given year and filter.
5. It sets various plot attributes, including labels, titles, legends, tick label sizes, grid lines, and background color.
6. Finally, it tightens the layout and updates the Tkinter canvas to display the plots.

In summary, this function allows you to compare the feat1 values month-wise for a specific year, using two different filter values for a specified column (filter). The result is two line plots side by side, each showing how feat1 varies over the months for a different filter condition.

Sales Data over the Months

In Helper_Plot class, define three new methods named color_month(), line_plot_month(), and sns_plot_month():

```python
def color_month(self, month):
    if month == 1:
        return 'January','blue'
```

```python
        elif month == 2:
            return 'February','green'
        elif month == 3:
            return 'March','orange'
        elif month == 4:
            return 'April','yellow'
        elif month == 5:
            return 'May','red'
        elif month == 6:
            return 'June','violet'
        elif month == 7:
            return 'July','purple'
        elif month == 8:
            return 'August','black'
        elif month == 9:
            return 'September','brown'
        elif month == 10:
            return 'October','darkblue'
        elif month == 11:
            return 'November','grey'
        else:
            return 'December','pink'

    def line_plot_month(self, month, data, ax):
        label, color = self.color_month(month)
        mdata = data[data.index.month == month]
        date_index = mdata.index.to_numpy()

        ax.plot(date_index, mdata.to_numpy(),
            marker='o', linestyle='-',
            color=color, linewidth=2, markersize=1, label=label)

    def sns_plot_month(self, monthly_data, title, figure, canvas):
        figure.clear()
        ax = figure.add_subplot(1, 1, 1)
        ax.set_title(title, fontsize=12)
        ax.set_xlabel('YEAR', fontsize=10)
        ax.set_ylabel("SALES", fontsize=10)

        for i in range(1,13):
            self.line_plot_month(i, monthly_data, ax)

        ax.legend(facecolor='#E6E6FA', edgecolor='black')
        ax.grid()
        ax.set_facecolor('#F0F0F0')
        figure.tight_layout()
        canvas.draw()
```

The code defines three functions related to plotting sales data over the months:

1. color_month(month)

      - This function takes a month (an integer from 1 to 12) as input and returns a tuple containing the name of the month and a corresponding color.
      - For example, if month is 1, it returns ('January', 'blue').
      - This function is used to assign colors to the different months.

2. line_plot_month(month, data, ax)
   - This function takes a month (an integer from 1 to 12), a DataFrame data, and a Matplotlib axes object ax as input.
   - It uses the color_month() function to get the label and color for the given month.
   - It then filters the data to include only records for the specified month and plots it on the provided axes.
3. sns_plot_month(monthly_data, title, figure, canvas)
   - This function takes monthly_data (a DataFrame containing monthly sales data), a title, a Matplotlib figure, and a Tkinter canvas as input.
   - It creates a subplot on the provided figure and sets the title and labels.
   - It then iterates over each month (from 1 to 12) and calls the line_plot_month() function to plot the sales data for that month.
   - Finally, it adds a legend, sets the background color, and tightens the layout before updating the Tkinter canvas to display the plot.

These functions work together to create a line plot showing sales data over the months, with each month represented by a different color. The sns_plot_month() function orchestrates the process, while the line_plot_month() function handles the actual plotting for each individual month. The color_month() function provides the mapping between months and colors.

Window to Visualize Sales Data on Month-Wise Basis

In Helper_Plot class, define three new methods named plot_month_wise(), plot_month_wise_mean_ewm(), and plot_month_wise_by_month():

```python
def plot_month_wise(self, df, feat1, year, filter, filter1, filter2):
    win = tk.Toplevel()
    form3 = Form3(win)
    self.line_plot_month_wise(df, feat1, year, filter,
        filter1, filter2, form3.figure1, form3.canvas1)

def plot_month_wise_mean_ewm(self, data_mean, data_ewm):
    win = tk.Toplevel()
    form3 = Form3(win)
    self.line_plot_data_mean_ewm(data_mean, data_ewm, form3.figure1,
form3.canvas1, "YEAR", "SALES")

def plot_month_wise_by_month(self, data_mean, title):
    win = tk.Toplevel()
    form3 = Form3(win)
    self.sns_plot_month(data_mean, title, form3.figure1, form3.canvas1)
```

These functions provide functionality to plot sales data month-wise:
   1. plot_month_wise(self, df, feat1, year, filter, filter1, filter2)

- This function takes a DataFrame df, a feature feat1, a specific year, a filter to apply (e.g., a category), and two filter values filter1 and filter2.
- It creates a new top-level window using Tkinter (tk.Toplevel()).
- Inside this window, it creates an instance of Form3.
- It then calls line_plot_month_wise() with the provided arguments to plot the data.

2. plot_month_wise_mean_ewm(self, data_mean, data_ewm)
   - This function takes data_mean and data_ewm.
   - It creates a new top-level window and an instance of Form3.
   - It calls line_plot_data_mean_ewm() with the provided arguments to plot the data.

3. plot_month_wise_by_month(self, data_mean, title)
   - This function takes data_mean (a DataFrame with monthly sales data) and a title.
   - It creates a new top-level window and an instance of Form3.
   - It calls sns_plot_month() with the provided arguments to plot the data.

These functions allow you to visualize sales data on a month-wise basis, providing different options for plotting and comparing data across months.

Monthly Sales Data for Different Regions over Time

In Helper_Plot class, define a new method named month_wise_region_based(). It visualizes the monthly sales data for different regions over time:

```python
def month_wise_region_based(self, df, figure, canvas):
    figure.clear()

    west_df = df.loc[df['Region'] == 'West']
    east_df = df.loc[df['Region'] == 'East']
    south_df = df.loc[df['Region'] == 'South']
    central_df = df.loc[df['Region'] == 'Central']

    west_monthly_sales = west_df['Sales'].resample('M').sum()
    west_monthly_sales = west_monthly_sales.round(2)

    east_monthly_sales = east_df['Sales'].resample('M').sum()
    east_monthly_sales = east_monthly_sales.round(2)

    south_monthly_sales = south_df['Sales'].resample('M').sum()
    south_monthly_sales = south_monthly_sales.round(2)

    central_monthly_sales = central_df['Sales'].resample('M').sum()
    central_monthly_sales = central_monthly_sales.round(2)

    ax1 = figure.add_subplot(1, 1, 1)
    ax1.plot(west_monthly_sales.index.to_numpy(), west_monthly_sales.values,
color="red", marker='o', linestyle='-', label="West")
    ax1.plot(east_monthly_sales.index.to_numpy(), east_monthly_sales.values,
color="blue", marker='o', linestyle='-', label="East")
```

```python
        ax1.plot(south_monthly_sales.index.to_numpy(), south_monthly_sales.values,
color="green", marker='o', linestyle='-', label="South")
        ax1.plot(central_monthly_sales.index.to_numpy(),
central_monthly_sales.values, color="black", marker='o', linestyle='-',
label="Central")

        ax1.set_title("Region-Based Monthly Sales", fontsize=12)
        ax1.legend(facecolor='#E6E6FA', edgecolor='black')
        ax1.set_xlabel("Date")
        ax1.set_ylabel("Sales")
        ax1.set_facecolor('#F0F0F0')
        ax1.grid(True)

        figure.tight_layout()
        canvas.draw()
```

The function takes a DataFrame df, a Matplotlib figure, and a Tkinter canvas as inputs. It performs the following tasks:

1. Extracts data for each region (West, East, South, Central) from the DataFrame df.
2. Resamples the monthly sales data for each region.
3. Rounds the sales values to 2 decimal places.
4. Creates a line plot with different colors for each region.
5. Sets the title, legend, labels, and background color for the plot.
6. Draws the plot on the canvas.

This function allows you to visualize the monthly sales data for different regions over time.

Monthly Sales Quantity for Different Product Categories over Time

In Helper_Plot class, define a new method named month_wise_category_based(). It visualizes the monthly sales quantities for different product categories over time:

```python
def month_wise_category_based(self, df, figure, canvas):
    figure.clear()

    #Creates a new column
    df['Quantity'] = 1

    office_supplies_df = df.loc[df['Category'] == 'Office Supplies']
    technology_df = df.loc[df['Category'] == 'Technology']
    furniture_df = df.loc[df['Category'] == 'Furniture']

    # Find how many quantities sold per month for each category
    monthly_office = office_supplies_df['Quantity'].resample('M').sum()
    monthly_technology = technology_df['Quantity'].resample('M').sum()
    monthly_furniture = furniture_df['Quantity'].resample('M').sum()

    ax1 = figure.add_subplot(1, 1, 1)
    ax1.plot(monthly_office.index.to_numpy(), monthly_office.values, color="red",
marker='o', linestyle='-', label="Office Products Sales Quantities by Month")
```

```python
        ax1.plot(monthly_technology.index.to_numpy(), monthly_technology.values,
color="blue", marker='o', linestyle='-', label="Technology Products Sales Quantities
by Month")
        ax1.plot(monthly_furniture.index.to_numpy(), monthly_furniture.values,
color="green", marker='o', linestyle='-', label="Furniture Products Sales Quantities
by Month")

        ax1.set_title("Category-Based Monthly Quantity", fontsize=12)
        ax1.legend(facecolor='#E6E6FA', edgecolor='black')
        ax1.set_xlabel("Date")
        ax1.set_ylabel("Quantity")
        ax1.set_facecolor('#F0F0F0')
        ax1.grid(True)

        figure.tight_layout()
        canvas.draw()
```

It takes a DataFrame df, a Matplotlib figure, and a Tkinter canvas as inputs. It performs the
following tasks:
1. Clears the existing content in the figure.
2. Adds a new column called 'Quantity' to the DataFrame df and initializes it with a value of
   1.
3. Filters the DataFrame for each category (Office Supplies, Technology, Furniture).
4. Calculates the monthly sales quantities for each category.
5. Creates a line plot with different colors for each category.
6. Sets the title, legend, labels, and background color for the plot.
7. Draws the plot on the canvas.

This function allows you to visualize the monthly sales quantities for different product categories
over time.

Monthly Sales Data for Different Segments over Time

In Helper_Plot class, define a new method named month_wise_segment_based(). It allows you to
visualize the monthly sales for different segments (Corporate, Home Office, Consumer) over time:

```python
    def month_wise_segment_based(self, df, figure, canvas):
        figure.clear()

        corp_df = df.loc[df['Segment'] == 'Corporate']
        office_df = df.loc[df['Segment'] == 'Home Office']
        cons_df = df.loc[df['Segment'] == 'Consumer']


        corp_monthly_sales = corp_df['Sales'].resample('M').sum()
        corp_monthly_sales = corp_monthly_sales.round(2)

        office_monthly_sales = office_df['Sales'].resample('M').sum()
        office_monthly_sales = office_monthly_sales.round(2)
```

```python
        cons_monthly_sales = cons_df['Sales'].resample('M').sum()
        cons_monthly_sales = cons_monthly_sales.round(2)

        ax1 = figure.add_subplot(1, 1, 1)
        ax1.plot(corp_monthly_sales.index.to_numpy(), corp_monthly_sales.values,
color="red", marker='o', linestyle='-', label="Corporate")
        ax1.plot(office_monthly_sales.index.to_numpy(), office_monthly_sales.values,
color="blue", marker='o', linestyle='-', label="Home Office")
        ax1.plot(cons_monthly_sales.index.to_numpy(), cons_monthly_sales.values,
color="green", marker='o', linestyle='-', label="Consumer")

        ax1.set_title("Segment-Based Monthly Sales", fontsize=12)
        ax1.legend(facecolor='#E6E6FA', edgecolor='black')
        ax1.set_xlabel("Date")
        ax1.set_ylabel("Sales")
        ax1.set_facecolor('#F0F0F0')
        ax1.grid(True)

        figure.tight_layout()
        canvas.draw()
```

It takes a DataFrame df, a Matplotlib figure, and a Tkinter canvas as inputs. It performs the
following tasks:
1. Clears the existing content in the figure.
2. Filters the DataFrame for each segment (Corporate, Home Office, Consumer).
3. Calculates the monthly sales for each segment.
4. Creates a line plot with different colors for each segment.
5. Sets the title, legend, labels, and background color for the plot.
6. Draws the plot on the canvas.

This function allows you to visualize the monthly sales for different segments (Corporate, Home
Office, Consumer) over time.

Monthly Sales Data for Different Cities over Time

In Helper_Plot class, define a new method named month_wise_city_based(). It visualizes the
monthly sales for different cities over time:

```python
    def month_wise_city_based(self, df, figure, canvas):
        figure.clear()

        los_df = df.loc[df['City'] == 'Los Angeles']
        york_df = df.loc[df['City'] == 'New York City']
        phil_df = df.loc[df['City'] == 'Philadelphia']
        san_df = df.loc[df['City'] == 'San Francisco']
        sea_df = df.loc[df['City'] == 'Seattle']
        chi_df = df.loc[df['City'] == 'Chicago']
        hou_df = df.loc[df['City'] == 'Houston']
        col_df = df.loc[df['City'] == 'Columbus']
```

```python
die_df = df.loc[df['City'] == 'San Diego']
spr_df = df.loc[df['City'] == 'Springfield']

los_monthly_sales = los_df['Sales'].resample('M').sum()
los_monthly_sales = los_monthly_sales.round(2)

york_monthly_sales = york_df['Sales'].resample('M').sum()
york_monthly_sales = york_monthly_sales.round(2)

phils_monthly_sales = phil_df['Sales'].resample('M').sum()
phils_monthly_sales = phils_monthly_sales.round(2)

san_monthly_sales = san_df['Sales'].resample('M').sum()
san_monthly_sales = san_monthly_sales.round(2)

sea_monthly_sales = sea_df['Sales'].resample('M').sum()
sea_monthly_sales = sea_monthly_sales.round(2)

ax1 = figure.add_subplot(1, 1, 1)
ax1.plot(los_monthly_sales.index.to_numpy(), los_monthly_sales.values,
color="red", marker='o', linestyle='-', label="Los Angeles")
ax1.plot(york_monthly_sales.index.to_numpy(), york_monthly_sales.values,
color="blue", marker='o', linestyle='-', label="New York City")
ax1.plot(phils_monthly_sales.index.to_numpy(), phils_monthly_sales.values,
color="green", marker='o', linestyle='-', label="Philadelphia")
ax1.plot(san_monthly_sales.index.to_numpy(), san_monthly_sales.values,
color="black", marker='o', linestyle='-', label="San Francisco")
ax1.plot(sea_monthly_sales.index.to_numpy(), sea_monthly_sales.values,
color="cyan", marker='o', linestyle='-', label="Seattle")

ax1.set_title("City-Based Monthly Sales", fontsize=12)
ax1.legend(facecolor='#E6E6FA', edgecolor='black')
ax1.set_xlabel("Date")
ax1.set_ylabel("Sales")
ax1.set_facecolor('#F0F0F0')
ax1.grid(True)

figure.tight_layout()
canvas.draw()
```

It takes a DataFrame df, a Matplotlib figure, and a Tkinter canvas as inputs. It performs the following tasks:

1. Clears the existing content in the figure.
2. Filters the DataFrame for each city (Los Angeles, New York City, Philadelphia, San Francisco, Seattle).
3. Calculates the monthly sales for each city.
4. Creates a line plot with different colors for each city.
5. Sets the title, legend, labels, and background color for the plot.
6. Draws the plot on the canvas.

This function allows you to visualize the monthly sales for different cities over time. The cities included in this function are Los Angeles, New York City, Philadelphia, San Francisco, and Seattle.

Monthly Sales Data for Different Shipping Modes over Time

In Helper_Plot class, define a new method named month_wise_shipmode_based(). It visualizes the monthly sales for different shipping modes over time:

```python
def month_wise_shipmode_based(self, df, figure, canvas):
    figure.clear()

    std_df = df.loc[df['Ship Mode'] == 'Standard Class']
    first_df = df.loc[df['Ship Mode'] == 'First Class']
    scd_df = df.loc[df['Ship Mode'] == 'Second Class']
    same_df = df.loc[df['Ship Mode'] == 'Same Day']

    std_monthly_sales = std_df['Sales'].resample('M').sum()
    std_monthly_sales = std_monthly_sales.round(2)

    first_monthly_sales = first_df['Sales'].resample('M').sum()
    first_monthly_sales = first_monthly_sales.round(2)

    scd_monthly_sales = scd_df['Sales'].resample('M').sum()
    scd_monthly_sales = scd_monthly_sales.round(2)

    same_monthly_sales = same_df['Sales'].resample('M').sum()
    same_monthly_sales = same_monthly_sales.round(2)

    ax1 = figure.add_subplot(1, 1, 1)
    ax1.plot(std_monthly_sales.index.to_numpy(), std_monthly_sales.values,
color="red", marker='o', linestyle='-', label="Standard Class")
    ax1.plot(first_monthly_sales.index.to_numpy(), first_monthly_sales.values,
color="blue", marker='o', linestyle='-', label="First Class")
    ax1.plot(scd_monthly_sales.index.to_numpy(), scd_monthly_sales.values,
color="green", marker='o', linestyle='-', label="Second Class")
    ax1.plot(same_monthly_sales.index.to_numpy(), same_monthly_sales.values,
color="cyan", marker='o', linestyle='-', label="Same Day")

    ax1.set_title("Ship Mode-Based Monthly Sales", fontsize=12)
    ax1.legend(facecolor='#E6E6FA', edgecolor='black')
    ax1.set_xlabel("Date")
    ax1.set_ylabel("Sales")
    ax1.set_facecolor('#F0F0F0')
    ax1.grid(True)

    figure.tight_layout()
    canvas.draw()
```

It takes a DataFrame df, a Matplotlib figure, and a Tkinter canvas as inputs. It performs the following tasks:

1. Clears the existing content in the figure.
2. Filters the DataFrame for each shipping mode (Standard Class, First Class, Second Class, Same Day).
3. Calculates the monthly sales for each shipping mode.
4. Creates a line plot with different colors for each shipping mode.
5. Sets the title, legend, labels, and background color for the plot.
6. Draws the plot on the canvas.

This function allows you to visualize the monthly sales for different shipping modes over time. The shipping modes included in this function are Standard Class, First Class, Second Class, and Same Day.

Monthly Sales Data for Different Product Names over Time

In Helper_Plot class, define a new method named month_wise_productname_based(). It allows you to visualize the monthly sales for different product names over time:

```python
def month_wise_productname_based(self, df, figure, canvas):
    figure.clear()

    env_df = df.loc[df['Product Name'] == 'Staple envelope']
    stp_df = df.loc[df['Product Name'] == 'Staples']
    eas_df = df.loc[df['Product Name'] == 'Easy-staple paper']
    ave_df = df.loc[df['Product Name'] == 'Avery Non-Stick Binders']
    rem_df = df.loc[df['Product Name'] == 'Staple remover']

    env_monthly_sales = env_df['Sales'].resample('M').sum()
    env_monthly_sales = env_monthly_sales.round(2)

    stp_monthly_sales = stp_df['Sales'].resample('M').sum()
    stp_monthly_sales = stp_monthly_sales.round(2)

    eas_monthly_sales = eas_df['Sales'].resample('M').sum()
    eas_monthly_sales = eas_monthly_sales.round(2)

    ave_monthly_sales = ave_df['Sales'].resample('M').sum()
    ave_monthly_sales = ave_monthly_sales.round(2)

    rem_monthly_sales = ave_df['Sales'].resample('M').sum()
    rem_monthly_sales = rem_monthly_sales.round(2)

    ax1 = figure.add_subplot(1, 1, 1)
    ax1.plot(env_monthly_sales.index.to_numpy(), env_monthly_sales.values,
            color="red", marker='o', linestyle='-', label="Staple envelope")
    ax1.plot(stp_monthly_sales.index.to_numpy(), stp_monthly_sales.values,
            color="blue", marker='o', linestyle='-', label="Staples")
    ax1.plot(eas_monthly_sales.index.to_numpy(), eas_monthly_sales.values,
            color="green", marker='o', linestyle='-', label="Easy-staple paper")
    ax1.plot(ave_monthly_sales.index.to_numpy(), ave_monthly_sales.values,
```

```
                color="cyan", marker='o', linestyle='-', label="Avery Non-Stick
Binders")
        ax1.plot(rem_monthly_sales.index.to_numpy(), rem_monthly_sales.values,
                color="black", marker='o', linestyle='-', label="Staple remover")

        ax1.set_title("Product Name-Based Monthly Sales", fontsize=12)
        ax1.legend(facecolor='#E6E6FA', edgecolor='black')
        ax1.set_xlabel("Date")
        ax1.set_ylabel("Sales")
        ax1.set_facecolor('#F0F0F0')
        ax1.grid(True)

        figure.tight_layout()
        canvas.draw()
```

It takes a DataFrame df, a Matplotlib figure, and a Tkinter canvas as inputs. It performs the following tasks:

1. Clears the existing content in the figure.
2. Filters the DataFrame for each product name (Staple envelope, Staples, Easy-staple paper, Avery Non-Stick Binders, Staple remover).
3. Calculates the monthly sales for each product name.
4. Creates a line plot with different colors for each product name.
5. Sets the title, legend, labels, and background color for the plot.
6. Draws the plot on the canvas.

This function allows you to visualize the monthly sales for different product names over time. The product names included in this function are Staple envelope, Staples, Easy-staple paper, Avery Non-Stick Binders, and Staple remover.

Monthly Sales Data for Different Sub-Categories over Time

In Helper_Plot class, define a new method named month_wise_productname_based(). It is designed to create a line plot that visualizes the monthly sales for different sub-categories of products:

```
def month_wise_subcategory_based(self, df, figure, canvas):
    figure.clear()

    bin_df = df.loc[df['Sub-Category'] == 'Binders']
    pap_df = df.loc[df['Sub-Category'] == 'Paper']
    pho_df = df.loc[df['Sub-Category'] == 'Phones']
    sto_df = df.loc[df['Sub-Category'] == 'Storage']
    fur_df = df.loc[df['Sub-Category'] == 'Furnishings']

    bin_monthly_sales = bin_df['Sales'].resample('M').sum()
    bin_monthly_sales = bin_monthly_sales.round(2)

    pap_monthly_sales = pap_df['Sales'].resample('M').sum()
    pap_monthly_sales = pap_monthly_sales.round(2)
```

```python
pho_monthly_sales = pho_df['Sales'].resample('M').sum()
pho_monthly_sales = pho_monthly_sales.round(2)

sto_monthly_sales = sto_df['Sales'].resample('M').sum()
sto_monthly_sales = sto_monthly_sales.round(2)

fur_monthly_sales = fur_df['Sales'].resample('M').sum()
fur_monthly_sales = fur_monthly_sales.round(2)

ax1 = figure.add_subplot(1, 1, 1)
ax1.plot(bin_monthly_sales.index.to_numpy(), bin_monthly_sales.values,
        color="red", marker='o', linestyle='-', label="Binders")
ax1.plot(pap_monthly_sales.index.to_numpy(), pap_monthly_sales.values,
        color="blue", marker='o', linestyle='-', label="Paper")
ax1.plot(pho_monthly_sales.index.to_numpy(), pho_monthly_sales.values,
        color="green", marker='o', linestyle='-', label="Phones")
ax1.plot(sto_monthly_sales.index.to_numpy(), sto_monthly_sales.values,
        color="black", marker='o', linestyle='-', label="Storage")
ax1.plot(fur_monthly_sales.index.to_numpy(), fur_monthly_sales.values,
        color="cyan", marker='o', linestyle='-', label="Furnishings")

ax1.set_title("Sub-Category-Based Monthly Sales", fontsize=12)
ax1.legend(facecolor='#E6E6FA', edgecolor='black')
ax1.set_xlabel("Date")
ax1.set_ylabel("Sales")
ax1.set_facecolor('#F0F0F0')
ax1.grid(True)

figure.tight_layout()
canvas.draw()
```

Let's break down the function step by step:
1. figure.clear(): This line ensures that any existing content in the provided figure is cleared before plotting new data. This helps prevent any overlap or confusion between old and new plots.
2. Sub-Category Filtering:
   The function first filters the DataFrame df to obtain specific subsets of data for different sub-categories. It does this using conditions like df.loc[df['Sub-Category'] == 'Binders'], df.loc[df['Sub-Category'] == 'Paper'], and so on. This means that for each sub-category (e.g., Binders, Paper, Phones, Storage, Furnishings), it extracts the relevant data.
3. Monthly Sales Calculation:
   For each sub-category, it then calculates the total sales for each month. This is done using the .resample('M').sum() method, which groups the data by month and sums up the sales.
4. Line Plot Creation:
   - After obtaining the monthly sales data for each sub-category, it creates a line plot using ax1.plot().
   - Each sub-category has its own line in a different color (red, blue, green, black, cyan).

- The x-axis represents the date (month), and the y-axis represents the sales.
5. Plot Customization:
    - ax1.set_title("Sub-Category-Based Monthly Sales", fontsize=12): Sets the title of the plot.
    - ax1.legend(facecolor='#E6E6FA', edgecolor='black'): Adds a legend to the plot, which indicates which color corresponds to which sub-category.
    - ax1.set_xlabel("Date") and ax1.set_ylabel("Sales"): Label the x and y axes, respectively.
    - ax1.set_facecolor('#F0F0F0'): Sets the background color of the plot.
    - ax1.grid(True): Adds a grid to the plot for better visualization.
6. Tight Layout and Drawing:
    - figure.tight_layout(): Adjusts the layout of the plot to make sure all elements fit properly.
    - canvas.draw(): Draws the plot on the canvas, making it visible in the GUI.

In summary, this function helps you visualize the monthly sales trends for different product sub-categories. Each sub-category has its own line, and you can see how their sales evolve over time. The legend allows you to identify which line corresponds to which sub-category.

Windows to Visualize Monthly Sales Data of Specific Category

In Helper_Plot class, define seven new methods. These functions are designed to open a new window using tk.Toplevel(), create an instance of Form3 (which is a class with a figure1 and canvas1 attribute), and then call specific plotting functions based on the type of data analysis you want to perform:

```python
def plot_month_wise_subcategory_based(self, df):
    win = tk.Toplevel()
    form3 = Form3(win)
    self.month_wise_subcategory_based(df, form3.figure1, form3.canvas1)

def plot_month_wise_productname_based(self, df):
    win = tk.Toplevel()
    form3 = Form3(win)
    self.month_wise_productname_based(df, form3.figure1, form3.canvas1)

def plot_month_wise_shipmode_based(self, df):
    win = tk.Toplevel()
    form3 = Form3(win)
    self.month_wise_shipmode_based(df, form3.figure1, form3.canvas1)

def plot_month_wise_city_based(self, df):
    win = tk.Toplevel()
    form3 = Form3(win)
    self.month_wise_city_based(df, form3.figure1, form3.canvas1)
```

```python
def plot_month_wise_region_based(self, df):
    win = tk.Toplevel()
    form3 = Form3(win)
    self.month_wise_region_based(df, form3.figure1, form3.canvas1)

def plot_month_wise_category_based(self, df):
    win = tk.Toplevel()
    form3 = Form3(win)
    self.month_wise_category_based(df, form3.figure1, form3.canvas1)

def plot_month_wise_segment_based(self, df):
    win = tk.Toplevel()
    form3 = Form3(win)
    self.month_wise_segment_based(df, form3.figure1, form3.canvas1)
```

Let's go over each function:

1. plot_month_wise_subcategory_based(df):
   - Opens a new window.
   - Creates an instance of Form3.
   - Calls the month_wise_subcategory_based() function, passing the DataFrame df, figure1, and canvas1 as arguments. This will generate a line plot based on sub-categories.
2. plot_month_wise_productname_based(df):
   Similar to the first function, but this time it calls month_wise_productname_based() to generate a line plot based on product names.
3. plot_month_wise_shipmode_based(df):
   Calls month_wise_shipmode_based() to generate a line plot based on different ship modes.
4. plot_month_wise_city_based(df):
   Calls month_wise_city_based() to generate a line plot based on different cities.
5. plot_month_wise_region_based(df):
   Calls month_wise_region_based() to generate a line plot based on different regions.
6. plot_month_wise_category_based(df):
   Calls month_wise_category_based() to generate a line plot based on different product categories.
7. plot_month_wise_segment_based(df):
   Calls month_wise_segment_based() to generate a line plot based on different market segments.

Each of these functions follows a similar pattern. They open a new window, create an instance of Form3, and then call a specific plotting function with the appropriate arguments. This allows you to visualize different aspects of your data in separate windows.

```python
    def binds_month_wise(self, window, df, data_mean, data_ewm):
        window.month_wise.entryconfigure("Sales Quarter 1 and 2 Year 2018",
            command = lambda:self.plot_month_wise(df, "Sales", 2018, "Quarter", "Jan-
March", "April-June"))

        window.month_wise.entryconfigure("Sales Quarter 3 and 4 Year 2018",
            command = lambda:self.plot_month_wise(df, "Sales", 2018, "Quarter",
"July-Sept", "Oct-Dec"))

        window.month_wise.entryconfigure("Sales Quarter 1 and 2 Year 2017",
            command = lambda:self.plot_month_wise(df, "Sales", 2017, "Quarter", "Jan-
March", "April-June"))

        window.month_wise.entryconfigure("Sales Quarter 3 and 4 Year 2017",
            command = lambda:self.plot_month_wise(df, "Sales", 2017, "Quarter",
"July-Sept", "Oct-Dec"))

        window.month_wise.entryconfigure("Sales Quarter 1 and 2 Year 2016",
            command = lambda:self.plot_month_wise(df, "Sales", 2016, "Quarter", "Jan-
March", "April-June"))

        window.month_wise.entryconfigure("Sales Quarter 3 and 4 Year 2016",
            command = lambda:self.plot_month_wise(df, "Sales", 2016, "Quarter",
"July-Sept", "Oct-Dec"))

        window.month_wise.entryconfigure("Sales Quarter 1 and 2 Year 2015",
            command = lambda:self.plot_month_wise(df, "Sales", 2015, "Quarter", "Jan-
March", "April-June"))

        window.month_wise.entryconfigure("Sales Quarter 3 and 4 Year 2015",
            command = lambda:self.plot_month_wise(df, "Sales", 2015, "Quarter",
"July-Sept", "Oct-Dec"))

        window.month_wise.entryconfigure("Sales Month 1 and 2 Year 2018",
            command = lambda:self.plot_month_wise(df, "Sales", 2018, "Month",
"January", "February"))

        window.month_wise.entryconfigure("Sales Month 3 and 4 Year 2017",
            command = lambda:self.plot_month_wise(df, "Sales", 2017, "Month",
"March", "April"))

        window.month_wise.entryconfigure("Sales Month 5 and 6 Year 2016",
            command = lambda:self.plot_month_wise(df, "Sales", 2016, "Month", "May",
"June"))

        window.month_wise.entryconfigure("Sales Month 7 and 8 Year 2015",
            command = lambda:self.plot_month_wise(df, "Sales", 2015, "Month", "July",
"August"))

        window.month_wise.entryconfigure("Month-Wise Sales Mean and EWM",
            command = lambda:self.plot_month_wise_mean_ewm(data_mean, data_ewm))

        window.month_wise.entryconfigure("Sales by Month",
```

```
        command = lambda:self.plot_month_wise_by_month(data_mean, "Sales by
Month"))

        window.month_wise.entryconfigure("Region-Based Monthly Sales",
            command = lambda:self.plot_month_wise_region_based(df))

        window.month_wise.entryconfigure("Category-Based Monthly Quantities",
            command = lambda:self.plot_month_wise_category_based(df))

        window.month_wise.entryconfigure("Segment-Based Monthly Sales",
            command = lambda:self.plot_month_wise_segment_based(df))

        window.month_wise.entryconfigure("City-Based Monthly Sales",
            command = lambda:self.plot_month_wise_city_based(df))

        window.month_wise.entryconfigure("Ship Mode-Based Monthly Sales",
            command = lambda:self.plot_month_wise_shipmode_based(df))

        window.month_wise.entryconfigure("Product Name-Based Monthly Sales",
            command = lambda:self.plot_month_wise_productname_based(df))

        window.month_wise.entryconfigure("Sub-Category-Based Monthly Sales",
            command = lambda:self.plot_month_wise_subcategory_based(df))
```

Setting Up the Menu Options Related to Month-Wise Analysis

In Helper_Plot class, define a new method named binds_month_wise(). It is set of functions and associated them with specific options. Each option in the dropdown menu corresponds to a specific analysis or visualization task:

```
    def binds_month_wise(self, window, df, data_mean, data_ewm):
        window.month_wise.entryconfigure("Sales Quarter 1 and 2 Year 2018",
            command = lambda:self.plot_month_wise(df, "Sales", 2018, "Quarter", "Jan-
March", "April-June"))

        window.month_wise.entryconfigure("Sales Quarter 3 and 4 Year 2018",
            command = lambda:self.plot_month_wise(df, "Sales", 2018, "Quarter",
"July-Sept", "Oct-Dec"))

        window.month_wise.entryconfigure("Sales Quarter 1 and 2 Year 2017",
            command = lambda:self.plot_month_wise(df, "Sales", 2017, "Quarter", "Jan-
March", "April-June"))

        window.month_wise.entryconfigure("Sales Quarter 3 and 4 Year 2017",
            command = lambda:self.plot_month_wise(df, "Sales", 2017, "Quarter",
"July-Sept", "Oct-Dec"))

        window.month_wise.entryconfigure("Sales Quarter 1 and 2 Year 2016",
            command = lambda:self.plot_month_wise(df, "Sales", 2016, "Quarter", "Jan-
March", "April-June"))

        window.month_wise.entryconfigure("Sales Quarter 3 and 4 Year 2016",
            command = lambda:self.plot_month_wise(df, "Sales", 2016, "Quarter",
"July-Sept", "Oct-Dec"))
```

```
    window.month_wise.entryconfigure("Sales Quarter 1 and 2 Year 2015",
        command = lambda:self.plot_month_wise(df, "Sales", 2015, "Quarter", "Jan-
March", "April-June"))

    window.month_wise.entryconfigure("Sales Quarter 3 and 4 Year 2015",
        command = lambda:self.plot_month_wise(df, "Sales", 2015, "Quarter",
"July-Sept", "Oct-Dec"))

    window.month_wise.entryconfigure("Sales Month 1 and 2 Year 2018",
        command = lambda:self.plot_month_wise(df, "Sales", 2018, "Month",
"January", "February"))

    window.month_wise.entryconfigure("Sales Month 3 and 4 Year 2017",
        command = lambda:self.plot_month_wise(df, "Sales", 2017, "Month",
"March", "April"))

    window.month_wise.entryconfigure("Sales Month 5 and 6 Year 2016",
        command = lambda:self.plot_month_wise(df, "Sales", 2016, "Month", "May",
"June"))

    window.month_wise.entryconfigure("Sales Month 7 and 8 Year 2015",
        command = lambda:self.plot_month_wise(df, "Sales", 2015, "Month", "July",
"August"))

    window.month_wise.entryconfigure("Month-Wise Sales Mean and EWM",
        command = lambda:self.plot_month_wise_mean_ewm(data_mean, data_ewm))

    window.month_wise.entryconfigure("Sales by Month",
        command = lambda:self.plot_month_wise_by_month(data_mean, "Sales by
Month"))

    window.month_wise.entryconfigure("Region-Based Monthly Sales",
        command = lambda:self.plot_month_wise_region_based(df))

    window.month_wise.entryconfigure("Category-Based Monthly Quantities",
        command = lambda:self.plot_month_wise_category_based(df))

    window.month_wise.entryconfigure("Segment-Based Monthly Sales",
        command = lambda:self.plot_month_wise_segment_based(df))

    window.month_wise.entryconfigure("City-Based Monthly Sales",
        command = lambda:self.plot_month_wise_city_based(df))

    window.month_wise.entryconfigure("Ship Mode-Based Monthly Sales",
        command = lambda:self.plot_month_wise_shipmode_based(df))

    window.month_wise.entryconfigure("Product Name-Based Monthly Sales",
        command = lambda:self.plot_month_wise_productname_based(df))

    window.month_wise.entryconfigure("Sub-Category-Based Monthly Sales",
        command = lambda:self.plot_month_wise_subcategory_based(df))
```

Let's break down some of the functions and their associated options:

    1. binds_month_wise():

This function is binding various options to specific commands in the GUI. When the user selects an option from the dropdown menu, the associated command will be executed. plot_month_wise():

2. This function generates a plot based on the selected year, quarter, and months. It takes the DataFrame (df) and specific data parameters as inputs. For example, it can plot the sales for the first and second quarters of 2018.

3. plot_month_wise_mean_ewm():
This function plots the mean and exponentially weighted moving average (EWM) of the data. It takes data_mean and data_ewm as inputs.

4. plot_month_wise_by_month():
This function is probably used to plot the sales data on a month-by-month basis. It takes data_mean and a title as inputs.

5. plot_month_wise_region_based():
This function generates a plot showing the region-based monthly sales. It takes the DataFrame (df) as input.

6. plot_month_wise_category_based():
This function generates a plot showing category-based monthly quantities. It takes the DataFrame (df) as input.

7. plot_month_wise_segment_based():
This function generates a plot showing segment-based monthly sales. It takes the DataFrame (df) as input.

8. plot_month_wise_city_based():
This function generates a plot showing city-based monthly sales. It takes the DataFrame (df) as input.

9. plot_month_wise_shipmode_based():
This function generates a plot showing ship mode-based monthly sales. It takes the DataFrame (df) as input.

10. plot_month_wise_productname_based():
This function generates a plot showing product name-based monthly sales. It takes the DataFrame (df) as input.

11. plot_month_wise_subcategory_based():
This function generates a plot showing subcategory-based monthly sales. It takes the DataFrame (df) as input.

Each of these functions is associated with a specific option in the dropdown menu. When a user selects an option, it triggers the corresponding function to perform the intended analysis or visualization. For example, if a user chooses "Region-Based Monthly Sales", it will execute the plot_month_wise_region_based() function to generate and display the corresponding plot.

This design allows users to interact with the GUI and perform a variety of data analyses and visualizations with ease.

Setting Up the Combobox Options Related to Month-Wise Analysis

In Helper_Plot class, define a new method named choose_month_wise(). It's designed to take various inputs and based on the value of chosen, it will call different methods to generate different types of plots:

```python
def choose_month_wise(self, df, data_mean, data_ewm,
        data_norm, chosen, figure1, canvas1, figure2, canvas2):
    if chosen == "Sales Quarter 1 and 2 Year 2018":
        self.line_plot_month_wise(df, "Sales", 2018,
            "Quarter", "Jan-March", "April-June", figure1, canvas1)

    if chosen == "Sales Quarter 3 and 4 Year 2018":
        self.line_plot_month_wise(df, "Sales", 2018,
            "Quarter", "July-Sept", "Oct-Dec", figure2, canvas2)

    if chosen == "Sales Quarter 1 and 2 Year 2017":
        self.line_plot_month_wise(df, "Sales", 2017,
            "Quarter", "Jan-March", "April-June", figure1, canvas1)

    if chosen == "Sales Quarter 3 and 4 Year 2017":
        self.line_plot_month_wise(df, "Sales", 2017,
            "Quarter", "July-Sept", "Oct-Dec", figure2, canvas2)

    if chosen == "Sales Quarter 1 and 2 Year 2016":
        self.line_plot_month_wise(df, "Sales", 2016,
            "Quarter", "Jan-March", "April-June", figure1, canvas1)

    if chosen == "Sales Quarter 3 and 4 Year 2016":
        self.line_plot_month_wise(df, "Sales", 2016,
            "Quarter", "July-Sept", "Oct-Dec", figure2, canvas2)

    if chosen == "Sales Quarter 1 and 2 Year 2015":
        self.line_plot_month_wise(df, "Sales", 2015,
            "Quarter", "Jan-March", "April-June", figure1, canvas1)

    if chosen == "Sales Quarter 3 and 4 Year 2015":
        self.line_plot_month_wise(df, "Sales", 2015,
            "Quarter", "July-Sept", "Oct-Dec", figure2, canvas2)

    if chosen == "Month-Wise Sales Mean and EWM":
        self.line_plot_data_mean_ewm(data_mean, data_ewm, figure1, canvas1,
"YEAR", "SALES")

    if chosen == "Sales by Month":
        self.sns_plot_month(data_mean, "Sales by Month", figure2, canvas2)

    if chosen == "Region-Based Monthly Sales":
        self.month_wise_region_based(df, figure1, canvas1)
```

```
if chosen == "Category-Based Monthly Quantities":
    self.month_wise_category_based(df, figure2, canvas2)

if chosen == "Segment-Based Monthly Sales":
    self.month_wise_segment_based(df, figure1, canvas1)

if chosen == "City-Based Monthly Sales":
    self.month_wise_city_based(df, figure2, canvas2)

if chosen == "Ship Mode-Based Monthly Sales":
    self.month_wise_shipmode_based(df, figure1, canvas1)

if chosen == "Product Name-Based Monthly Sales":
    self.month_wise_productname_based(df, figure2, canvas2)

if chosen == "Sub-Category-Based Monthly Sales":
    self.month_wise_subcategory_based(df, figure1, canvas1)
```

Here's what each block of the function does:
1. Sales Quarters and Years:

   For example, if chosen is "Sales Quarter 1 and 2 Year 2018", it calls line_plot_month_wise() with specific arguments to plot sales for the first and second quarters of 2018.
2. Month-Wise Sales Mean and EWM:

   If chosen is "Month-Wise Sales Mean and EWM", it calls line_plot_data_mean_ewm() to generate a plot for the mean and exponentially weighted moving average of the data.
3. Sales by Month:

   If chosen is "Sales by Month", it calls sns_plot_month() to generate a plot showing sales by month.
4. Region-Based Monthly Sales:

   If chosen is "Region-Based Monthly Sales", it calls month_wise_region_based() to generate a plot showing region-based monthly sales.
5. Category-Based Monthly Quantities:

   If chosen is "Category-Based Monthly Quantities", it calls month_wise_category_based() to generate a plot showing category-based monthly quantities.
6. Segment-Based Monthly Sales:

   If chosen is "Segment-Based Monthly Sales", it calls month_wise_segment_based() to generate a plot showing segment-based monthly sales.
7. City-Based Monthly Sales:

   If chosen is "City-Based Monthly Sales", it calls month_wise_city_based() to generate a plot showing city-based monthly sales.
8. Ship Mode-Based Monthly Sales:

   If chosen is "Ship Mode-Based Monthly Sales", it calls month_wise_shipmode_based() to generate a plot showing ship mode-based monthly sales.
9. Product Name-Based Monthly Sales:

If chosen is "Product Name-Based Monthly Sales", it calls month_wise_productname_based() to generate a plot showing product name-based monthly sales.

10. Sub-Category-Based Monthly Sales:
    If chosen is "Sub-Category-Based Monthly Sales", it calls month_wise_subcategory_based() to generate a plot showing subcategory-based monthly sales.

This function provides a central mechanism for generating different types of plots based on the user's selection. It's a flexible way to handle various data visualization tasks within your application.

Window to Visualize RFM Case Distribution

In Helper_Plot class, define a new method named plot_rfm_distribution(). It is responsible for generating a visualization that depicts the distribution of a variable var1 within a DataFrame df:

```python
def plot_rfm_distribution(self, df, var1, title=""):
    win = tk.Toplevel()
    form3 = Form3(win)
    win.title(title)
    self.plot_piechart(df, var1, form3.figure1, form3.canvas1, "Case Distribution
of " + var1)
```

Here's a breakdown of the steps it takes:
1. win = tk.Toplevel(): This line creates a new window within the Tkinter application.
2. form3 = Form3(win): It instantiates an object of the Form3 class within the newly created window. Form3 contains elements for plotting.
3. win.title(title): If a title argument is provided (which is optional), this line sets the title of the window to the value of title. This allows for customization of the window title.
4. self.plot_piechart(df, var1, form3.figure1, form3.canvas1, "Case Distribution of " + var1): This line calls another method named plot_piechart with the following arguments:
   - df: The DataFrame containing the data to be visualized.
   - var1: The variable of interest within the DataFrame.
   - form3.figure1: A figure element from the Form3 object, used for plotting.
   - form3.canvas1: A canvas element from the Form3 object, used for displaying the plot.
   - "Case Distribution of " + var1: A string that serves as a label or title for the visualization.

Overall, this method sets up a new window, instantiates a form for plotting, potentially customizes the window title, and then calls a method to generate the pie chart based on the provided DataFrame and variable.

Window to Visualize RFM Grouped Distribution

In Helper_Plot class, define a new method named plot_grouped_rfm_distribution(). It is responsible for generating a grouped visualization that shows the distribution of one variable (var2) within categories defined by another variable (var1) in a DataFrame df:

```python
def plot_grouped_rfm_distribution(self, df, var1="", var2="", title1="",
label=""):
    win = tk.Toplevel()
    form3 = Form3(win)
    win.title("Distribution of " + var2 + " by " + var1)
    sum_by_cat = df.groupby(var1)[var2].sum()
    self.plot_piechart_group(sum_by_cat, form3.figure1, form3.canvas1, title1,
label)
```

Let's break down the steps:

1. win = tk.Toplevel(): This line creates a new window within the Tkinter application.
2. form3 = Form3(win): It instantiates an object of the Form3 class within the newly created window. This suggests that Form3 contains elements necessary for plotting.
3. win.title("Distribution of " + var2 + " by " + var1): This line sets the title of the window. The title is constructed based on the values of var1 and var2. This provides context for the visualization.
4. sum_by_cat = df.groupby(var1)[var2].sum(): This line groups the DataFrame df by the values of var1 and calculates the sum of var2 within each group. sum_by_cat holds the grouped data.
5. self.plot_piechart_group(sum_by_cat, form3.figure1, form3.canvas1, title1, label): This line calls another method named plot_piechart_group() with the following arguments:
    - sum_by_cat: The grouped data that was calculated in step 4.
    - form3.figure1: A figure element from the Form3 object, used for plotting.
    - form3.canvas1: A canvas element from the Form3 object, used for displaying the plot.
    - title1: A title or label for the visualization (passed as an argument).
    - label: A label for the data being visualized (passed as an argument).

Overall, this method sets up a new window, instantiates a form for plotting, customizes the window title, performs grouping and aggregation on the data, and then calls a method to generate the grouped pie chart based on the provided DataFrame and variables.

In Helper_Plot class, define a new method named plot_grouped_rfm_distribution(). It generates a line plot to visualize monthly sales based on different customer segments derived from RFM (Recency, Frequency, Monetary) analysis:

```python
def month_wise_rfm_based(self, df, figure, canvas):
    figure.clear()

    top_df = df.loc[df['Customer Segment'] == 'Top Customer']
    high_df = df.loc[df['Customer Segment'] == 'High Value Customer']
    med_df = df.loc[df['Customer Segment'] == 'Medium Value Customer']
    low_df = df.loc[df['Customer Segment'] == 'Low Value Customer']
    lost_df = df.loc[df['Customer Segment'] == 'Lost Customer']

    top_monthly_sales = top_df['Sales'].resample('M').sum()
    top_monthly_sales = top_monthly_sales.round(2)

    high_monthly_sales = high_df['Sales'].resample('M').sum()
    high_monthly_sales = high_monthly_sales.round(2)

    med_monthly_sales = med_df['Sales'].resample('M').sum()
    med_monthly_sales = med_monthly_sales.round(2)

    low_monthly_sales = low_df['Sales'].resample('M').sum()
    low_monthly_sales = low_monthly_sales.round(2)

    lost_monthly_sales = lost_df['Sales'].resample('M').sum()
    lost_monthly_sales = lost_monthly_sales.round(2)

    ax1 = figure.add_subplot(1, 1, 1)
    ax1.plot(top_monthly_sales.index.to_numpy(), top_monthly_sales.values,
            color="red", marker='o', linestyle='-', label="Top Customer")
    ax1.plot(high_monthly_sales.index.to_numpy(), high_monthly_sales.values,
            color="blue", marker='o', linestyle='-', label="High Value
Customer")
    ax1.plot(med_monthly_sales.index.to_numpy(), med_monthly_sales.values,
            color="green", marker='o', linestyle='-', label="Medium Value
Customer")
    ax1.plot(low_monthly_sales.index.to_numpy(), low_monthly_sales.values,
            color="black", marker='o', linestyle='-', label="Low Value
Customer")
    ax1.plot(lost_monthly_sales.index.to_numpy(), lost_monthly_sales.values,
            color="orange", marker='o', linestyle='-', label="Lost Customer")

    ax1.set_title("RFM-Based Monthly Sales", fontsize=12)
    ax1.legend(facecolor='#E6E6FA', edgecolor='black')
    ax1.set_xlabel("Date")
    ax1.set_ylabel("Sales")
    ax1.set_facecolor('#F0F0F0')
    ax1.grid(True)

    figure.tight_layout()
    canvas.draw()
```

Here's an explanation of how it works:

1. Data Preparation: The function starts by clearing any existing content from the provided figure.
2. Data Segmentation by Customer Segment:

   It separates the original dataset into five groups based on the 'Customer Segment': 'Top Customer', 'High Value Customer', 'Medium Value Customer', 'Low Value Customer', and 'Lost Customer'. This categorization helps analyze sales trends for different types of customers.
3. Monthly Sales Calculation:

   For each customer segment, it calculates the total sales for each month. This is done by aggregating sales data using the .resample('M').sum() method, which groups the data by month and sums up the sales.
4. Data Rounding:

   The calculated monthly sales values are rounded to two decimal places. This ensures a cleaner representation of the data.
5. Plot Creation:

   The function creates a single subplot in the provided figure.
6. Line Plotting:

   For each customer segment, it plots a line representing the monthly sales over time. Each line has a distinct color ('red', 'blue', 'green', 'black', 'orange') for differentiation. Circular markers ('o') indicate specific data points.
7. Plot Customization:

   It sets various attributes for the plot, including the title, legend properties, labels for the x and y-axes, background color, and grid visibility.
8. Layout Adjustment:

   The layout of the figure is adjusted, and the canvas is redrawn to ensure proper display.

In summary, this function allows users to analyze and compare the monthly sales trends across different customer segments based on RFM analysis. The resulting plot provides a visual representation of how sales vary over time for each segment.

Window to Visualize Monthly Sales Based on Different Customer Segments

In Helper_Plot class, define a new method named plot_month_wise_rfm_based(). It creates a new window (Toplevel) and a corresponding instance of Form3. Then, it calls the month_wise_rfm_based() method, passing the provided DataFrame (df) along with the figure and canvas from Form3. This action will generate a line plot visualizing monthly sales based on RFM customer segments in the newly opened window:

```
def plot_month_wise_rfm_based(self, df):
    win = tk.Toplevel()
    form3 = Form3(win)
    self.month_wise_rfm_based(df, form3.figure1, form3.canvas1)
```

Setting Up the Menu Options Related to RFM Analysis

In Helper_Plot class, define a new method named binds_month_wise(). It provides several menu entries are configured for the rfm_analysis submenu:

1. Customer Segment: This command triggers the plot_rfm_distribution() method with the DataFrame and the variable "Customer Segment". It generates a pie chart showing the distribution of cases among different customer segments.

2. Sales by Customer Segment: This command triggers the plot_grouped_rfm_distribution() method with the DataFrame, using "Customer Segment" as the first variable and "Sales" as the second. It generates a pie chart illustrating the distribution of sales among different customer segments.

3. Customer Segment by Year and Quarter: This command triggers the plot_categorized_distribution() method with the DataFrame. It categorizes data by "Year" and "Customer Segment" first, and then by "Quarter" and "Customer Segment". It generates two pie charts showing the distribution of cases in customer segments across years and quarters.

4. Customer Segment by Day and Month: This command triggers the plot_categorized_distribution() method with the DataFrame. It categorizes data by "Day" and "Customer Segment" first, and then by "Month" and "Customer Segment". It generates two pie charts showing the distribution of cases in customer segments across days and months.

5. Customer Segment by Segment and Sub-Category: This command triggers the plot_categorized_distribution() method with the DataFrame. It categorizes data by "Segment" and "Customer Segment" first, and then by "Sub-Category" and "Customer Segment". It generates two pie charts showing the distribution of cases in customer segments across segments and sub-categories.

6. Customer Segment by Region and State: This command triggers the plot_categorized_distribution() method with the DataFrame. It categorizes data by "Region" and "Customer Segment" first, and then by "State" and "Customer Segment". It generates two pie charts showing the distribution of cases in customer segments across regions and states.

7. RFM-Based Monthly Sales: This command triggers the plot_month_wise_rfm_based() method. It generates a line plot visualizing monthly sales based on RFM customer segments.

```python
def binds_rfm_distribution(self, window, df):
    window.rfm_analysis.entryconfigure("Customer Segment",
        command = lambda:self.plot_rfm_distribution(df, "Customer Segment",
            "The Case Distribution of Customer Segment"))

    window.rfm_analysis.entryconfigure("Sales by Customer Segment",
        command = lambda:self.plot_grouped_rfm_distribution(df, "Customer
Segment",
            "Sales", "Sales Distribution by Customer Segment"))

    window.rfm_analysis.entryconfigure("Customer Segment by Year and Quarter",
        command = lambda:self.plot_categorized_distribution(df, "Year", "Customer
Segment",
            "Quarter", "Customer Segment",
            "The Case Distribution of Customer Segment by Year",
            "The Case Distribution of Customer Segment by Quarter"))

    window.rfm_analysis.entryconfigure("Customer Segment by Day and Month",
        command = lambda:self.plot_categorized_distribution(df, "Day", "Customer
Segment",
            "Month", "Customer Segment",
            "The Case Distribution of Customer Segment by Day",
            "The Case Distribution of Customer Segment by Month"))

    window.rfm_analysis.entryconfigure("Customer Segment by Segment and Sub-
Category",
        command = lambda:self.plot_categorized_distribution(df, "Segment",
"Customer Segment",
            "Sub-Category", "Customer Segment",
            "The Case Distribution of Customer Segment by Segment",
            "The Case Distribution of Customer Segment by Sub-Category"))

    window.rfm_analysis.entryconfigure("Customer Segment by Region and State",
        command = lambda:self.plot_categorized_distribution(df, "Region",
"Customer Segment",
            "State", "Customer Segment",
            "The Case Distribution of Customer Segment by Region",
            "The Case Distribution of Customer Segment by State"))

    window.rfm_analysis.entryconfigure("RFM-Based Monthly Sales",
        command = lambda:self.plot_month_wise_rfm_based(df))
```

Setting Up the Combobox Options Related to RFM Analysis

In Helper_Plot class, define a new method named choose_rfm_distribution(). In it, different actions are defined based on the chosen parameter, which represents the user's selection from a combobox.

1. Customer Segment: If this option is chosen, it triggers the plot_piechart() method. This method plots a pie chart illustrating the distribution of cases among different customer segments.

2. Sales by Customer Segment: If selected, it calculates the sum of sales grouped by customer segments, and then triggers the plot_piechart_group() method. This method generates a pie chart showing the distribution of sales among different customer segments.

3. Customer Segment by Year and Quarter: If chosen, it triggers the dist_one_vs_another_plot() method twice, once for "Year" and once for "Quarter". This method creates two distribution plots showing the distribution of customer segments across years and quarters.

4. Customer Segment by Day and Month: Similarly, if selected, it triggers the dist_one_vs_another_plot() method twice, once for "Day" and once for "Month". This method creates two distribution plots showing the distribution of customer segments across days and months.

5. Customer Segment by Segment and Sub-Category: It also triggers the dist_one_vs_another_plot() method twice, once for "Segment" and once for "Sub-Category". This method creates two distribution plots showing the distribution of customer segments across segments and sub-categories.

6. Customer Segment by Region and State: Similarly, if selected, it triggers the dist_one_vs_another_plot() method twice, once for "Region" and once for "State". This method creates two distribution plots showing the distribution of customer segments across regions and states.

7. RFM-Based Monthly Sales: If this option is chosen, it triggers the month_wise_rfm_based() method. This method generates a line plot visualizing monthly sales based on RFM customer segments.

```python
    def choose_rfm_distribution(self, df, chosen, figure1, canvas1, figure2,
canvas2):
        if chosen == "Customer Segment":
            self.plot_piechart(df, chosen, figure1, canvas1,
                "Case Distribution of " + chosen)

        if chosen == "Sales by Customer Segment":
            sum_by_cat = df.groupby("Customer Segment")["Sales"].sum()
            self.plot_piechart_group(sum_by_cat, figure2, canvas2, chosen)

        if chosen == "Customer Segment by Year and Quarter":
            self.dist_one_vs_another_plot(df, "Year", "Customer Segment",
                figure1, canvas1, "Customer Segment by Year")
            self.dist_one_vs_another_plot(df, "Quarter", "Customer Segment",
                figure2, canvas2, "Customer Segment by Quarter")

        if chosen == "Customer Segment by Day and Month":
            self.dist_one_vs_another_plot(df, "Day", "Customer Segment",
                figure1, canvas1, "Customer Segment by Day")
            self.dist_one_vs_another_plot(df, "Month", "Customer Segment",
                figure2, canvas2, "Customer Segment by Month")

        if chosen == "Customer Segment by Segment and Sub-Category":
```

```python
        self.dist_one_vs_another_plot(df, "Segment", "Customer Segment",
            figure1, canvas1, "Customer Segment by Segment")
        self.dist_one_vs_another_plot(df, "Sub-Category", "Customer Segment",
            figure2, canvas2, "Customer Segment by Sub-Category")

    if chosen == "Customer Segment by Region and State":
        self.dist_one_vs_another_plot(df, "Region", "Customer Segment",
            figure1, canvas1, "Customer Segment by Region")
        self.dist_one_vs_another_plot(df, "State", "Customer Segment",
            figure2, canvas2, "Customer Segment by State")

    if chosen == "RFM-Based Monthly Sales":
        self.month_wise_rfm_based(df, figure1, canvas1)
```

Visualizing Random Forest Feature Importance

In Helper_Plot class, define two new methods named rf_importance() and plot_rf_importance().
The code is related to visualizing the feature importance calculated from a Random Forest model:

```python
def rf_importance(self, X, y, figure, canvas):
    result_rf = self.obj_data.feat_importance_rf(X, y)
    figure.clear()
    ax1 = figure.add_subplot(1,1,1)
    sns.set_color_codes("pastel")
    ax=sns.barplot(x = 'Values',y = 'Features', data=result_rf, color="orange",
ax=ax1)
    ax1.set_title('Random Forest Features Importance', fontweight
="bold",fontsize=14)

    ax1.set_xlabel('Features Importance',  fontsize=10)
    ax1.set_ylabel('Feature Labels',  fontsize=10)
    # Set font for tick labels
    ax1.tick_params(axis='both', which='major', labelsize=10)
    ax1.tick_params(axis='both', which='minor', labelsize=10)
    ax1.set_facecolor('#F0F0F0')
    ax1.grid(True)
    figure.tight_layout()
    canvas.draw()

def plot_rf_importance(self, X, y):
    win = tk.Toplevel()
    form3 = Form3(win)
    win.title("Random Forest Feature Importance")
    self.rf_importance(X, y, form3.figure1, form3.canvas1)
```

Let's break down the functions:

1. rf_importance(self, X, y, figure, canvas):
   - This function takes four parameters: X (features), y (target variable), figure, and
     canvas.
   - It first calls a method feat_importance_rf() from an object self.obj_data,
     presumably to calculate the feature importance using a Random Forest model.

- It then clears the existing content of the figure.
- A new subplot (ax1) is added to the figure.
- A bar plot is created using Seaborn (sns.barplot) to visualize the feature importance values ('Values') associated with each feature ('Features').
- The title, x-label, and y-label of the plot are set.
- Tick labels for both major and minor ticks are adjusted to a font size of 10.
- The background color of the plot is set to a light gray.
- The plot is displayed with a grid, and the figure is tightly laid out.
- Finally, canvas.draw() is called to update the canvas with the new plot.

2. plot_rf_importance(self, X, y):
   - This function takes X (features) and y (target variable) as parameters.
   - It creates a new Tkinter Toplevel window (win) and a Form3 instance (form3) within that window.
   - The title of the window is set to "Random Forest Feature Importance".
   - The rf_importance() function is then called with X, y, and the figure and canvas from form3.

Overall, these functions are used to visualize the importance of features in a Random Forest model. They generate a bar plot showing the relative importance of different features in predicting the target variable.

Visualizing Extra Trees Feature Importance

In Helper_Plot class, define two new methods named et_importance() and plot_et_importance(). The code is related to visualizing the feature importance calculated from an extra trees model:

```python
def et_importance(self, X, y, figure, canvas):
    result_rf = self.obj_data.feat_importance_et(X, y)
    figure.clear()
    ax1 = figure.add_subplot(1,1,1)
    sns.set_color_codes("pastel")
    ax=sns.barplot(x = 'Values',y = 'Features', data=result_rf, color="Red",
ax=ax1)
    ax1.set_title('Extra Trees Features Importance', fontweight
="bold",fontsize=14)

    ax1.set_xlabel('Features Importance',  fontsize=10)
    ax1.set_ylabel('Feature Labels',  fontsize=10)
    # Set font for tick labels
    ax1.tick_params(axis='both', which='major', labelsize=10)
    ax1.tick_params(axis='both', which='minor', labelsize=10)
    ax1.set_facecolor('#F0F0F0')
    ax1.grid(True)
    figure.tight_layout()
    canvas.draw()
```

```python
def plot_et_importance(self, X, y):
    win = tk.Toplevel()
    form3 = Form3(win)
    win.title("Extra Trees Feature Importance")
    self.et_importance(X, y, form3.figure1, form3.canvas1)
```

Let's go through them:
1. et_importance(self, X, y, figure, canvas):
    - This function calculates the feature importance using an Extra Trees model. It takes in four parameters: X (features), y (target variable), figure, and canvas.
    - It first calls a method feat_importance_et() from an object self.obj_data, presumably to calculate the feature importance using an Extra Trees model.
    - Then, it clears the existing content of the figure.
    - A new subplot (ax1) is added to the figure.
    - A bar plot is created using Seaborn (sns.barplot) to visualize the feature importance values ('Values') associated with each feature ('Features').
    - The title, x-label, and y-label of the plot are set.
    - Tick labels for both major and minor ticks are adjusted to a font size of 10.
    - The background color of the plot is set to a light gray.
    - The plot is displayed with a grid, and the figure is tightly laid out.
    - Finally, canvas.draw() is called to update the canvas with the new plot.
2. plot_et_importance(self, X, y):
    - This function takes X (features) and y (target variable) as parameters.
    - It creates a new Tkinter Toplevel window (win) and a Form3 instance (form3) within that window.
    - The title of the window is set to "Extra Trees Feature Importance".
    - The et_importance() function is then called with X, y, and the figure and canvas from form3.

These functions serve the purpose of visualizing the importance of features in an Extra Trees model in a similar manner to how it was done for the Random Forest model. They generate a bar plot showing the relative importance of different features in predicting the target variable.

Visualizing Recursive Feature Elimination Feature Importance

In Helper_Plot class, define two new methods named rfe_importance() and plot_rfe_importance(). The code is related to visualizing the feature importance calculated from a Recursive Feature Elimination model:

```python
def rfe_importance(self, X, y, figure, canvas):
    result_lg = self.obj_data.feat_importance_rfe(X, y)
```

```python
        figure.clear()
        ax1 = figure.add_subplot(1,1,1)
        sns.set_color_codes("pastel")
        ax=sns.barplot(x = 'Ranking',y = 'Features', data=result_lg, color="green",
ax=ax1)
        ax1.set_title('RFE Features Importance', fontweight ="bold",fontsize=14)

        ax1.set_xlabel('Features Importance',  fontsize=10)
        ax1.set_ylabel('Feature Labels',  fontsize=10)
        # Set font for tick labels
        ax1.tick_params(axis='both', which='major', labelsize=10)
        ax1.tick_params(axis='both', which='minor', labelsize=10)
        ax1.set_facecolor('#F0F0F0')
        ax1.grid(True)
        figure.tight_layout()
        canvas.draw()

    def plot_rfe_importance(self, X, y):
        win = tk.Toplevel()
        form3 = Form3(win)
        win.title("RFE Feature Importance")
        self.rfe_importance(X, y, form3.figure1, form3.canvas1)
```

Let's go through them:

1. rfe_importance(self, X, y, figure, canvas):
    - This function calculates the feature importance using RFE. It takes in four parameters: X (features), y (target variable), figure, and canvas.
    - It first calls a method feat_importance_rfe() from an object self.obj_data, presumably to calculate the feature importance using RFE.
    - Then, it clears the existing content of the figure.
    - A new subplot (ax1) is added to the figure.
    - A bar plot is created using Seaborn (sns.barplot) to visualize the feature importance values ('Ranking') associated with each feature ('Features').
    - The title, x-label, and y-label of the plot are set.
    - Tick labels for both major and minor ticks are adjusted to a font size of 10.
    - The background color of the plot is set to a light gray.
    - The plot is displayed with a grid, and the figure is tightly laid out.
    - Finally, canvas.draw() is called to update the canvas with the new plot.

2. plot_rfe_importance(self, X, y):
    - This function takes X (features) and y (target variable) as parameters.
    - It creates a new Tkinter Toplevel window (win) and a Form3 instance (form3) within that window.
    - The title of the window is set to "RFE Feature Importance".
    - The rfe_importance() function is then called with X, y, and the figure and canvas from form3.

These functions serve the purpose of visualizing the importance of features determined by the Recursive Feature Elimination process. They generate a bar plot showing the ranking of different features based on their importance in predicting the target variable.

Visualizing Correlation Coefficients

In Helper_Plot class, define two new methods named corr_coeffs() and plot_corr_coeffs(). The functions are used to calculate and visualize the correlation coefficients between different features and a target variable named 'Churn':

```python
def corr_coeffs(self, df, figure, canvas):
    figure.clear()
    ax = figure.add_subplot(1,1,1)

    #correlation coefficient of every column with Summary column
    all_corr = df.corr().abs()['Churn'].sort_values(ascending = False)

    # Filters correlations greater than 0.01
    filtered_corr = all_corr[all_corr > 0.01]

    # Define a custom color palette (replace with your preferred colors)
    custom_palette = sns.color_palette("Set1", len(filtered_corr))
    filtered_corr.plot(kind='barh', ax=ax, color=custom_palette)
    ax.set_title("Correlation Coefficient of Features with Churn (Threshold > 0.01)", fontsize = 9)
    ax.set_ylabel("Coefficient")
    ax.set_facecolor('#F0F0F0')

    # Set font for tick labels
    ax.tick_params(axis='both', which='major', labelsize=10)
    ax.tick_params(axis='both', which='minor', labelsize=10)

    ax.grid(True)
    figure.tight_layout()
    canvas.draw()

def plot_corr_coeffs(self, df):
    win = tk.Toplevel()
    form3 = Form3(win)
    win.title("Correlation Coefficients")
    self.corr_coeffs(df, form3.figure1, form3.canvas1)
```

Here's an explanation:
1. corr_coeffs(self, df, figure, canvas):
    - This function calculates and visualizes the correlation coefficients between features and the 'Churn' variable.
    - It takes three parameters: df (the DataFrame containing the dataset), figure, and canvas.
    - It first clears the existing content of the figure.

- A new subplot (ax) is added to the figure.
- The correlation coefficients of each column with respect to the 'Churn' column are calculated and sorted in descending order (all_corr).
- Correlations greater than 0.01 are selected (filtered_corr).
- A custom color palette is defined.
- A horizontal bar plot is created with the filtered correlations. Each feature is represented on the y-axis, and its correlation coefficient is represented on the x-axis. The bars are colored using the custom palette.
- The title, y-label, and background color of the plot are set.
- Tick labels for both major and minor ticks are adjusted to a font size of 10.
- The plot is displayed with a grid, and the figure is tightly laid out.
- Finally, canvas.draw() is called to update the canvas with the new plot.

2. plot_corr_coeffs(self, df):
    - This function takes df (the DataFrame containing the dataset) as a parameter.
    - It creates a new Tkinter Toplevel window (win) and a Form3 instance (form3) within that window.
    - The title of the window is set to "Correlation Coefficients".
    - The corr_coeffs() function is then called with df, and the figure and canvas from form3.

These functions serve the purpose of visualizing the correlation coefficients between features and the 'Churn' variable. The horizontal bar plot provides a quick overview of which features have the highest absolute correlation with 'Churn'.

Visualizing Correlation Matrix

In Helper_Plot class, define two new methods named corr_mat() and plot_corr_mat(). These functions are used to generate a heatmap representing the correlation matrix between numeric features in the dataset, with correlations greater than 0.01 considered. The resulting visualization provides insights into the relationships between different numeric variables:

```python
def corr_mat(self, df, figure, canvas):
    figure.clear()
    ax = figure.add_subplot(1,1,1)
    categorical_columns = df.select_dtypes(include=['object',
'category']).columns
    df_removed = df.drop(columns=categorical_columns)
    corrdata = df_removed.corr()

    annot_kws = {"size": 8, "color":"black"}
    # Filter correlations greater than 0.01
    mask = abs(corrdata) > 0.01
    filtered_corr = corrdata[mask]
```

```python
        # Drops features that don't meet the threshold
        filtered_corr = filtered_corr.dropna(axis=0, how='all')
        filtered_corr = filtered_corr.dropna(axis=1, how='all')

        sns.heatmap(filtered_corr, ax = ax, lw=1, annot=True, cmap="Set1",
annot_kws=annot_kws)
        ax.set_title('Correlation Matrix (Threshold > 0.01)', fontweight="bold",
fontsize=12)

        # Set font for x and y labels
        ax.set_xlabel('Features', fontweight="bold", fontsize=12)
        ax.set_ylabel('Features', fontweight="bold", fontsize=12)

        # Set font for tick labels
        ax.tick_params(axis='both', which='major', labelsize=8)
        ax.tick_params(axis='both', which='minor', labelsize=8)

        figure.tight_layout()
        canvas.draw()

    def plot_corr_mat(self, df):
        win = tk.Toplevel()
        form3 = Form3(win)
        win.title("Correlation Matrix")
        self.corr_mat(df, form3.figure1, form3.canvas1)
```

The code defines two functions related to correlation matrices:

1. corr_mat(self, df, figure, canvas):
   - This function calculates and visualizes the correlation matrix between numeric features in the dataset.
   - It takes three parameters: df (the DataFrame containing the dataset), figure, and canvas.
   - The existing content of the figure is cleared.
   - A new subplot (ax) is added to the figure.
   - Categorical columns are identified and removed from the dataset to focus on numeric features.
   - The correlation matrix is calculated for the remaining numeric features.
   - Annotation keyword arguments (annot_kws) for the heatmap are defined, specifying the font size and color.
   - A mask is created to filter correlations greater than 0.01.
   - The correlations that don't meet the threshold are dropped.
   - The filtered correlation matrix is visualized as a heatmap using Seaborn (sns.heatmap()).
   - The title, x-label, and y-label are set, along with font sizes for labels and tick labels.
   - The figure is tightly laid out.

2. plot_corr_mat(self, df):
    - This function takes df (the DataFrame containing the dataset) as a parameter.
    - It creates a new Tkinter Toplevel window (win) and a Form3 instance (form3) within that window.
    - The title of the window is set to "Correlation Matrix".
    - The corr_mat() function is then called with df, and the figure and canvas from form3.

Setting Up the Menu Options Related to Feature Importance

In Helper_Plot class, define a new method named binds_feat_importance(). This method sets up the functionality for various options in a feature engineering menu:

```python
def binds_feat_importance(self, window, df, X, y):
    window.feat_eng.entryconfigure("Correlation Matrix",
        command = lambda:self.plot_corr_mat(df))

    window.feat_eng.entryconfigure("Correlation Coefficients",
        command = lambda:self.plot_corr_coeffs(df))

    window.feat_eng.entryconfigure("Random Forest Feature Importance",
        command = lambda:self.plot_rf_importance(X, y))

    window.feat_eng.entryconfigure("Extra Trees Feature Importance",
        command = lambda:self.plot_et_importance(X, y))

    window.feat_eng.entryconfigure("RFE Feature Importance",
        command = lambda:self.plot_rfe_importance(X, y))
```

Here's an explanation of what each option does:
1. "Correlation Matrix":
   When selected, this option triggers the display of a correlation matrix heatmap. This heatmap shows the correlations between numeric features in the dataset.
2. "Correlation Coefficients":
   When selected, this option triggers the display of a bar chart showing the correlation coefficients between each feature and a target variable (Churn based on the code you provided).
3. "Random Forest Feature Importance":
   When selected, this option triggers the display of a bar chart showing the feature importance as determined by a Random Forest algorithm. This helps identify which features have the most impact on the target variable.
4. "Extra Trees Feature Importance":

When selected, this option triggers the display of a bar chart showing the feature importance as determined by an Extra Trees algorithm. This is similar to the Random Forest feature importance, but computed with a different algorithm.

5. "RFE Feature Importance":

   When selected, this option triggers the display of a bar chart showing the feature importance as determined by Recursive Feature Elimination (RFE). RFE is a method that recursively removes the least important features and builds the model until a specified number of features is reached.

Each of these options is associated with a command, which specifies what action to take when the option is selected. The actions include calling specific functions (e.g., plot_corr_mat(), plot_corr_coeffs(), plot_rf_importance(), plot_et_importance(), plot_rfe_importance()) with appropriate arguments.

Overall, these options provide a range of feature engineering and visualization tools to analyze and understand the dataset. They help in identifying important features and understanding their relationships with the target variable.

Actual versus Predicted Values of a Regression Model

In Helper_Plot class, define a new method named scatter_train_test_regression(). It creates a pair of scatter plots to visualize the relationship between actual and predicted values in a regression model. It operates on both the training and test sets:

```python
def scatter_train_test_regression(self, ytrain, ytest, predictions_train,
predictions_test, figure, canvas, label):
        # Visualizes the training set results in a scatter plot
        figure.clear()
        ax1 = figure.add_subplot(2, 1, 1)
        ax1.scatter(x=ytrain, y=predictions_train, color='red', label='Training
Data')
        ax1.set_title('The actual versus predicted (Training set): ' + label,
fontweight='bold', fontsize=10)
        ax1.set_xlabel('Actual Train Set', fontsize=8)
        ax1.set_ylabel('Predicted Train Set', fontsize=8)
        ax1.plot([ytrain.min(), ytrain.max()], [ytrain.min(), ytrain.max()], 'b--',
linewidth=2, label='Perfect Prediction')
        ax1.grid(True)
        ax1.set_facecolor('#F0F0F0')
        ax1.legend(facecolor='#E6E6FA', edgecolor='black')

        ax2 = figure.add_subplot(2, 1, 2)
        ax2.scatter(x=ytest, y=predictions_test, color='red', label='Test Data')
        ax2.set_title('The actual versus predicted (Test set): ' + label,
fontweight='bold', fontsize=10)
        ax2.set_xlabel('Actual Test Set', fontsize=8)
        ax2.set_ylabel('Predicted Test Set', fontsize=8)
```

```
    ax2.plot([ytest.min(), ytest.max()], [ytest.min(), ytest.max()], 'b--',
linewidth=2, label='Perfect Prediction')
    ax2.grid(True)
    ax2.set_facecolor('#F0F0F0')
    ax2.legend(facecolor='#E6E6FA', edgecolor='black')

    figure.tight_layout()
    canvas.draw()
```

Here's a breakdown of the function:

1. It takes as input:
    - ytrain: The actual target values for the training set.
    - ytest: The actual target values for the test set.
    - predictions_train: The predicted target values for the training set.
    - predictions_test: The predicted target values for the test set.
    - figure: The area where the plots will be displayed.
    - canvas: The canvas where the figure will be drawn.
    - label: A label that will be included in the titles of the plots.
2. The function first clears any existing content from the figure.
3. It creates two subplots: one for the training set and one for the test set. Each subplot contains a scatter plot.
4. For the training set:
    - The scatter plot displays the actual target values (ytrain) on the x-axis and the predicted values (predictions_train) on the y-axis. The points are shown in red, representing the training data.
    - A title is set, incorporating the provided label.
    - Labels for the x and y axes are defined.
    - A dashed blue line is drawn to represent perfect predictions.
    - A grid is added to the plot.
    - The background color is set, and a legend is added.
5. For the test set:
    - The scatter plot displays the actual target values (ytest) on the x-axis and the predicted values (predictions_test) on the y-axis. The points are shown in red, representing the test data.
    - A title is set, similar to the training set subplot.
    - Labels for the x and y axes are defined.
    - A dashed blue line is drawn to represent perfect predictions.
    - A grid is added to the plot.
    - The background color is set, and a legend is added.
6. The layout of the figure is adjusted for better visualization, and the canvas is redrawn.

In summary, this function helps visualize how well the regression model's predictions align with the actual values, both in the training and test sets.

Regression Model's Performance

In Helper_Plot class, define a new method named lineplot_train_test_regression(). This function generates a set of four line plots to visualize the performance of a regression model on different subsets of data:

```python
def lineplot_train_test_regression(self, ytrain, ytest, yval, yfinal,
        predictions_train, predictions_test, predictions_val, all_pred, figure,
canvas, label):
    figure.clear()
    ax1 = figure.add_subplot(4, 1, 1)
    ax1.plot(ytrain.index.to_numpy(), ytrain.to_numpy(), color="blue",
linewidth=2, linestyle="-", label='Actual')
    ax1.plot(ytrain.index.to_numpy(), predictions_train, color="red",
linewidth=2, linestyle="-", label='Predicted')
    ax1.set_title('Actual and Predicted Training Set: ' + label, fontsize=10)
    ax1.set_xlabel('Date', fontsize=8)
    ax1.set_ylabel("Sales", fontsize=8)
    ax1.legend(prop={'size': 8},facecolor='#E6E6FA', edgecolor='black')
    ax1.grid(True)
    ax1.set_facecolor('#F0F0F0')
    # Set font for tick labels
    ax1.tick_params(axis='both', which='major', labelsize=8)
    ax1.tick_params(axis='both', which='minor', labelsize=8)

    ax2 = figure.add_subplot(4, 1, 2)
    ax2.plot(ytest.index.to_numpy(), ytest.to_numpy(), color="blue", linewidth=2,
linestyle="-", label='Actual')
    ax2.plot(ytest.index.to_numpy(), predictions_test, color="red", linewidth=2,
linestyle="-", label='Predicted')
    ax2.set_title('Actual and Predicted Test Set: ' + label, fontsize=10)
    ax2.set_xlabel('Date', fontsize=8)
    ax2.set_ylabel("Sales", fontsize=8)
    ax2.legend(prop={'size': 8}, facecolor='#E6E6FA', edgecolor='black')
    ax2.grid(True)
    ax2.set_facecolor('#F0F0F0')
    # Set font for tick labels
    ax2.tick_params(axis='both', which='major', labelsize=8)
    ax2.tick_params(axis='both', which='minor', labelsize=8)

    ax3 = figure.add_subplot(4, 1, 3)
    ax3.plot(yval.index.to_numpy(), yval.to_numpy(), color="blue", linewidth=2,
linestyle="-", label='Actual')
    ax3.plot(yval.index.to_numpy(), predictions_val, color="red", linewidth=2,
linestyle="-", label='Predicted')
    ax3.set_title('Actual and Predicted Validation Set (90 days forecasting) ' +
label, fontsize=8)
    ax3.set_xlabel('Date', fontsize=8)
    ax3.set_ylabel("Sales", fontsize=8)
    ax3.legend(prop={'size': 8}, facecolor='#E6E6FA', edgecolor='black')
```

```python
        ax3.grid(True)
        ax3.set_facecolor('#F0F0F0')
        # Set font for tick labels
        ax3.tick_params(axis='both', which='major', labelsize=8)
        ax3.tick_params(axis='both', which='minor', labelsize=8)

        ax4 = figure.add_subplot(4, 1, 4)
        ax4.plot(yfinal.index.to_numpy(), yfinal.to_numpy(), color="blue",
linewidth=2, linestyle="-", label='Actual')
        ax4.plot(yfinal.index.to_numpy(), all_pred, color="red", linewidth=2,
linestyle="-", label='Predicted')
        ax4.set_title('Actual and Predicted All Set ' + label, fontsize=8)
        ax4.set_xlabel('Date', fontsize=8)
        ax4.set_ylabel("Adj Close", fontsize=8)
        ax4.legend(prop={'size': 8}, facecolor='#E6E6FA', edgecolor='black')
        ax4.grid(True)
        ax4.set_facecolor('#F0F0F0')
        # Set font for tick labels
        ax4.tick_params(axis='both', which='major', labelsize=8)
        ax4.tick_params(axis='both', which='minor', labelsize=8)

        figure.tight_layout()
        canvas.draw()
```

Here's an explanation of the function:

1. The function takes the following inputs:
    - ytrain: The actual target values for the training set.
    - ytest: The actual target values for the test set.
    - yval: The actual target values for the validation set.
    - yfinal: The actual target values for the final set.
    - predictions_train: The predicted target values for the training set.
    - predictions_test: The predicted target values for the test set.
    - predictions_val: The predicted target values for the validation set.
    - all_pred: The predicted target values for all sets.
    - figure: The area where the plots will be displayed.
    - canvas: The canvas where the figure will be drawn.
    - label: A label that will be included in the titles of the plots.
2. The function first clears any existing content from the figure.
3. It creates four subplots, each representing a different data set (training, test, validation, and final).
4. For each subplot:
    - It plots the actual target values (ytrain, ytest, yval, yfinal) in blue and the predicted values (predictions_train, predictions_test, predictions_val, all_pred) in red.
    - A title is set, incorporating the provided label.
    - Labels for the x and y axes are defined.
    - A legend is added to differentiate between actual and predicted values.

- A grid is added to the plot.
- The background color is set.

5. The layout of the figure is adjusted for better visualization, and the canvas is redrawn.

In summary, this function provides a comprehensive view of the model's performance on different subsets of data, allowing for easy comparison between actual and predicted values.

Performing Various Regression Models

In Helper_Plot class, define a new method named choose_plot_regression(). It performs several tasks based on the value of chosen:

1. If chosen is "Linear Regression":
   - Trains a linear regression model on the training data.
   - Makes predictions on different data sets.
   - Calls scatter_train_test_regression() and lineplot_train_test_regression() to visualize the model's performance.
2. If chosen is "RF Regression":
   - Trains a random forest regression model on the training data.
   - Makes predictions on different data sets.
   - Calls scatter_train_test_regression() and lineplot_train_test_regression() to visualize the model's performance.
3. If chosen is "Decision Trees Regression":
   - Trains a decision tree regression model on the training data.
   - Makes predictions on different data sets.
   - Calls scatter_train_test_regression() and lineplot_train_test_regression() to visualize the model's performance.
4. If chosen is "Gradient Boosting Regression":
   - Trains a gradient boosting regression model on the training data.
   - Makes predictions on different data sets.
   - Calls scatter_train_test_regression() and lineplot_train_test_regression() to visualize the model's performance.
5. If chosen is "XGB Regression":
   - Trains an XGBoost regression model on the training data.
   - Makes predictions on different data sets.
   - Calls scatter_train_test_regression() and lineplot_train_test_regression() to visualize the model's performance.
6. If chosen is "MLP Regression":
   - Trains a multi-layer perceptron (MLP) regression model on the training data.
   - Makes predictions on different data sets.

- Calls scatter_train_test_regression() and lineplot_train_test_regression() to visualize the model's performance.

7. If chosen is "Lasso Regression":
    - Trains a Lasso regression model on the training data.
    - Makes predictions on different data sets.
    - Calls scatter_train_test_regression() and lineplot_train_test_regression() to visualize the model's performance.

8. If chosen is "Ridge Regression":
    - Trains a Ridge regression model on the training data.
    - Makes predictions on different data sets.
    - Calls scatter_train_test_regression() and lineplot_train_test_regression() to visualize the model's performance.

9. If chosen is "AdaBoost Regression":
    - Trains an AdaBoost regression model on the training data.
    - Makes predictions on different data sets.
    - Calls scatter_train_test_regression() and lineplot_train_test_regression() to visualize the model's performance.

10. If chosen is "KNN Regression":
    - Trains a K-Nearest Neighbors (KNN) regression model on the training data.
    - Makes predictions on different data sets.
    - Calls scatter_train_test_regression() and lineplot_train_test_regression() to visualize the model's performance.

This function serves as a central control for training and visualizing regression models based on the chosen algorithm.

```python
def choose_plot_regression(self, chosen, X_final_reg, X_train_reg,
        X_test_reg, X_val_reg, y_final_reg, y_train_reg, y_test_reg, y_val_reg,
        figure1, canvas1, figure2, canvas2):
    if chosen == "Linear Regression":
        best_lin_reg = self.obj_reg.linear_regression(X_train_reg, y_train_reg)
        predictions_test, predictions_train, predictions_val, all_pred =
self.obj_reg.perform_regression(best_lin_reg, X_final_reg, y_final_reg,
            X_train_reg, y_train_reg, X_test_reg, y_test_reg, X_val_reg,
y_val_reg, chosen)

        self.scatter_train_test_regression(y_train_reg, y_test_reg,
            predictions_train, predictions_test, figure1, canvas1, chosen)

        self.lineplot_train_test_regression(y_train_reg,
            y_test_reg, y_val_reg, y_final_reg, predictions_train,
predictions_test, predictions_val, all_pred,
            figure2, canvas2, chosen)

    if chosen == "RF Regression":
        best_rf_reg = self.obj_reg.rf_regression(X_train_reg, y_train_reg)
```

```python
                predictions_test, predictions_train, predictions_val, all_pred = \
        self.obj_reg.perform_regression(best_rf_reg, X_final_reg, y_final_reg,
                X_train_reg, y_train_reg, X_test_reg, y_test_reg, X_val_reg,
        y_val_reg, chosen)

            self.scatter_train_test_regression(y_train_reg, y_test_reg,
                predictions_train, predictions_test, figure1, canvas1, chosen)

            self.lineplot_train_test_regression(y_train_reg,
                y_test_reg, y_val_reg, y_final_reg, predictions_train,
        predictions_test, predictions_val, all_pred,
                figure2, canvas2, chosen)

        if chosen == "Decision Trees Regression":
            best_dt_reg = self.obj_reg.dt_regression(X_train_reg, y_train_reg)
            predictions_test, predictions_train, predictions_val, all_pred = \
        self.obj_reg.perform_regression(best_dt_reg, X_final_reg, y_final_reg,
                X_train_reg, y_train_reg, X_test_reg, y_test_reg, X_val_reg,
        y_val_reg, chosen)

            self.scatter_train_test_regression(y_train_reg, y_test_reg,
                predictions_train, predictions_test, figure1, canvas1, chosen)

            self.lineplot_train_test_regression(y_train_reg,
                y_test_reg, y_val_reg, y_final_reg, predictions_train,
        predictions_test, predictions_val, all_pred,
                figure2, canvas2, chosen)

        if chosen == "Gradient Boosting Regression":
            best_gb_reg = self.obj_reg.gb_regression(X_train_reg, y_train_reg)
            predictions_test, predictions_train, predictions_val, all_pred = \
        self.obj_reg.perform_regression(best_gb_reg, X_final_reg, y_final_reg,
                X_train_reg, y_train_reg, X_test_reg, y_test_reg, X_val_reg,
        y_val_reg, chosen)

            self.scatter_train_test_regression(y_train_reg, y_test_reg,
                predictions_train, predictions_test, figure1, canvas1, chosen)

            self.lineplot_train_test_regression(y_train_reg,
                y_test_reg, y_val_reg, y_final_reg, predictions_train,
        predictions_test, predictions_val, all_pred,
                figure2, canvas2, chosen)

        if chosen == "XGB Regression":
            best_xgb_reg = self.obj_reg.xgb_regression(X_train_reg, y_train_reg)
            predictions_test, predictions_train, predictions_val, all_pred = \
        self.obj_reg.perform_regression(best_xgb_reg, X_final_reg, y_final_reg,
                X_train_reg, y_train_reg, X_test_reg, y_test_reg, X_val_reg,
        y_val_reg, chosen)

            self.scatter_train_test_regression(y_train_reg, y_test_reg,
                predictions_train, predictions_test, figure1, canvas1, chosen)

            self.lineplot_train_test_regression(y_train_reg,
                y_test_reg, y_val_reg, y_final_reg, predictions_train,
        predictions_test, predictions_val, all_pred,
                figure2, canvas2, chosen)
```

```python
        if chosen == "MLP Regression":
            best_mlp_reg = self.obj_reg.mlp_regression(X_train_reg, y_train_reg)
            predictions_test, predictions_train, predictions_val, all_pred =
self.obj_reg.perform_regression(best_mlp_reg, X_final_reg, y_final_reg,
                X_train_reg, y_train_reg, X_test_reg, y_test_reg, X_val_reg,
y_val_reg, chosen)

            self.scatter_train_test_regression(y_train_reg, y_test_reg,
                predictions_train, predictions_test, figure1, canvas1, chosen)

            self.lineplot_train_test_regression(y_train_reg,
                y_test_reg, y_val_reg, y_final_reg, predictions_train,
predictions_test, predictions_val, all_pred,
                figure2, canvas2, chosen)

        if chosen == "Lasso Regression":
            best_lasso_reg = self.obj_reg.lasso_regression(X_train_reg, y_train_reg)
            predictions_test, predictions_train, predictions_val, all_pred =
self.obj_reg.perform_regression(best_lasso_reg, X_final_reg, y_final_reg,
                X_train_reg, y_train_reg, X_test_reg, y_test_reg, X_val_reg,
y_val_reg, chosen)

            self.scatter_train_test_regression(y_train_reg, y_test_reg,
                predictions_train, predictions_test, figure1, canvas1, chosen)

            self.lineplot_train_test_regression(y_train_reg,
                y_test_reg, y_val_reg, y_final_reg, predictions_train,
predictions_test, predictions_val, all_pred,
                figure2, canvas2, chosen)

        if chosen == "Ridge Regression":
            best_ridge_reg = self.obj_reg.ridge_regression(X_train_reg, y_train_reg)
            predictions_test, predictions_train, predictions_val, all_pred =
self.obj_reg.perform_regression(best_ridge_reg, X_final_reg, y_final_reg,
                X_train_reg, y_train_reg, X_test_reg, y_test_reg, X_val_reg,
y_val_reg, chosen)

            self.scatter_train_test_regression(y_train_reg, y_test_reg,
                predictions_train, predictions_test, figure1, canvas1, chosen)

            self.lineplot_train_test_regression(y_train_reg,
                y_test_reg, y_val_reg, y_final_reg, predictions_train,
predictions_test, predictions_val, all_pred,
                figure2, canvas2, chosen)

        if chosen == "AdaBoost Regression":
            best_ada_reg = self.obj_reg.adaboost_regression(X_train_reg, y_train_reg)
            predictions_test, predictions_train, predictions_val, all_pred =
self.obj_reg.perform_regression(best_ada_reg, X_final_reg, y_final_reg,
                X_train_reg, y_train_reg, X_test_reg, y_test_reg, X_val_reg,
y_val_reg, chosen)

            self.scatter_train_test_regression(y_train_reg, y_test_reg,
                predictions_train, predictions_test, figure1, canvas1, chosen)

            self.lineplot_train_test_regression(y_train_reg,
                y_test_reg, y_val_reg, y_final_reg, predictions_train,
predictions_test, predictions_val, all_pred,
```

```
            figure2, canvas2, chosen)

    if chosen == "KNN Regression":
            best_knn_reg = self.obj_reg.knn_regression(X_train_reg, y_train_reg)
            predictions_test, predictions_train, predictions_val, all_pred =
self.obj_reg.perform_regression(best_knn_reg, X_final_reg, y_final_reg,
            X_train_reg, y_train_reg, X_test_reg, y_test_reg, X_val_reg,
y_val_reg, chosen)

        self.scatter_train_test_regression(y_train_reg, y_test_reg,
            predictions_train, predictions_test, figure1, canvas1, chosen)

        self.lineplot_train_test_regression(y_train_reg,
            y_test_reg, y_val_reg, y_final_reg, predictions_train,
predictions_test, predictions_val, all_pred,
            figure2, canvas2, chosen)
```

Visualizing Confusion Matrix and ROC

In Helper_Plot class, define a new method named plot_cm_roc():

```python
def plot_cm_roc(self, model, X_test, y_test, ypred, name, figure, canvas):
    figure.clear()

    #Plots confusion matrix
    ax1 = figure.add_subplot(2,1,1)
    cm = confusion_matrix(y_test, ypred, )
    sns.heatmap(cm, annot=True, linewidth=2, linecolor='black', fmt='g',
cmap="cool", annot_kws={"size": 14}, ax=ax1)
    ax1.set_title('Confusion Matrix' + " of " + name, fontsize=12)
    ax1.set_xlabel('Y predict', fontsize=10)
    ax1.set_ylabel('Y test', fontsize=10)
    ax1.xaxis.set_ticklabels(['Churn = 1', 'Churn = 0'], fontsize=10)
    ax1.yaxis.set_ticklabels(['Churn = 1', 'Churn = 0'], fontsize=10)
    ax1.set_facecolor('#F0F0F0')

    #Plots ROC
    ax2 = figure.add_subplot(2,1,2)
    Y_pred_prob = model.predict_proba(X_test)
    Y_pred_prob = Y_pred_prob[:, 1]

    fpr, tpr, thresholds = roc_curve(y_test, Y_pred_prob)
    ax2.plot([0,1],[0,1], color='navy', linestyle='--', linewidth=3,
label='Random Guess')
    ax2.plot(fpr,tpr, color='red', linewidth=3, label='ROC Curve')
    ax2.set_xlabel('False Positive Rate', fontsize=10)
    ax2.set_ylabel('True Positive Rate', fontsize=10)
    ax2.set_title('ROC Curve of ' + name , fontsize=12)
    ax2.grid(True)
    ax2.legend(facecolor='#E6E6FA', edgecolor='black')
    ax2.set_facecolor('#F0F0F0')

    figure.tight_layout()
    canvas.draw()
```

The plot_cm_roc() function serves as a visualization tool for evaluating the performance of a classification model. It first prepares the canvas by clearing any existing content. The upper subplot is dedicated to the Confusion Matrix, a crucial metric in classification tasks. This matrix provides insights into how well the model predicts the true and false positives and negatives. The function employs seaborn's heatmap to generate a clear visual representation of the confusion matrix. It customizes labels and titles to ensure clarity and provides a distinctive color scheme for better interpretation. Additionally, it sets the background color of the plot to enhance visibility.

Moving to the lower subplot, the function focuses on plotting the Receiver Operating Characteristic (ROC) curve. This curve is fundamental in assessing a model's ability to discriminate between the classes. It calculates the true positive rate and false positive rate, then visualizes them on the plot. The curve is superimposed on a dashed line representing random guessing, offering a clear reference point. The function handles axis labels and titles, ensuring they are appropriately sized for easy comprehension. It also applies grid lines for better visualization of the curve's trajectory.

Once both subplots are prepared, the function tightens the layout to optimize the arrangement of elements. Finally, it draws the canvas to display the finished plots. In summary, plot_cm_roc() is an indispensable tool for visualizing the performance of a classification model, providing valuable insights through the Confusion Matrix and ROC curve. It ensures that the plots are well-organized, labeled, and presented in a visually appealing manner for effective evaluation.

Visualizing Learning Curve and True Values versus Predicted Values of a Classifier

In Helper_Plot class, define a new method named plot_real_pred_val_learning_curve():

```python
#Plots true values versus predicted values diagram and learning curve
def plot_real_pred_val_learning_curve(self, model, X_train, y_train, X_test,
y_test, ypred, name, figure, canvas):
    figure.clear()

    #Plots true values versus predicted values diagram
    ax1 = figure.add_subplot(2,1,1)
    acc=accuracy_score(y_test, ypred)
    ax1.scatter(range(len(ypred)),ypred,color="blue", lw=2,label="Predicted")
    ax1.scatter(range(len(y_test)),
        y_test, color="red", label="Actual")
    ax1.set_title("Predicted Values vs True Values of " + name, fontsize=12)
    ax1.set_xlabel("Accuracy: " + str(round((acc*100),3)) + "%")
    ax1.legend(facecolor='#E6E6FA', edgecolor='black')
    ax1.grid(True, alpha=0.75, lw=1, ls='-.')
    ax1.set_facecolor('#F0F0F0')

    #Plots learning curve
```

```python
        train_sizes=np.linspace(.1, 1.0, 5)
        train_sizes, train_scores, test_scores, fit_times, _ = learning_curve(model,
            X_train, y_train, cv=None, n_jobs=None, train_sizes=train_sizes,
return_times=True)
        train_scores_mean = np.mean(train_scores, axis=1)
        train_scores_std = np.std(train_scores, axis=1)
        test_scores_mean = np.mean(test_scores, axis=1)
        test_scores_std = np.std(test_scores, axis=1)

        ax2 = figure.add_subplot(2,1,2)
        ax2.fill_between(train_sizes, train_scores_mean - train_scores_std,
            train_scores_mean + train_scores_std, alpha=0.1, color="r")
        ax2.fill_between(train_sizes, test_scores_mean - test_scores_std,
            test_scores_mean + test_scores_std, alpha=0.1, color="g")
        ax2.plot(train_sizes, train_scores_mean, 'o-',
            color="b", label="Training score")
        ax2.plot(train_sizes, test_scores_mean, 'o-',
            color="r", label="Cross-validation score")
        ax2.legend(loc="best", facecolor='#E6E6FA', edgecolor='black')
        ax2.set_title("Learning curve of " + name, fontsize=12)
        ax2.set_xlabel("fit_times")
        ax2.set_ylabel("Score")
        ax2.grid(True, alpha=0.75, lw=1, ls='-.')
        ax2.set_facecolor('#F0F0F0')

        figure.tight_layout()
        canvas.draw()
```

The plot_real_pred_val_learning_curve() function is a multifaceted visualization tool used for evaluating the performance of a machine learning model. It is designed to provide comprehensive insights into how well the model's predictions align with actual values. The upper subplot focuses on creating a scatter plot that juxtaposes predicted values against their corresponding true values. It employs distinct colors to differentiate between the predicted and actual data points. The title of the plot clearly indicates its purpose, emphasizing the comparison between predictions and reality. Additionally, the accuracy of the model is prominently displayed on the x-axis, offering a quantitative assessment of its performance. To enhance clarity, a legend is included to distinguish between predicted and actual values. The function also incorporates grid lines for better visualization and sets an appropriate background color for improved contrast.

The lower subplot of the function is dedicated to plotting the learning curve. This curve illustrates the model's performance as training data size increases. It assesses both training and cross-validation scores, shedding light on how well the model generalizes to new data. The plot employs shaded areas around the curves to represent the standard deviation, providing insights into the variance of the scores. Different colors are used to clearly distinguish between training and cross-validation scores. The legend is strategically placed for optimal visibility. Additionally, grid lines are applied to aid in the interpretation of the curve's progression. The title of the plot succinctly conveys its purpose, emphasizing the learning curve of the model.

The function concludes by ensuring that the layout of the subplots is well-organized and optimized. It then draws the canvas to display the finished plots. In summary, the plot_real_pred_val_learning_curve() function is a versatile visualization tool that combines a scatter plot for visualizing predictions with actual values and a learning curve for assessing the model's performance with changing data sizes. It ensures that the plots are accurately labeled, visually appealing, and presented in an organized manner for effective model evaluation.

Predicting Churn Customers Using Machine Learning Classifier

In Helper_Plot class, define a new method named choose_plot_ML():

```python
    def choose_plot_ML(self, root, chosen, X_train, X_test, y_train, y_test,
figure1, canvas1, figure2, canvas2):
        if chosen == "Logistic Regression":
            best_model, y_pred = self.obj_ml.implement_LR(chosen, X_train, X_test,
y_train, y_test)

            #Plots confusion matrix and ROC
            self.plot_cm_roc(best_model, X_test, y_test, y_pred, chosen, figure1,
canvas1)

            #Plots true values versus predicted values diagram and learning curve
            self.plot_real_pred_val_learning_curve(best_model, X_train, y_train,
                X_test, y_test, y_pred, chosen, figure2, canvas2)

            #Shows table of result
            df_lr = self.obj_data.read_dataset("results_LR.csv")
            self.shows_table(root, df_lr, 350, 750, "Y_test and Y_pred of Logistic
Regression")

        if chosen == "Random Forest":
            best_model, y_pred = self.obj_ml.implement_RF(chosen, X_train, X_test,
y_train, y_test)

            #Plots confusion matrix and ROC
            self.plot_cm_roc(best_model, X_test, y_test, y_pred, chosen, figure1,
canvas1)

            #Plots true values versus predicted values diagram and learning curve
            self.plot_real_pred_val_learning_curve(best_model, X_train, y_train,
                X_test, y_test, y_pred, chosen, figure2, canvas2)

            #Shows table of result
            df_rf = self.obj_data.read_dataset("results_RF.csv")
            self.shows_table(root, df_rf, 350, 750, "Y_test and Y_pred of Random
Forest")

        if chosen == "K-Nearest Neighbors":
            best_model, y_pred = self.obj_ml.implement_KNN(chosen, X_train, X_test,
y_train, y_test)

            #Plots confusion matrix and ROC
```

```python
        self.plot_cm_roc(best_model, X_test, y_test, y_pred, chosen, figure1,
canvas1)

        #Plots true values versus predicted values diagram and learning curve
        self.plot_real_pred_val_learning_curve(best_model, X_train, y_train,
            X_test, y_test, y_pred, chosen, figure2, canvas2)

        #Shows table of result
        df_knn = self.obj_data.read_dataset("results_KNN.csv")
        self.shows_table(root, df_knn, 350, 750, "Y_test and Y_pred of KNN")

    if chosen == "Decision Trees":
        best_model, y_pred = self.obj_ml.implement_DT(chosen, X_train, X_test,
y_train, y_test)

        #Plots confusion matrix and ROC
        self.plot_cm_roc(best_model, X_test, y_test, y_pred, chosen, figure1,
canvas1)

        #Plots true values versus predicted values diagram and learning curve
        self.plot_real_pred_val_learning_curve(best_model, X_train, y_train,
            X_test, y_test, y_pred, chosen, figure2, canvas2)

        #Shows table of result
        df_dt = self.obj_data.read_dataset("results_DT.csv")
        self.shows_table(root, df_dt, 350, 750, "Y_test and Y_pred of Decision
Trees")

    if chosen == "Gradient Boosting":
        best_model, y_pred = self.obj_ml.implement_GB(chosen, X_train, X_test,
y_train, y_test)

        #Plots confusion matrix and ROC
        self.plot_cm_roc(best_model, X_test, y_test, y_pred, chosen, figure1,
canvas1)

        #Plots true values versus predicted values diagram and learning curve
        self.plot_real_pred_val_learning_curve(best_model, X_train, y_train,
            X_test, y_test, y_pred, chosen, figure2, canvas2)

        #Shows table of result
        df_gb = self.obj_data.read_dataset("results_GB.csv")
        self.shows_table(root, df_gb, 350, 750, "Y_test and Y_pred of Gradient
Boosting")

    if chosen == "Extreme Gradient Boosting":
        best_model, y_pred = self.obj_ml.implement_XGB(chosen, X_train, X_test,
y_train, y_test)

        #Plots confusion matrix and ROC
        self.plot_cm_roc(best_model, X_test, y_test, y_pred, chosen, figure1,
canvas1)

        #Plots true values versus predicted values diagram and learning curve
        self.plot_real_pred_val_learning_curve(best_model, X_train, y_train,
            X_test, y_test, y_pred, chosen, figure2, canvas2)

        #Shows table of result
```

```python
            df_xgb = self.obj_data.read_dataset("results_XGB.csv")
            self.shows_table(root, df_xgb, 350, 750, "Y_test and Y_pred of Extreme
Gradient Boosting")

        if chosen == "Multi-Layer Perceptron":
            best_model, y_pred = self.obj_ml.implement_MLP(chosen, X_train, X_test,
y_train, y_test)

            #Plots confusion matrix and ROC
            self.plot_cm_roc(best_model, X_test, y_test, y_pred, chosen, figure1,
canvas1)

            #Plots true values versus predicted values diagram and learning curve
            self.plot_real_pred_val_learning_curve(best_model, X_train, y_train,
                X_test, y_test, y_pred, chosen, figure2, canvas2)

            #Shows table of result
            df_mlp = self.obj_data.read_dataset("results_MLP.csv")
            self.shows_table(root, df_mlp, 350, 750, "Y_test and Y_pred of Multi-
Layer Perceptron")

        if chosen == "Support Vector Classifier":
            best_model, y_pred = self.obj_ml.implement_SVC(chosen, X_train, X_test,
y_train, y_test)

            #Plots confusion matrix and ROC
            self.plot_cm_roc(best_model, X_test, y_test, y_pred, chosen, figure1,
canvas1)

            #Plots true values versus predicted values diagram and learning curve
            self.plot_real_pred_val_learning_curve(best_model, X_train, y_train,
                X_test, y_test, y_pred, chosen, figure2, canvas2)

            #Shows table of result
            df_svc = self.obj_data.read_dataset("results_SVC.csv")
            self.shows_table(root, df_svc, 350, 750, "Y_test and Y_pred of Support
Vector Classifier")

        if chosen == "AdaBoost":
            best_model, y_pred = self.obj_ml.implement_ADA(chosen, X_train, X_test,
y_train, y_test)

            #Plots confusion matrix and ROC
            self.plot_cm_roc(best_model, X_test, y_test, y_pred, chosen, figure1,
canvas1)

            #Plots true values versus predicted values diagram and learning curve
            self.plot_real_pred_val_learning_curve(best_model, X_train, y_train,
                X_test, y_test, y_pred, chosen, figure2, canvas2)

            #Shows table of result
            df_ada = self.obj_data.read_dataset("results_ADA.csv")
            self.shows_table(root, df_ada, 350, 750, "Y_test and Y_pred of AdaBoost
Classifier")
```

The choose_plot_ML() function acts as a dispatcher for plotting visualizations related to various machine learning models. It takes in parameters such as the chosen model, training and testing data, figure objects, and canvas objects for displaying plots. Each conditional block corresponds to a specific machine learning model and its associated tasks.

For example, when the chosen model is "Logistic Regression", the function calls the implement_LR() method to train the logistic regression model, obtaining the best model and its predictions. It then proceeds to generate and display a confusion matrix and ROC curve through the plot_cm_roc method. Additionally, it creates a scatter plot comparing true values with predicted values and a learning curve, both visualized through the plot_real_pred_val_learning_curve method. Finally, it retrieves the results for logistic regression from a dataset and displays it as a table using the shows_table method.

Similar sequences of operations occur for other machine learning models such as "Random Forest", "K-Nearest Neighbors", "Decision Trees", "Gradient Boosting", "Extreme Gradient Boosting", "Multi-Layer Perceptron", "Support Vector Classifier", and "AdaBoost". In each case, the appropriate model is trained, predictions are generated, and visualizations are created and displayed.

This function effectively streamlines the process of evaluating and visualizing the performance of different machine learning models, ensuring consistency and clarity in the generated plots and tables.

PLOTTING THE RESULTS

Completing the Main Class

The main class starts by importing necessary modules like os (for interacting with the operating system), pandas (for data manipulation), tkinter (for creating GUIs), and various classes from other Python scripts (e.g., Main_Window, Helper_Plot, Process_Data, Regression, Machine_Learning, and Form1).

1. The Main_Sales class is defined. This class acts as a controller for the application.
2. __init__() method: The initialization method doesn't do anything except calling initialize() method.
3. initialize() method:
   - This method is responsible for setting up the main GUI window. It configures the window's size, title, and creates instances of various classes (e.g., Main_Window, Helper_Plot, Process_Data, Regression, Machine_Learning).
   - It then calls the add_widgets method of obj_window to place widgets in the root window.
   - The method then performs various data preprocessing operations (e.g., filling missing values, creating dummy datasets, normalizing data), which are essential for the subsequent analysis.
   - It also binds events to various widgets using the binds_event method.
4. binds_event() method:
   This method associates specific functions with events triggered by widgets. For example, clicking buttons or selecting items in comboboxes triggers the associated functions.

5. Event Handling Methods:
   choose_list_widget(), choose_combo_year(), choose_combobox_month(), and choose_combo_rfm() are methods that handle events triggered by selecting items from listboxes and comboboxes. These functions call other methods to generate and display specific visualizations based on the selected items.

6. split_regression() and split_prediction() methods:
   These methods handle the splitting of data for regression and prediction tasks, respectively. They ensure that the data is appropriately split before any modeling is performed.

7. choose_combo_reg() and choose_combo_pred() methods:
   These methods handle events triggered by selecting regression and prediction models from comboboxes. They call other methods to generate and display visualizations for the selected models.

8. if __name__ == "__main__":
   - This conditional block ensures that the code is only executed when the script is run directly (not when it's imported as a module).
   - It creates a tkinter root window and an instance of the Main_Sales class, which kicks off the application.

Overall, this script serves as the main controller for the application, managing the initialization, GUI setup, event handling, and interactions between different components of the program.

```python
#main_sales.py
import os
import pandas as pd
import tkinter as tk
from tkinter import *
from main_window import Main_Window
from helper_plot import Helper_Plot
from process_data import Process_Data
from regression import Regression
from machine_learning import Machine_Learning
from form1 import Form1

class Main_Sales():
    def __init__(self, root):
        #super().__init__()
        self.initialize()

    def initialize(self):
        self.root = root
        width = 1560
        height = 790
        self.root.geometry(f"{width}x{height}")
        self.root.title("TIME-SERIES SUPERSTORE SALES FORECASTING AND PREDICTION
USING MACHINE LEARNING")
```

```python
        #Creates necessary objects
        self.obj_window = Main_Window()
        self.obj_plot = Helper_Plot()
        self.obj_data = Process_Data()
        self.obj_reg = Regression()
        self.obj_ML = Machine_Learning()

        #Places widgets in root
        self.obj_window.add_widgets(self.root)

        #Reads dataset
        self.df_before_fill, self.df_after_fill = self.obj_data.preprocess()

        #Creates dummy dataset for visualization
        self.df_dummy = self.df_after_fill.copy()
        self.df_dummy = self.obj_data.create_dummy(self.df_dummy)

        #Normalizes year-wise data
        self.year_data_mean, self.year_data_ewm, self.year_norm =
self.obj_data.normalize_year_wise_data(self.df_after_fill)

        #Normalizes month-wise data
        self.month_data_mean, self.month_data_ewm, self.month_norm =
self.obj_data.normalize_month_wise_data(self.df_after_fill)

        #Calculates RFM
        self.rfm_df, self.rank_df, self.merged_rank_dummy =
self.obj_data.calculate_RFM(self.df_after_fill, self.df_dummy)

        #Finds churn customer
        self.df_final = self.obj_data.find_churn_customer(self.df_dummy, self.rfm_df,
self.rank_df)

        #For machine learning
        self.df_final, self.X1, self.y1, self.X2, self.y2 =
self.obj_data.encode_df(self.df_final)

        #Extracts input and output variables for regression
        self.obj_reg.splitting_data_regression(self.X2, self.y2)

        #Extracts input and output variables for prediction
        self.obj_ML.oversampling_splitting(self.df_final)

        #turns off combo_reg and combo_pred after splitting is done
        self.obj_window.combo_reg['state'] = 'disabled'
        self.obj_window.combo_pred['state'] = 'disabled'

        #Binds events
        self.binds_event()
        self.obj_plot.binds_menu_open_dataset(self.df_before_fill,
self.df_after_fill, self.root, self.obj_window)
        self.obj_plot.binds_features_distribution(self.obj_window,
self.df_before_fill, self.df_after_fill, self.df_dummy)
        self.obj_plot.binds_categories_distribution(self.obj_window, self.df_dummy)
        self.obj_plot.binds_year_wise(self.obj_window, self.df_dummy,
self.year_data_mean, self.year_data_ewm)
        self.obj_plot.binds_month_wise(self.obj_window, self.df_dummy,
self.month_data_mean, self.month_data_ewm)
```

```python
        self.obj_plot.binds_rfm_distribution(self.obj_window, self.merged_rank_dummy)
        self.obj_plot.binds_feat_importance(self.obj_window, self.df_final, self.X1,
self.y1)

    def binds_event(self):
        #Shows table if user clicks LOAD DATASET
        self.obj_window.btn_load.config(command =
lambda:self.obj_plot.shows_table(self.root,
            self.merged_rank_dummy, 1250, 600, "Superstore Dataset"))

        #Binds listbox to choose_list_widget() function
        self.obj_window.listbox.bind("<<ListboxSelect>>", self.choose_list_widget)

        # Binds combo_year to choose_combo_year()
        self.obj_window.combo_year.bind("<<ComboboxSelected>>",
self.choose_combo_year)

        # Binds combo_month to choose_combobox_month()
        self.obj_window.combo_month.bind("<<ComboboxSelected>>",
self.choose_combobox_month)

        # Binds combo_tech to choose_combo_rfm()
        self.obj_window.combo_rfm.bind("<<ComboboxSelected>>", self.choose_combo_rfm)

        #Binds btn_reg to split_regression() function
        self.obj_window.btn_reg.config(command = self.split_regression)

        # Binds combo_reg to choose_combo_reg()
        self.obj_window.combo_reg.bind("<<ComboboxSelected>>", self.choose_combo_reg)

        #Binds combo_pred to split_prediction() function
        self.obj_window.btn_pred.config(command = self.split_prediction)

        # Binds combo_pred to choose_combo_pred()
        self.obj_window.combo_pred.bind("<<ComboboxSelected>>",
self.choose_combo_pred)

    def choose_list_widget(self, event):
        chosen = self.obj_window.listbox.get(self.obj_window.listbox.curselection())
        print(chosen)
        self.obj_plot.choose_plot(self.df_after_fill, self.df_dummy, chosen,
            self.obj_window.figure1, self.obj_window.canvas1,
            self.obj_window.figure2, self.obj_window.canvas2)

    def choose_combo_year(self, event):
        chosen = self.obj_window.combo_year.get()
        self.obj_plot.choose_year_wise(self.df_after_fill, self.year_data_mean,
self.year_data_ewm, self.year_norm, chosen,
            self.obj_window.figure1, self.obj_window.canvas1,
            self.obj_window.figure2, self.obj_window.canvas2)

    def choose_combobox_month(self, event):
        chosen = self.obj_window.combo_month.get()
        self.obj_plot.choose_month_wise(self.df_dummy,
            self.month_data_mean, self.month_data_ewm, self.month_norm, chosen,
            self.obj_window.figure1, self.obj_window.canvas1,
            self.obj_window.figure2, self.obj_window.canvas2)
```

```python
    def choose_combo_rfm(self, event):
        chosen = self.obj_window.combo_rfm.get()
        self.obj_plot.choose_rfm_distribution(self.merged_rank_dummy, chosen,
            self.obj_window.figure1,
            self.obj_window.canvas1, self.obj_window.figure2,
            self.obj_window.canvas2)

    def split_regression(self):
        file_path = os.getcwd()+"/X_final_reg.pkl"
        if os.path.exists(file_path):
            self.X_Ori, self.X_final_reg, self.X_train_reg, self.X_test_reg, \
            self.X_val_reg, self.y_final_reg, self.y_train_reg, \
            self.y_test_reg, self.y_val_reg = self.obj_reg.load_regression_files()
        else:
            self.obj_reg.splitting_data_regression(self.df_final)
            self.X_Ori, self.X_final_reg, self.X_train_reg, self.X_test_reg,
            self.X_val_reg, self.y_final_reg, self.y_train_reg,
            self.y_test_reg, self.y_val_reg = self.obj_reg.load_regression_files()

        print("Loading regression files done...")

        #turns on combo_reg after splitting is done
        self.obj_window.combo_reg['state'] = 'normal'

        self.obj_window.btn_reg.config(state="disabled")

    def choose_combo_reg(self, event):
        chosen = self.obj_window.combo_reg.get()

        self.obj_plot.choose_plot_regression(chosen, self.X_final_reg,
            self.X_train_reg, self.X_test_reg, self.X_val_reg,
            self.y_final_reg, self.y_train_reg, self.y_test_reg,
            self.y_val_reg,
            self.obj_window.figure1, self.obj_window.canvas1,
            self.obj_window.figure2, self.obj_window.canvas2)

    def split_prediction(self):
        file_path = os.getcwd()+"/X_train.pkl"
        if os.path.exists(file_path):
            self.X_train, self.X_test, self.y_train, self.y_test =
self.obj_ML.load_files()
        else:
            self.obj_ML.oversampling_splitting(self.df_final)
            self.X_train, self.X_test, self.y_train, self.y_test =
self.obj_ML.load_files()

        print("Loading files done...")

        #turns on combo_pred after splitting is done
        self.obj_window.combo_pred['state'] = 'normal'

        self.obj_window.btn_pred.config(state="disabled")

    def choose_combo_pred(self, event):
        chosen = self.obj_window.combo_pred.get()
        self.obj_plot.choose_plot_ML(self.root, chosen, self.X_train, self.X_test,
            self.y_train, self.y_test, self.obj_window.figure1,
            self.obj_window.canvas1, self.obj_window.figure2,
```

```python
            self.obj_window.canvas2)

if __name__ == "__main__":
    root = tk.Tk()
    app = Main_Sales(root)
    root.mainloop()
```

The Result of Viewing Dataset

Run the main_sales.py script. From About Dataset menu, choose View Dataset. The dataset will be displayed as shown in figure 6.1.

	Order ID	Order Date	Ship Date	Ship Mode	Customer ID	Customer Name	S
1	CA-2015-103800	2015-01-03 00:00:00	2015-01-07 00:00:00	Standard Class	DP-13000	Darren Powers	C
2	CA-2015-112326	2015-01-04 00:00:00	2015-01-08 00:00:00	Standard Class	PO-19195	Phillina Ober	H
3	CA-2015-112326	2015-01-04 00:00:00	2015-01-08 00:00:00	Standard Class	PO-19195	Phillina Ober	H
4	CA-2015-112326	2015-01-04 00:00:00	2015-01-08 00:00:00	Standard Class	PO-19195	Phillina Ober	H
5	CA-2015-141817	2015-01-05 00:00:00	2015-01-12 00:00:00	Standard Class	MB-18085	Mick Brown	C
6	CA-2015-167199	2015-01-06 00:00:00	2015-01-10 00:00:00	Standard Class	ME-17320	Maria Etezadi	H
7	CA-2015-167199	2015-01-06 00:00:00	2015-01-10 00:00:00	Standard Class	ME-17320	Maria Etezadi	H
8	CA-2015-130813	2015-01-06 00:00:00	2015-01-08 00:00:00	Second Class	LS-17230	Lycoris Saunders	C
9	CA-2015-167199	2015-01-06 00:00:00	2015-01-10 00:00:00	Standard Class	ME-17320	Maria Etezadi	H
10	CA-2015-167199	2015-01-06 00:00:00	2015-01-10 00:00:00	Standard Class	ME-17320	Maria Etezadi	H
11	CA-2015-167199	2015-01-06 00:00:00	2015-01-10 00:00:00	Standard Class	ME-17320	Maria Etezadi	H
12	CA-2015-106054	2015-01-06 00:00:00	2015-01-07 00:00:00	First Class	JO-15145	Jack O'Briant	C
13	CA-2015-167199	2015-01-06 00:00:00	2015-01-10 00:00:00	Standard Class	ME-17320	Maria Etezadi	H
14	CA-2015-167199	2015-01-06 00:00:00	2015-01-10 00:00:00	Standard Class	ME-17320	Maria Etezadi	H
15	CA-2015-105417	2015-01-07 00:00:00	2015-01-12 00:00:00	Standard Class	VS-21820	Vivek Sundaresam	C
16	CA-2015-105417	2015-01-07 00:00:00	2015-01-12 00:00:00	Standard Class	VS-21820	Vivek Sundaresam	C
17	CA-2015-135405	2015-01-09 00:00:00	2015-01-13 00:00:00	Standard Class	MS-17830	Melanie Seite	C
18	CA-2015-135405	2015-01-09 00:00:00	2015-01-13 00:00:00	Standard Class	MS-17830	Melanie Seite	C
19	CA-2015-149020	2015-01-10 00:00:00	2015-01-15 00:00:00	Standard Class	AJ-10780	Anthony Jacobs	C
20	CA-2015-149020	2015-01-10 00:00:00	2015-01-15 00:00:00	Standard Class	AJ-10780	Anthony Jacobs	C
21	CA-2015-130092	2015-01-11 00:00:00	2015-01-14 00:00:00	First Class	SV-20365	Seth Vernon	C
22	CA-2015-162775	2015-01-13 00:00:00	2015-01-15 00:00:00	Second Class	CS-12250	Chris Selesnick	C
23	CA-2015-162775	2015-01-13 00:00:00	2015-01-15 00:00:00	Second Class	CS-12250	Chris Selesnick	C
24	CA-2015-162775	2015-01-13 00:00:00	2015-01-15 00:00:00	Second Class	CS-12250	Chris Selesnick	C

9800 rows x 22 columns

Figure 6.1 The dataset

Then, from About Dataset menu, choose Dataset Information. The dataset information will be displayed as shown in figure 6.2.

```
Dataset Information                                                    —  □  ×
<class 'pandas.core.frame.DataFrame'>
DatetimeIndex: 9800 entries, 2015-01-03 to 2018-12-30
Data columns (total 22 columns):
 #   Column         Non-Null Count  Dtype
---  ------         --------------  -----
 0   Order ID       9800 non-null   object
 1   Order Date     9800 non-null   datetime64[ns]
 2   Ship Date      9800 non-null   datetime64[ns]
 3   Ship Mode      9800 non-null   object
 4   Customer ID    9800 non-null   object
 5   Customer Name  9800 non-null   object
 6   Segment        9800 non-null   object
 7   Country        9800 non-null   object
 8   City           9800 non-null   object
 9   State          9800 non-null   object
 10  Postal Code    9800 non-null   float64
 11  Region         9800 non-null   object
 12  Product ID     9800 non-null   object
 13  Category       9800 non-null   object
 14  Sub-Category   9800 non-null   object
 15  Product Name   9800 non-null   object
 16  Sales          9800 non-null   float64
 17  Day            9800 non-null   int32
 18  Month          9800 non-null   int32
 19  Year           9800 non-null   int32
 20  Week           9800 non-null   UInt32
 21  Quarter        9800 non-null   int32
dtypes: UInt32(1), datetime64[ns](2), float64(2), int32(4), object(13)
memory usage: 1.5+ MB
```

Figure 6.2 The dataset information

Then, from About Dataset menu, choose Statistical Description. The statistical description will be displayed as shown in figure 6.3.

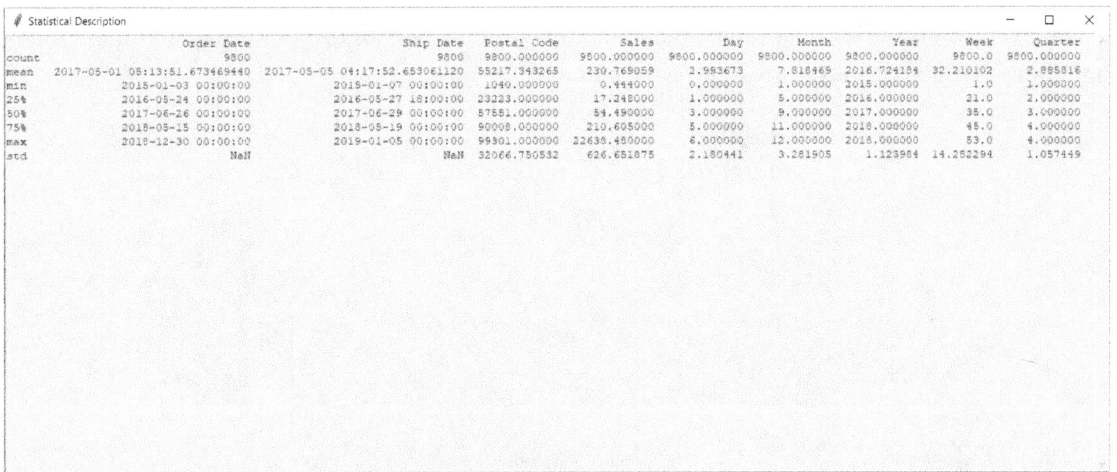

Figure 6.3 The statistical description

The Result of Case Distribution

Run the main_sales.py script. Then, from Features Distribution menu, choose Missing Values item. The result will be displayed as shown in figure 6.4.

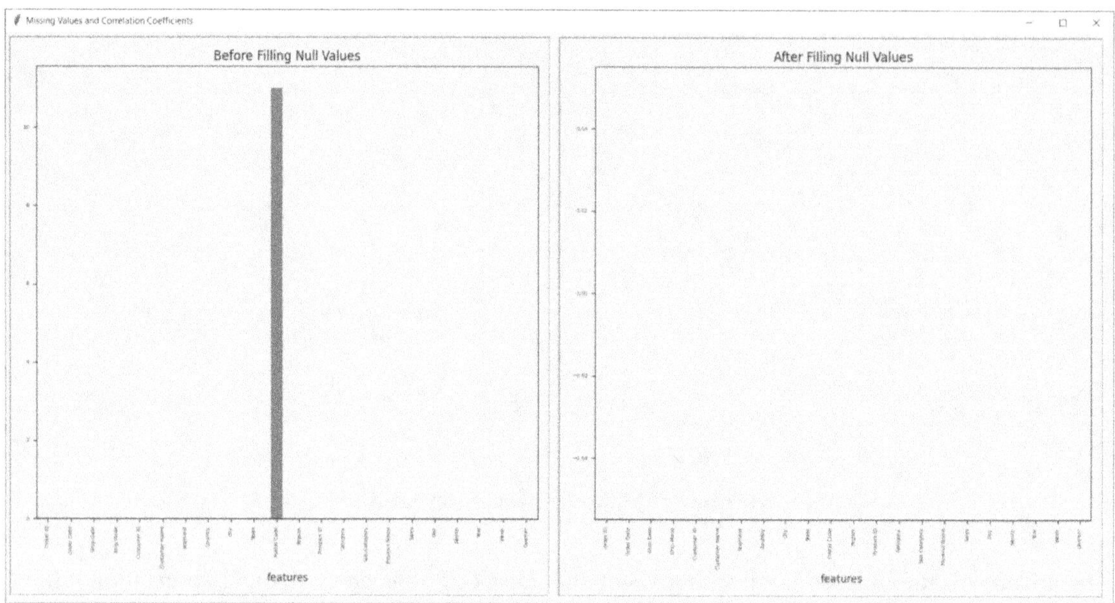

Figure 6.4 The missing values

Then, from Features Distribution menu, choose Day and Month item. The case distribution of day and month will be displayed as shown in figure 6.6.

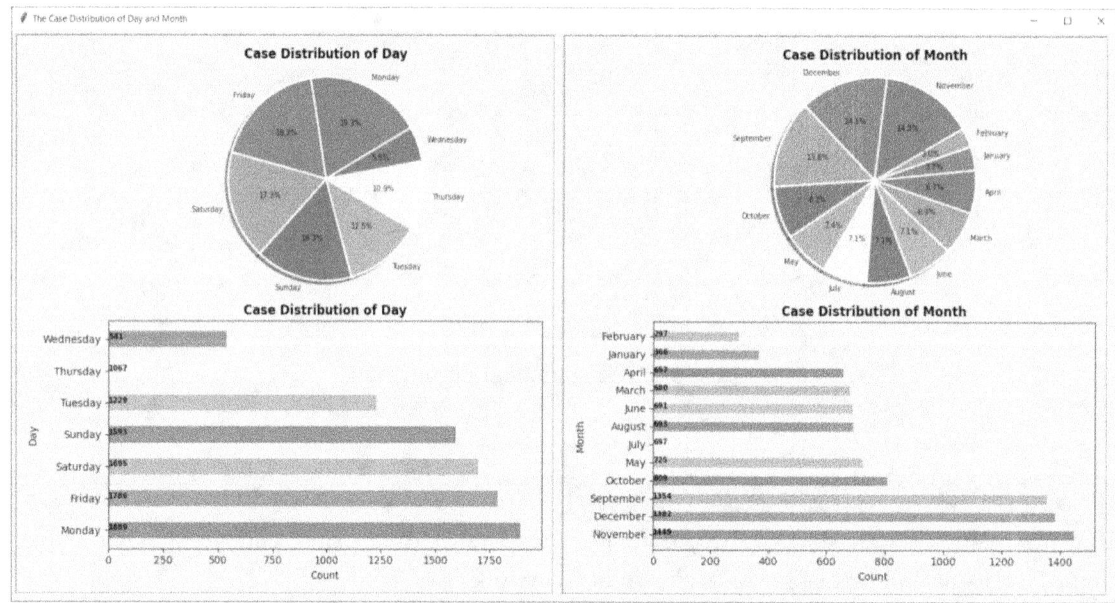

Figure 6.6 The case distribution of dataset by day and month

Then, from Features Distribution menu, choose Quarter and Year item. The case distribution of day and month will be displayed as shown in figure 6.7.

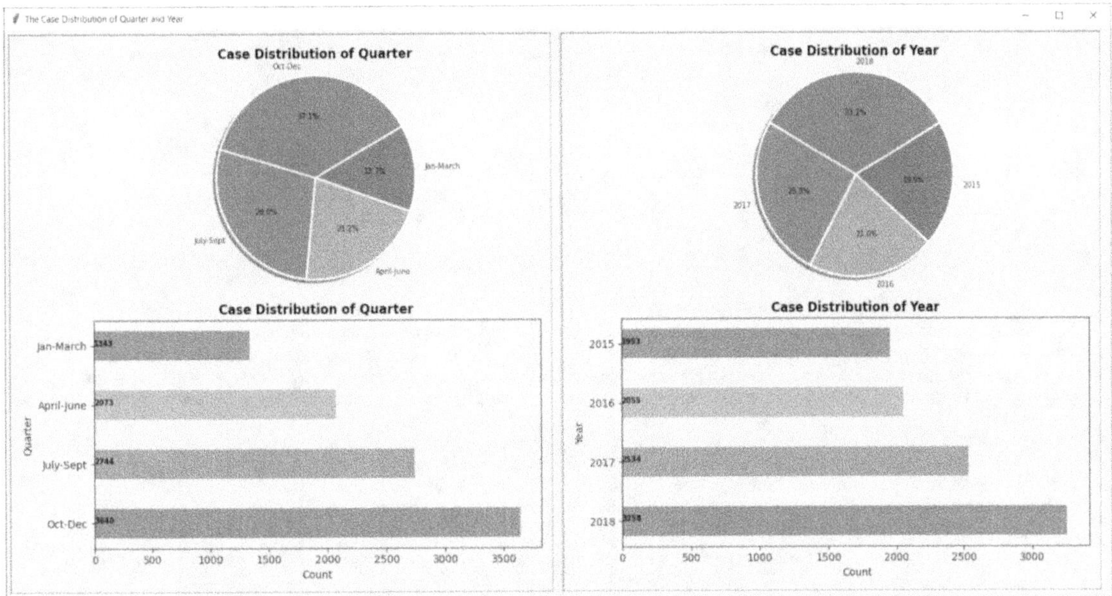

Figure 6.7 The case distribution of dataset by quarter and year

Next, from Features Distribution menu, choose State and Region item. The case distribution of day and month will be displayed as shown in figure 6.8.

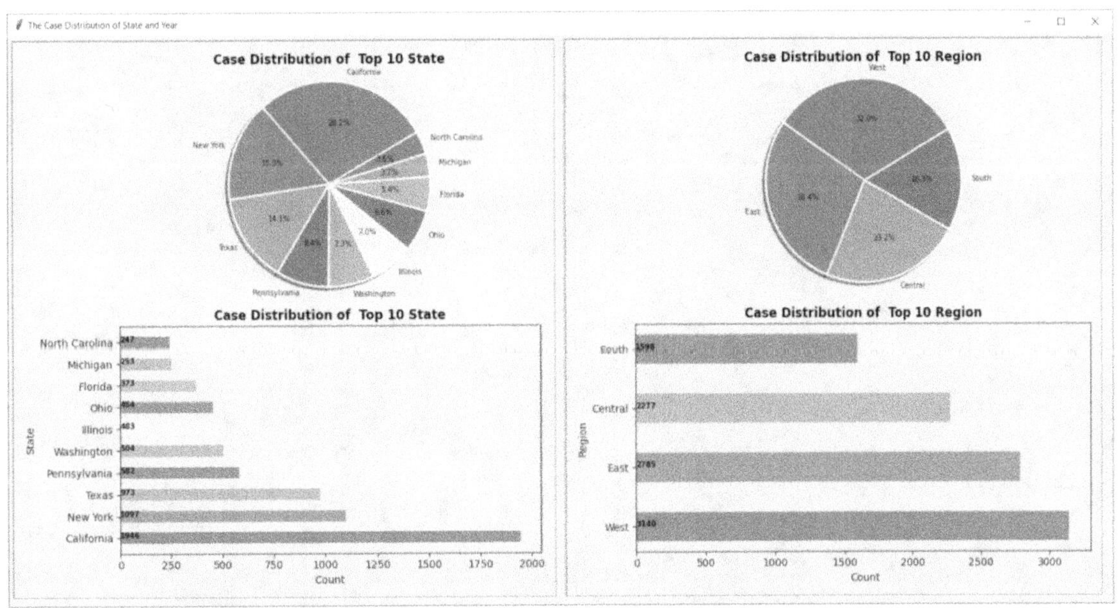

Figure 6.8 The case distribution of dataset by state and region

Next, from Features Distribution menu, choose Customer Name and Customer ID item. The case distribution of day and month will be displayed as shown in figure 6.9.

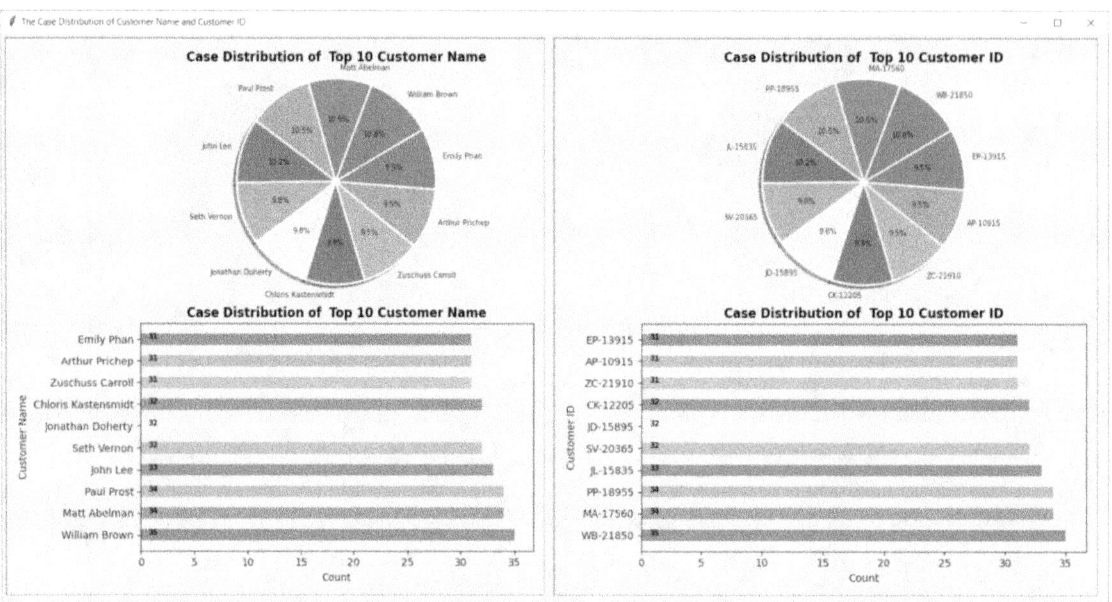

Figure 6.9 The case distribution of dataset by customer and customer id

Next, from Features Distribution menu, choose Ship Mode and Segment item. The case distribution of day and month will be displayed as shown in figure 6.10.

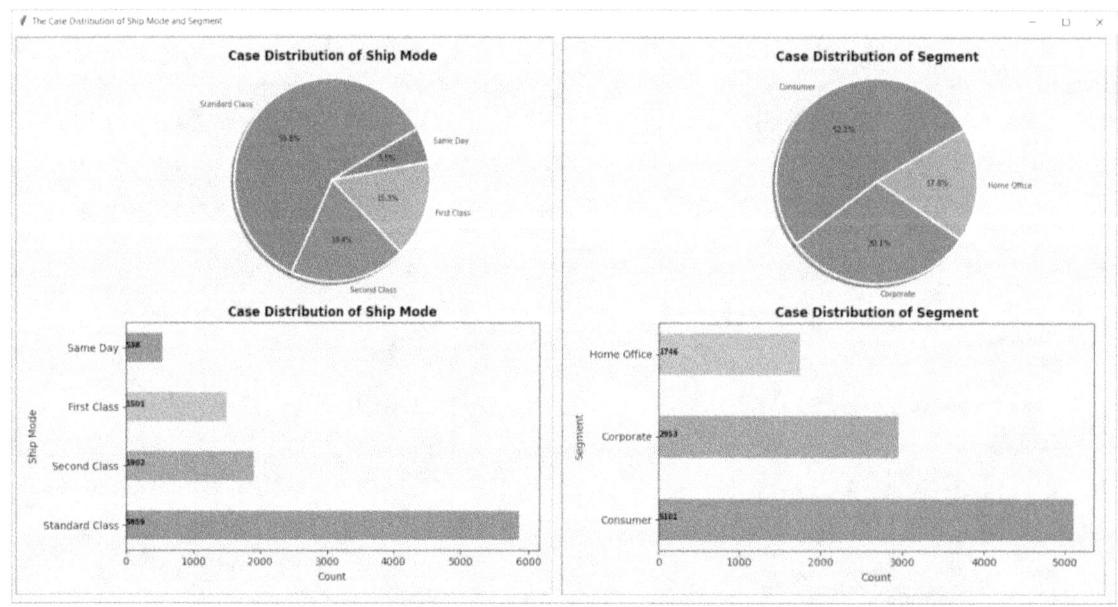

Figure 6.10 The case distribution of dataset by ship mode and segment

Next, from Features Distribution menu, choose Product Name and Product ID item. The case distribution of day and month will be displayed as shown in figure 6.11.

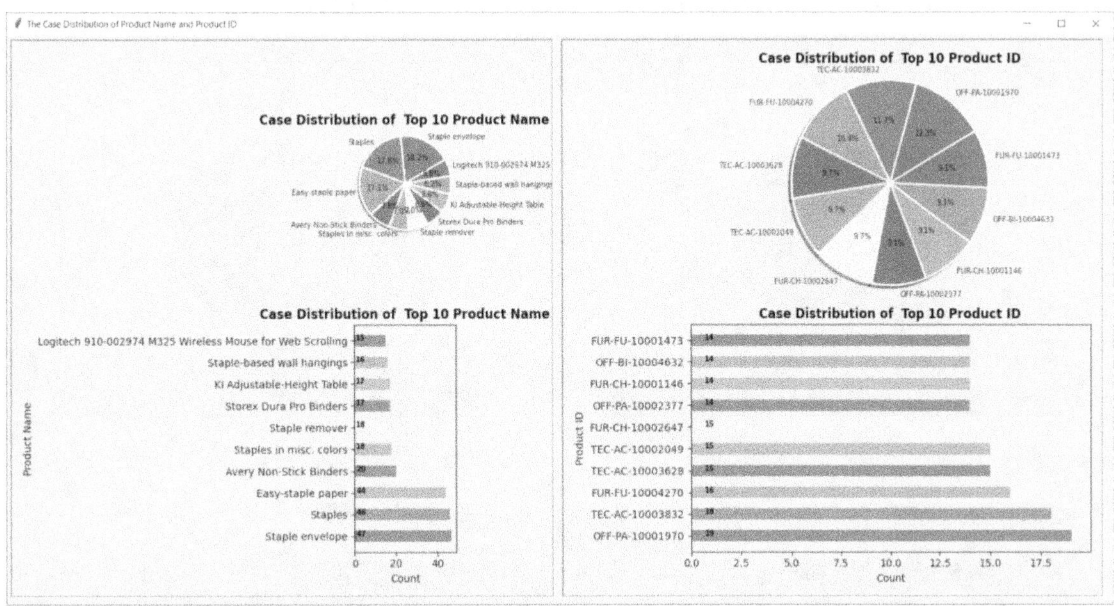

Figure 6.11 The case distribution of dataset by product name and product id

Next, from Features Distribution menu, choose Category and Sub-Category item. The case distribution of day and month will be displayed as shown in figure 6.12.

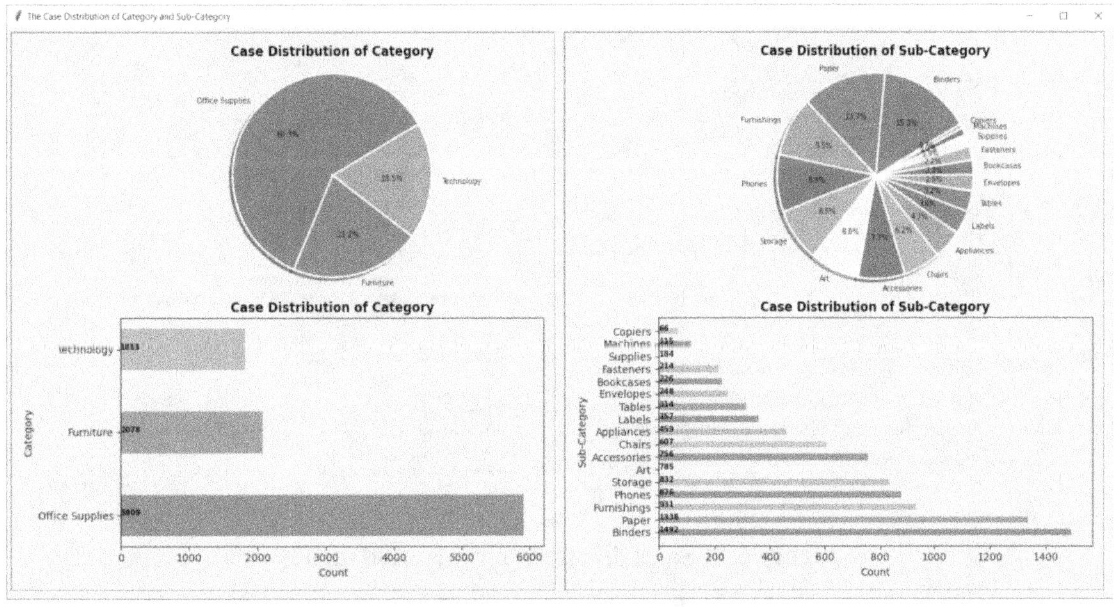

Figure 6.12 The case distribution of dataset by category and sub-category

The Result of Sales Distribution

Run the main_sales.py script. Then, from Categorized Distribution menu, choose Sales by Year and Quarter item. The result will be displayed as shown in figure 6.13.

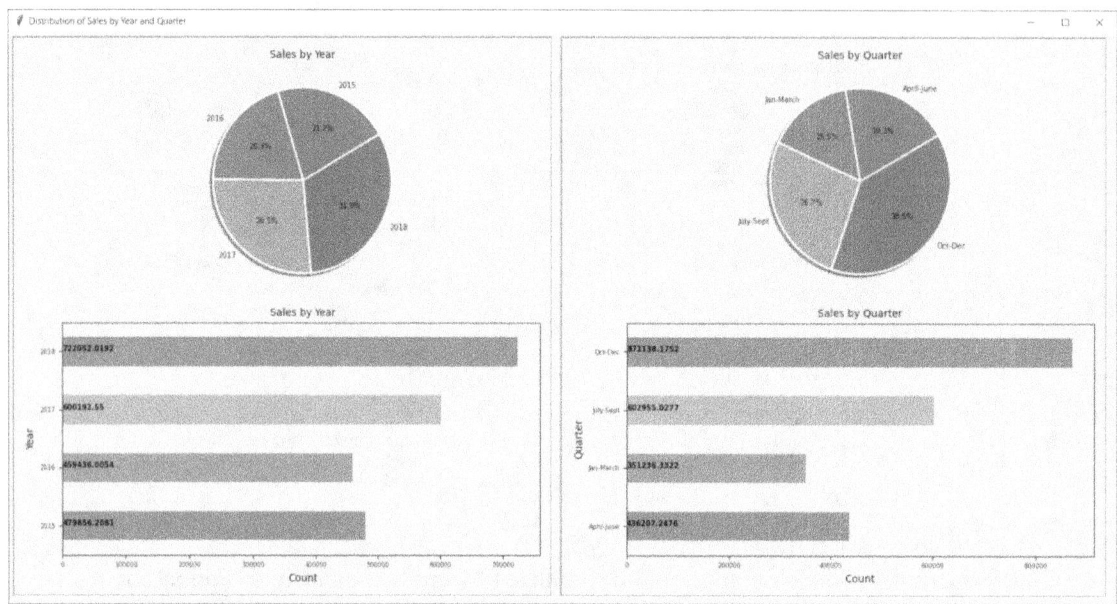

Figure 6.13 Sales distribution by year and quarter

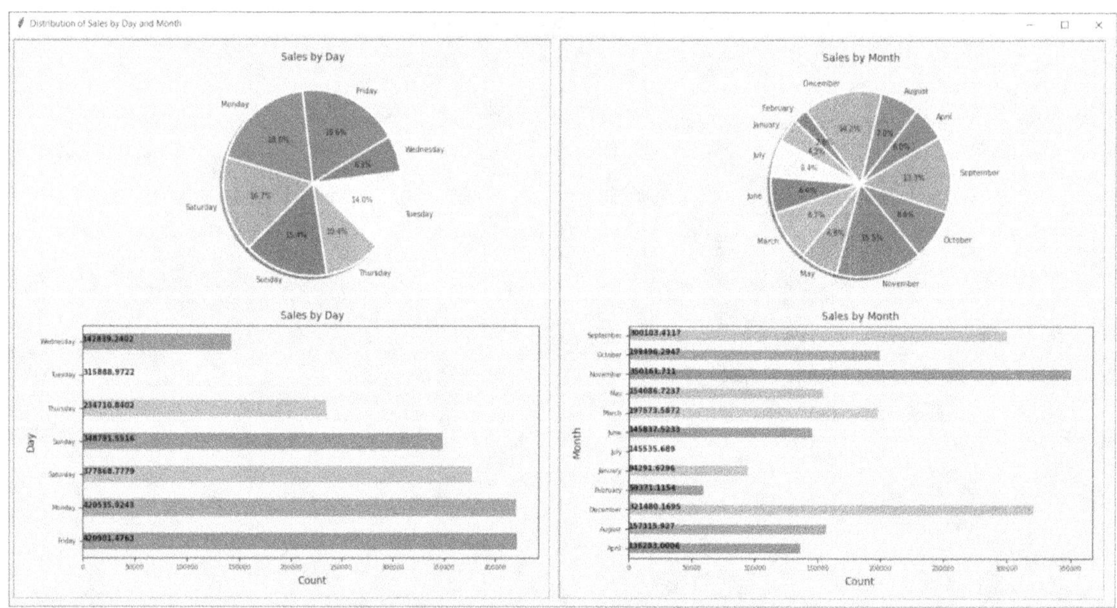

Figure 6.14 Sales distribution by day and month

Next, from Categorized Distribution menu, choose Sales by Day and Month item. The result will be displayed as shown in figure 6.14. Then, from Categorized Distribution menu, choose Sales by Ship Mode and Segment item. The result will be displayed as shown in figure 6.15.

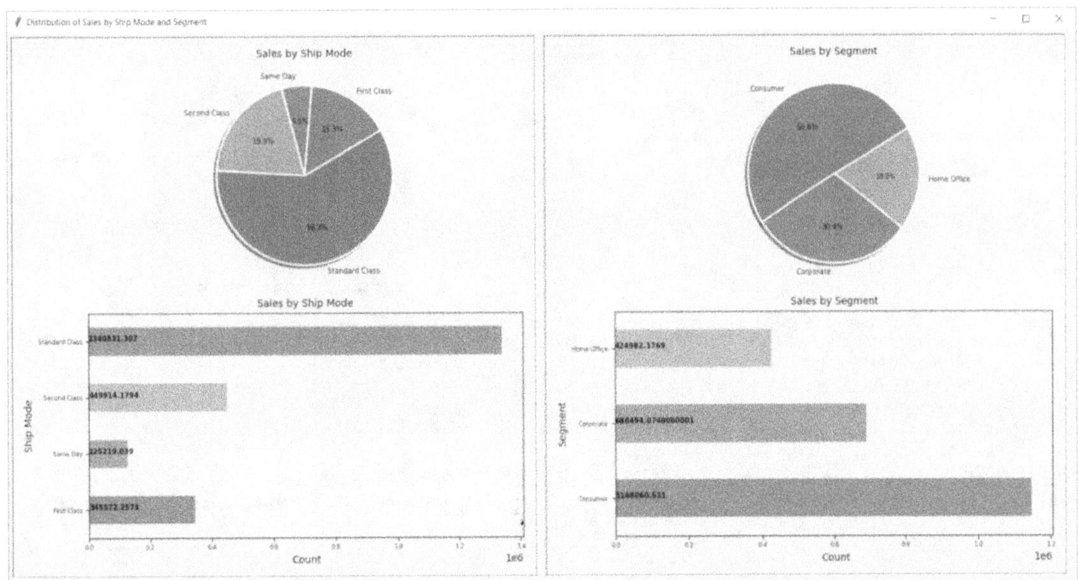

Figure 6.15 Sales distribution by ship mode and segment

Next, from Categorized Distribution menu, choose Sales by Category and Sub-Category item. The result will be displayed as shown in figure 6.15.

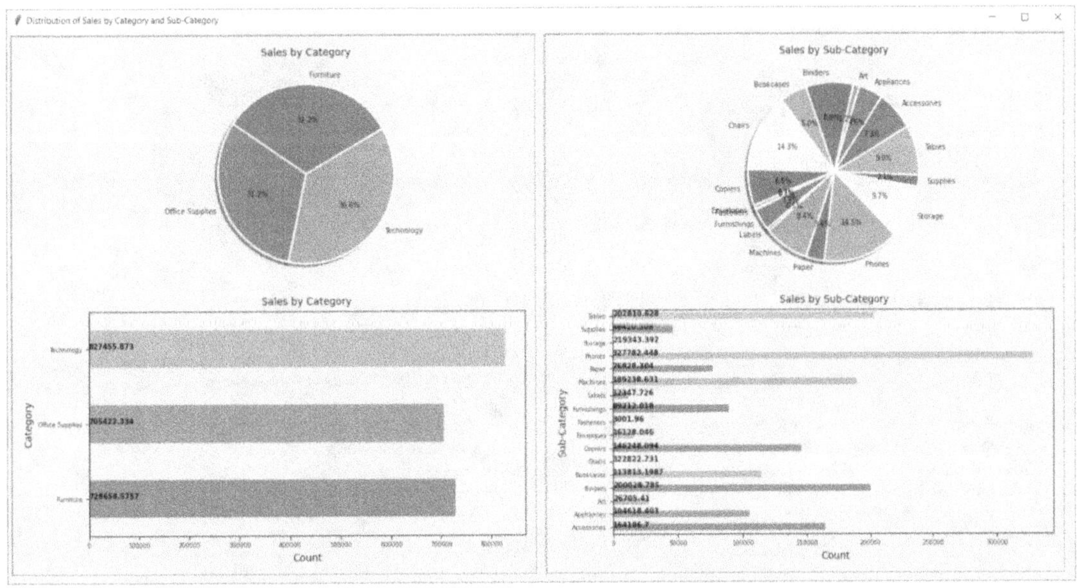

Figure 6.16 Sales distribution by category and sub-category

Next, from Categorized Distribution menu, choose Sales by Product Name and Product ID item. The result will be displayed as shown in figure 6.17.

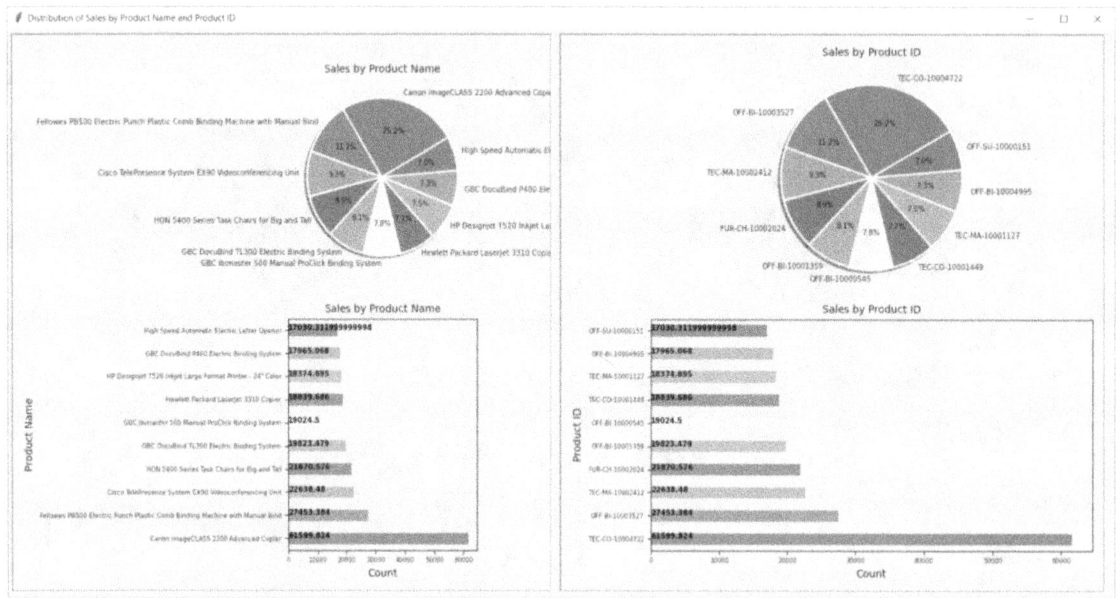

Figure 6.17 Sales distribution by product name and product id

Next, from Categorized Distribution menu, choose Sales by Customer Name and Customer ID item. The result will be displayed as shown in figure 6.18.

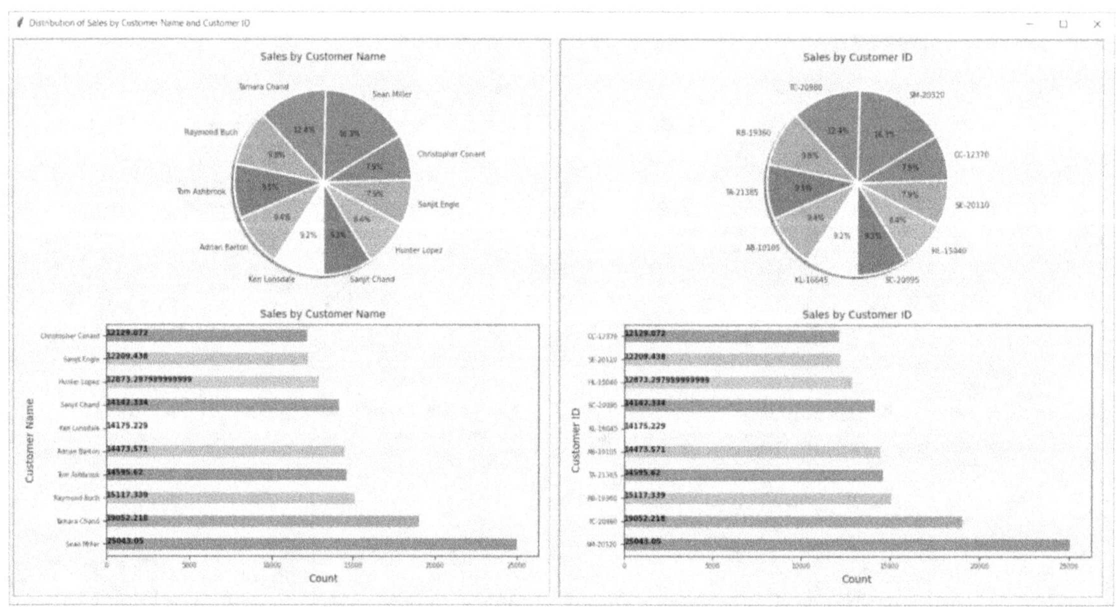

Figure 6.18 Sales distribution by customer name and customer id

Next, from Categorized Distribution menu, choose Sales by City and State item. The result will be displayed as shown in figure 6.19.

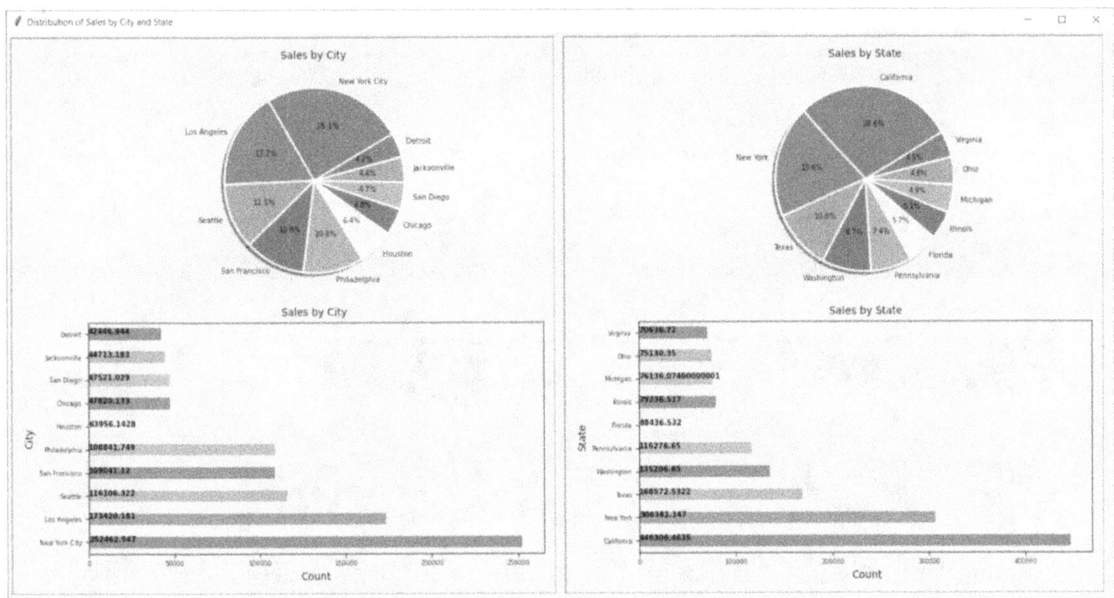

Figure 6.19 Sales distribution by city and state

Next, from Categorized Distribution menu, choose Sales by Categorized Sales item. The result will be displayed as shown in figure 6.20.

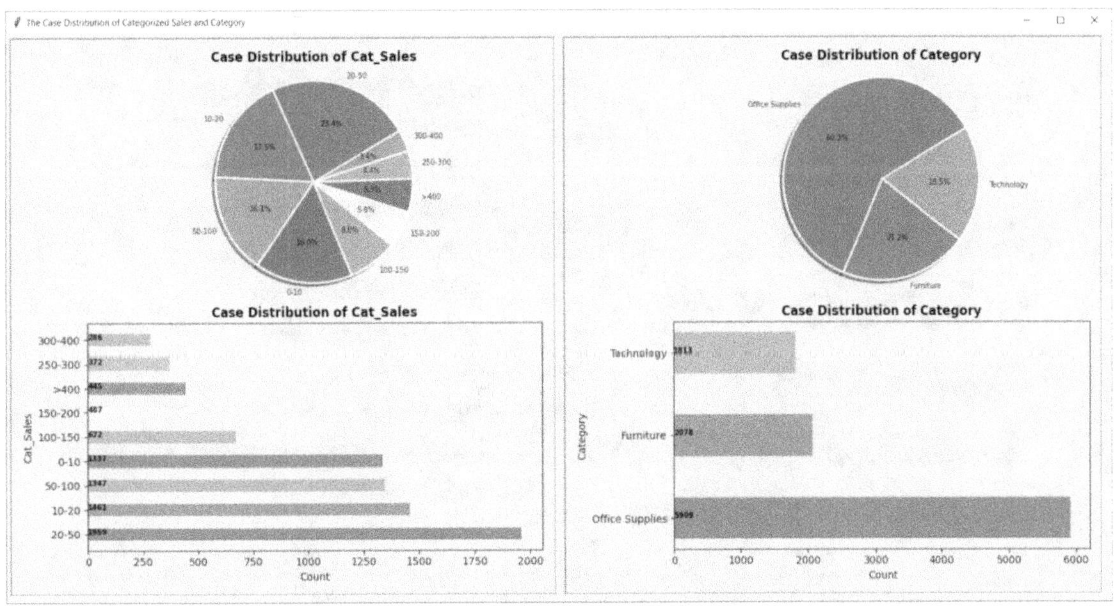

Figure 6.20 The distribution of categorized sales

Next, from Categorized Distribution menu, choose Sales by Categorized Sales by Year and Quarter item. The result will be displayed as shown in figure 6.21.

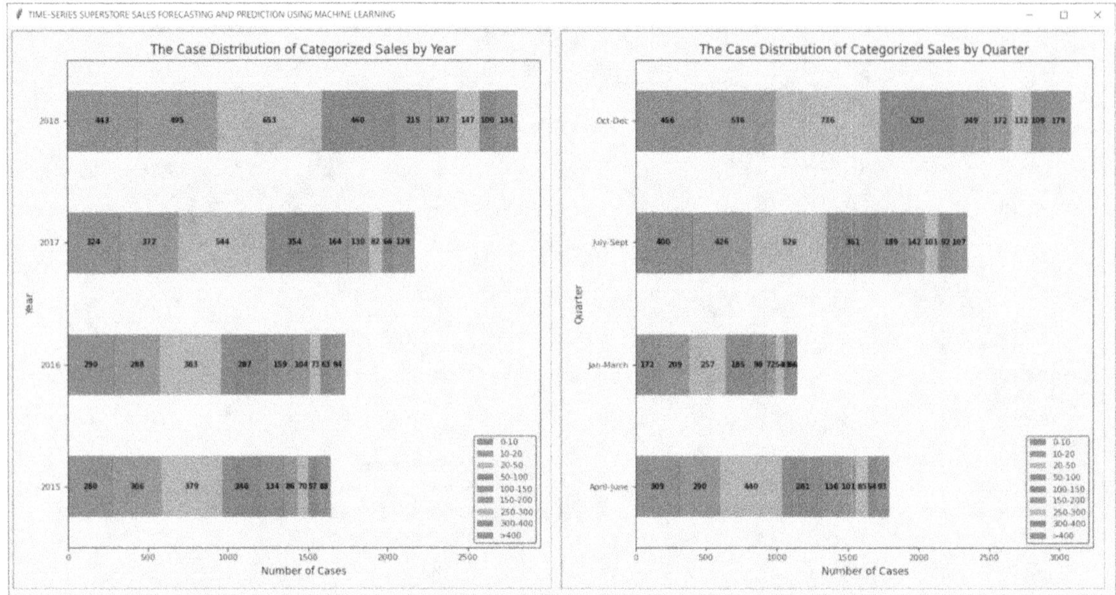

Figure 6.21 The distribution of categorized sales by year and quarter

Next, from Categorized Distribution menu, choose Sales by Categorized Sales by Day and Month item. The result will be displayed as shown in figure 6.22.

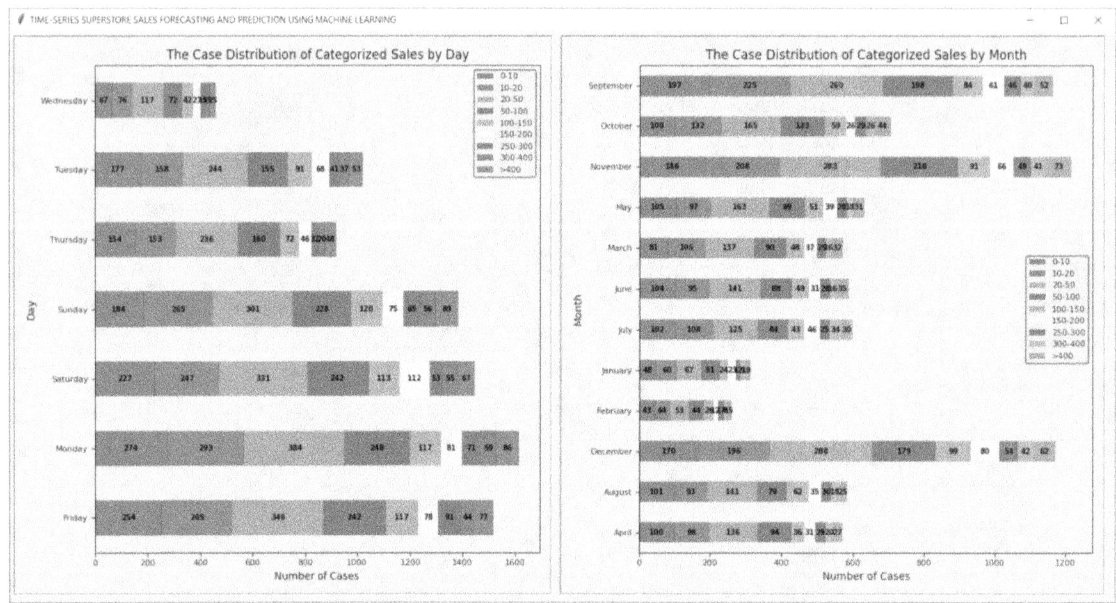

Figure 6.22 The distribution of categorized sales by day and month

Next, from Categorized Distribution menu, choose Sales by Categorized Sales by Segment and Sub-Category item. The result will be displayed as shown in figure 6.23.

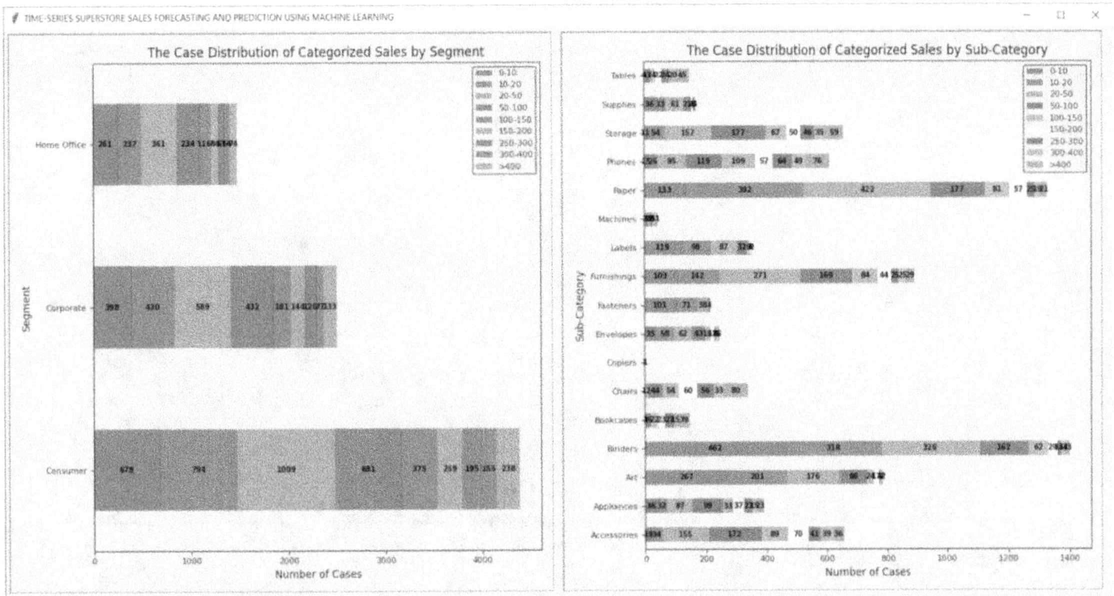

Figure 6.23 The distribution of categorized sales by segment and sub-category

Next, from Categorized Distribution menu, choose Sales by Categorized Sales by Region and State item. The result will be displayed as shown in figure 6.24.

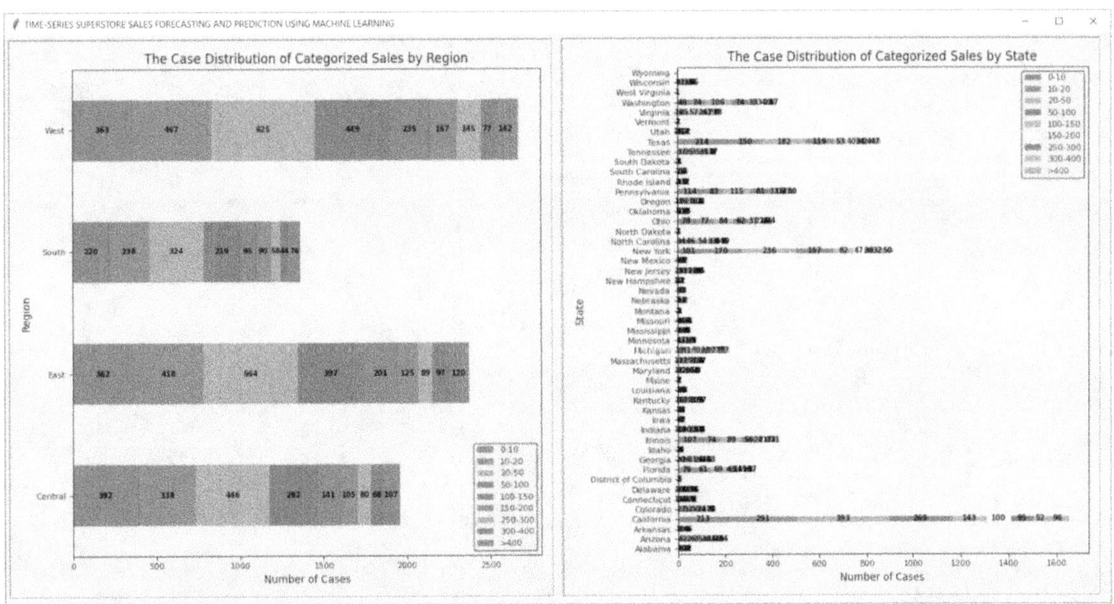

Figure 6.24 The distribution of categorized sales by region and state

Next, from Categorized Distribution menu, choose Sales by Day versus Sales per Category item. The result will be displayed as shown in figure 6.25.

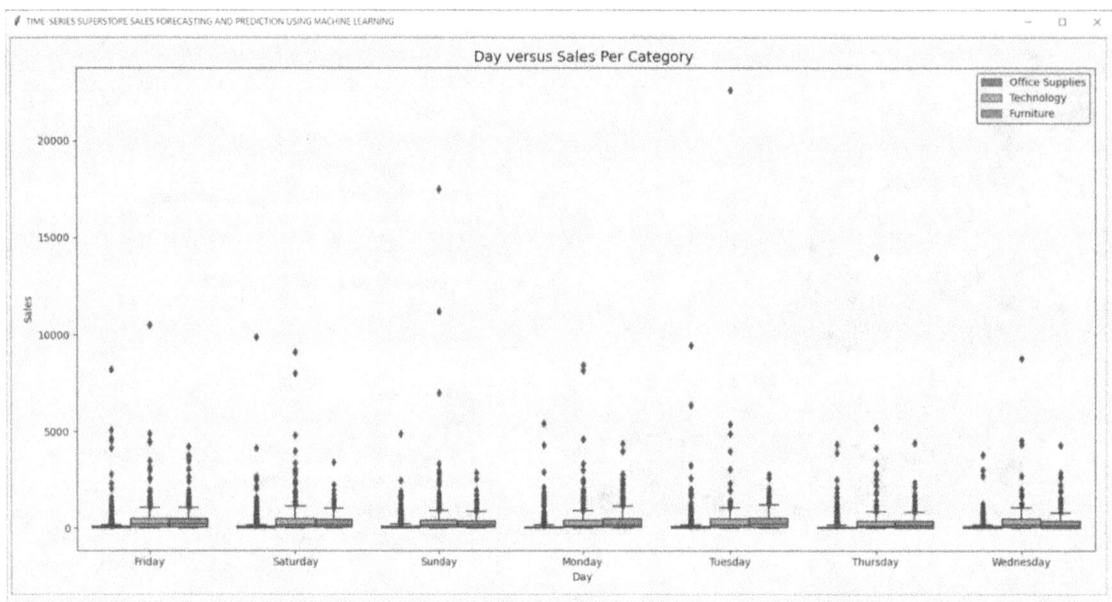

Figure 6.25 The distribution of sales by day per category

Next, from Categorized Distribution menu, choose Sales by Month versus Sales per Segment item. The result will be displayed as shown in figure 6.26.

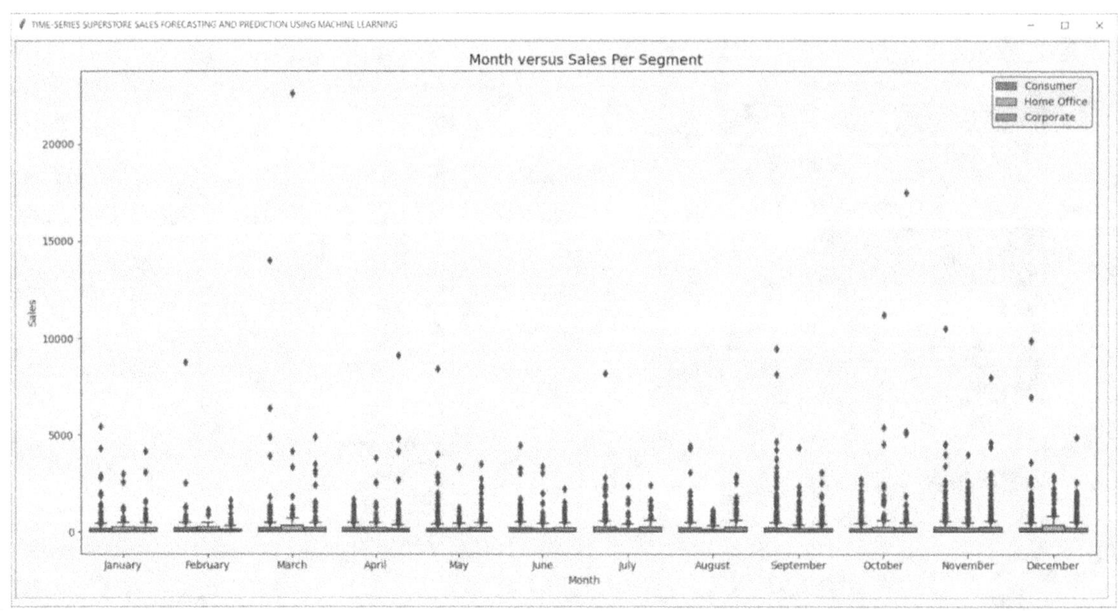

Figure 6.26 The distribution of sales by month per segment

Next, from Categorized Distribution menu, choose Sales by Region versus Sales per Quarter item. The result will be displayed as shown in figure 6.27.

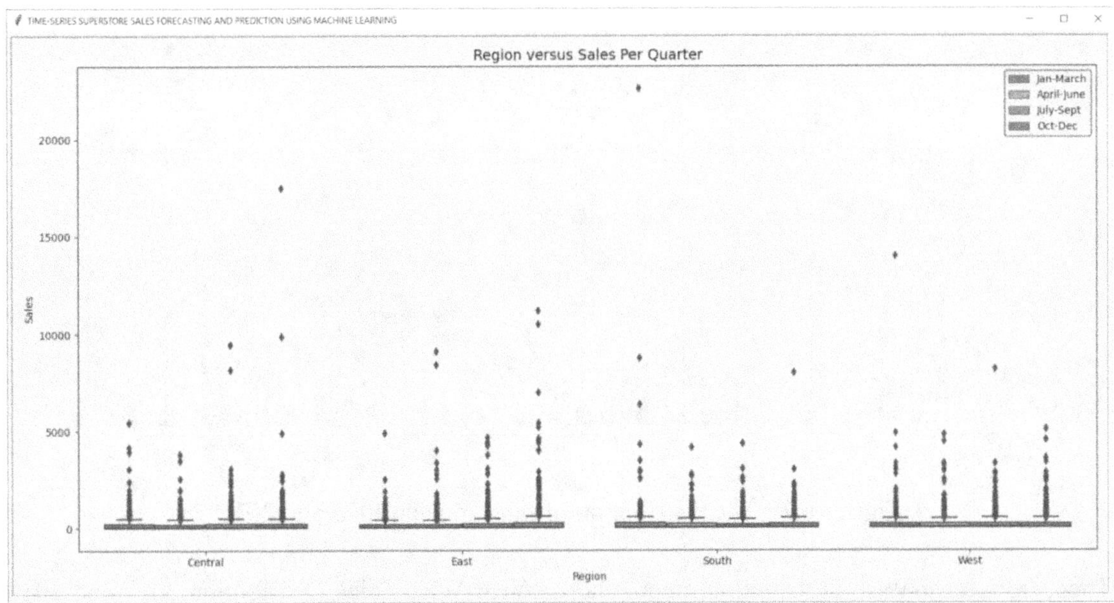

Figure 6.27 The distribution of sales by region per quarter

The Result of Year-Wise Sales Distribution

Run the main_sales.py script. Then, from Year-Wise Distribution menu, choose Year-Wise Sales Distribution 2015 and 2016 item. The result will be displayed as shown in figure 6.28.

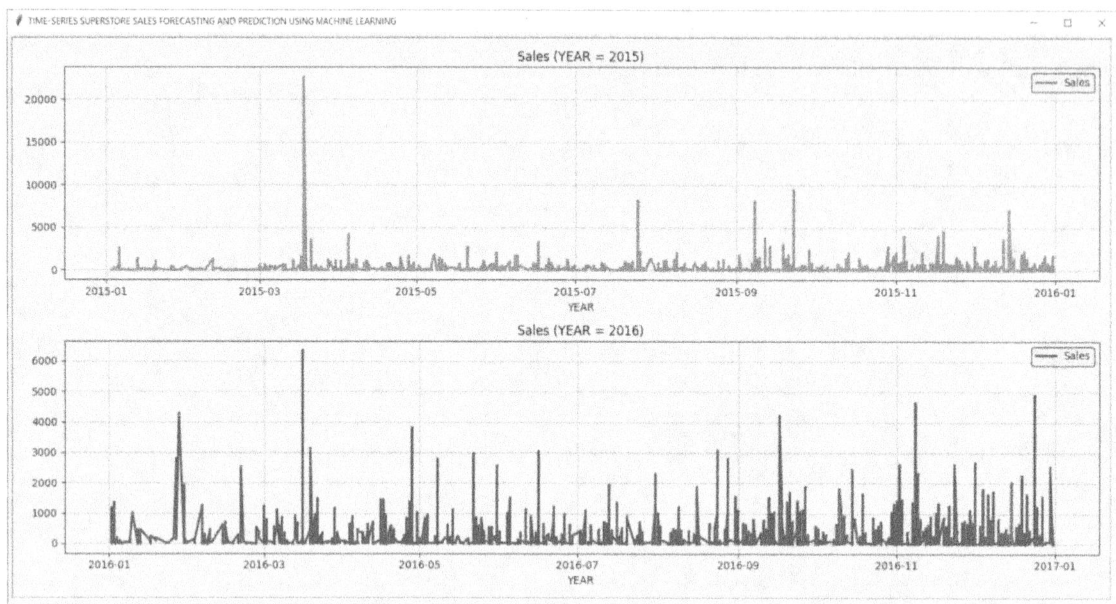

Figure 6.28 The distribution of sales in year 2015 and 2016

Then, from Year-Wise Distribution menu, choose Year-Wise Sales Distribution 2017 and 2018 item. The result will be displayed as shown in figure 6.29.

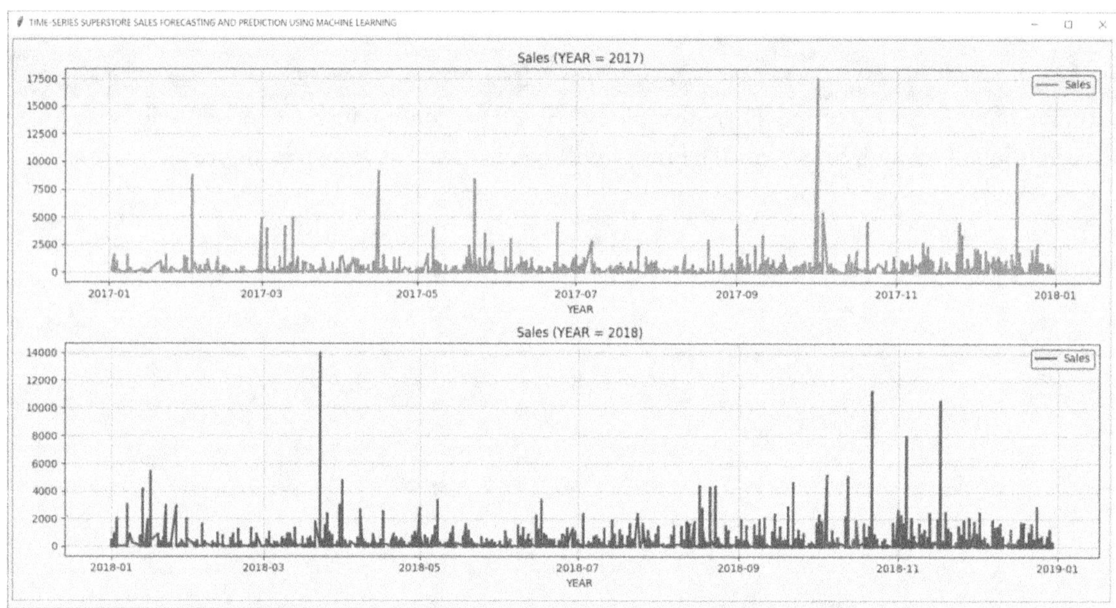

Figure 6.29 The distribution of sales in year 2017 and 2018

Next, from Year-Wise Distribution menu, choose Year-Wise Sales Mean and EWM item. The result will be displayed as shown in figure 6.30.

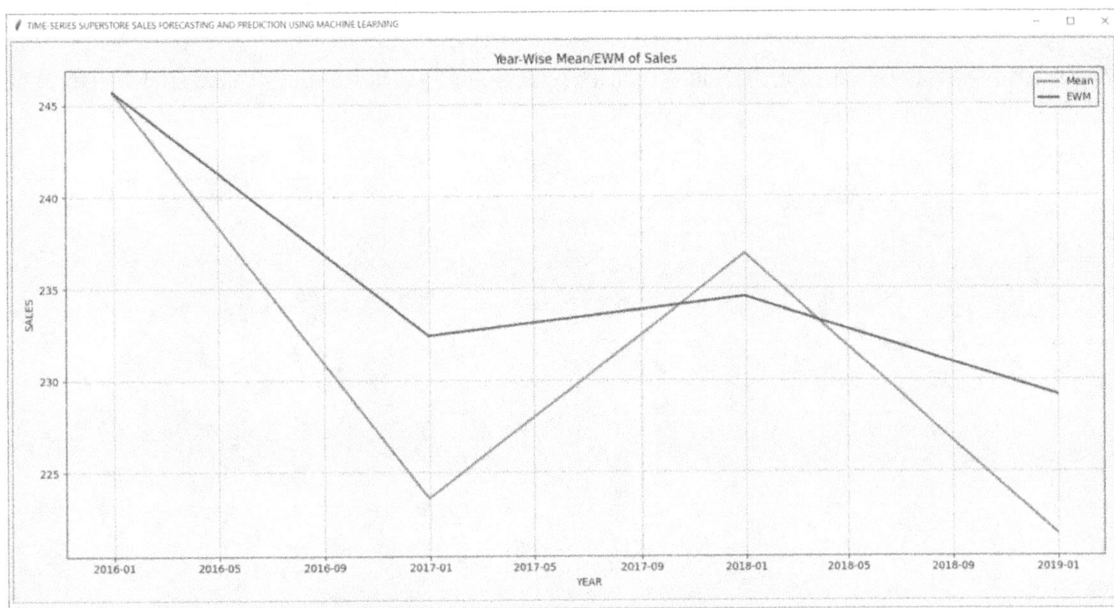

Figure 6.30 Year-wise sales by mean and EWM

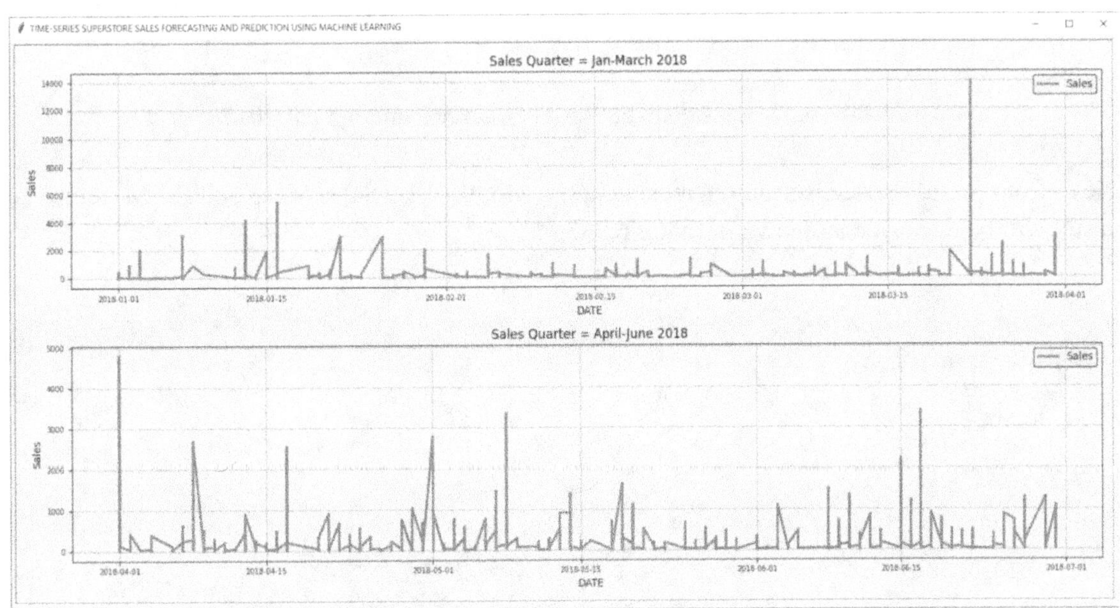

Figure 6.31 Sales distribution in Quarter 1 and 2 Year 2018

The Result of Month-Wise Sales Distribution

Run the main_sales.py script. Then, from Month-Wise Distribution menu, choose Sales Quarter 1 and 2 Year 2018 item. The result will be displayed as shown in figure 6.31.

Next, from Month-Wise Distribution menu, choose Sales Quarter 3 and 4 Year 2017 item. The result will be displayed as shown in figure 6.32.

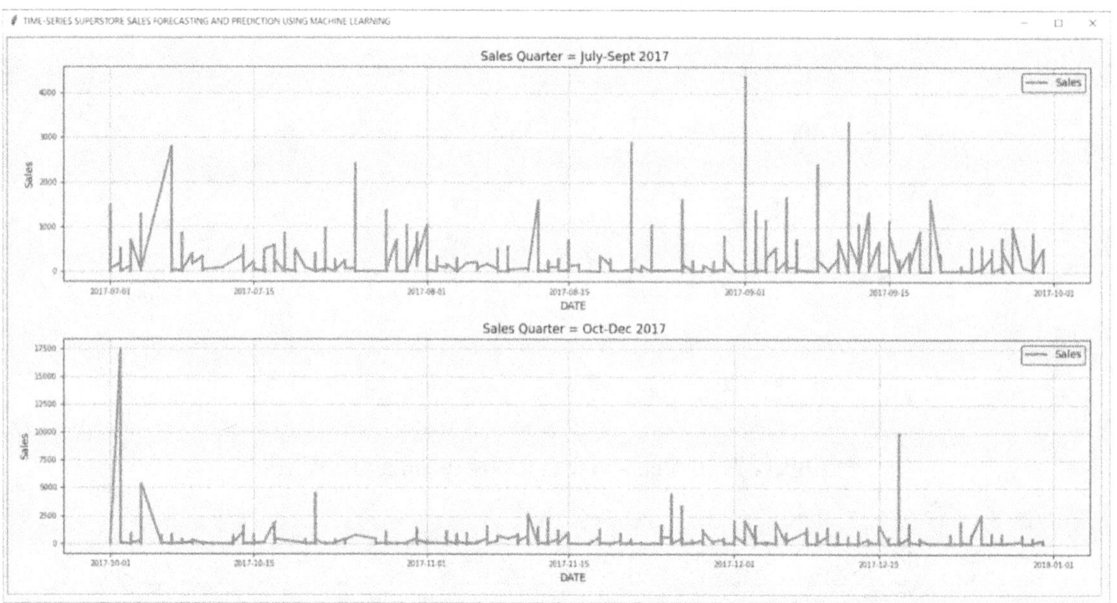

Figure 6.32 Sales distribution in Quarter 3 and 4 Year 2017

Next, from Month-Wise Distribution menu, choose Month-Wise Sales Mean and EWM item. The result will be displayed as shown in figure 6.33.

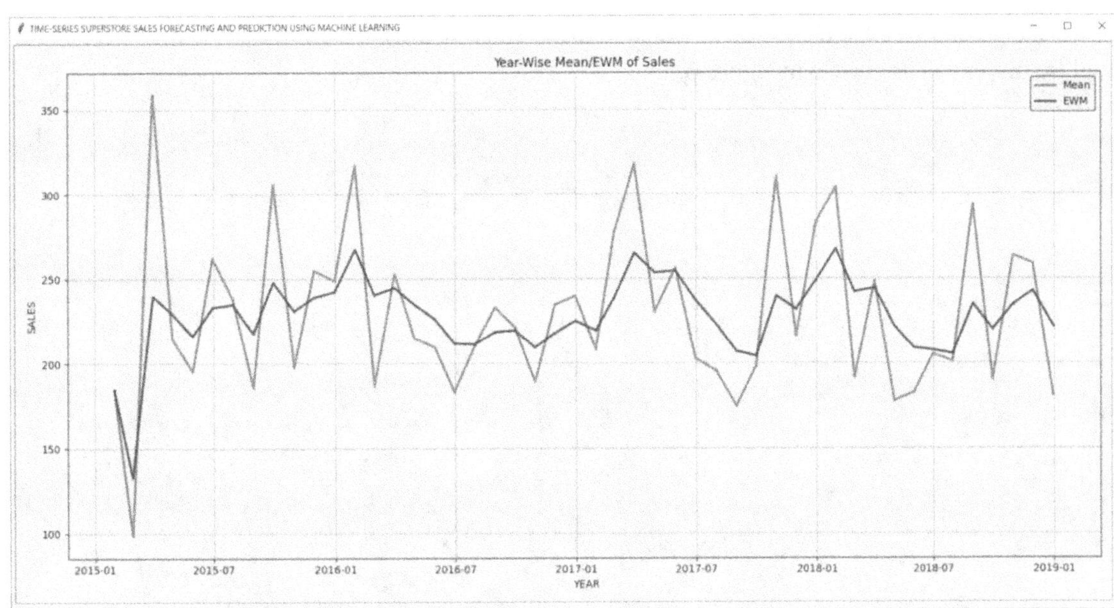

Figure 6.33 Sales Month-Wise Sales by Mean and EWM

Next, from Month-Wise Distribution menu, choose Sales by Month item. The result will be displayed as shown in figure 6.34.

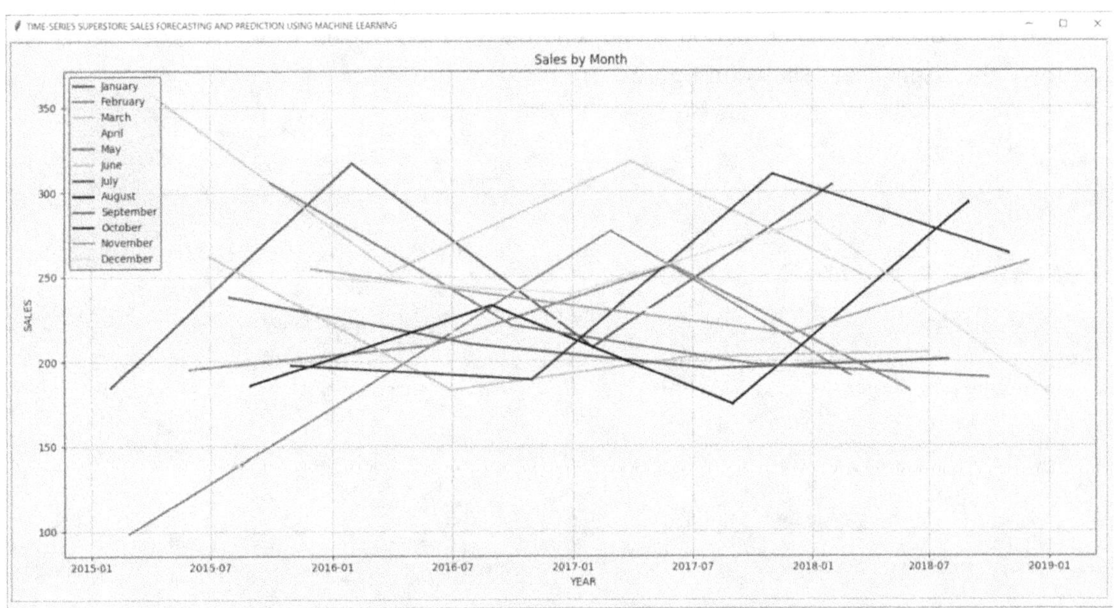

Figure 6.34 The sales distribution by month across years

Next, from Month-Wise Distribution menu, choose Region-Based Monthly Sales item. The result will be displayed as shown in figure 6.35.

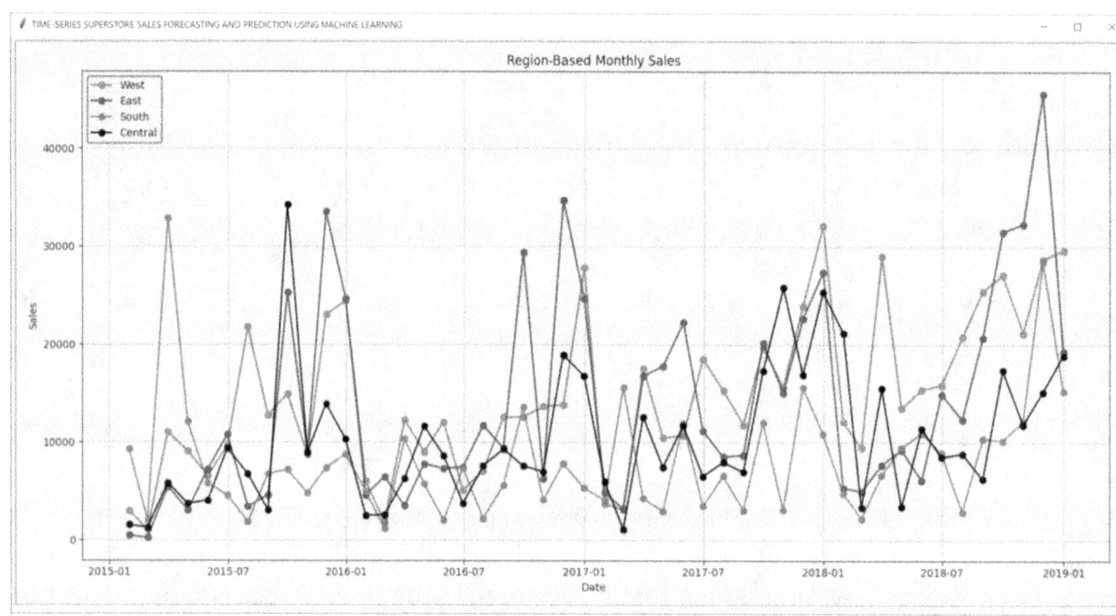

Figure 6.35 The region-based monthly sales

Next, from Month-Wise Distribution menu, choose Segment-Based Monthly Sales item. The result will be displayed as shown in figure 6.36.

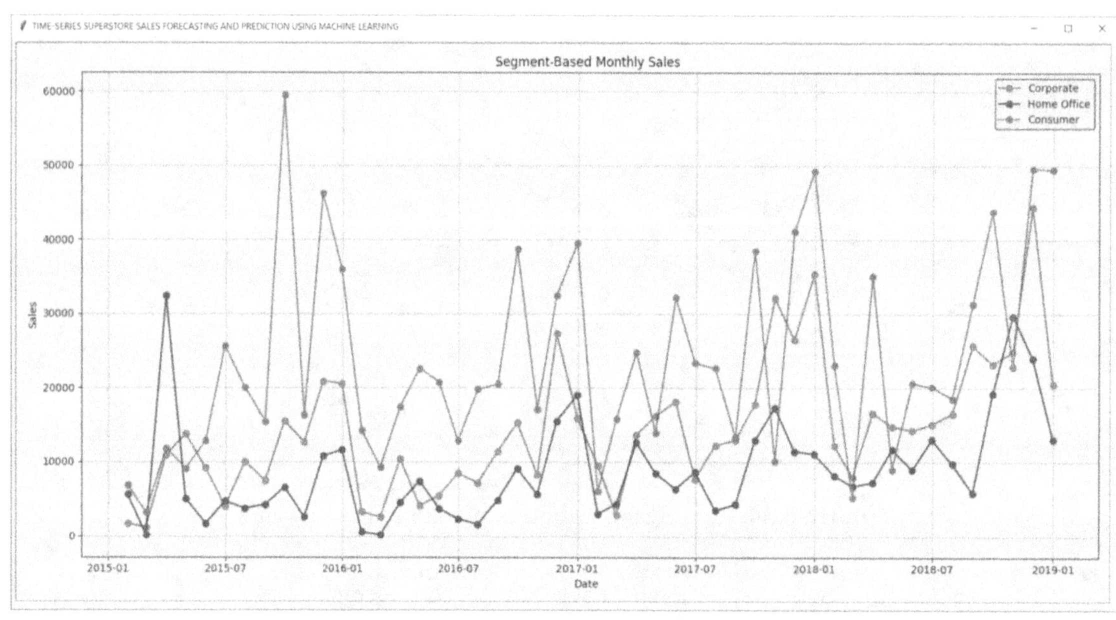

Figure 6.36 The segment-based monthly sales

Next, from Month-Wise Distribution menu, choose City-Based Monthly Sales item. The result will be displayed as shown in figure 6.37.

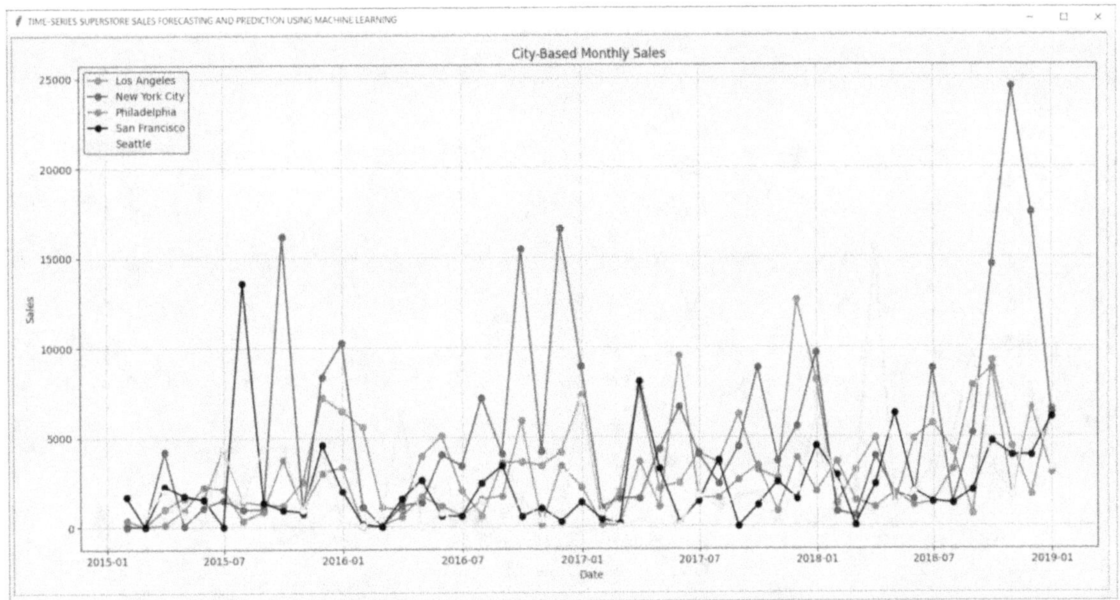

Figure 6.37 The city-based monthly sales

Next, from Month-Wise Distribution menu, choose Ship Mode-Based Monthly Sales item. The result will be displayed as shown in figure 6.38.

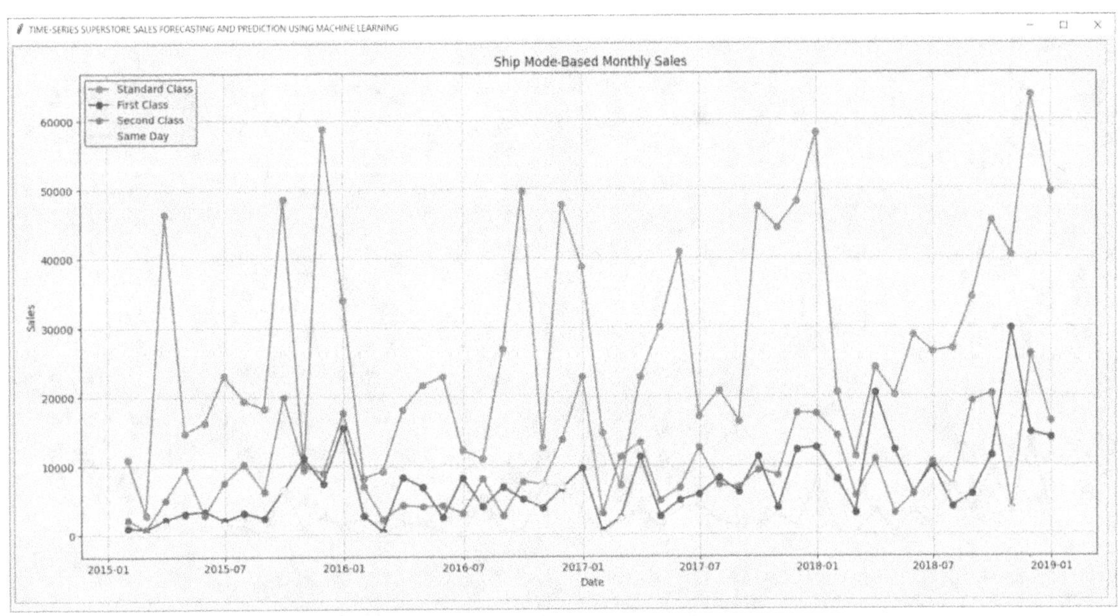

Figure 6.38 The ship mode-based monthly sales

Next, from Month-Wise Distribution menu, choose Product Name-Based Monthly Sales item. The result will be displayed as shown in figure 6.39.

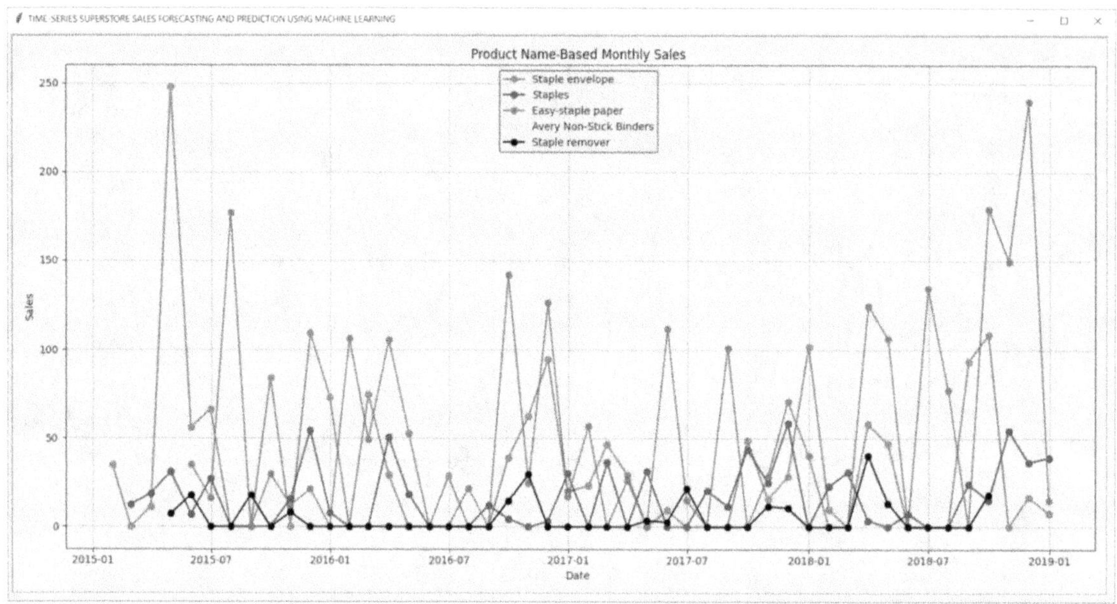

Figure 6.39 The product name-based monthly sales

Next, from Month-Wise Distribution menu, choose Sub-Category-Based Monthly Sales item. The result will be displayed as shown in figure 6.40.

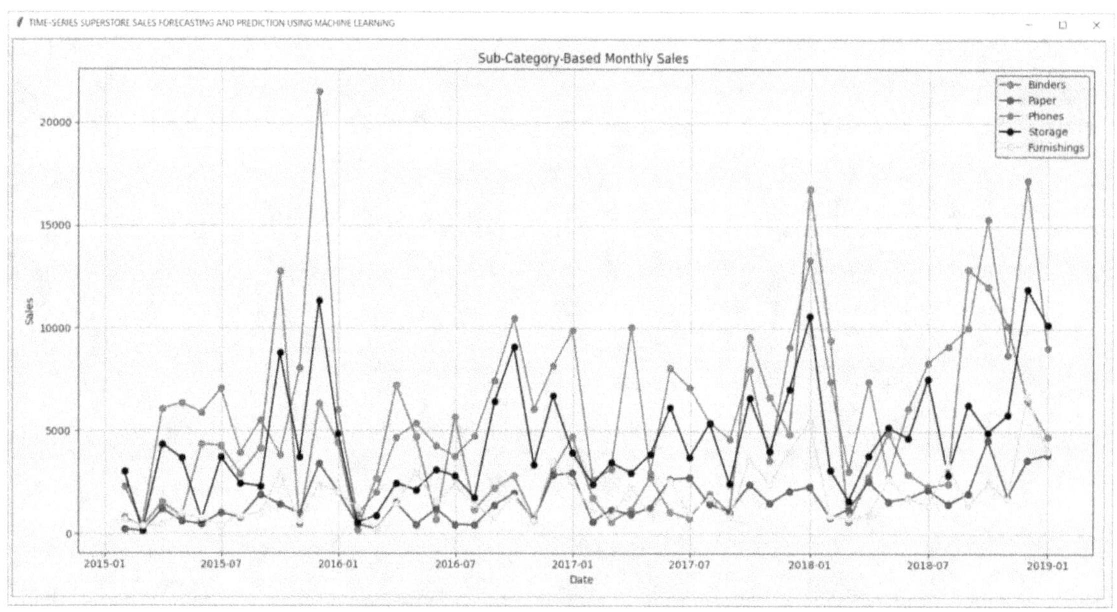

Figure 6.40 The sub-category-based monthly sales

The Result of RFM Analysis

The Result of RFM Analysis

Run the main_sales.py script. Then, from RFM and Product Analysis menu, choose Customer Segment item. The result will be displayed as shown in figure 6.41.

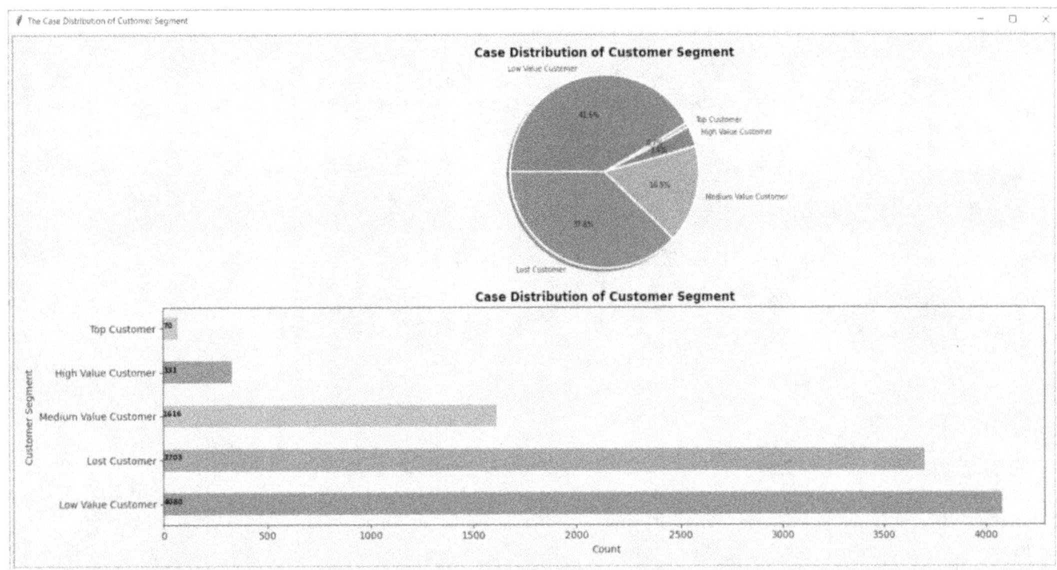

Figure 6.41 The customer segments as a product of RFM analysis

Then, from RFM and Product Analysis menu, choose Sales by Customer Segment item. The result will be displayed as shown in figure 6.42.

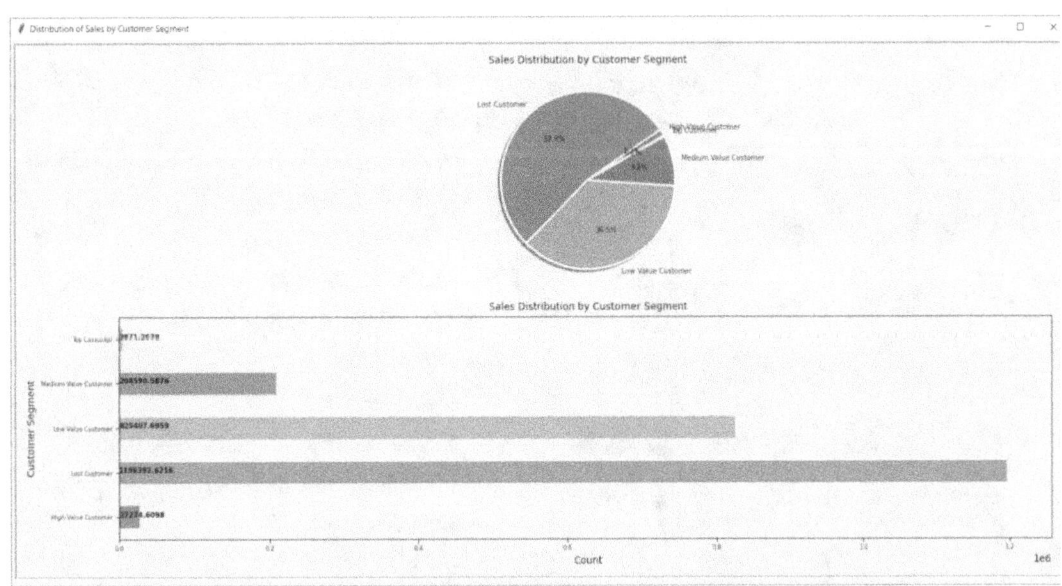

Figure 6.42 The sales distribution by customer segments

Next, from RFM and Product Analysis menu, choose Customer Segment by Year and Quarter item. The result will be displayed as shown in figure 6.43.

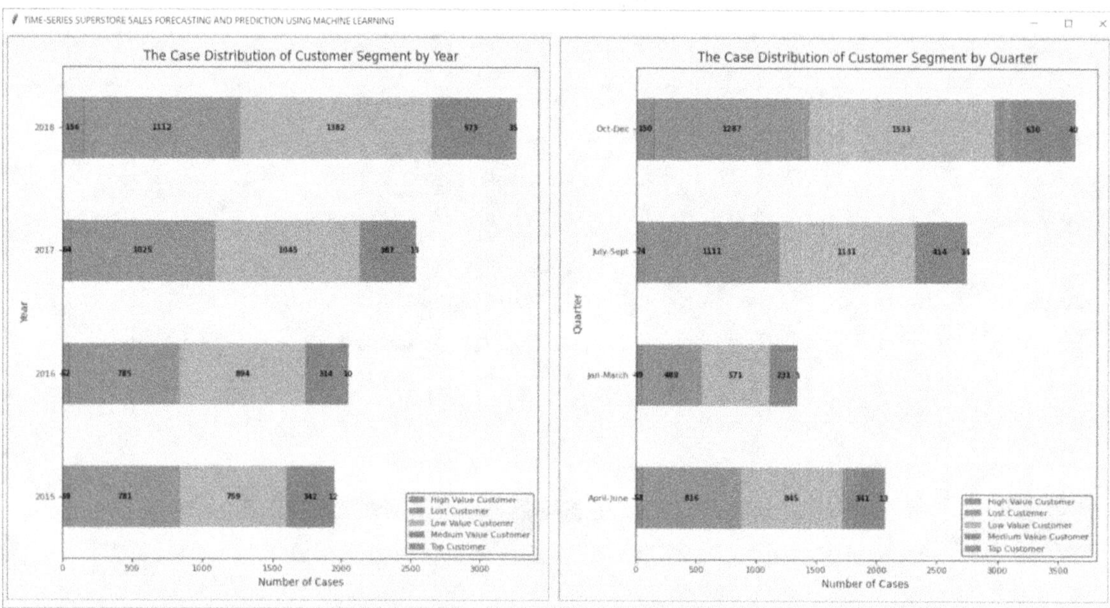

Figure 6.43 The case distribution of customer segments by year and quarter

Next, from RFM and Product Analysis menu, choose Customer Segment by Day and Month item. The result will be displayed as shown in figure 6.44.

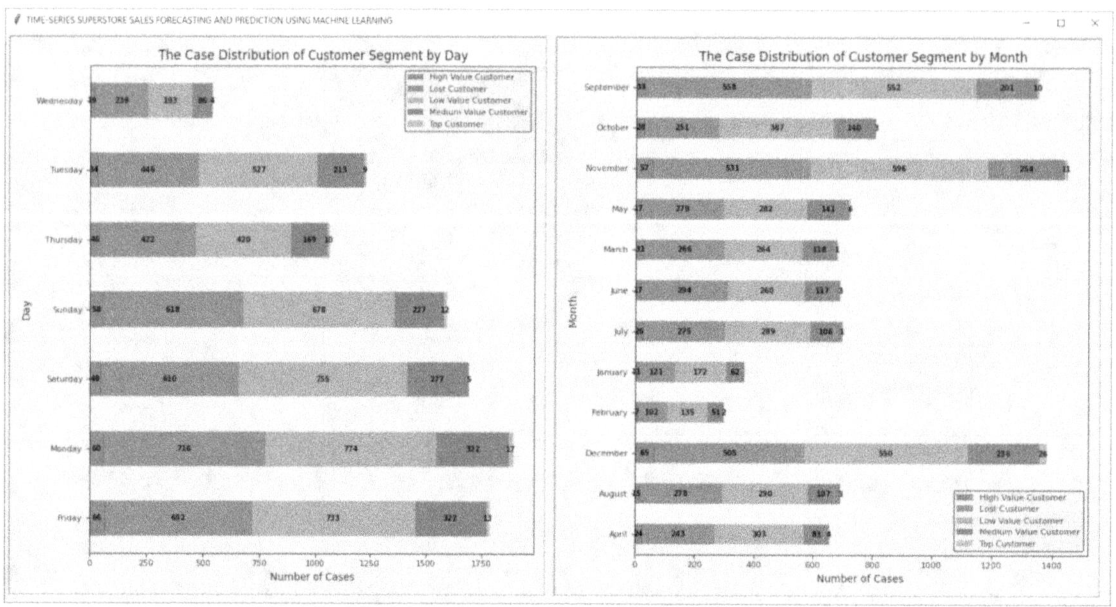

Figure 6.44 The case distribution of customer segments by day and month

Next, from RFM and Product Analysis menu, choose Customer Segment by Segment and Sub-Category item. The result will be displayed as shown in figure 6.45.

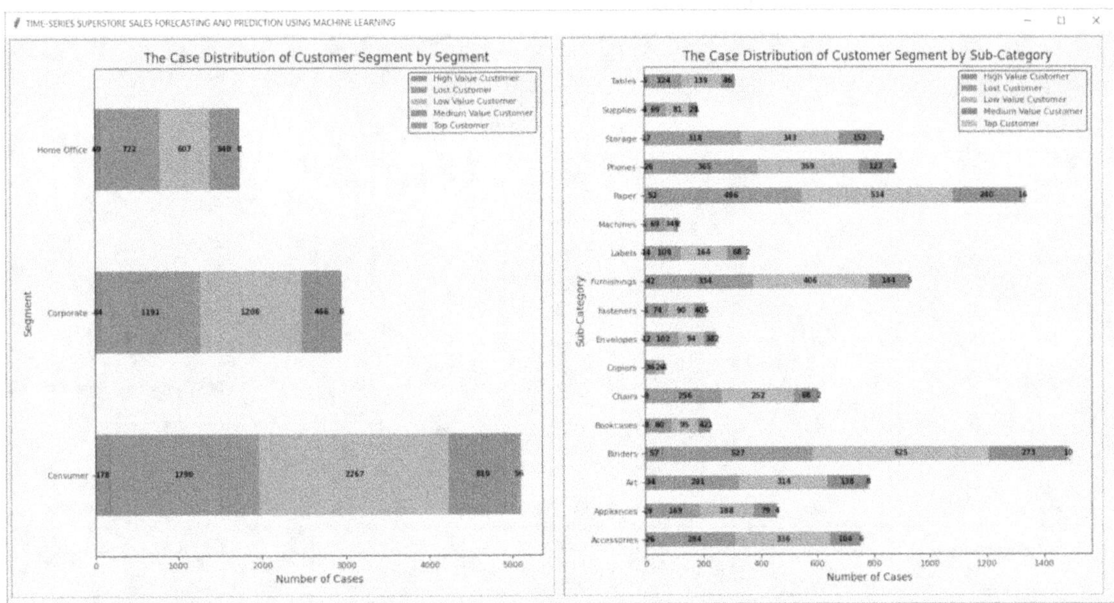

Figure 6.45 The case distribution of customer segments by segment and sub-category

Next, from RFM and Product Analysis menu, choose Customer Segment by Region and State item. The result will be displayed as shown in figure 6.46.

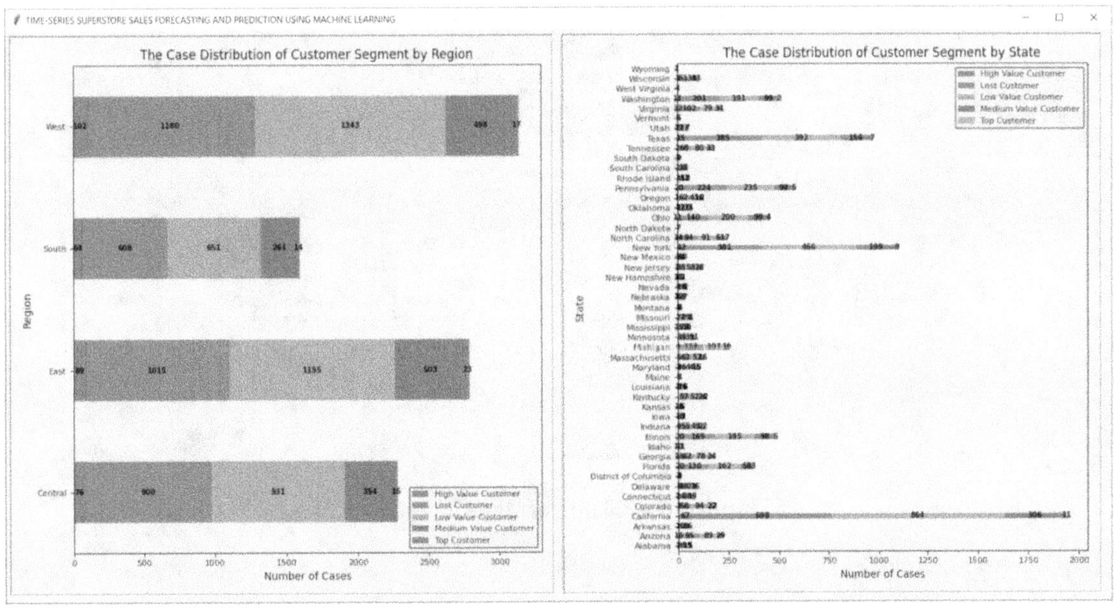

Figure 6.46 The case distribution of customer segments by region and state

Next, from RFM and Product Analysis menu, choose RFM-Based Monthly Sales item. The result will be displayed as shown in figure 6.47.

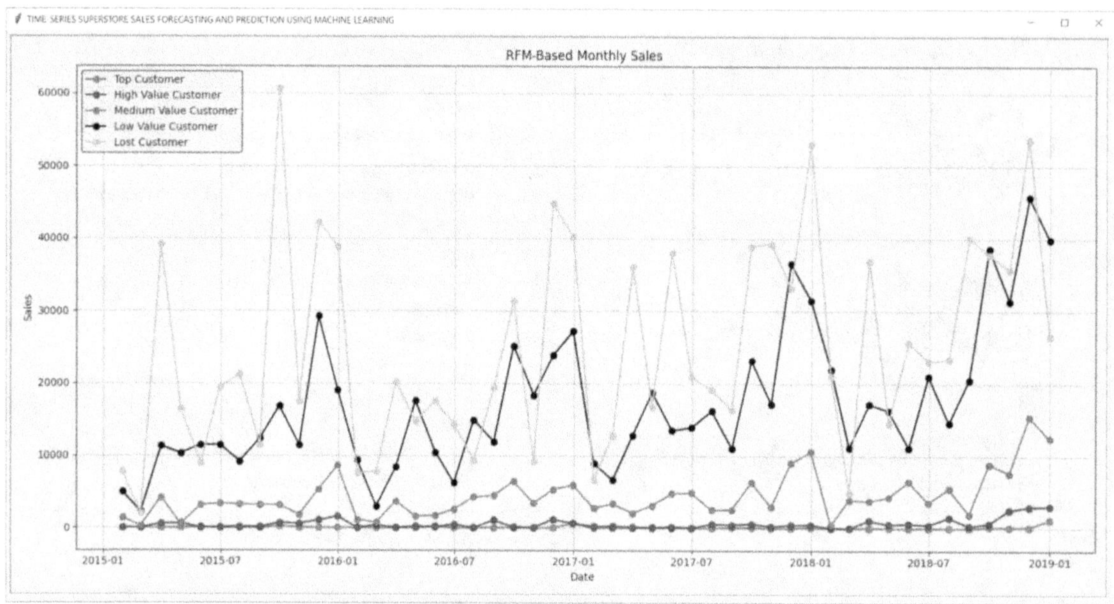

Figure 6.47 The sales distribution of customer segments by month

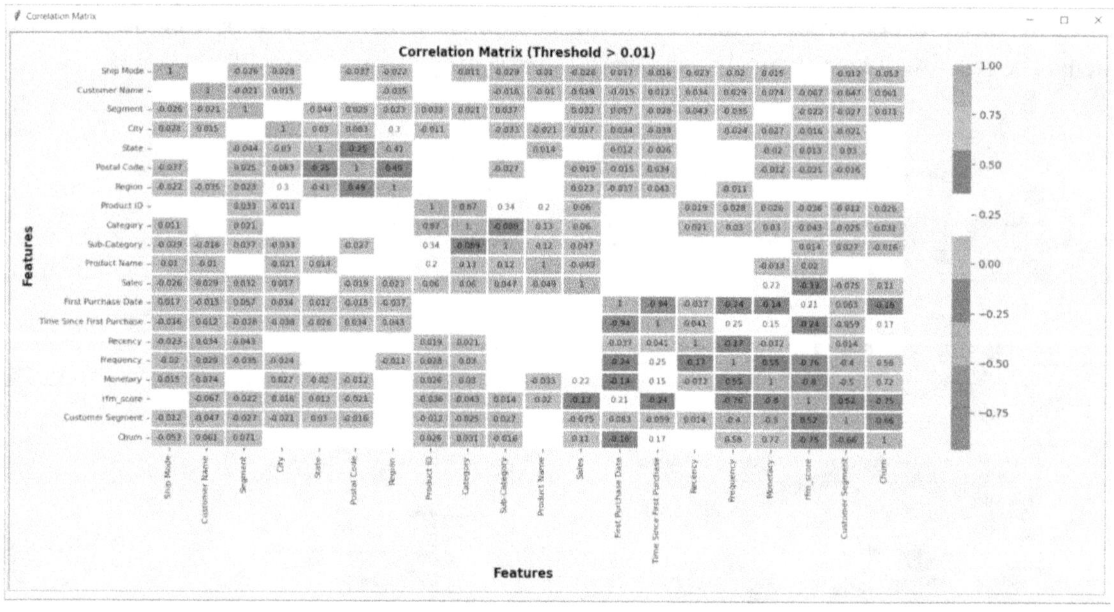

Figure 6.48 The correlation matrix

The Result of Feature Analysis

Run the main_sales.py script. Then, from Feature Importance menu, choose Correlation Matrix item. The result will be displayed as shown in figure 6.48.

Next, from Feature Importance menu, choose Correlation Coefficients item. The result will be displayed as shown in figure 6.49.

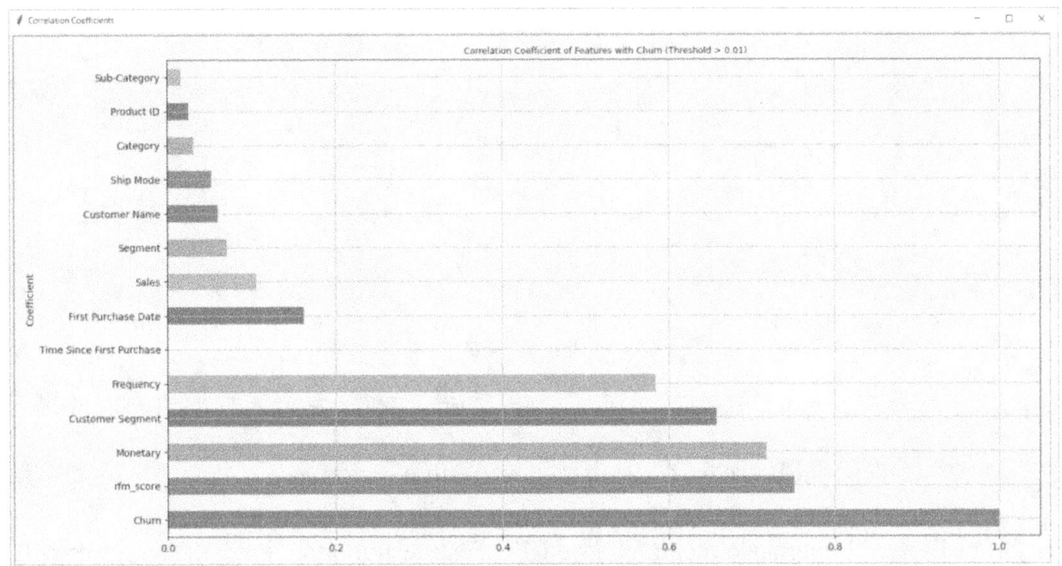

Figure 6.49 The correlation coefficients

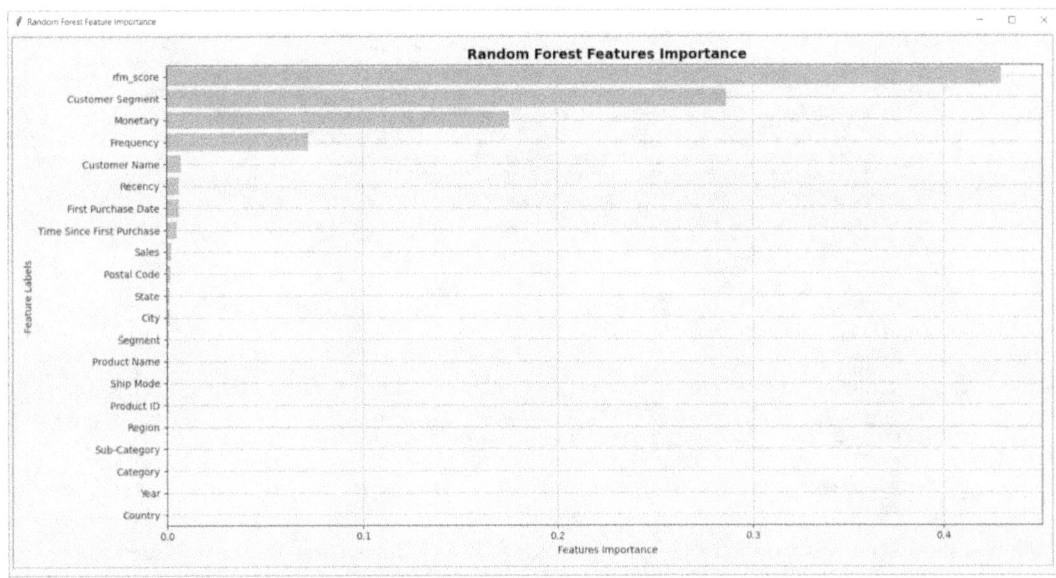

Figure 6.50 The random forest feature importance

Next, from Feature Importance menu, choose Random Forest Feature Importance item. The result will be displayed as shown in figure 6.50. Then, from Feature Importance menu, choose Extra Trees Feature Importance item. The result will be displayed as shown in figure 6.51.

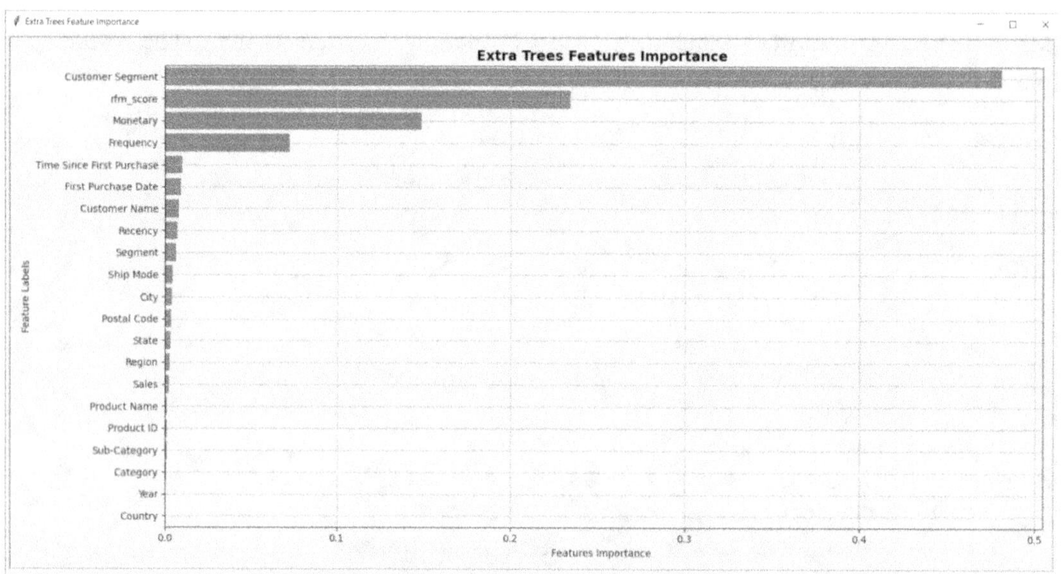

Figure 6.51 The extra trees feature importance

Then, from Feature Importance menu, choose RFE Feature Importance item. The result will be displayed as shown in figure 6.52.

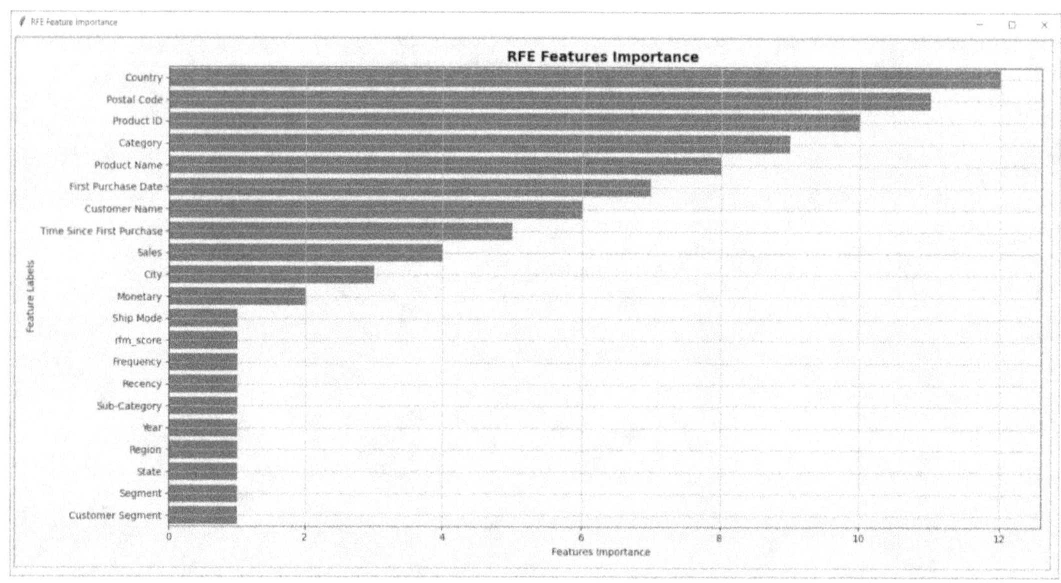

Figure 6.52 The RFE feature importance

The Result of Regression

Run the main_sales.py script. Click SPLIT DATA FOR FORECASTING button. Then, from the combobox, choose Linear Regression item. The result will be displayed as shown in figure 6.53.

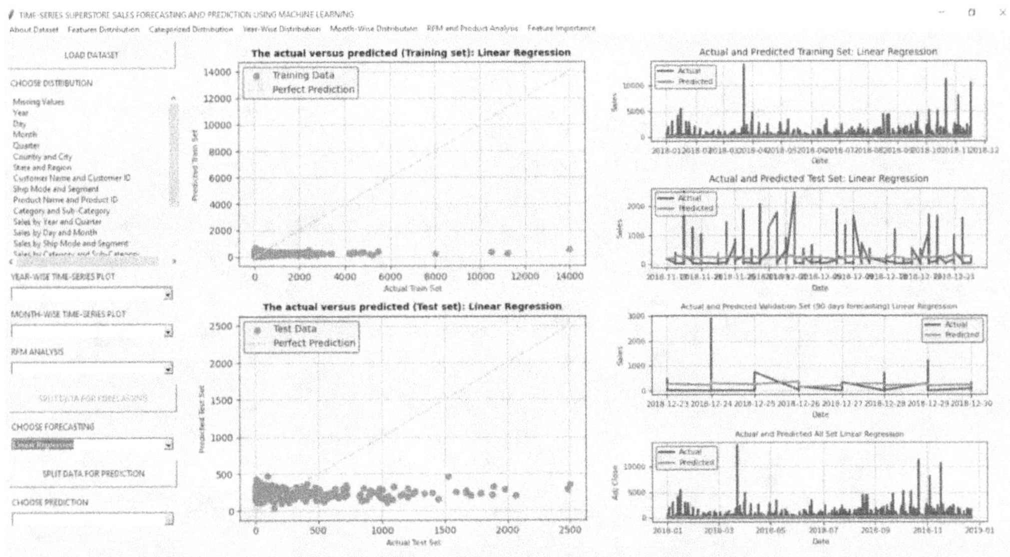

Figure 6.53 The result of linear regressor

Then, from the combobox, choose Decision Trees Regression item. The result will be displayed as shown in figure 6.54.

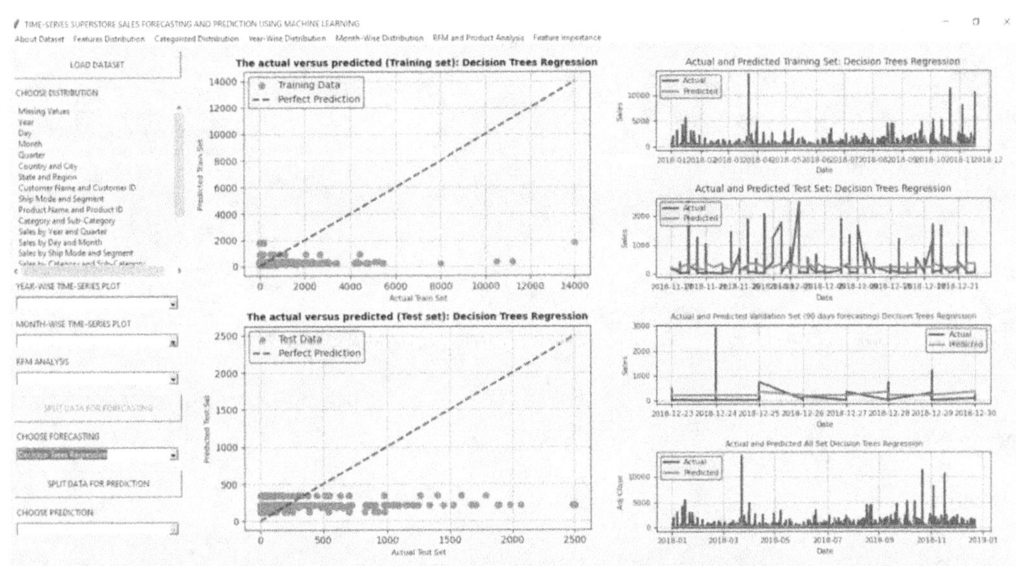

Figure 6.54 The result of decision tree regressor

Then, from the combobox, choose KNN Regression item. The result will be displayed as shown in figure 6.55.

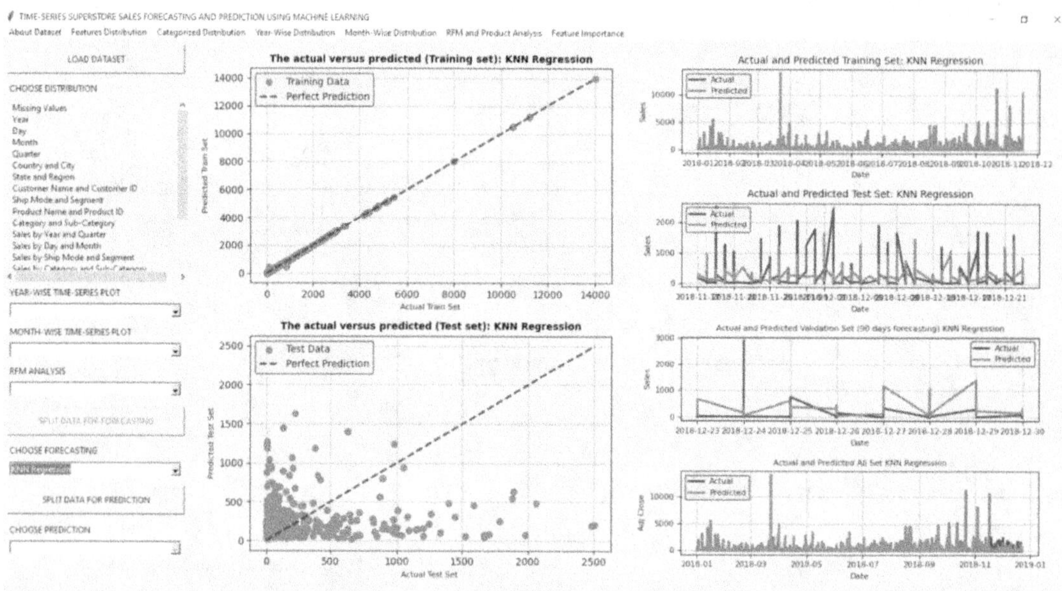

Figure 6.55 The result of k-nearest neighbors regressor

Then, from the combobox, choose Lasso Regression item. The result will be displayed as shown in figure 6.56.

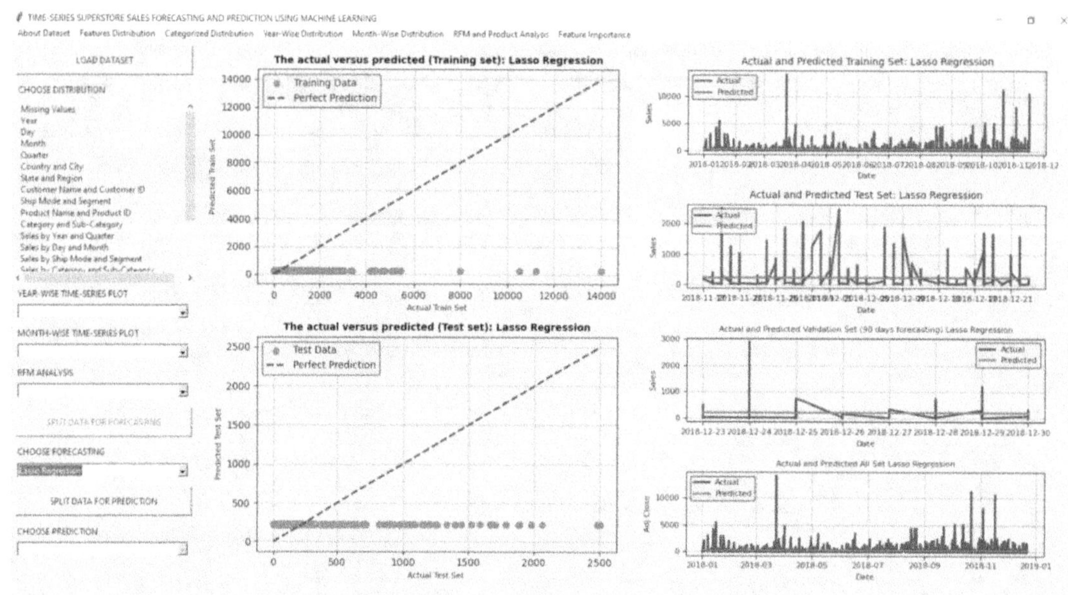

Figure 6.56 The result lasso regressor

Then, from the combobox, choose Ridge Regression item. The result will be displayed as shown in figure 6.57.

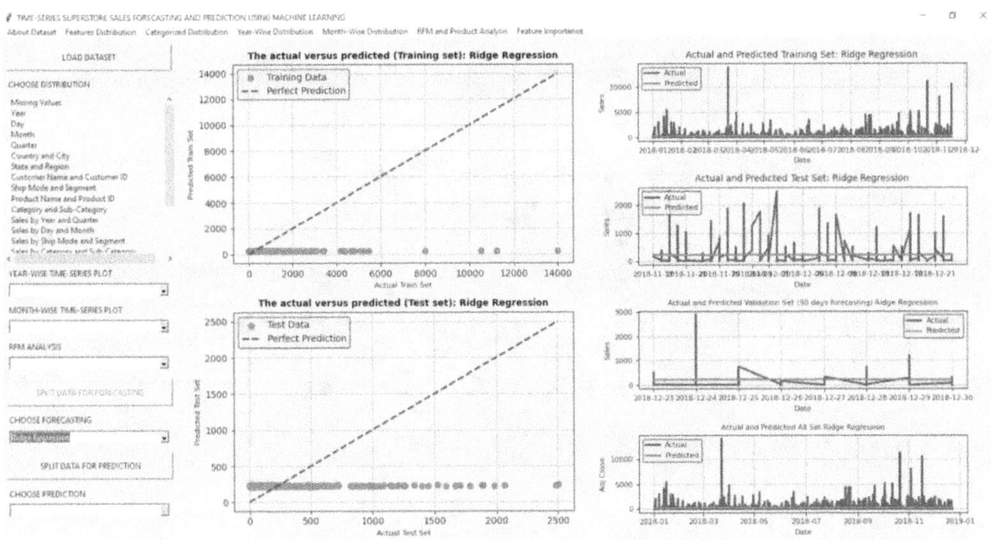

Figure 6.57 The result ridge regressor

The Result of Prediction

Run the main_sales.py script. Click SPLIT DATA FOR PREDICTION button. Then, from the combobox, choose Logistic Regression item. The result will be displayed as shown in figure 6.58.

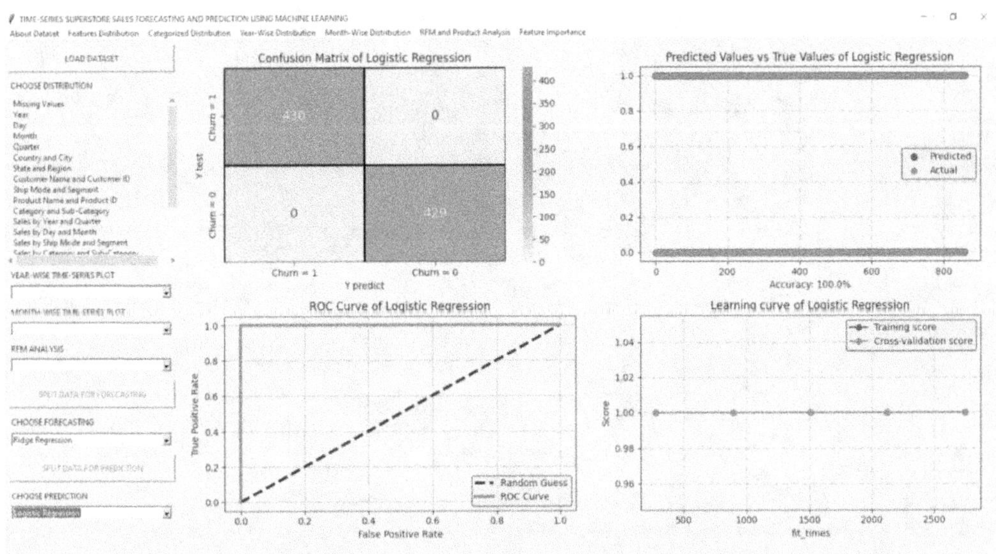

Figure 6.58 The result logistic regression classifier

Then, from the combobox, choose Random Forest item. The result will be displayed as shown in figure 6.59.

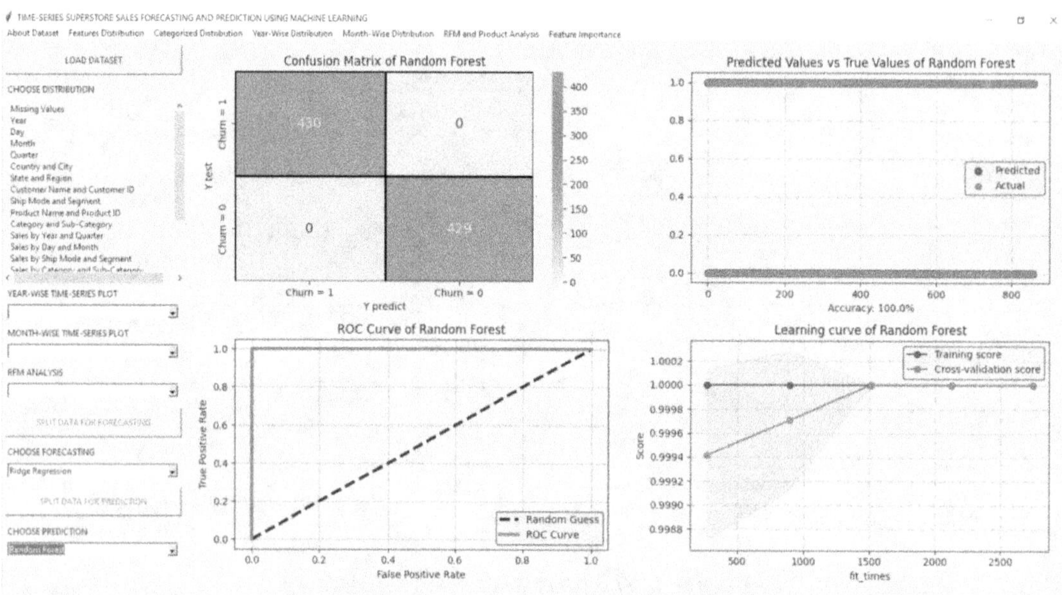

Figure 6.59 The result random forest classifier

Next, from the combobox, choose Decision Trees item. The result will be displayed as shown in figure 6.60.

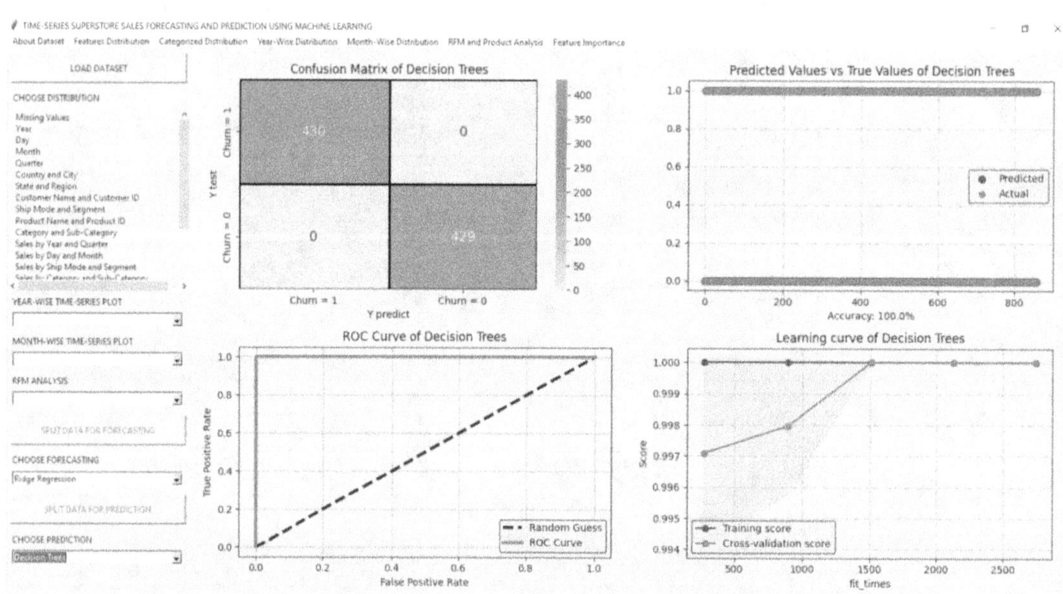

Figure 6.60 The result decision trees classifier

Next, from the combobox, choose K-Nearest Neighbors item. The result will be displayed as shown in figure 6.61.

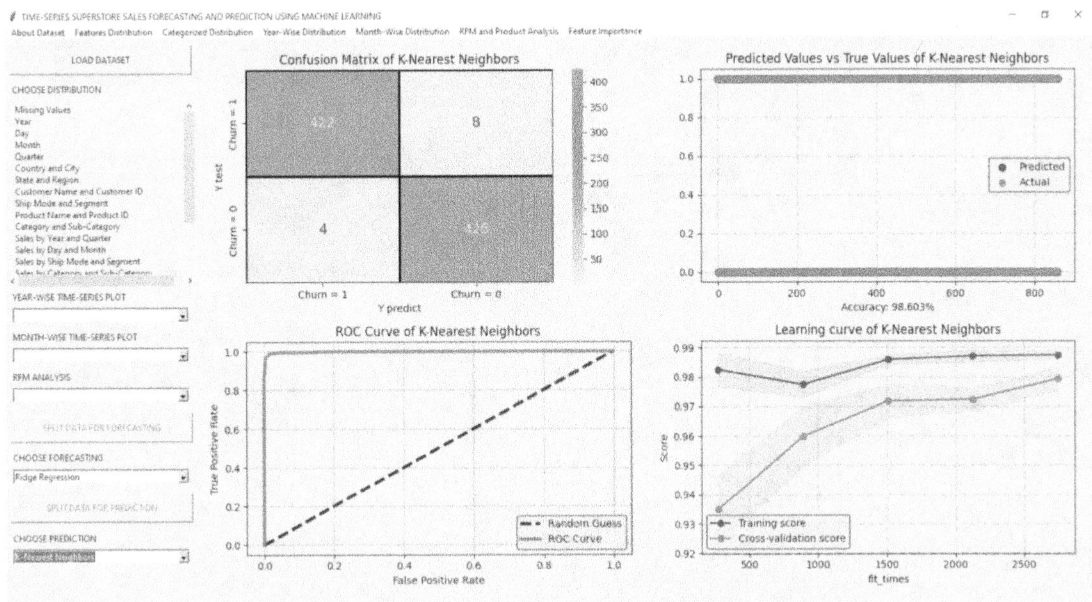

Figure 6.61 The result k-nearest neighbors classifier

Next, from the combobox, choose AdaBoost item. The result will be displayed as shown in figure 6.62.

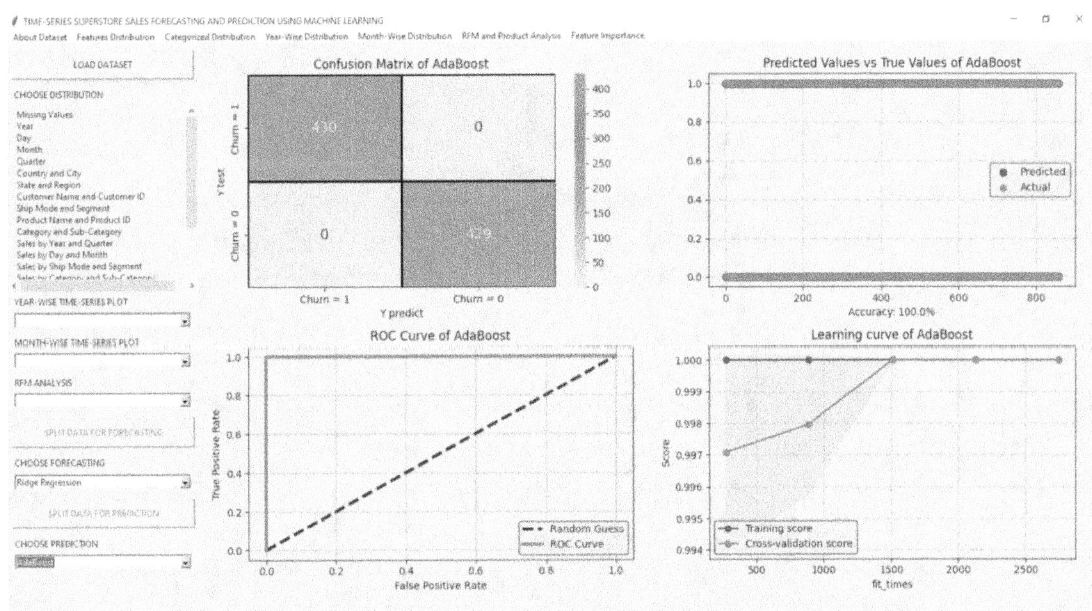

Figure 6.62 The result AdaBoost classifier

Next, from the combobox, choose Gradient Boosting item. The result will be displayed as shown in figure 6.63.

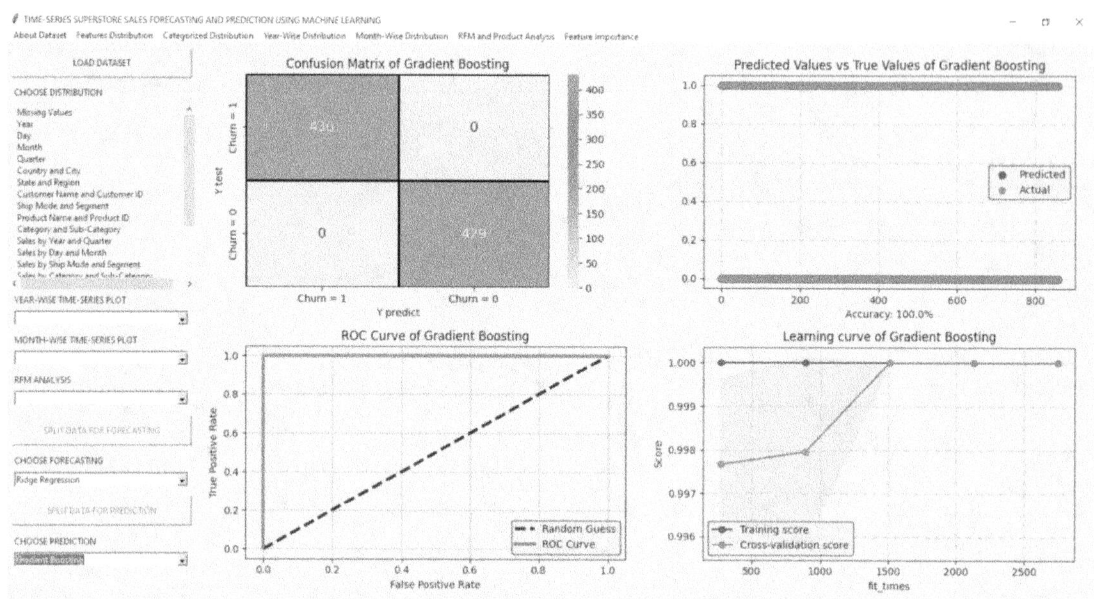

Figure 6.63 The result Gradient Boosting classifier

Next, from the combobox, choose Extreme Gradient Boosting item. The result will be displayed as shown in figure 6.64.

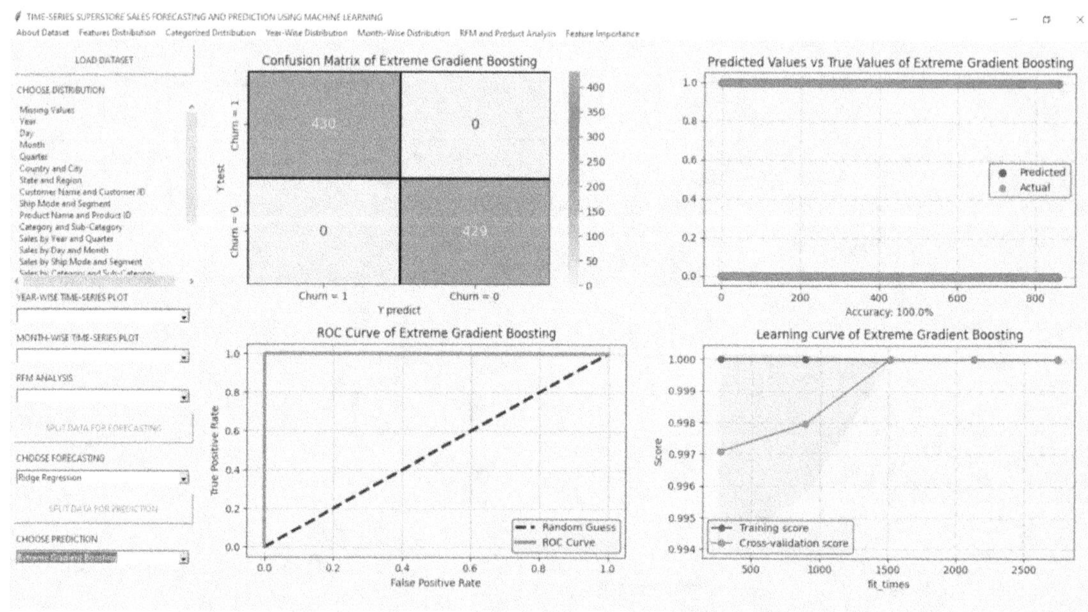

Figure 6.64 The result Extreme Gradient Boosting classifier

Next, from the combobox, choose Multi-Layer Perceptron item. The result will be displayed as shown in figure 6.65.

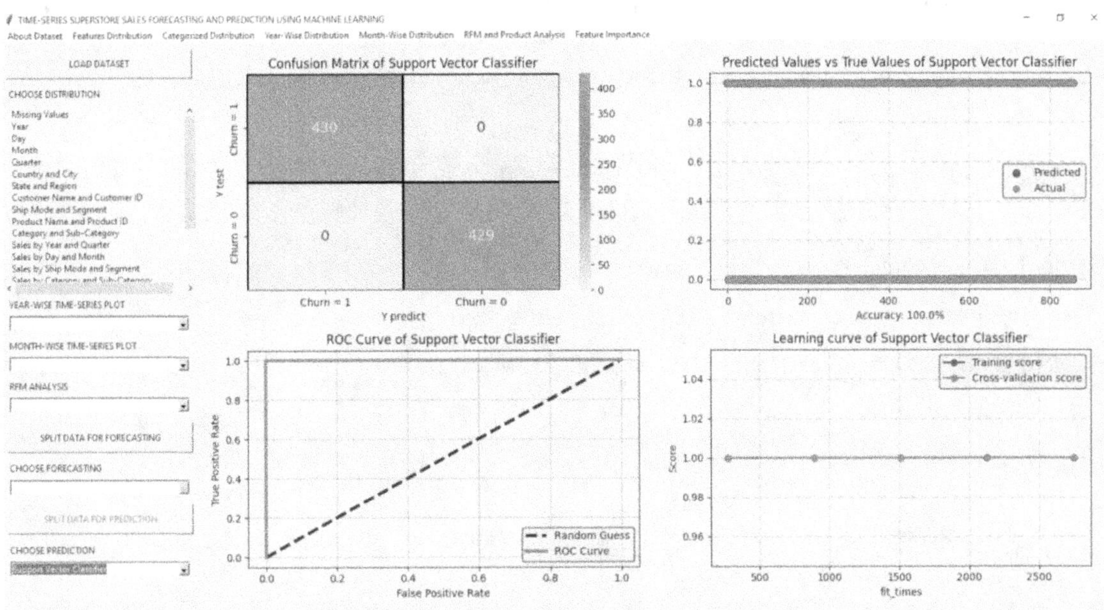

Figure 6.64 The result Support Vector classifier

FULL SOURCE CODE:

```
#main_sales.py
import os
import pandas as pd
import tkinter as tk
from tkinter import *
from main_window import Main_Window
from helper_plot import Helper_Plot
from process_data import Process_Data
from regression import Regression
from machine_learning import Machine_Learning
from form1 import Form1

class Main_Sales():
    def __init__(self, root):
        #super().__init__()
        self.initialize()

    def initialize(self):
        self.root = root
        width = 1560
        height = 790
        self.root.geometry(f"{width}x{height}")
        self.root.title("TIME-SERIES SUPERSTORE SALES FORECASTING AND PREDICTION USING MACHINE
LEARNING")

        #Creates necessary objects
        self.obj_window = Main_Window()
        self.obj_plot = Helper_Plot()
        self.obj_data = Process_Data()
```

```python
        self.obj_reg = Regression()
        self.obj_ML = Machine_Learning()

        #Places widgets in root
        self.obj_window.add_widgets(self.root)

        #Reads dataset
        self.df_before_fill, self.df_after_fill = self.obj_data.preprocess()

        #Creates dummy dataset for visualization
        self.df_dummy = self.df_after_fill.copy()
        self.df_dummy = self.obj_data.create_dummy(self.df_dummy)

        #Normalizes year-wise data
        self.year_data_mean, self.year_data_ewm, self.year_norm = 
self.obj_data.normalize_year_wise_data(self.df_after_fill)

        #Normalizes month-wise data
        self.month_data_mean, self.month_data_ewm, self.month_norm = 
self.obj_data.normalize_month_wise_data(self.df_after_fill)

        #Calculates RFM
        self.rfm_df, self.rank_df, self.merged_rank_dummy = 
self.obj_data.calculate_RFM(self.df_after_fill, self.df_dummy)

        #Finds churn customer
        self.df_final = self.obj_data.find_churn_customer(self.df_dummy, self.rfm_df,
self.rank_df)

        #For machine learning
        self.df_final, self.X1, self.y1, self.X2, self.y2 = 
self.obj_data.encode_df(self.df_final)

        #Extracts input and output variables for regression
        self.obj_reg.splitting_data_regression(self.X2, self.y2)

        #Extracts input and output variables for prediction
        self.obj_ML.oversampling_splitting(self.df_final)

        #turns off combo_reg and combo_pred after splitting is done
        self.obj_window.combo_reg['state'] = 'disabled'
        self.obj_window.combo_pred['state'] = 'disabled'

        #Binds events
        self.binds_event()
        self.obj_plot.binds_menu_open_dataset(self.df_before_fill, self.df_after_fill,
self.root, self.obj_window)
        self.obj_plot.binds_features_distribution(self.obj_window, self.df_before_fill,
self.df_after_fill, self.df_dummy)
        self.obj_plot.binds_categories_distribution(self.obj_window, self.df_dummy)
        self.obj_plot.binds_year_wise(self.obj_window, self.df_dummy, self.year_data_mean,
self.year_data_ewm)
        self.obj_plot.binds_month_wise(self.obj_window, self.df_dummy, self.month_data_mean,
self.month_data_ewm)
        self.obj_plot.binds_rfm_distribution(self.obj_window, self.merged_rank_dummy)
        self.obj_plot.binds_feat_importance(self.obj_window, self.df_final, self.X1, self.y1)

    def binds_event(self):
        #Shows table if user clicks LOAD DATASET
        self.obj_window.btn_load.config(command = lambda:self.obj_plot.shows_table(self.root,
            self.merged_rank_dummy, 1250, 600, "Superstore Dataset"))

        #Binds listbox to choose_list_widget() function
        self.obj_window.listbox.bind("<<ListboxSelect>>", self.choose_list_widget)
```

```python
        # Binds combo_year to choose_combo_year()
        self.obj_window.combo_year.bind("<<ComboboxSelected>>", self.choose_combo_year)

        # Binds combo_month to choose_combobox_month()
        self.obj_window.combo_month.bind("<<ComboboxSelected>>", self.choose_combobox_month)

        # Binds combo_tech to choose_combo_rfm()
        self.obj_window.combo_rfm.bind("<<ComboboxSelected>>", self.choose_combo_rfm)

        #Binds btn_reg to split_regression() function
        self.obj_window.btn_reg.config(command = self.split_regression)

        # Binds combo_reg to choose_combo_reg()
        self.obj_window.combo_reg.bind("<<ComboboxSelected>>", self.choose_combo_reg)

        #Binds combo_pred to split_prediction() function
        self.obj_window.btn_pred.config(command = self.split_prediction)

        # Binds combo_pred to choose_combo_pred()
        self.obj_window.combo_pred.bind("<<ComboboxSelected>>", self.choose_combo_pred)

    def choose_list_widget(self, event):
        chosen = self.obj_window.listbox.get(self.obj_window.listbox.curselection())
        print(chosen)
        self.obj_plot.choose_plot(self.df_after_fill, self.df_dummy, chosen,
            self.obj_window.figure1, self.obj_window.canvas1,
            self.obj_window.figure2, self.obj_window.canvas2)

    def choose_combo_year(self, event):
        chosen = self.obj_window.combo_year.get()
        self.obj_plot.choose_year_wise(self.df_after_fill, self.year_data_mean,
self.year_data_ewm, self.year_norm, chosen,
            self.obj_window.figure1, self.obj_window.canvas1,
            self.obj_window.figure2, self.obj_window.canvas2)

    def choose_combobox_month(self, event):
        chosen = self.obj_window.combo_month.get()
        self.obj_plot.choose_month_wise(self.df_dummy,
            self.month_data_mean, self.month_data_ewm, self.month_norm, chosen,
            self.obj_window.figure1, self.obj_window.canvas1,
            self.obj_window.figure2, self.obj_window.canvas2)

    def choose_combo_rfm(self, event):
        chosen = self.obj_window.combo_rfm.get()
        self.obj_plot.choose_rfm_distribution(self.merged_rank_dummy, chosen,
            self.obj_window.figure1,
            self.obj_window.canvas1, self.obj_window.figure2,
            self.obj_window.canvas2)

    def split_regression(self):
        file_path = os.getcwd()+"/X_final_reg.pkl"
        if os.path.exists(file_path):
            self.X_Ori, self.X_final_reg, self.X_train_reg, self.X_test_reg, \
            self.X_val_reg, self.y_final_reg, self.y_train_reg, \
            self.y_test_reg, self.y_val_reg = self.obj_reg.load_regression_files()
        else:
            self.obj_reg.splitting_data_regression(self.df_final)
            self.X_Ori, self.X_final_reg, self.X_train_reg, self.X_test_reg,
            self.X_val_reg, self.y_final_reg, self.y_train_reg,
            self.y_test_reg, self.y_val_reg = self.obj_reg.load_regression_files()

        print("Loading regression files done...")
```

```python
        #turns on combo_reg after splitting is done
        self.obj_window.combo_reg['state'] = 'normal'

        self.obj_window.btn_reg.config(state="disabled")

    def choose_combo_reg(self, event):
        chosen = self.obj_window.combo_reg.get()

        self.obj_plot.choose_plot_regression(chosen, self.X_final_reg,
            self.X_train_reg, self.X_test_reg, self.X_val_reg,
            self.y_final_reg, self.y_train_reg, self.y_test_reg,
            self.y_val_reg,
            self.obj_window.figure1, self.obj_window.canvas1,
            self.obj_window.figure2, self.obj_window.canvas2)

    def split_prediction(self):
        file_path = os.getcwd()+"/X_train.pkl"
        if os.path.exists(file_path):
            self.X_train, self.X_test, self.y_train, self.y_test = self.obj_ML.load_files()
        else:
            self.obj_ML.oversampling_splitting(self.df_final)
            self.X_train, self.X_test, self.y_train, self.y_test = self.obj_ML.load_files()

        print("Loading files done...")

        #turns on combo_pred after splitting is done
        self.obj_window.combo_pred['state'] = 'normal'

        self.obj_window.btn_pred.config(state="disabled")

    def choose_combo_pred(self, event):
        chosen = self.obj_window.combo_pred.get()
        self.obj_plot.choose_plot_ML(self.root, chosen, self.X_train, self.X_test,
            self.y_train, self.y_test, self.obj_window.figure1,
            self.obj_window.canvas1, self.obj_window.figure2,
            self.obj_window.canvas2)

if __name__ == "__main__":
    root = tk.Tk()
    app = Main_Sales(root)
    root.mainloop()


#main_window.py
import tkinter as tk
from tkinter import ttk
from matplotlib.figure import Figure
from matplotlib.backends.backend_tkagg import FigureCanvasTkAgg

class Main_Window:
    def add_widgets(self, root):
        #Set styles
        self.set_style(root)

        #Adds menu
        self.add_menu(root)

        #Adds button(s)
        self.add_buttons(root)

        #Adds canvasses
        self.add_canvas(root)

        #Adds labels
```

```python
        self.add_labels(root)

        #Adds listbox widget
        self.add_listboxes(root)

        #Adds combobox widget
        self.add_comboboxes(root)

    def set_style(self, root):
        # variables created for colors
        ebg = '#404040'
        fg = '#FFFFFF'

        style = ttk.Style()

        # Be sure to include this or style.map() won't function as expected.
        style.theme_use('alt')

        # the following alters the Listbox
        root.option_add('*TCombobox*Listbox.Background', ebg)
        root.option_add('*TCombobox*Listbox.Foreground', fg)
        root.option_add('*TCombobox*Listbox.selectBackground', fg)
        root.option_add('*TCombobox*Listbox.selectForeground', ebg)

        # the following alters the Combobox entry field
        style.map('TCombobox', fieldbackground=[('readonly', ebg)])
        style.map('TCombobox', selectbackground=[('readonly', ebg)])
        style.map('TCombobox', selectforeground=[('readonly', fg)])
        style.map('TCombobox', background=[('readonly', ebg)])
        style.map('TCombobox', foreground=[('readonly', fg)])

    def add_menu(self, root):
        self.menu_bar = tk.Menu(root)

        #Creates a Dataset menu
        self.dataset_menu = tk.Menu(self.menu_bar, tearoff=0)
        self.dataset_menu.add_command(label="View Dataset")
        self.dataset_menu.add_command(label="Dataset Information")
        self.dataset_menu.add_command(label="Statistical Description")
        self.dataset_menu.add_command(label="Null Values")
        self.dataset_menu.add_command(label="Postal Code Null Values")
        self.menu_bar.add_cascade(label="About Dataset", menu=self.dataset_menu)

        #Creates a feature distribution menu
        self.dist_menu = tk.Menu(self.menu_bar, tearoff=0)
        self.dist_menu.add_command(label="Missing Values")
        self.dist_menu.add_command(label="Day and Month")
        self.dist_menu.add_command(label="Quarter and Year")
        self.dist_menu.add_command(label="Country and City")
        self.dist_menu.add_command(label="State and Region")
        self.dist_menu.add_command(label="Customer Name and Customer ID")
        self.dist_menu.add_command(label="Ship Mode and Segment")
        self.dist_menu.add_command(label="Product Name and Product ID")
        self.dist_menu.add_command(label="Category and Sub-Category")
        self.menu_bar.add_cascade(label="Features Distribution", menu=self.dist_menu)

        #Creates category distribution menu
        self.dist_cat = tk.Menu(self.menu_bar, tearoff=0)
        self.dist_cat.add_command(label="Sales by Year and Quarter")
        self.dist_cat.add_command(label="Sales by Day and Month")
        self.dist_cat.add_command(label="Sales by Ship Mode and Segment")
        self.dist_cat.add_command(label="Sales by Category and Sub-Category")
        self.dist_cat.add_command(label="Sales by Product Name and Product ID")
        self.dist_cat.add_command(label="Sales by Customer Name and Customer ID")
```

```python
self.dist_cat.add_command(label="Sales by City and State")
self.dist_cat.add_command(label="Categorized Sales")
self.dist_cat.add_command(label="Categorized Sales by Year and Quarter")
self.dist_cat.add_command(label="Categorized Sales by Day and Month")
self.dist_cat.add_command(label="Categorized Sales by Segment and Sub-Category")
self.dist_cat.add_command(label="Categorized Sales by Region and State")
self.dist_cat.add_command(label="Day versus Sales Per Category")
self.dist_cat.add_command(label="Month versus Sales Per Segment")
self.dist_cat.add_command(label="Sub-Category versus Sales Per Year")
self.dist_cat.add_command(label="Region versus Sales Per Quarter")
self.menu_bar.add_cascade(label="Categorized Distribution", menu=self.dist_cat)

#Creates year-wise distribution menu
self.year_wise = tk.Menu(self.menu_bar, tearoff=0)
self.year_wise.add_command(label="Year-Wise Sales Distribution 2015 and 2016")
self.year_wise.add_command(label="Year-Wise Sales Distribution 2017 and 2018")
self.year_wise.add_command(label="Year-Wise Sales Mean and EWM")
self.year_wise.add_command(label="Sales by Year")
self.year_wise.add_command(label="Sales by Quarter")
self.year_wise.add_command(label="Sales by Month")
self.year_wise.add_command(label="Sales by Day")
self.year_wise.add_command(label="Sales by Week")
self.menu_bar.add_cascade(label="Year-Wise Distribution", menu=self.year_wise)

#Creates month-wise distribution menu
self.month_wise = tk.Menu(self.menu_bar, tearoff=0)
self.month_wise.add_command(label="Sales Quarter 1 and 2 Year 2018")
self.month_wise.add_command(label="Sales Quarter 3 and 4 Year 2018")
self.month_wise.add_command(label="Sales Quarter 1 and 2 Year 2017")
self.month_wise.add_command(label="Sales Quarter 3 and 4 Year 2017")
self.month_wise.add_command(label="Sales Quarter 1 and 2 Year 2016")
self.month_wise.add_command(label="Sales Quarter 3 and 4 Year 2016")
self.month_wise.add_command(label="Sales Quarter 1 and 2 Year 2015")
self.month_wise.add_command(label="Sales Quarter 3 and 4 Year 2015")
self.month_wise.add_command(label="Sales Month 1 and 2 Year 2018")
self.month_wise.add_command(label="Sales Month 3 and 4 Year 2017")
self.month_wise.add_command(label="Sales Month 5 and 6 Year 2016")
self.month_wise.add_command(label="Sales Month 7 and 8 Year 2015")
self.month_wise.add_command(label="Month-Wise Sales Mean and EWM")
self.month_wise.add_command(label="Sales by Month")
self.month_wise.add_command(label="Region-Based Monthly Sales")
self.month_wise.add_command(label="Category-Based Monthly Quantities")
self.month_wise.add_command(label="Segment-Based Monthly Sales")
self.month_wise.add_command(label="City-Based Monthly Sales")
self.month_wise.add_command(label="Ship Mode-Based Monthly Sales")
self.month_wise.add_command(label="Product Name-Based Monthly Sales")
self.month_wise.add_command(label="Sub-Category-Based Monthly Sales")
self.menu_bar.add_cascade(label="Month-Wise Distribution", menu=self.month_wise)

#Creates RFM distribution menu
self.rfm_analysis = tk.Menu(self.menu_bar, tearoff=0)
self.rfm_analysis.add_command(label="Customer Segment")
self.rfm_analysis.add_command(label="Sales by Customer Segment")
self.rfm_analysis.add_command(label="Customer Segment by Year and Quarter")
self.rfm_analysis.add_command(label="Customer Segment by Day and Month")
self.rfm_analysis.add_command(label="Customer Segment by Segment and Sub-Category")
self.rfm_analysis.add_command(label="Customer Segment by Region and State")
self.rfm_analysis.add_command(label="RFM-Based Monthly Sales")
self.menu_bar.add_cascade(label="RFM and Product Analysis", menu=self.rfm_analysis)

#Creates feature engineering
self.feat_eng = tk.Menu(self.menu_bar, tearoff=0)
self.feat_eng.add_command(label="Correlation Matrix")
self.feat_eng.add_command(label="Correlation Coefficients")
```

```python
        self.feat_eng.add_command(label="Random Forest Feature Importance")
        self.feat_eng.add_command(label="Extra Trees Feature Importance")
        self.feat_eng.add_command(label="RFE Feature Importance")
        self.menu_bar.add_cascade(label="Feature Importance", menu=self.feat_eng)

        root.config(menu=self.menu_bar)

    def add_buttons(self, root):
        #Adds button
        self.btn_load = tk.Button(root, height=2, width=35, text="LOAD DATASET")
        self.btn_load.grid(row=0, column=0, padx=5, pady=5, sticky="w")

        self.btn_reg = tk.Button(root, height=2, width=35, text="SPLIT DATA FOR FORECASTING")
        self.btn_reg.grid(row=9, column=0, padx=5, pady=5, sticky="w")

        self.btn_pred = tk.Button(root, height=2, width=35, text="SPLIT DATA FOR PREDICTION")
        self.btn_pred.grid(row=12, column=0, padx=5, pady=5, sticky="w")

    def add_labels(self, root):
        #Adds labels
        self.label1 = tk.Label(root, text = "CHOOSE DISTRIBUTION")
        self.label1.grid(row=1, column=0, padx=5, pady=1, sticky="w")

        self.label2 = tk.Label(root, text = "YEAR-WISE TIME-SERIES PLOT")
        self.label2.grid(row=3, column=0, padx=5, pady=1, sticky="w")

        self.label3 = tk.Label(root, text = "MONTH-WISE TIME-SERIES PLOT")
        self.label3.grid(row=5, column=0, padx=5, pady=1, sticky="w")

        self.label4 = tk.Label(root, text = "RFM ANALYSIS")
        self.label4.grid(row=7, column=0, padx=5, pady=1, sticky="w")

        self.label5 = tk.Label(root, text = "CHOOSE FORECASTING")
        self.label5.grid(row=10, column=0, padx=5, pady=1, sticky="w")

        self.label6 = tk.Label(root, text = "CHOOSE PREDICTION")
        self.label6.grid(row=13, column=0, padx=5, pady=1, sticky="w")

    def add_canvas(self, root):
        #Menambahkan canvas1 widget pada root untuk menampilkan hasil
        self.figure1 = Figure(figsize=(6.2, 7.6), dpi=100)
        self.figure1.patch.set_facecolor('#F0F0F0')
        self.canvas1 = FigureCanvasTkAgg(self.figure1, master=root)
        self.canvas1.get_tk_widget().grid(row=0, column=1, columnspan=1,
            rowspan=25, padx=5, pady=5, sticky="n")

        #Menambahkan canvas2 widget pada root untuk menampilkan hasil
        self.figure2 = Figure(figsize=(6.2, 7.6), dpi=100)
        self.figure2.patch.set_facecolor('#F0F0F0')
        self.canvas2 = FigureCanvasTkAgg(self.figure2, master=root)
        self.canvas2.get_tk_widget().grid(row=0, column=2, columnspan=1,
            rowspan=25, padx=5, pady=5, sticky="n")

    def add_listboxes(self, root):
        #Creates list widget
        self.listbox = tk.Listbox(root, height=15, selectmode=tk.SINGLE, width=40,
            fg ="black", bg="#F0F0F0",
            highlightcolor="black", selectbackground="red",relief="flat",
            borderwidth=5, highlightthickness=0)
        self.listbox.grid(row=2, column=0, sticky='n', padx=5, pady=1)

        self.scrollbar_v = tk.Scrollbar(root, orient="vertical",command=self.listbox.yview)
        self.scrollbar_v.grid(row=2, column=0, sticky='nse')
```

```python
        self.scrollbar_h = tk.Scrollbar(root, orient="horizontal",command=self.listbox.xview)
        self.scrollbar_h.grid(row=2, column=0, sticky='ews')

        self.listbox.config(yscrollcommand=self.scrollbar_v.set,
xscrollcommand=self.scrollbar_h.set)

        # Menyisipkan item ke dalam list widget
        items = ["Missing Values",
                "Year", "Day",
                "Month", "Quarter",
                "Country and City",
                "State and Region",
                "Customer Name and Customer ID",
                "Ship Mode and Segment",
                "Product Name and Product ID",
                "Category and Sub-Category",
                "Sales by Year and Quarter",
                "Sales by Day and Month",
                "Sales by Ship Mode and Segment",
                "Sales by Category and Sub-Category",
                "Sales by Product Name and Product ID",
                "Sales by Customer Name and Customer ID",
                "Sales by City and State",
                "Categorized Sales by Year and Quarter",
                "Categorized Sales by Day and Month",
                "Categorized Sales by Segment and Sub-Category",
                "Categorized Sales by Region and State"]
        for item in items:
            self.listbox.insert(tk.END, item)

    def add_comboboxes(self, root):
        # Create ComboBoxes
        self.combo_year = ttk.Combobox(root, width=38)
        self.combo_year["values"] = ["Year-Wise Sales Distribution 2017 and 2018",
            "Year-Wise Sales Distribution 2015 and 2016",
            "Year-Wise Sales Mean and EWM",
            "Normalized Year-Wise Data"]
        self.combo_year.grid(row=4, column=0, padx=5, pady=1, sticky="n")

        self.combo_month = ttk.Combobox(root, width=38, style='TCombobox')
        self.combo_month["values"] = ["Sales Quarter 1 and 2 Year 2018",
            "Sales Quarter 3 and 4 Year 2018",
            "Sales Quarter 1 and 2 Year 2017",
            "Sales Quarter 3 and 4 Year 2017",
            "Sales Quarter 1 and 2 Year 2016",
            "Sales Quarter 3 and 4 Year 2016",
            "Sales Quarter 1 and 2 Year 2015",
            "Sales Quarter 3 and 4 Year 2015",
            "Month-Wise Sales Mean and EWM",
            "Sales by Month",
            "Region-Based Monthly Sales",
            "Category-Based Monthly Quantities",
            "Segment-Based Monthly Sales",
            "City-Based Monthly Sales",
            "Ship Mode-Based Monthly Sales",
            "Product Name-Based Monthly Sales",
            "Sub-Category-Based Monthly Sales"]
        self.combo_month.grid(row=6, column=0, padx=5, pady=1, sticky="n")

        self.combo_rfm = ttk.Combobox(root, width=38, style='TCombobox')
        self.combo_rfm["values"] = ["Customer Segment",
            "Sales by Customer Segment",
            "Customer Segment by Year and Quarter",
            "Customer Segment by Day and Month",
```

```python
            "Customer Segment by Segment and Sub-Category",
            "Customer Segment by Region and State",
            "RFM-Based Monthly Sales"]
        self.combo_rfm.grid(row=8, column=0, padx=5, pady=1, sticky="n")

        self.combo_reg = ttk.Combobox(root, width=38, style='TCombobox')
        self.combo_reg["values"] = ["Linear Regression", "RF Regression",
            "Decision Trees Regression", "KNN Regression",
            "AdaBoost Regression", "Gradient Boosting Regression",
            "MLP Regression", "SVR Regression", "Lasso Regression", "Ridge Regression"]
        self.combo_reg.grid(row=11, column=0, padx=5, pady=1, sticky="n")

        self.combo_pred = ttk.Combobox(root, width=38, style='TCombobox')
        self.combo_pred["values"] = ["Logistic Regression", "Random Forest",
            "Decision Trees", "K-Nearest Neighbors",
            "AdaBoost", "Gradient Boosting",
            "Extreme Gradient Boosting", "Light Gradient Boosting",
            "Multi-Layer Perceptron", "Support Vector Classifier"]
        self.combo_pred.grid(row=14, column=0, padx=5, pady=1, sticky="n")


#process_data.py
import os
import pandas as pd
from datetime import datetime
import numpy as np
from sklearn.preprocessing import LabelEncoder
from sklearn.ensemble import RandomForestClassifier, ExtraTreesClassifier
from sklearn.linear_model import LogisticRegression
from sklearn.feature_selection import RFE

class Process_Data:
    def read_dataset(self, filename):
        #Reads dataset
        curr_path = os.getcwd()
        path = os.path.join(curr_path, filename)
        df = pd.read_csv(path)

        return df

    def preprocess(self):
        df = self.read_dataset("train.csv")

        #Extracts day, month, week, quarter, and year from order date
        df['Date'] = pd.to_datetime(df['Order Date'], format="%d/%m/%Y")
        df['Day'] = df['Date'].dt.weekday
        df['Month'] = df['Date'].dt.month
        df['Year']  = df['Date'].dt.year
        df['Week'] = df['Date'].dt.isocalendar().week
        df['Quarter']= df['Date'].dt.quarter

        #Sets Date column as index
        df = df.set_index("Date")

        #Converts data types to datetime
        df['Order Date'] = pd.to_datetime(df['Order Date'], format="%d/%m/%Y")
        df['Ship Date'] = pd.to_datetime(df['Ship Date'], format="%d/%m/%Y")

        # Drop columns
        df = df.drop(['Row ID'],axis=1)

        # Sort values by order date
        df.sort_values('Order Date', ascending=True, inplace=True)
```

```python
        # Fillna values in 'Postal Code' with correct postal code
        df2 = df.copy()
        df2['Postal Code'] = df['Postal Code'].fillna(5401)

        return df, df2

    def create_dummy(self, df):
        #Creates a dummy dataframe for visualization
        df_dummy=df.copy()

        #Converts days and months from numerics to meaningful string
        days = {0:'Sunday',1:'Monday',2:'Tuesday',3:'Wednesday',
                4:'Thursday',5: 'Friday',6:'Saturday'}
        df_dummy['Day'] = df_dummy['Day'].map(days)

        months={1:'January',2:'February',3:'March',4:'April',
                5:'May',6:'June',7:'July',8:'August',9:'September',
                10:'October',11:'November',12:'December'}
        df_dummy['Month']= df_dummy['Month'].map(months)

        quarters = {1:'Jan-March', 2:'April-June',3:'July-Sept',
                    4:'Oct-Dec'}
        df_dummy['Quarter'] = df_dummy['Quarter'].map(quarters)

        #Categorizes Sales feature
        labels = ['0-10', '10-20',  '20-50', '50-100', '100-150', '150-200','250-300','300-400', '>400']
        df_dummy['Cat_Sales'] = pd.cut(df_dummy['Sales'],
            [0, 10, 20, 50, 100, 150, 200, 250, 300, 400], labels=labels)

        return df_dummy

    def normalize_year_wise_data(self, df):
        #Normalizes year-wise data
        year_data_mean = df["Sales"].resample('y').mean()
        year_data_ewm = year_data_mean.ewm(span=5).mean()
        year_norm = (year_data_mean - year_data_mean.min()) / (year_data_mean.max() - year_data_mean.min())

        return year_data_mean, year_data_ewm, year_norm

    def normalize_month_wise_data(self, df):
        month_data_mean = df["Sales"].resample('m').mean()
        month_data_ewm = month_data_mean.ewm(span=5).mean()

        month_norm = (month_data_mean - month_data_mean.min()) / (month_data_mean.max() - month_data_mean.min())

        return month_data_mean, month_data_ewm, month_norm

    def calculate_RFM(self, df, df_dummy):
        # Calculating recency
        recency_df = df.groupby('Customer Name', as_index=False)['Order Date'].max()
        recent_date = recency_df['Order Date'].max()
        recency_df['Recency'] = recency_df['Order Date'].apply(
            lambda x: (recent_date - x).days)
        recency_df.rename(columns={'Order Date':'Last Purchase Date'}, inplace=True)

        # Calculating Frequency
        frequency_df = df.groupby('Customer Name', as_index=False)['Order Date'].count()
        frequency_df.rename(columns={'Order Date':'Frequency'}, inplace=True)

        # Calculating monetary
        monetary_df = df.groupby('Customer Name', as_index=False)['Sales'].sum()
```

```python
        monetary_df.rename(columns={'Sales':'Monetary'}, inplace=True)

        # Merging all three df in one df
        rfm_df = recency_df.merge(frequency_df, on='Customer Name')
        rfm_df = rfm_df.merge(monetary_df, on='Customer Name')
        rfm_df['Monetary'] = rfm_df['Monetary'].round(2)
        rfm_df.drop(['Last Purchase Date'], axis=1, inplace=True)

        rank_df = rfm_df.copy() # We make copy of rfm_df because we will need RFM features
later

        # Normalizing the rank of the customers
        rank_df['r_rank'] = rank_df['Recency'].rank(ascending=False)
        rank_df['f_rank'] = rank_df['Frequency'].rank(ascending=False)
        rank_df['m_rank'] = rank_df['Monetary'].rank(ascending=False)

        rank_df['r_rank_norm'] = (rank_df['r_rank'] / rank_df['r_rank'].max()) * 100
        rank_df['f_rank_norm'] = (rank_df['f_rank'] / rank_df['f_rank'].max()) * 100
        rank_df['m_rank_norm'] = (rank_df['m_rank'] / rank_df['m_rank'].max()) * 100

        rank_df.drop(['r_rank','f_rank','m_rank'], axis=1, inplace=True)

        # Calculating RFM scores
        rank_df['rfm_score'] = (0.15*rank_df['r_rank_norm']) + (0.28*rank_df['f_rank_norm']) +
(0.57*rank_df['m_rank_norm'])
        rank_df = rank_df[['Customer Name','rfm_score']]
        rank_df['rfm_score'] = round(rank_df['rfm_score']*0.05, 2)

        # Masking all customers rfm scores by rating conditions to set customer segments easily
        top_customer_mask = (rank_df['rfm_score'] >= 4.5)
        high_value_mask = ((rank_df['rfm_score']<4.5) & (rank_df['rfm_score']>=4))
        medium_value_mask = ((rank_df['rfm_score']<4) & (rank_df['rfm_score']>=3))
        low_value_mask = ((rank_df['rfm_score']<3) & (rank_df['rfm_score']>=1.6))
        lost_mask = (rank_df['rfm_score'] < 1.6)

        rank_df.loc[top_customer_mask, 'Customer Segment'] = 'Top Customer'
        rank_df.loc[high_value_mask, 'Customer Segment'] = 'High Value Customer'
        rank_df.loc[medium_value_mask, 'Customer Segment'] = 'Medium Value Customer'
        rank_df.loc[low_value_mask, 'Customer Segment'] = 'Low Value Customer'
        rank_df.loc[lost_mask, 'Customer Segment'] = 'Lost Customer'

        # Merge the DataFrames on 'Customer Name'
        merged_rank_dummy = rank_df.merge(df_dummy, on='Customer Name', how='inner')

        # Convert index to datetime
        merged_rank_dummy.index = pd.to_datetime(merged_rank_dummy.index)

        # Set 'Order Date' as the index
        merged_rank_dummy.set_index('Order Date', inplace=True)

        return rfm_df, rank_df, merged_rank_dummy

    def find_churn_customer(self, df, rfm_df, rank_df):
        #Find time since first purchase for every customer
        first_purchase_df = df.groupby('Customer Name', as_index=False)['Order Date'].min()
        first_purchase_df.rename(columns={'Order Date':'First Purchase Date'}, inplace=True)

        df_final = df.copy() # Make sure changes we will make doesn't affect original df so we
copy it
        df_final = df_final.merge(first_purchase_df, on='Customer Name',how='left')
        df_final['Time Since First Purchase'] = (df_final['Order Date'].max() -
                                    df_final['First Purchase Date']).dt.days
```

```python
        # Add recancy,frequency,monetary and segment columns to df. We found those features in
the previous section
        df_final = df_final.merge(rfm_df, on='Customer Name', how='left')
        df_final = df_final.merge(rank_df, on='Customer Name', how='left')

        # Find churned and not churned customers
        churned = (df_final['Customer Segment'] == 'Lost Customer')
        not_churned = (df_final['Customer Segment'] != 'Lost Customer')

        df_final.loc[churned, 'Churned'] = 1
        df_final.loc[not_churned, 'Churned'] = 0
        df_final['Churned'] = df_final['Churned'].astype('int64')

        #Rename Churned column to Churn
        df_final.rename(columns={'Churned':'Churn'}, inplace=True)

        # Convert index to datetime
        df_final.index = pd.to_datetime(df_final.index)

        # Set 'Order Date' as the index
        df_final.set_index('Order Date', inplace=True)

        return df_final

    def encode_df(self, df):
        #Drops Daily Summary column
        df.drop(['Order ID', 'Ship Date', 'Customer ID', 'Cat_Sales', 'Day', 'Month', 'Week',
'Quarter'], axis=1, inplace=True)

        #Controls the size of dataset for regression and prediction to suit your computing
power
        df=df[df["Year"] == 2018]
        #df = df[(df["Year"] == 2016) & (df["Month"] >= 3) & (df["Month"] <= 7)]
        #Selects data in year 2015-2016, because very big dataset
        #df = df[df['Year'].isin([2015, 2016])]

        # Encodes all non-numeric columns
        non_numeric_columns = df.select_dtypes(exclude=['number']).columns
        label_encoder = LabelEncoder()
        for column in non_numeric_columns:
            df[column] = label_encoder.fit_transform(df[column])

        print(df.head().to_string())

        #Extracts output and input variables for prediction
        y1 = df['Churn'] # Target for the model
        X1 = df.drop(['Churn'], axis = 1)

        y2 = df['Sales'] # Target for regression
        X2 = df.drop(['Sales'], axis = 1)

        return df, X1, y1, X2, y2

    def feat_importance_rf(self, X, y):
        names = X.columns
        rf = RandomForestClassifier()
        rf.fit(X, y)

        result_rf = pd.DataFrame()
        result_rf['Features'] = X.columns
        result_rf ['Values'] = rf.feature_importances_
        result_rf.sort_values('Values', inplace = True, ascending = False)

        return result_rf
```

```python
    def feat_importance_et(self, X, y):
        model = ExtraTreesClassifier()
        model.fit(X, y)

        result_et = pd.DataFrame()
        result_et['Features'] = X.columns
        result_et ['Values'] = model.feature_importances_
        result_et.sort_values('Values', inplace=True, ascending =False)

        return result_et

    def feat_importance_rfe(self, X, y):
        model = LogisticRegression()
        #Creates the RFE model
        rfe = RFE(model)
        rfe = rfe.fit(X, y)

        result_lg = pd.DataFrame()
        result_lg['Features'] = X.columns
        result_lg ['Ranking'] = rfe.ranking_
        result_lg.sort_values('Ranking', inplace=True , ascending = False)

        return result_lg

    def save_result(self, y_test, y_pred, fname):
        # Convert y_test and y_pred to pandas Series for easier handling
        y_test_series = pd.Series(y_test)
        y_pred_series = pd.Series(y_pred)

        # Calculate y_result_series
        y_result_series = pd.Series(y_pred - y_test == 0)
        y_result_series = y_result_series.map({True: 'True', False: 'False'})

        # Create a DataFrame to hold y_test, y_pred, and y_result
        data = pd.DataFrame({'y_test': y_test_series, 'y_pred': y_pred_series, 'result':
y_result_series})

        # Save the DataFrame to a CSV file
        data.to_csv(fname, index=False)

#regression.py
import pandas as pd
import numpy as np
from sklearn.preprocessing import MinMaxScaler
import joblib
from sklearn.metrics import mean_squared_error, mean_absolute_error
from sklearn.metrics import roc_auc_score,roc_curve, r2_score, explained_variance_score
from sklearn.linear_model import LinearRegression
from sklearn.ensemble import RandomForestRegressor, GradientBoostingRegressor,
AdaBoostRegressor
from sklearn.model_selection import GridSearchCV
from sklearn.tree import DecisionTreeRegressor
from xgboost import XGBRegressor
from sklearn.neural_network import MLPRegressor
from sklearn.linear_model import LassoCV
from sklearn.linear_model import RidgeCV
from sklearn.neighbors import KNeighborsRegressor

class Regression:
    def splitting_data_regression(self, X, y_final):
        #Normalizes data
        scaler = MinMaxScaler()
        X_minmax_data = scaler.fit_transform(X)
```

```python
X_final = pd.DataFrame(columns=X.columns, data=X_minmax_data, index=X.index)
print('Shape of features : ', X_final.shape)
print('Shape of target : ', y_final.shape)

#Shifts target array to predict the n + 1 samples
n=90
y_final = y_final.shift(-1)
y_val = y_final[-n:-1]
y_final = y_final[:-n]

#Takes last n rows of data to be validation set
X_val = X_final[-n:-1]
X_final = X_final[:-n]

print("\n -----After process------ \n")
print('Shape of features : ', X_final.shape)
print('Shape of target : ', y_final.shape)
print(y_final.tail().to_string())

y_final=y_final.astype('float64')

#Splits data into training and test data at 80% and 20% respectively
split_idx=round(0.8*len(X))
print("split_idx=",split_idx)
X_train_reg = X_final[:split_idx]
y_train_reg = y_final[:split_idx]
X_test_reg = X_final[split_idx:]
y_test_reg = y_final[split_idx:]

#Saves into pkl files
joblib.dump(X, 'X_Ori.pkl')
joblib.dump(X_final, 'X_final_reg.pkl')
joblib.dump(X_train_reg, 'X_train_reg.pkl')
joblib.dump(X_test_reg, 'X_test_reg.pkl')
joblib.dump(X_val, 'X_val_reg.pkl')
joblib.dump(y_final, 'y_final_reg.pkl')
joblib.dump(y_train_reg, 'y_train_reg.pkl')
joblib.dump(y_test_reg, 'y_test_reg.pkl')
joblib.dump(y_val, 'y_val_reg.pkl')

def load_regression_files(self):
    X_Ori = joblib.load('X_Ori.pkl')
    X_final_reg = joblib.load('X_final_reg.pkl')
    X_train_reg = joblib.load('X_train_reg.pkl')
    X_test_reg = joblib.load('X_test_reg.pkl')
    X_val_reg = joblib.load('X_val_reg.pkl')
    y_final_reg = joblib.load('y_final_reg.pkl')
    y_train_reg = joblib.load('y_train_reg.pkl')
    y_test_reg = joblib.load('y_test_reg.pkl')
    y_val_reg = joblib.load('y_val_reg.pkl')

    return X_Ori, X_final_reg, X_train_reg, X_test_reg, X_val_reg, y_final_reg,
y_train_reg, y_test_reg, y_val_reg

def perform_regression(self, model, X, y, xtrain, ytrain, xtest, ytest, xval, yval,
label):
    model.fit(xtrain, ytrain)
    predictions_test = model.predict(xtest)
    predictions_train = model.predict(xtrain)
    predictions_val = model.predict(xval)

    # Convert ytest and predictions_test to NumPy arrays
    ytest_np = ytest.to_numpy().flatten()
    predictions_test_np = predictions_test.flatten()
```

```python
        str_label = 'RMSE using ' + label
        print(str_label + f': {np.sqrt(mean_squared_error(ytest_np, predictions_test_np))}')
        print("mean square error: ", mean_squared_error(ytest_np, predictions_test_np))
        print("variance or r-squared: ", explained_variance_score(ytest_np,
predictions_test_np))
        print("mean absolute error (MAE): ", mean_absolute_error(ytest_np,
predictions_test_np))
        print("R2 (R-squared): ", r2_score(ytest_np, predictions_test_np))
        print("Adjusted R2: ", 1 - (1-r2_score(ytest_np, predictions_test_np))*(len(ytest_np)-
1)/(len(ytest_np)-xtest.shape[1]-1))

        mean_percentage_error = np.mean((ytest_np - predictions_test_np) / ytest_np) * 100
        print("Mean Percentage Error (MPE): ", mean_percentage_error)

        mean_absolute_percentage_error = np.mean(np.abs((ytest_np - predictions_test_np) /
ytest_np)) * 100
        print("Mean Absolute Percentage Error (MAPE): ", mean_absolute_percentage_error)

        print('ACTUAL: Avg. ' + f': {ytest_np.mean()}')
        print('ACTUAL: Median ' + f': {np.median(ytest_np)}')
        print('PREDICTED: Avg. ' + f': {predictions_test_np.mean()}')
        print('PREDICTED: Median ' + f': {np.median(predictions_test_np)}')

        # Evaluation of regression on all dataset
        all_pred = model.predict(X)
        print("mean square error (whole dataset): ", mean_squared_error(y, all_pred))
        print("variance or r-squared (whole dataset): ", explained_variance_score(y,
all_pred))

        return predictions_test, predictions_train, predictions_val, all_pred

    def linear_regression(self, X_train, y_train):
        #Linear Regression
        #Creates a Linear Regression model
        lin_reg = LinearRegression()

        #Defines the hyperparameter grid to search
        param_grid = {
            'fit_intercept': [True, False],    # Try both True and False for fit_intercept
            'normalize': [True, False]         # Try both True and False for normalize
        }

        #Creates GridSearchCV with the Linear Regression model and the hyperparameter grid
        grid_search = GridSearchCV(lin_reg, param_grid, cv=5, scoring='neg_mean_squared_error')

        #Fits the GridSearchCV to the training data
        grid_search.fit(X_train, y_train)

        #Gets the best Linear Regression model from the grid search
        best_lin_reg = grid_search.best_estimator_

        #Prints the best hyperparameters found
        print("Best Hyperparameters for Linear Regression:")
        print(grid_search.best_params_)

        return best_lin_reg

    def rf_regression(self, X_train, y_train):
        #Random Forest Regression
        # Create a RandomForestRegressor model
        rf_reg = RandomForestRegressor()

        # Define the hyperparameter grid to search
```

```python
        param_grid = {
            'n_estimators': [50, 100, 150],            # Number of trees in the forest
            'max_depth': [None, 5, 10],                # Maximum depth of the tree
            'min_samples_split': [2, 5, 10],           # Minimum number of samples required to
split an internal node
            'min_samples_leaf': [1, 2, 4],             # Minimum number of samples required to
be at a leaf node
            'bootstrap': [True, False]                 # Whether bootstrap samples are used
when building trees
        }

        # Create GridSearchCV with the RandomForestRegressor model and the hyperparameter grid
        grid_search = GridSearchCV(rf_reg, param_grid, cv=5, scoring='neg_mean_squared_error')

        # Fit the GridSearchCV to the training data
        grid_search.fit(X_train, y_train)

        # Get the best RandomForestRegressor model from the grid search
        best_rf_reg = grid_search.best_estimator_

        # Print the best hyperparameters found
        print("Best Hyperparameters for RandomForestRegressor:")
        print(grid_search.best_params_)

        return best_rf_reg

    def dt_regression(self, X_train, y_train):
        #Decision Tree (DT) regression
        # Create a DecisionTreeRegressor model
        dt_reg = DecisionTreeRegressor(random_state=100)

        # Define the hyperparameter grid to search
        param_grid = {
            'max_depth': [None, 5, 10, 15],            # Maximum depth of the tree
            'min_samples_split': [2, 5, 10],           # Minimum number of samples required to
split an internal node
            'min_samples_leaf': [1, 2, 4, 6],          # Minimum number of samples required to
be at a leaf node
        }

        # Create GridSearchCV with the DecisionTreeRegressor model and the hyperparameter grid
        grid_search = GridSearchCV(dt_reg, param_grid, cv=5, scoring='neg_mean_squared_error')

        # Fit the GridSearchCV to the training data
        grid_search.fit(X_train, y_train)

        # Get the best DecisionTreeRegressor model from the grid search
        best_dt_reg = grid_search.best_estimator_

        # Print the best hyperparameters found
        print("Best Hyperparameters for DecisionTreeRegressor:")
        print(grid_search.best_params_)

        return best_dt_reg

    def gb_regression(self, X_train, y_train):
        #Gradient Boosting regression
        # Create the GradientBoostingRegressor model
        gb_reg = GradientBoostingRegressor()

        # Define the hyperparameter grid to search
        param_grid = {
            'n_estimators': [50, 100, 150],                 # Number of boosting stages (trees)
to build
```

```python
            'learning_rate': [0.01, 0.1, 0.5],           # Step size at each boosting
iteration
            'max_depth': [3, 5, 7],                      # Maximum depth of the individual
trees
            'min_samples_split': [2, 5, 10],             # Minimum number of samples
required to split an internal node
            'min_samples_leaf': [1, 2, 4],               # Minimum number of samples
required to be at a leaf node
        }

        # Create GridSearchCV with the GradientBoostingRegressor model and the hyperparameter
grid
        grid_search = GridSearchCV(gb_reg, param_grid, cv=5, scoring='neg_mean_squared_error')

        # Fit the GridSearchCV to the training data
        grid_search.fit(X_train, y_train)

        # Get the best GradientBoostingRegressor model from the grid search
        best_gb_reg = grid_search.best_estimator_

        # Print the best hyperparameters found
        print("Best Hyperparameters for GradientBoostingRegressor:")
        print(grid_search.best_params_)

        return best_gb_reg

    def xgb_regression(self, X_train, y_train):
        #Extreme Gradient Boosting (XGB)
        # Create the XGBRegressor model
        xgb_reg = XGBRegressor()

        # Define the hyperparameter grid to search
        param_grid = {
            'n_estimators': [50, 100, 150],              # Number of boosting stages (trees) to
build
            'learning_rate': [0.01, 0.1, 0.5],           # Step size at each boosting iteration
            'max_depth': [3, 5, 7],                      # Maximum depth of the individual
trees
            'min_child_weight': [1, 2, 4],               # Minimum sum of instance weight
(hessian) needed in a child
            'gamma': [0, 0.1, 0.2],                      # Minimum loss reduction required to
make a further partition on a leaf node
            'subsample': [0.8, 1.0],                     # Subsample ratio of the training
instances
            'colsample_bytree': [0.8, 1.0]              # Subsample ratio of columns when
constructing each tree
        }

        # Create GridSearchCV with the XGBRegressor model and the hyperparameter grid
        grid_search = GridSearchCV(xgb_reg, param_grid, cv=5, scoring='neg_mean_squared_error')

        # Fit the GridSearchCV to the training data
        grid_search.fit(X_train, y_train)

        # Get the best XGBRegressor model from the grid search
        best_xgb_reg = grid_search.best_estimator_

        # Print the best hyperparameters found
        print("Best Hyperparameters for XGBRegressor:")
        print(grid_search.best_params_)

        return best_xgb_reg

    def mlp_regression(self, X_train, y_train):
```

```python
#MLP regression
# Create the MLPRegressor model
mlp_reg = MLPRegressor()

# Define the hyperparameter grid to search
param_grid = {
    'hidden_layer_sizes': [(50,), (100,), (50, 50), (100, 50)],   # Number of neurons
in each hidden layer
    'activation': ['relu', 'tanh'],                               # Activation
function for the hidden layers
    'solver': ['adam', 'sgd'],                                    # Solver for weight
optimization
    'learning_rate': ['constant', 'invscaling', 'adaptive'],      # Learning rate
schedule
    'learning_rate_init': [0.01, 0.001],                          # Initial learning
rate
    'max_iter': [100, 200, 300],                                  # Maximum number of
iterations
}

# Create GridSearchCV with the MLPRegressor model and the hyperparameter grid
grid_search = GridSearchCV(mlp_reg, param_grid, cv=5, scoring='neg_mean_squared_error')

# Fit the GridSearchCV to the training data
grid_search.fit(X_train, y_train)

# Get the best MLPRegressor model from the grid search
best_mlp_reg = grid_search.best_estimator_

# Print the best hyperparameters found
print("Best Hyperparameters for MLPRegressor:")
print(grid_search.best_params_)

return best_mlp_reg

def lasso_regression(self, X_train, y_train):
    # Create the LassoCV model
    lasso_reg = LassoCV(n_alphas=1000, max_iter=3000, random_state=0)

    # Define the hyperparameter grid to search
    param_grid = {
        'normalize': [True, False],        # Whether to normalize the features before
fitting the model
        'fit_intercept': [True, False]     # Whether to calculate the intercept for this
model
    }

    # Create GridSearchCV with the LassoCV model and the hyperparameter grid
    grid_search = GridSearchCV(lasso_reg, param_grid, cv=5,
scoring='neg_mean_squared_error')

    # Fit the GridSearchCV to the training data
    grid_search.fit(X_train, y_train)

    # Get the best LassoCV model from the grid search
    best_lasso_reg = grid_search.best_estimator_

    # Print the best hyperparameters found
    print("Best Hyperparameters for Lasso Regression:")
    print(grid_search.best_params_)

    return best_lasso_reg

def ridge_regression(self, X_train, y_train):
```

```python
        #Ridge regression
        ridge_reg = RidgeCV(gcv_mode='auto')

        # Define the hyperparameter grid to search (optional if you want to include other
hyperparameters)
        param_grid = {
            'normalize': [True, False],          # Whether to normalize the features before
fitting the model
            'fit_intercept': [True, False]       # Whether to calculate the intercept for this
model
        }

        # Create GridSearchCV with the RidgeCV model and the hyperparameter grid (optional if
you include the param_grid)
        grid_search = GridSearchCV(ridge_reg, param_grid, cv=5,
scoring='neg_mean_squared_error')

        # Fit the GridSearchCV to the training data
        grid_search.fit(X_train, y_train)

        # Get the best RidgeCV model from the grid search
        best_ridge_reg = grid_search.best_estimator_

        # Print the best hyperparameters found (optional if you included the param_grid)
        print("Best Hyperparameters for Ridge Regression:")
        print(grid_search.best_params_)

        return best_ridge_reg

    def adaboost_regression(self, X_train, y_train):
        #Adaboost regression
        # Create the AdaBoostRegressor model
        ada_reg = AdaBoostRegressor()

        # Define the hyperparameter grid to search
        param_grid = {
            'n_estimators': [50, 100, 150],          # Number of boosting stages (trees) to
build
            'learning_rate': [0.01, 0.1, 0.5],       # Step size at each boosting iteration
            'loss': ['linear', 'square', 'exponential'] # Loss function to use when updating
weights
        }

        # Create GridSearchCV with the AdaBoostRegressor model and the hyperparameter grid
        grid_search = GridSearchCV(ada_reg, param_grid, cv=5, scoring='neg_mean_squared_error')

        # Fit the GridSearchCV to the training data
        grid_search.fit(X_train, y_train)

        # Get the best AdaBoostRegressor model from the grid search
        best_ada_reg = grid_search.best_estimator_

        # Print the best hyperparameters found
        print("Best Hyperparameters for AdaBoostRegressor:")
        print(grid_search.best_params_)

        return best_ada_reg

    def knn_regression(self, X_train, y_train):
        #KNN regression
        # Create a KNeighborsRegressor model
        knn_reg = KNeighborsRegressor()

        # Define the hyperparameter grid to search
```

```python
        param_grid = {
            'n_neighbors': [3, 5, 7, 9],                # Number of neighbors to use for
regression
            'weights': ['uniform', 'distance'],        # Weight function used in prediction
            'algorithm': ['auto', 'ball_tree', 'kd_tree', 'brute']  # Algorithm used to compute
the nearest neighbors
        }

        # Create GridSearchCV with the KNeighborsRegressor model and the hyperparameter grid
        grid_search = GridSearchCV(knn_reg, param_grid, cv=5, scoring='neg_mean_squared_error')

        # Fit the GridSearchCV to the training data
        grid_search.fit(X_train, y_train)

        # Get the best KNeighborsRegressor model from the grid search
        best_knn_reg = grid_search.best_estimator_

        # Print the best hyperparameters found
        print("Best Hyperparameters for KNeighborsRegressor:")
        print(grid_search.best_params_)

        return best_knn_reg


#machine_learning.py
import numpy as np
from imblearn.over_sampling import SMOTE
from sklearn.model_selection import train_test_split, RandomizedSearchCV, GridSearchCV,
StratifiedKFold
from sklearn.preprocessing import StandardScaler
import joblib
from sklearn.linear_model import LogisticRegression
from sklearn.metrics import confusion_matrix, accuracy_score, recall_score, precision_score
from sklearn.metrics import classification_report, f1_score, plot_confusion_matrix
from sklearn.ensemble import RandomForestClassifier
from sklearn.neighbors import KNeighborsClassifier
from sklearn.tree import DecisionTreeClassifier
from sklearn.ensemble import AdaBoostClassifier, GradientBoostingClassifier
from xgboost import XGBClassifier
from sklearn.neural_network import MLPClassifier
from sklearn.svm import SVC
import os
import joblib
import pandas as pd
from process_data import Process_Data

class Machine_Learning:
    def __init__(self):
        self.obj_data = Process_Data()

    def oversampling_splitting(self, df):
        #Sets target column
        y = df["Churn"]

        #Ensures y is of integer type
        y = np.array([1 if i>0 else 0 for i in y]).astype(int)

        #Drops irrelevant column
        X = df.drop(["Churn"], axis =1)

        #Checks null values because of technical indicators
        print(X.isnull().sum().to_string())
        print('Total number of null values: ', X.isnull().sum().sum())
```

```python
    #Fills each null value in every column with mean value
    cols = list(X.columns)
    for n in cols:
        X[n].fillna(X[n].mean(),inplace = True)

    #Checks again null values
    print(X.isnull().sum().to_string())
    print('Total number of null values: ', X.isnull().sum().sum())

    # Check and convert data types
    X = X.astype(float)
    y = y.astype(int)

    sm = SMOTE(random_state=42)
    X,y = sm.fit_resample(X, y)

    #Splits the data into training and testing
    X_train, X_test, y_train, y_test = train_test_split(X, y, test_size = 0.2,
random_state = 2021, stratify=y)

    #Use Standard Scaler
    scaler = StandardScaler()
    X_train_stand = scaler.fit_transform(X_train)
    X_test_stand = scaler.transform(X_test)

    #Saves into pkl files
    joblib.dump(X_train_stand, 'X_train.pkl')
    joblib.dump(X_test_stand, 'X_test.pkl')
    joblib.dump(y_train, 'y_train.pkl')
    joblib.dump(y_test, 'y_test.pkl')

def load_files(self):
    X_train = joblib.load('X_train.pkl')
    X_test = joblib.load('X_test.pkl')
    y_train = joblib.load('y_train.pkl')
    y_test = joblib.load('y_test.pkl')

    return X_train, X_test, y_train, y_test

def train_model(self, model, X, y):
    model.fit(X, y)
    return model

def predict_model(self, model, X, proba=False):
    if ~proba:
        y_pred = model.predict(X)
    else:
        y_pred_proba = model.predict_proba(X)
        y_pred = np.argmax(y_pred_proba, axis=1)

    return y_pred

def run_model(self, name, model, X_train, X_test, y_train, y_test, proba=False):
    y_pred = self.predict_model(model, X_test, proba)

    accuracy = accuracy_score(y_test, y_pred)
    recall = recall_score(y_test, y_pred, average='weighted')
    precision = precision_score(y_test, y_pred, average='weighted')
    f1 = f1_score(y_test, y_pred, average='weighted')

    print(name)
    print('accuracy: ', accuracy)
    print('recall: ', recall)
    print('precision: ', precision)
```

```python
        print('f1: ', f1)
        print(classification_report(y_test, y_pred))

        return y_pred

    def logistic_regression(self, name, X_train, X_test, y_train, y_test):
        #Logistic Regression Classifier
        # Define the parameter grid for the grid search
        param_grid = {
            'C': [0.01, 0.1, 1, 10],
            'penalty': ['none', 'l2'],
            'solver': ['newton-cg', 'lbfgs', 'liblinear', 'saga'],
        }

        # Initialize the Logistic Regression model
        logreg = LogisticRegression(max_iter=5000, random_state=2021)

        # Create GridSearchCV with the Logistic Regression model and the parameter grid
        grid_search = GridSearchCV(logreg, param_grid, cv=3, scoring='accuracy', n_jobs=-1)

        # Train and perform grid search
        grid_search.fit(X_train, y_train)

        # Get the best Logistic Regression model from the grid search
        best_model = grid_search.best_estimator_

        #Saves model
        joblib.dump(best_model, 'LR_Model.pkl')

        # Print the best hyperparameters found
        print(f"Best Hyperparameters for LR:")
        print(grid_search.best_params_)

        return best_model

    def implement_LR(self, chosen, X_train, X_test, y_train, y_test):
        file_path = os.getcwd()+"/LR_Model.pkl"
        if os.path.exists(file_path):
            model = joblib.load('LR_Model.pkl')
            y_pred = self.run_model(chosen, model, X_train, X_test, y_train, y_test,
proba=True)
        else:
            model = self.logistic_regression(chosen, X_train, X_test, y_train, y_test)
            y_pred = self.run_model(chosen, model, X_train, X_test, y_train, y_test,
proba=True)

        #Saves result into excel file
        self.obj_data.save_result(y_test, y_pred, "results_LR.csv")

        print("Training Logistic Regression done...")
        return model, y_pred

    def random_forest(self, name, X_train, X_test, y_train, y_test):
        #Random Forest Classifier
        # Define the parameter grid for the grid search
        param_grid = {
            'n_estimators': [100, 200, 300],
            'max_depth': [10, 20, 30, 40, 50],
            'min_samples_split': [2, 5, 10],
            'min_samples_leaf': [1, 2, 4]
        }

        # Initialize the RandomForestClassifier model
        rf = RandomForestClassifier(random_state=2021)
```

```python
    # Create GridSearchCV with the RandomForestClassifier model and the parameter grid
    grid_search = GridSearchCV(rf, param_grid, cv=3, scoring='accuracy', n_jobs=-1)

    # Train and perform grid search
    grid_search.fit(X_train, y_train)

    # Get the best RandomForestClassifier model from the grid search
    best_model = grid_search.best_estimator_

    #Saves model
    joblib.dump(best_model, 'RF_Model.pkl')

    # Print the best hyperparameters found
    print(f"Best Hyperparameters for RF:")
    print(grid_search.best_params_)

    return best_model

def implement_RF(self, chosen, X_train, X_test, y_train, y_test):
    file_path = os.getcwd()+"/RF_Model.pkl"
    if os.path.exists(file_path):
        model = joblib.load('RF_Model.pkl')
        y_pred = self.run_model(chosen, model, X_train, X_test, y_train, y_test,
proba=True)
    else:
        model = self.random_forest(chosen, X_train, X_test, y_train, y_test)
        y_pred = self.run_model(chosen, model, X_train, X_test, y_train, y_test,
proba=True)

    #Saves result into excel file
    self.obj_data.save_result(y_test, y_pred, "results_RF.csv")

    print("Training Random Forest done...")
    return model, y_pred

def knearest_neigbors(self, name, X_train, X_test, y_train, y_test):
    #KNN Classifier
    # Define the parameter grid for the grid search
    param_grid = {
        'n_neighbors': list(range(2, 10))
    }

    # Initialize the KNN Classifier
    knn = KNeighborsClassifier()

    # Create GridSearchCV with the KNN model and the parameter grid
    grid_search = GridSearchCV(knn, param_grid, cv=3, scoring='accuracy', n_jobs=-1)

    # Train and perform grid search
    grid_search.fit(X_train, y_train)

    # Get the best KNN model from the grid search
    best_model = grid_search.best_estimator_

    #Saves model
    joblib.dump(best_model, 'KNN_Model.pkl')

    # Print the best hyperparameters found
    print(f"Best Hyperparameters for KNN:")
    print(grid_search.best_params_)

    return best_model
```

```python
    def implement_KNN(self, chosen, X_train, X_test, y_train, y_test):
        file_path = os.getcwd()+"/KNN_Model.pkl"
        if os.path.exists(file_path):
            model = joblib.load('KNN_Model.pkl')
            y_pred = self.run_model(chosen, model, X_train, X_test, y_train, y_test,
proba=True)
        else:
            model = self.knearest_neigbors(chosen, X_train, X_test, y_train, y_test)
            y_pred = self.run_model(chosen, model, X_train, X_test, y_train, y_test,
proba=True)

        #Saves result into excel file
        self.obj_data.save_result(y_test, y_pred, "results_KNN.csv")

        print("Training KNN done...")
        return model, y_pred

    def decision_trees(self, name, X_train, X_test, y_train, y_test):
        # Initialize the DecisionTreeClassifier model
        dt_clf = DecisionTreeClassifier(random_state=2021)

        # Define the parameter grid for the grid search
        param_grid = {
            'max_depth': np.arange(1, 51, 1),
            'criterion': ['gini', 'entropy'],
            'min_samples_split': [2, 5, 10],
            'min_samples_leaf': [1, 2, 4],
        }

        # Create GridSearchCV with the DecisionTreeClassifier model and the parameter grid
        grid_search = GridSearchCV(dt_clf, param_grid, cv=3, scoring='accuracy', n_jobs=-1)

        # Train and perform grid search
        grid_search.fit(X_train, y_train)

        # Get the best DecisionTreeClassifier model from the grid search
        best_model = grid_search.best_estimator_

        #Saves model
        joblib.dump(best_model, 'DT_Model.pkl')

        # Print the best hyperparameters found
        print(f"Best Hyperparameters for DT:")
        print(grid_search.best_params_)

        return best_model

    def implement_DT(self, chosen, X_train, X_test, y_train, y_test):
        file_path = os.getcwd()+"/DT_Model.pkl"
        if os.path.exists(file_path):
            model = joblib.load('DT_Model.pkl')
            y_pred = self.run_model(chosen, model, X_train, X_test, y_train, y_test,
proba=True)
        else:
            model = self.decision_trees(chosen, X_train, X_test, y_train, y_test)
            y_pred = self.run_model(chosen, model, X_train, X_test, y_train, y_test,
proba=True)

        #Saves result into excel file
        self.obj_data.save_result(y_test, y_pred, "results_DT.csv")

        print("Training Decision Trees done...")
        return model, y_pred
```

```python
    def gradient_boosting(self, name, X_train, X_test, y_train, y_test):
        #Gradient Boosting Classifier
        # Initialize the GradientBoostingClassifier model
        gbt = GradientBoostingClassifier(random_state=2021)

        # Define the parameter grid for the grid search
        param_grid = {
            'n_estimators': [100, 200, 300],
            'max_depth': [10, 20, 30],
            'subsample': [0.6, 0.8, 1.0],
            'max_features': [0.2, 0.4, 0.6, 0.8, 1.0],
        }

        # Create GridSearchCV with the GradientBoostingClassifier model and the parameter grid
        grid_search = GridSearchCV(gbt, param_grid, cv=3, scoring='accuracy', n_jobs=-1)

        # Train and perform grid search
        grid_search.fit(X_train, y_train)

        # Get the best GradientBoostingClassifier model from the grid search
        best_model = grid_search.best_estimator_

        #Saves model
        joblib.dump(best_model, 'GB_Model.pkl')

        # Print the best hyperparameters found
        print(f"Best Hyperparameters for GB:")
        print(grid_search.best_params_)

        return best_model

    def implement_GB(self, chosen, X_train, X_test, y_train, y_test):
        file_path = os.getcwd()+"/GB_Model.pkl"
        if os.path.exists(file_path):
            model = joblib.load('GB_Model.pkl')
            y_pred = self.run_model(chosen, model, X_train, X_test, y_train, y_test,
proba=True)
        else:
            model = self.gradient_boosting(chosen, X_train, X_test, y_train, y_test)
            y_pred = self.run_model(chosen, model, X_train, X_test, y_train, y_test,
proba=True)

        #Saves result into excel file
        self.obj_data.save_result(y_test, y_pred, "results_GB.csv")

        print("Training Gradient Boosting done...")
        return model, y_pred

    def extreme_gradient_boosting(self, name, X_train, X_test, y_train, y_test):
        # Define the parameter grid for the grid search
        param_grid = {
            'n_estimators': [100, 200, 300],
            'max_depth': [10, 20, 30],
            'learning_rate': [0.01, 0.1, 0.2],
            'subsample': [0.6, 0.8, 1.0],
            'colsample_bytree': [0.6, 0.8, 1.0],
        }

        # Initialize the XGBoost classifier
        xgb = XGBClassifier(random_state=2021, use_label_encoder=False,
eval_metric='mlogloss')

        # Create GridSearchCV with the XGBoost classifier and the parameter grid
        grid_search = GridSearchCV(xgb, param_grid, cv=3, scoring='accuracy', n_jobs=-1)
```

```python
    # Train and perform grid search
    grid_search.fit(X_train, y_train)

    # Get the best XGBoost classifier model from the grid search
    best_model = grid_search.best_estimator_

    #Saves model
    joblib.dump(best_model, 'XGB_Model.pkl')

    # Print the best hyperparameters found
    print(f"Best Hyperparameters for XGB:")
    print(grid_search.best_params_)

    return best_model

def implement_XGB(self, chosen, X_train, X_test, y_train, y_test):
    file_path = os.getcwd()+"/XGB_Model.pkl"
    if os.path.exists(file_path):
        model = joblib.load('XGB_Model.pkl')
        y_pred = self.run_model(chosen, model, X_train, X_test, y_train, y_test,
proba=True)
    else:
        model = self.extreme_gradient_boosting(chosen, X_train, X_test, y_train, y_test)
        y_pred = self.run_model(chosen, model, X_train, X_test, y_train, y_test,
proba=True)

    #Saves result into excel file
    self.obj_data.save_result(y_test, y_pred, "results_XGB.csv")

    print("Training Extreme Gradient Boosting done...")
    return model, y_pred

def multi_layer_perceptron(self, name, X_train, X_test, y_train, y_test):
    # Define the parameter grid for the grid search
    param_grid = {
        'hidden_layer_sizes': [(50,), (100,), (50, 50), (100, 50), (100, 100)],
        'activation': ['logistic', 'relu'],
        'solver': ['adam', 'sgd'],
        'alpha': [0.0001, 0.001, 0.01],
        'learning_rate': ['constant', 'invscaling', 'adaptive'],
    }

    # Initialize the MLP Classifier
    mlp = MLPClassifier(random_state=2021)

    # Create GridSearchCV with the MLP Classifier and the parameter grid
    grid_search = GridSearchCV(mlp, param_grid, cv=3, scoring='accuracy', n_jobs=-1)

    # Train and perform grid search
    grid_search.fit(X_train, y_train)

    # Get the best MLP Classifier model from the grid search
    best_model = grid_search.best_estimator_

    #Saves model
    joblib.dump(best_model, 'MLP_Model.pkl')

    # Print the best hyperparameters found
    print(f"Best Hyperparameters for MLP:")
    print(grid_search.best_params_)

    return best_model
```

```python
    def implement_MLP(self, chosen, X_train, X_test, y_train, y_test):
        file_path = os.getcwd()+"/MLP_Model.pkl"
        if os.path.exists(file_path):
            model = joblib.load('MLP_Model.pkl')
            y_pred = self.run_model(chosen, model, X_train, X_test, y_train, y_test,
proba=True)
        else:
            model = self.multi_layer_perceptron(chosen, X_train, X_test, y_train, y_test)
            y_pred = self.run_model(chosen, model, X_train, X_test, y_train, y_test,
proba=True)

        #Saves result into excel file
        self.obj_data.save_result(y_test, y_pred, "results_MLP.csv")

        print("Training Multi-Layer Perceptron done...")
        return model, y_pred

    def support_vector(self, name, X_train, X_test, y_train, y_test):
        #Support Vector Classifier
        # Define the parameter grid for the grid search
        param_grid = {
            'C': [0.1, 1, 10],
            'kernel': ['linear', 'poly', 'rbf'],
            'gamma': ['scale', 'auto', 0.1, 1],
        }

        # Initialize the SVC model
        model_svc = SVC(random_state=2021, probability=True)

        # Create GridSearchCV with the SVC model and the parameter grid
        grid_search = GridSearchCV(model_svc, param_grid, cv=3, scoring='accuracy', n_jobs=-1,
refit=True)

        # Train and perform grid search
        grid_search.fit(X_train, y_train)

        # Get the best MLP Classifier model from the grid search
        best_model = grid_search.best_estimator_

        #Saves model
        joblib.dump(best_model, 'SVC_Model.pkl')

        # Print the best hyperparameters found
        print(f"Best Hyperparameters for SVC:")
        print(grid_search.best_params_)

        return best_model

    def implement_SVC(self, chosen, X_train, X_test, y_train, y_test):
        file_path = os.getcwd()+"/SVC_Model.pkl"
        if os.path.exists(file_path):
            model = joblib.load('SVC_Model.pkl')
            y_pred = self.run_model(chosen, model, X_train, X_test, y_train, y_test,
proba=True)
        else:
            model = self.support_vector(chosen, X_train, X_test, y_train, y_test)
            y_pred = self.run_model(chosen, model, X_train, X_test, y_train, y_test,
proba=True)

        #Saves result into excel file
        self.obj_data.save_result(y_test, y_pred, "results_SVC.csv")

        print("Training Support Vector Classifier done...")
        return model, y_pred
```

```python
    def adaboost_classifier(self, name, X_train, X_test, y_train, y_test):
        # Define the parameter grid for the grid search
        param_grid = {
            'n_estimators': [50, 100, 150],
            'learning_rate': [0.01, 0.1, 0.2],
        }

        # Initialize the AdaBoost classifier
        adaboost = AdaBoostClassifier(random_state=2021)

        # Create GridSearchCV with the AdaBoost classifier and the parameter grid
        grid_search = GridSearchCV(adaboost, param_grid, cv=3, scoring='accuracy', n_jobs=-1)

        # Train and perform grid search
        grid_search.fit(X_train, y_train)

        # Get the best AdaBoost Classifier model from the grid search
        best_model = grid_search.best_estimator_

        #Saves model
        joblib.dump(best_model, 'ADA_Model.pkl')

        # Print the best hyperparameters found
        print(f"Best Hyperparameters for AdaBoost:")
        print(grid_search.best_params_)

        return best_model

    def implement_ADA(self, chosen, X_train, X_test, y_train, y_test):
        file_path = os.getcwd()+"/ADA_Model.pkl"
        if os.path.exists(file_path):
            model = joblib.load('ADA_Model.pkl')
            y_pred = self.run_model(chosen, model, X_train, X_test, y_train, y_test,
proba=True)
        else:
            model = self.adaboost_classifier(chosen, X_train, X_test, y_train, y_test)
            y_pred = self.run_model(chosen, model, X_train, X_test, y_train, y_test,
proba=True)

        #Saves result into excel file
        self.obj_data.save_result(y_test, y_pred, "results_ADA.csv")

        print("Training AdaBoost done...")
        return model, y_pred

#helper_plot.py
import matplotlib.pyplot as plt
import tkinter as tk
from tkinter import *
import seaborn as sns
import numpy as np
import pandas as pd
import sys
from pandastable import Table
from io import StringIO
from sklearn.metrics import confusion_matrix, roc_curve, accuracy_score
from sklearn.model_selection import learning_curve
from process_data import Process_Data
from main_window import Main_Window
from form1 import Form1
from form2 import Form2
from form3 import Form3
```

```python
from machine_learning import Machine_Learning
from regression import Regression

class Helper_Plot:
    def __init__(self):
        self.obj_window = Main_Window()
        self.obj_data = Process_Data()
        self.obj_reg = Regression()
        self.obj_ml = Machine_Learning()

    def shows_table(self, root, df, width, height, title):
        frame = Toplevel(root) #new window
        self.table = Table(frame, dataframe=df, showtoolbar=True, showstatusbar=True)

        # Sets dimension of Toplevel
        frame.geometry(f"{width}x{height}")
        frame.title(title)
        self.table.show()

    def plot_missing_values(self, df, figure, canvas, title=""):
        figure.clear()
        ax = figure.add_subplot(1,1,1)
        #Plots null values
        missing = df.isna().sum().reset_index()
        missing.columns = ['features', 'total_missing']
        missing['percent'] = (missing['total_missing'] / len(df)) * 100
        missing.index = missing['features']
        del missing['features']
        missing['total_missing'].plot(kind = 'bar', ax=ax)
        ax.set_title(title, fontsize = 12)
        ax.set_facecolor('#F0F0F0')

        # Set font for tick labels
        ax.tick_params(axis='both', which='major', labelsize=5)
        ax.tick_params(axis='both', which='minor', labelsize=5)
        figure.tight_layout()
        canvas.draw()

    # Defines function to create pie chart and bar plot as subplots
    def plot_piechart(self, df, var, figure, canvas, title='', top_ten=False):
        figure.clear()

        # Optionally filter the DataFrame to consider only the top ten values
        if top_ten:
            value_counts = df[var].value_counts().nlargest(10)
        else:
            value_counts = df[var].value_counts()

        # Pie Chart (top subplot)
        ax1 = figure.add_subplot(2,1,1)
        label_list = list(value_counts.index)
        colors = sns.color_palette("Set1", len(label_list))
        _, _, autopcts = ax1.pie(value_counts, autopct="%1.1f%%", colors=colors,
            startangle=30, labels=label_list,
            wedgeprops={"linewidth": 2, "edgecolor": "white"},  # Add white edge
            shadow=True, textprops={'fontsize': 7})
        ax1.set_title(title, weight="bold", fontsize=12)

        # Bar Plot (bottom subplot)
        ax2 = figure.add_subplot(2,1,2)
        ax = value_counts.plot(kind="barh", color=colors, alpha=0.8, ax = ax2)
        for i, j in enumerate(value_counts.values):
            ax.text(.7, i, j, weight="bold", fontsize=7)
```

```python
        ax2.set_title(title, weight="bold", fontsize=12)
        ax2.set_xlabel("Count")
        ax2.set_facecolor('#F0F0F0')
        figure.tight_layout()

        # Autoscale the subplots
        ax1.autoscale()
        ax2.autoscale()

        canvas.draw()

    def plot_piechart_group(self, df, figure, canvas, title="", label=""):
        figure.clear()

        # Pie Chart (top subplot)
        ax1 = figure.add_subplot(2,1,1)
        label_list = list(df.index)
        print(label_list)
        colors = sns.color_palette("Set1", len(label_list))
        _, _, autopcts = ax1.pie(df.values, autopct="%1.1f%%", colors=colors,
            startangle=30, labels=label_list,
            wedgeprops={"linewidth": 2, "edgecolor": "white"},   # Add white edge
            shadow=True, textprops={'fontsize': 7})
        ax1.set_title(title, fontsize=10)

        # Bar Plot (bottom subplot)
        ax2 = figure.add_subplot(2,1,2)
        ax = df.plot(kind="barh", color=colors, alpha=0.8, ax = ax2)
        for i, j in enumerate(df.values):
            ax.text(.7, i, j, weight="bold", fontsize=7)

        ax2.set_title(title, fontsize=10)
        ax2.set_xlabel("Count")
        ax2.set_facecolor('#F0F0F0')

        # Set font for tick labels
        ax.tick_params(axis='both', which='major', labelsize=6)
        ax.tick_params(axis='both', which='minor', labelsize=6)
        figure.tight_layout()
        canvas.draw()

    #Puts label inside stacked bar
    def put_label_stacked_bar(self, ax,fontsize):
        #patches is everything inside of the chart
        for rect in ax.patches:
            # Find where everything is located
            height = rect.get_height()
            width = rect.get_width()
            x = rect.get_x()
            y = rect.get_y()

            # The height of the bar is the data value and can be used as the label
            label_text = f'{width:.0f}'

            # ax.text(x, y, text)
            label_x = x + width / 2
            label_y = y + height / 2

            # plots only when height is greater than specified value
            if width > 0:
                ax.text(label_x, label_y, label_text, \
                    ha='center', va='center', \
                    weight = "bold",fontsize=fontsize)
```

```python
#Plots one variable against another variable
def dist_one_vs_another_plot(self, df, cat1, cat2, figure, canvas, title):
    figure.clear()
    ax1 = figure.add_subplot(1,1,1)

    group_by_stat = df.groupby([cat1, cat2]).size()
    colors = sns.color_palette("Set1", len(df[cat1].unique()))
    group_by_stat.unstack().plot(kind='barh', stacked=True, ax=ax1,color=colors)
    ax1.set_title(title, fontsize=12)
    ax1.set_xlabel('Number of Cases', fontsize=10)
    ax1.set_ylabel(cat1, fontsize=10)
    self.put_label_stacked_bar(ax1,7)

    # Set font for tick labels
    ax1.tick_params(axis='both', which='major', labelsize=8)
    ax1.tick_params(axis='both', which='minor', labelsize=8)
    ax1.legend(facecolor='#E6E6FA', edgecolor='black', fontsize=8)
    ax1.set_facecolor('#F0F0F0')
    figure.tight_layout()
    canvas.draw()

def box_plot(self, df, x, y, hue, figure, canvas, title):
    figure.clear()
    ax1 = figure.add_subplot(1,1,1)

    sns.boxplot(data = df, x = x, y = y, hue = hue, ax=ax1)
    ax1.set_title(title, fontsize=14)
    ax1.set_xlabel(x, fontsize=10)
    ax1.set_ylabel(y, fontsize=10)
    ax1.set_facecolor('#F0F0F0')
    ax1.legend(facecolor='#E6E6FA', edgecolor='black')
    figure.tight_layout()
    canvas.draw()

def dataset_info(self, df):
    win = tk.Toplevel()
    form2 = Form2(win)
    win.title("Dataset Information")

    # Capture sys.stdout
    original_stdout = sys.stdout
    sys.stdout = StringIO()

    # Get df.info() output
    df.info()

    # Get the string value
    info_string = sys.stdout.getvalue()

    # Reset sys.stdout
    sys.stdout = original_stdout

    # Insert the info string into the Text widget
    form2.text.insert(tk.END, info_string)

def dataset_describe(self, df):
    win = tk.Toplevel()
    form2 = Form2(win)
    win.title("Statistical Description")

    # Capture df.describe() output as a string
    describe_string_io = StringIO()
    df.describe().to_string(buf=describe_string_io)
```

```python
        # Get the string value
        describe_string = describe_string_io.getvalue()

        # Insert the info string into the Text widget
        form2.text.insert(tk.END, describe_string)

    def display_null_counts(self, df):
        win = tk.Toplevel()
        form2 = Form2(win)
        win.title("Null Value Counts")

        # Capture sys.stdout
        original_stdout = sys.stdout
        sys.stdout = StringIO()

        # Get df.isnull().sum() output
        null_counts = df.isnull().sum()

        # Get the string value
        null_counts_string = null_counts.to_string()

        # Reset sys.stdout
        sys.stdout = original_stdout

        # Insert the info string into the Text widget
        form2.text.insert(tk.END, null_counts_string)

    def display_null_postal_code_rows(self, df):
        win = tk.Toplevel()
        form2 = Form2(win)
        win.title("Postal Code Null Value Counts")

        # Filter rows where "Postal Code" is null
        null_postal_code_df = df[df["Postal Code"].isnull()]

        # Convert DataFrame to string representation
        null_postal_code_str = null_postal_code_df.to_string(index=False)

        # Insert the string into the ScrolledText widget
        form2.text.insert(tk.END, null_postal_code_str)

    def plot_missing_values_and_coeff(self, df0, df1):
        win = tk.Toplevel()
        form1 = Form1(win)
        win.title("Missing Values and Correlation Coefficients")
        self.plot_missing_values(df0, form1.figure1, form1.canvas1, "Before Filling Null
Values")
        self.plot_missing_values(df1, form1.figure2, form1.canvas2, "After Filling Null
Values")

    def plot_case_distribution(self, df, var1, var2, title="", label="", top_ten=False):
        win = tk.Toplevel()
        form1 = Form1(win)
        win.title(title)
        self.plot_piechart(df, var1, form1.figure1, form1.canvas1, "Case Distribution of " +
label + var1, top_ten)
        self.plot_piechart(df, var2, form1.figure2, form1.canvas2, "Case Distribution of " +
label + var2, top_ten)

    def binds_menu_open_dataset(self, df_before, df_after, root, window):
        window.dataset_menu.entryconfigure("View Dataset",
            command =lambda:self.shows_table(root, df_after, 1250, 600, "Superstore Sales
Dataset"))
```

```python
        window.dataset_menu.entryconfigure("Dataset Information",
            command =lambda:self.dataset_info(df_after))

        window.dataset_menu.entryconfigure("Statistical Description",
            command =lambda:self.dataset_describe(df_after))

        window.dataset_menu.entryconfigure("Null Values",
            command =lambda:self.display_null_counts(df_before))

        window.dataset_menu.entryconfigure("Postal Code Null Values",
            command =lambda:self.display_null_postal_code_rows(df_before))

    def binds_features_distribution(self, window, df0, df1, df2):
        window.dist_menu.entryconfigure("Missing Values",
            command = lambda:self.plot_missing_values_and_coeff(df0, df1))

        window.dist_menu.entryconfigure("Day and Month",
            command = lambda:self.plot_case_distribution(df2, "Day", "Month",
                "The Case Distribution of Day and Month"))

        window.dist_menu.entryconfigure("Quarter and Year",
            command = lambda:self.plot_case_distribution(df2, "Quarter", "Year",
                "The Case Distribution of Quarter and Year"))

        window.dist_menu.entryconfigure("Country and City",
            command = lambda:self.plot_case_distribution(df2, "Country", "City",
                "The Case Distribution of Top Ten Country and Year", " Top 10 ", top_ten=True))

        window.dist_menu.entryconfigure("State and Region",
            command = lambda:self.plot_case_distribution(df2, "State", "Region",
                "The Case Distribution of State and Year", " Top 10 ", top_ten=True))

        window.dist_menu.entryconfigure("Customer Name and Customer ID",
            command = lambda:self.plot_case_distribution(df2, "Customer Name", "Customer ID",
                "The Case Distribution of Customer Name and Customer ID", " Top 10 ",
top_ten=True))

        window.dist_menu.entryconfigure("Ship Mode and Segment",
            command = lambda:self.plot_case_distribution(df2, "Ship Mode", "Segment",
                "The Case Distribution of Ship Mode and Segment"))

        window.dist_menu.entryconfigure("Product Name and Product ID",
            command = lambda:self.plot_case_distribution(df2, "Product Name", "Product ID",
                "The Case Distribution of Product Name and Product ID", " Top 10 ",
top_ten=True))

        window.dist_menu.entryconfigure("Category and Sub-Category",
            command = lambda:self.plot_case_distribution(df2, "Category", "Sub-Category",
                "The Case Distribution of Category and Sub-Category"))

    def plot_box_distribution(self, df, var1="", var2="", var3="", title=""):
        win = tk.Toplevel()
        form3 = Form3(win)
        self.box_plot(df, var1, var2, var3, form3.figure1, form3.canvas1, title)

    def plot_categorized_distribution(self, df, var1="", var2="", var3="",
        var4="", title1="", title2=""):
        win = tk.Toplevel()
        form1 = Form1(win)

        self.dist_one_vs_another_plot(df, var1, var2, form1.figure1, form1.canvas1, title1)
        self.dist_one_vs_another_plot(df, var3, var4, form1.figure2, form1.canvas2, title2)

    def plot_grouped_distribution(self, df, var1="", var2="", var3="",
```

```python
                var4="", title1="", title2="", label="", mode=""):
        win = tk.Toplevel()
        form1 = Form1(win)
        win.title("Distribution of " + var2 + " by " + var1 + " and " + var3)
        sum_by_cat1 = df.groupby(var1)[var2].sum()
        sum_by_cat_top_ten1 = sum_by_cat1.nlargest(10)
        sum_by_cat2 = df.groupby(var3)[var4].sum()
        sum_by_cat_top_ten2 = sum_by_cat2.nlargest(10)

        if mode == "":
            self.plot_piechart_group(sum_by_cat1, form1.figure1, form1.canvas1, title1, label)
            self.plot_piechart_group(sum_by_cat2, form1.figure2, form1.canvas2, title2, label)
        else:
            self.plot_piechart_group(sum_by_cat_top_ten1, form1.figure1, form1.canvas1, title1,
label)
            self.plot_piechart_group(sum_by_cat_top_ten2, form1.figure2, form1.canvas2, title2,
label)

    def binds_categories_distribution(self, window, df):
        window.dist_cat.entryconfigure("Sales by Year and Quarter",
            command = lambda:self.plot_grouped_distribution(df, "Year", "Sales",
            "Quarter", "Sales", "Sales by Year", "Sales by Quarter", "Sales"))

        window.dist_cat.entryconfigure("Sales by Day and Month",
            command = lambda:self.plot_grouped_distribution(df, "Day", "Sales",
            "Month", "Sales", "Sales by Day", "Sales by Month", "Sales"))

        window.dist_cat.entryconfigure("Sales by Ship Mode and Segment",
            command = lambda:self.plot_grouped_distribution(df, "Ship Mode", "Sales",
            "Segment", "Sales", "Sales by Ship Mode", "Sales by Segment", "Sales"))

        window.dist_cat.entryconfigure("Sales by Category and Sub-Category",
            command = lambda:self.plot_grouped_distribution(df, "Category", "Sales",
            "Sub-Category", "Sales", "Sales by Category", "Sales by Sub-Category", "Sales"))

        window.dist_cat.entryconfigure("Sales by Product Name and Product ID",
            command = lambda:self.plot_grouped_distribution(df, "Product Name", "Sales",
            "Product ID", "Sales", "Sales by Product Name", "Sales by Product ID", "Sales",
"top-ten"))

        window.dist_cat.entryconfigure("Sales by Customer Name and Customer ID",
            command = lambda:self.plot_grouped_distribution(df, "Customer Name", "Sales",
            "Customer ID", "Sales", "Sales by Customer Name", "Sales by Customer ID", "Sales",
"top-ten"))

        window.dist_cat.entryconfigure("Sales by City and State",
            command = lambda:self.plot_grouped_distribution(df, "City", "Sales",
            "State", "Sales", "Sales by City", "Sales by State", "Sales", "top-ten"))

        window.dist_cat.entryconfigure("Categorized Sales",
            command = lambda:self.plot_case_distribution(df, "Cat_Sales", "Category",
                "The Case Distribution of Categorized Sales and Category"))

        window.dist_cat.entryconfigure("Categorized Sales by Year and Quarter",
            command = lambda:self.plot_categorized_distribution(df, "Year", "Cat_Sales",
                "Quarter", "Cat_Sales",
                "The Case Distribution of Categorized Sales by Year",
                "The Case Distribution of Categorized Sales by Quarter"))

        window.dist_cat.entryconfigure("Categorized Sales by Day and Month",
            command = lambda:self.plot_categorized_distribution(df, "Day", "Cat_Sales",
                "Month", "Cat_Sales",
                "The Case Distribution of Categorized Sales by Day",
                "The Case Distribution of Categorized Sales by Month"))
```

```python
        window.dist_cat.entryconfigure("Categorized Sales by Segment and Sub-Category",
            command = lambda:self.plot_categorized_distribution(df, "Segment", "Cat_Sales",
                "Sub-Category", "Cat_Sales",
                "The Case Distribution of Categorized Sales by Segment",
                "The Case Distribution of Categorized Sales by Sub-Category"))

        window.dist_cat.entryconfigure("Categorized Sales by Region and State",
            command = lambda:self.plot_categorized_distribution(df, "Region", "Cat_Sales",
                "State", "Cat_Sales",
                "The Case Distribution of Categorized Sales by Region",
                "The Case Distribution of Categorized Sales by State"))

        window.dist_cat.entryconfigure("Day versus Sales Per Category",
            command = lambda:self.plot_box_distribution(df, "Day", "Sales", "Category",
                "Day versus Sales Per Category"))

        window.dist_cat.entryconfigure("Month versus Sales Per Segment",
            command = lambda:self.plot_box_distribution(df, "Month", "Sales", "Segment",
                "Month versus Sales Per Segment"))

        window.dist_cat.entryconfigure("Sub-Category versus Sales Per Year",
            command = lambda:self.plot_box_distribution(df, "Sub-Category", "Sales", "Year",
                "Sub-Category versus Sales Per Year"))

        window.dist_cat.entryconfigure("Region versus Sales Per Quarter",
            command = lambda:self.plot_box_distribution(df, "Region", "Sales", "Quarter",
                "Region versus Sales Per Quarter"))

    def choose_plot(self, df1, df2, chosen, figure1, canvas1, figure2, canvas2):
        print(chosen)
        if chosen == "Day":
            self.plot_piechart(df2, "Day", figure1, canvas1, "Case Distribution of Day")

        elif chosen == "Month":
            self.plot_piechart(df2, "Month", figure2, canvas2, "Case Distribution of Month")

        elif chosen == "Quarter":
            self.plot_piechart(df2, "Quarter", figure1, canvas1, "Case Distribution of
Quarter")

        elif chosen == "Year":
            self.plot_piechart(df2, "Year", figure2, canvas2, "Case Distribution of Year")

        elif chosen == "Missing Values":
            self.plot_missing_values(df1, figure1, canvas1)

        elif chosen == "Correlation Coefficient":
            self.plot_corr_coeffs(df1, figure2, canvas2)

        elif chosen == "Country and City":
            self.plot_piechart(df2, "Country", figure1, canvas1, "Case Distribution of
Country")
            self.plot_piechart(df2, "City", figure2, canvas2, "Case Distribution of City",
top_ten=True)

        elif chosen == "State and Region":
            self.plot_piechart(df2, "State", figure1, canvas1, "Case Distribution of State",
top_ten=True)
            self.plot_piechart(df2, "Region", figure2, canvas2, "Case Distribution of Region")

        elif chosen == "Customer Name and Customer ID":
            self.plot_piechart(df2, "Customer Name", figure1, canvas1, "Case Distribution of
Customer Name", top_ten=True)
```

```python
        self.plot_piechart(df2, "Customer ID", figure2, canvas2, "Case Distribution of
Customer ID", top_ten=True)

    elif chosen == "Ship Mode and Segment":
        self.plot_piechart(df2, "Ship Mode", figure1, canvas1, "Case Distribution of Ship
Mode")
        self.plot_piechart(df2, "Segment", figure2, canvas2, "Case Distribution of
Segment")

    elif chosen == "Product Name and Product ID":
        self.plot_piechart(df2, "Product Name", figure1, canvas1, "Case Distribution of
Product Name", top_ten=True)
        self.plot_piechart(df2, "Product ID", figure2, canvas2, "Case Distribution of
Product ID", top_ten=True)

    elif chosen == "Category and Sub-Category":
        self.plot_piechart(df2, "Category", figure1, canvas1, "Case Distribution of
Category", top_ten=True)
        self.plot_piechart(df2, "Sub-Category", figure2, canvas2, "Case Distribution of
Sub-Category", top_ten=True)

    elif chosen == "Sales by Year and Quarter":
        self.plot_piechart_group(df2.groupby('Year')['Sales'].sum(), figure1, canvas1,
"Sales by Year")
        self.plot_piechart_group(df2.groupby('Quarter')['Sales'].sum(), figure2, canvas2,
"Sales by Quarter")

    elif chosen == "Sales by Day and Month":
        self.plot_piechart_group(df2.groupby('Day')['Sales'].sum(), figure1, canvas1,
"Sales by Day")
        self.plot_piechart_group(df2.groupby('Month')['Sales'].sum(), figure2, canvas2,
"Sales by Month")

    elif chosen == "Sales by Ship Mode and Segment":
        self.plot_piechart_group(df2.groupby('Ship Mode')['Sales'].sum(), figure1, canvas1,
"Sales by Ship Mode")
        self.plot_piechart_group(df2.groupby('Segment')['Sales'].sum(), figure2, canvas2,
"Sales by Segment")

    elif chosen == "Sales by Category and Sub-Category":
        self.plot_piechart_group(df2.groupby('Category')['Sales'].sum(), figure1, canvas1,
"Sales by Category")
        self.plot_piechart_group(df2.groupby('Sub-Category')['Sales'].sum(), figure2,
canvas2, "Sales by Sub-Category")

    elif chosen == "Sales by Product Name and Product ID":
        self.plot_piechart_group(df2.groupby('Product Name')['Sales'].sum().nlargest(10),
figure1, canvas1, "Sales by Product Name")
        self.plot_piechart_group(df2.groupby('Product ID')['Sales'].sum().nlargest(10),
figure2, canvas2, "Sales by Product ID")

    elif chosen == "Sales by Customer Name and Customer ID":
        self.plot_piechart_group(df2.groupby('Customer Name')['Sales'].sum().nlargest(10),
            figure1, canvas1, "Sales by Customer Name")
        self.plot_piechart_group(df2.groupby('Customer ID')['Sales'].sum().nlargest(10),
            figure2, canvas2, "Sales by Customer ID")

    elif chosen == "Sales by City and State":
        self.plot_piechart_group(df2.groupby('City')['Sales'].sum().nlargest(10),
            figure1, canvas1, "Sales by City")
        self.plot_piechart_group(df2.groupby('State')['Sales'].sum().nlargest(10),
            figure2, canvas2, "Sales by State")

    elif chosen == "Categorized Sales by Year and Quarter":
```

```python
            self.dist_one_vs_another_plot(df2, "Year", "Cat_Sales", figure1, canvas1,
"Categorized Sales by Year")
            self.dist_one_vs_another_plot(df2, "Quarter", "Cat_Sales", figure2, canvas2,
"Categorized Sales by Quarter")

        elif chosen == "Categorized Sales by Day and Month":
            self.dist_one_vs_another_plot(df2, "Day", "Cat_Sales", figure1, canvas1,
"Categorized Sales by Day")
            self.dist_one_vs_another_plot(df2, "Month", "Cat_Sales", figure2, canvas2,
"Categorized Sales by Month")

        elif chosen == "Categorized Sales by Segment and Sub-Category":
            self.dist_one_vs_another_plot(df2, "Segment", "Cat_Sales", figure1, canvas1,
"Categorized Sales by Segment")
            self.dist_one_vs_another_plot(df2, "Sub-Category", "Cat_Sales", figure2, canvas2,
"Categorized Sales by Sub-Category")

        elif chosen == "Categorized Sales by Region and State":
            self.dist_one_vs_another_plot(df2, "Region", "Cat_Sales", figure1, canvas1,
"Categorized Sales by Region")
            self.dist_one_vs_another_plot(df2, "State", "Cat_Sales", figure2, canvas2,
"Categorized Sales by State")

        if chosen == "Correlation Matrix":
            self.plot_corr_mat(df1, figure1, canvas1)

    def line_plot_year_wise(self, df, feat, year1, year2, figure, canvas):
        figure.clear()
        ax1 = figure.add_subplot(2, 1, 1)
        data1 = df[df["Year"]==year1]
        data2 = df[df["Year"]==year2]
        # Convert the column and index to NumPy arrays
        date_index1 = data1.index.to_numpy()
        date_index2 = data2.index.to_numpy()

        # Line plot
        ax1.plot(date_index1, data1[feat].to_numpy(),
            color="red", marker='o', linestyle='-', linewidth=2, markersize=1, label=feat)
        ax1.set_xlabel('YEAR')
        ax1.set_title(feat + ' (YEAR = ' + str(year1) + ')', fontsize=12)
        ax1.legend(facecolor='#E6E6FA', edgecolor='black')
        ax1.set_facecolor('#F0F0F0')
        ax1.grid(True)

        ax2 = figure.add_subplot(2, 1, 2)
        ax2.plot(date_index2, data2[feat].to_numpy(),
            color="blue", marker='o', linestyle='-', linewidth=2, markersize=1, label=feat)
        ax2.set_xlabel('YEAR')
        ax2.set_title(feat + ' (YEAR = ' + str(year2) + ')', fontsize=12)
        ax2.legend(facecolor='#E6E6FA', edgecolor='black')
        ax2.set_facecolor('#F0F0F0')
        ax2.grid(True)

        figure.tight_layout()
        canvas.draw()

    def line_plot_norm_data(self, norm_data, figure, canvas, label, title):
        figure.clear()
        ax = figure.add_subplot(1, 1, 1)

        # Convert the column and index to NumPy arrays
        date_index = norm_data.index.to_numpy()

        values = norm_data.to_numpy()
```

```python
        ax.plot(values, date_index, marker='o', linestyle='-',
                        linewidth=3, markersize=2, label="SALES")

        ax.set_ylabel(label)
        ax.set_title(title, fontsize=12)
        ax.legend(fontsize=7, facecolor='#E6E6FA', edgecolor='black')
        ax.set_facecolor('#F0F0F0')
        ax.grid(True)

        figure.tight_layout()
        canvas.draw()

    def line_plot_data_mean_ewm(self, data_mean, data_ewm, figure, canvas, xlabel, ylabel):
        figure.clear()
        ax1 = figure.add_subplot(1, 1, 1)

        # Convert the column and index to NumPy arrays
        date_index = data_mean.index.to_numpy()

        # Line plot
        ax1.plot(date_index, data_mean.to_numpy(),
            color="red", marker='o', linestyle='-', linewidth=2, markersize=1, label="Mean")
        ax1.plot(date_index,data_ewm.to_numpy(),
            color="blue", marker='o', linestyle='-', linewidth=2, markersize=1, label="EWM")
        ax1.set_title("Year-Wise Mean/EWM of Sales", fontsize=12)
        ax1.legend(facecolor='#E6E6FA', edgecolor='black')
        ax1.set_xlabel(xlabel)
        ax1.set_ylabel(ylabel)
        ax1.set_facecolor('#F0F0F0')
        ax1.grid(True)

        figure.tight_layout()
        canvas.draw()

    def plot_year_wise(self, df, feat, year1, year2):
        win = tk.Toplevel()
        form3 = Form3(win)
        self.line_plot_year_wise(df, feat, year1, year2, form3.figure1, form3.canvas1)

    def plot_year_wise_mean_ewm(self, data_mean, data_ewm):
        win = tk.Toplevel()
        form3 = Form3(win)
        self.line_plot_data_mean_ewm(data_mean, data_ewm, form3.figure1, form3.canvas1, "YEAR",
"SALES")

    def box_violin_strip_heat(self, data, filter, feat1, figure1, canvas1, figure2, canvas2,
title):
        figure1.clear()
        ax1 = figure1.add_subplot(2, 1, 1)
        sns.boxplot(x = filter, y = feat1, data = data, ax=ax1)
        ax1.set_title("Box Plot of " + feat1 + " by " + filter, fontsize=12)
        # Set font for tick labels
        ax1.tick_params(axis='both', which='major', labelsize=6)
        ax1.tick_params(axis='both', which='minor', labelsize=6)
        ax1.grid(True)
        ax1.set_facecolor('#F0F0F0')

        ax2 = figure1.add_subplot(2, 1, 2)
        sns.violinplot(x = filter, y = feat1, data = data, ax=ax2)
        ax2.set_title("Violin Plot of " + feat1 + " by " + filter, fontsize=12)
        # Set font for tick labels
        ax2.tick_params(axis='both', which='major', labelsize=6)
        ax2.tick_params(axis='both', which='minor', labelsize=6)
        ax2.grid(True)
```

```python
        ax2.set_facecolor('#F0F0F0')
        figure1.tight_layout()
        canvas1.draw()

        figure2.clear()
        ax3 = figure2.add_subplot(2, 1, 1)
        sns.stripplot(x = filter, y = feat1, data = data, ax=ax3)
        ax3.set_title("Strip Plot of " + feat1 + " by " + filter, fontsize=12)
        # Set font for tick labels
        ax3.tick_params(axis='both', which='major', labelsize=6)
        ax3.tick_params(axis='both', which='minor', labelsize=6)
        ax3.set_facecolor('#F0F0F0')
        ax3.grid(True)

        ax4 = figure2.add_subplot(2, 1, 2)
        sns.swarmplot(x = filter, y = feat1, data = data, ax=ax4)
        ax4.set_title("Swarm Plot of " + feat1 + " by " + filter, fontsize=12)
        # Set font for tick labels
        ax4.tick_params(axis='both', which='major', labelsize=6)
        ax4.tick_params(axis='both', which='minor', labelsize=6)
        ax4.grid(True)
        ax4.set_facecolor('#F0F0F0')
        figure2.tight_layout()
        canvas2.draw()

    def plot_year_trends(self, df, var1, var2, title=""):
        win = tk.Toplevel()
        form1 = Form1(win)
        self.box_violin_strip_heat(df, var1, var2, form1.figure1, form1.canvas1,
            form1.figure2, form1.canvas2, title)

    def binds_year_wise(self, window, df, data_mean, data_ewm):
        window.year_wise.entryconfigure("Year-Wise Sales Distribution 2017 and 2018",
            command = lambda:self.plot_year_wise(df, "Sales", 2017, 2018))

        window.year_wise.entryconfigure("Year-Wise Sales Distribution 2015 and 2016",
            command = lambda:self.plot_year_wise(df, "Sales", 2015, 2016))

        window.year_wise.entryconfigure("Year-Wise Sales Mean and EWM",
            command = lambda:self.plot_year_wise_mean_ewm(data_mean, data_ewm))

        window.year_wise.entryconfigure("Sales by Year",
            command = lambda:self.plot_year_trends(df, "Year", "Sales"))

        window.year_wise.entryconfigure("Sales by Quarter",
            command = lambda:self.plot_year_trends(df, "Quarter", "Sales"))

        window.year_wise.entryconfigure("Sales by Month",
            command = lambda:self.plot_year_trends(df, "Month", "Sales"))

        window.year_wise.entryconfigure("Sales by Day",
            command = lambda:self.plot_year_trends(df, "Day", "Sales"))

        window.year_wise.entryconfigure("Sales by Week",
            command = lambda:self.plot_year_trends(df, "Week", "Sales"))


    def choose_year_wise(self, df, data_mean, data_ewm, data_norm, chosen, figure1, canvas1,
figure2, canvas2):
        if chosen == "Year-Wise Sales Distribution 2017 and 2018":
            self.line_plot_year_wise(df, "Sales", 2017, 2018, figure1, canvas1)

        if chosen == "Year-Wise Sales Distribution 2015 and 2016":
            self.line_plot_year_wise(df, "Sales", 2015, 2016, figure2, canvas2)
```

```python
        if chosen == "Year-Wise Sales Mean and EWM":
            self.line_plot_data_mean_ewm(data_mean, data_ewm, figure1, canvas1, "YEAR", chosen)

        if chosen == "Normalized Year-Wise Data":
            self.line_plot_norm_data(data_norm, figure2, canvas2, "YEAR", chosen)

    def line_plot_month_wise(self, df, feat1, year, filter, filter1, filter2, figure, canvas):
        figure.clear()
        ax1 = figure.add_subplot(2, 1, 1)

        data1 = df[(df["Year"]==year)&(df[filter]==filter1)]
        data2 = df[(df["Year"]==year)&(df[filter]==filter2)]

        # Convert the column and index to NumPy arrays
        date_index1 = data1.index.to_numpy()
        date_index2 = data2.index.to_numpy()

        # Line plot
        ax1.plot(date_index1, data1[feat1].to_numpy(),
            color="red", marker='o', linestyle='-', linewidth=2, markersize=1, label=feat1)
        ax1.set_xlabel('DATE')
        ax1.set_ylabel(feat1)
        ax1.set_title(feat1 + " " + filter + " = " + filter1 + " " + str(year), fontsize=12)
        ax1.legend(facecolor='#E6E6FA', edgecolor='black')
        ax1.set_facecolor('#F0F0F0')
        ax1.grid(True)

        # Set font for tick labels
        ax1.tick_params(axis='both', which='major', labelsize=7)
        ax1.tick_params(axis='both', which='minor', labelsize=7)

        ax2 = figure.add_subplot(2, 1, 2)
        ax2.plot(date_index2, data2[feat1].to_numpy(),
            color="red", marker='o', linestyle='-', linewidth=2, markersize=1, label=feat1)
        ax2.set_xlabel('DATE')
        ax2.set_ylabel(feat1)
        ax2.set_title(feat1 + " " + filter + " = " + filter2 + " " + str(year), fontsize=12)
        ax2.legend(facecolor='#E6E6FA', edgecolor='black')
        ax2.set_facecolor('#F0F0F0')
        ax2.grid(True)

        # Set font for tick labels
        ax2.tick_params(axis='both', which='major', labelsize=7)
        ax2.tick_params(axis='both', which='minor', labelsize=7)

        figure.tight_layout()
        canvas.draw()

    def color_month(self, month):
        if month == 1:
            return 'January','blue'
        elif month == 2:
            return 'February','green'
        elif month == 3:
            return 'March','orange'
        elif month == 4:
            return 'April','yellow'
        elif month == 5:
            return 'May','red'
        elif month == 6:
            return 'June','violet'
        elif month == 7:
            return 'July','purple'
```

```python
        elif month == 8:
            return 'August','black'
        elif month == 9:
            return 'September','brown'
        elif month == 10:
            return 'October','darkblue'
        elif month == 11:
            return 'November','grey'
        else:
            return 'December','pink'

    def line_plot_month(self, month, data, ax):
        label, color = self.color_month(month)
        mdata = data[data.index.month == month]
        date_index = mdata.index.to_numpy()

        ax.plot(date_index, mdata.to_numpy(),
            marker='o', linestyle='-',
            color=color, linewidth=2, markersize=1, label=label)

    def sns_plot_month(self, monthly_data, title, figure, canvas):
        figure.clear()
        ax = figure.add_subplot(1, 1, 1)
        ax.set_title(title, fontsize=12)
        ax.set_xlabel('YEAR', fontsize=10)
        ax.set_ylabel("SALES", fontsize=10)

        for i in range(1,13):
            self.line_plot_month(i, monthly_data, ax)

        ax.legend(facecolor='#E6E6FA', edgecolor='black')
        ax.grid()
        ax.set_facecolor('#F0F0F0')
        figure.tight_layout()
        canvas.draw()

    def plot_month_wise(self, df, feat1, year, filter, filter1, filter2):
        win = tk.Toplevel()
        form3 = Form3(win)
        self.line_plot_month_wise(df, feat1, year, filter,
            filter1, filter2, form3.figure1, form3.canvas1)

    def plot_month_wise_mean_ewm(self, data_mean, data_ewm):
        win = tk.Toplevel()
        form3 = Form3(win)
        self.line_plot_data_mean_ewm(data_mean, data_ewm, form3.figure1, form3.canvas1, "YEAR",
"SALES")

    def plot_month_wise_by_month(self, data_mean, title):
        win = tk.Toplevel()
        form3 = Form3(win)
        self.sns_plot_month(data_mean, title, form3.figure1, form3.canvas1)

    def month_wise_region_based(self, df, figure, canvas):
        figure.clear()

        west_df = df.loc[df['Region'] == 'West']
        east_df = df.loc[df['Region'] == 'East']
        south_df = df.loc[df['Region'] == 'South']
        central_df = df.loc[df['Region'] == 'Central']

        west_monthly_sales = west_df['Sales'].resample('M').sum()
        west_monthly_sales = west_monthly_sales.round(2)
```

```python
        east_monthly_sales = east_df['Sales'].resample('M').sum()
        east_monthly_sales = east_monthly_sales.round(2)

        south_monthly_sales = south_df['Sales'].resample('M').sum()
        south_monthly_sales = south_monthly_sales.round(2)

        central_monthly_sales = central_df['Sales'].resample('M').sum()
        central_monthly_sales = central_monthly_sales.round(2)

        ax1 = figure.add_subplot(1, 1, 1)
        ax1.plot(west_monthly_sales.index.to_numpy(), west_monthly_sales.values, color="red",
marker='o', linestyle='-', label="West")
        ax1.plot(east_monthly_sales.index.to_numpy(), east_monthly_sales.values, color="blue",
marker='o', linestyle='-', label="East")
        ax1.plot(south_monthly_sales.index.to_numpy(), south_monthly_sales.values,
color="green", marker='o', linestyle='-', label="South")
        ax1.plot(central_monthly_sales.index.to_numpy(), central_monthly_sales.values,
color="black", marker='o', linestyle='-', label="Central")

        ax1.set_title("Region-Based Monthly Sales", fontsize=12)
        ax1.legend(facecolor='#E6E6FA', edgecolor='black')
        ax1.set_xlabel("Date")
        ax1.set_ylabel("Sales")
        ax1.set_facecolor('#F0F0F0')
        ax1.grid(True)

        figure.tight_layout()
        canvas.draw()

    def month_wise_category_based(self, df, figure, canvas):
        figure.clear()

        #Creates a new column
        df['Quantity'] = 1

        office_supplies_df = df.loc[df['Category'] == 'Office Supplies']
        technology_df = df.loc[df['Category'] == 'Technology']
        furniture_df = df.loc[df['Category'] == 'Furniture']

        # Find how many quantities sold per month for each category
        monthly_office = office_supplies_df['Quantity'].resample('M').sum()
        monthly_technology = technology_df['Quantity'].resample('M').sum()
        monthly_furniture = furniture_df['Quantity'].resample('M').sum()

        ax1 = figure.add_subplot(1, 1, 1)
        ax1.plot(monthly_office.index.to_numpy(), monthly_office.values, color="red",
marker='o', linestyle='-', label="Office Products Sales Quantities by Month")
        ax1.plot(monthly_technology.index.to_numpy(), monthly_technology.values, color="blue",
marker='o', linestyle='-', label="Technology Products Sales Quantities by Month")
        ax1.plot(monthly_furniture.index.to_numpy(), monthly_furniture.values, color="green",
marker='o', linestyle='-', label="Furniture Products Sales Quantities by Month")

        ax1.set_title("Category-Based Monthly Quantity", fontsize=12)
        ax1.legend(facecolor='#E6E6FA', edgecolor='black')
        ax1.set_xlabel("Date")
        ax1.set_ylabel("Quantity")
        ax1.set_facecolor('#F0F0F0')
        ax1.grid(True)

        figure.tight_layout()
        canvas.draw()

    def month_wise_segment_based(self, df, figure, canvas):
        figure.clear()
```

```python
        corp_df = df.loc[df['Segment'] == 'Corporate']
        office_df = df.loc[df['Segment'] == 'Home Office']
        cons_df = df.loc[df['Segment'] == 'Consumer']


        corp_monthly_sales = corp_df['Sales'].resample('M').sum()
        corp_monthly_sales = corp_monthly_sales.round(2)

        office_monthly_sales = office_df['Sales'].resample('M').sum()
        office_monthly_sales = office_monthly_sales.round(2)

        cons_monthly_sales = cons_df['Sales'].resample('M').sum()
        cons_monthly_sales = cons_monthly_sales.round(2)

        ax1 = figure.add_subplot(1, 1, 1)
        ax1.plot(corp_monthly_sales.index.to_numpy(), corp_monthly_sales.values, color="red",
marker='o', linestyle='-', label="Corporate")
        ax1.plot(office_monthly_sales.index.to_numpy(), office_monthly_sales.values,
color="blue", marker='o', linestyle='-', label="Home Office")
        ax1.plot(cons_monthly_sales.index.to_numpy(), cons_monthly_sales.values, color="green",
marker='o', linestyle='-', label="Consumer")

        ax1.set_title("Segment-Based Monthly Sales", fontsize=12)
        ax1.legend(facecolor='#E6E6FA', edgecolor='black')
        ax1.set_xlabel("Date")
        ax1.set_ylabel("Sales")
        ax1.set_facecolor('#F0F0F0')
        ax1.grid(True)

        figure.tight_layout()
        canvas.draw()

    def month_wise_city_based(self, df, figure, canvas):
        figure.clear()

        los_df = df.loc[df['City'] == 'Los Angeles']
        york_df = df.loc[df['City'] == 'New York City']
        phil_df = df.loc[df['City'] == 'Philadelphia']
        san_df = df.loc[df['City'] == 'San Francisco']
        sea_df = df.loc[df['City'] == 'Seattle']
        chi_df = df.loc[df['City'] == 'Chicago']
        hou_df = df.loc[df['City'] == 'Houston']
        col_df = df.loc[df['City'] == 'Columbus']
        die_df = df.loc[df['City'] == 'San Diego']
        spr_df = df.loc[df['City'] == 'Springfield']

        los_monthly_sales = los_df['Sales'].resample('M').sum()
        los_monthly_sales = los_monthly_sales.round(2)

        york_monthly_sales = york_df['Sales'].resample('M').sum()
        york_monthly_sales = york_monthly_sales.round(2)

        phils_monthly_sales = phil_df['Sales'].resample('M').sum()
        phils_monthly_sales = phils_monthly_sales.round(2)

        san_monthly_sales = san_df['Sales'].resample('M').sum()
        san_monthly_sales = san_monthly_sales.round(2)

        sea_monthly_sales = sea_df['Sales'].resample('M').sum()
        sea_monthly_sales = sea_monthly_sales.round(2)

        ax1 = figure.add_subplot(1, 1, 1)
```

```python
        ax1.plot(los_monthly_sales.index.to_numpy(), los_monthly_sales.values, color="red",
marker='o', linestyle='-', label="Los Angeles")
        ax1.plot(york_monthly_sales.index.to_numpy(), york_monthly_sales.values, color="blue",
marker='o', linestyle='-', label="New York City")
        ax1.plot(phils_monthly_sales.index.to_numpy(), phils_monthly_sales.values,
color="green", marker='o', linestyle='-', label="Philadelphia")
        ax1.plot(san_monthly_sales.index.to_numpy(), san_monthly_sales.values, color="black",
marker='o', linestyle='-', label="San Francisco")
        ax1.plot(sea_monthly_sales.index.to_numpy(), sea_monthly_sales.values, color="cyan",
marker='o', linestyle='-', label="Seattle")

        ax1.set_title("City-Based Monthly Sales", fontsize=12)
        ax1.legend(facecolor='#E6E6FA', edgecolor='black')
        ax1.set_xlabel("Date")
        ax1.set_ylabel("Sales")
        ax1.set_facecolor('#F0F0F0')
        ax1.grid(True)

        figure.tight_layout()
        canvas.draw()

    def month_wise_shipmode_based(self, df, figure, canvas):
        figure.clear()

        std_df = df.loc[df['Ship Mode'] == 'Standard Class']
        first_df = df.loc[df['Ship Mode'] == 'First Class']
        scd_df = df.loc[df['Ship Mode'] == 'Second Class']
        same_df = df.loc[df['Ship Mode'] == 'Same Day']

        std_monthly_sales = std_df['Sales'].resample('M').sum()
        std_monthly_sales = std_monthly_sales.round(2)

        first_monthly_sales = first_df['Sales'].resample('M').sum()
        first_monthly_sales = first_monthly_sales.round(2)

        scd_monthly_sales = scd_df['Sales'].resample('M').sum()
        scd_monthly_sales = scd_monthly_sales.round(2)

        same_monthly_sales = same_df['Sales'].resample('M').sum()
        same_monthly_sales = same_monthly_sales.round(2)

        ax1 = figure.add_subplot(1, 1, 1)
        ax1.plot(std_monthly_sales.index.to_numpy(), std_monthly_sales.values, color="red",
marker='o', linestyle='-', label="Standard Class")
        ax1.plot(first_monthly_sales.index.to_numpy(), first_monthly_sales.values,
color="blue", marker='o', linestyle='-', label="First Class")
        ax1.plot(scd_monthly_sales.index.to_numpy(), scd_monthly_sales.values, color="green",
marker='o', linestyle='-', label="Second Class")
        ax1.plot(same_monthly_sales.index.to_numpy(), same_monthly_sales.values, color="cyan",
marker='o', linestyle='-', label="Same Day")

        ax1.set_title("Ship Mode-Based Monthly Sales", fontsize=12)
        ax1.legend(facecolor='#E6E6FA', edgecolor='black')
        ax1.set_xlabel("Date")
        ax1.set_ylabel("Sales")
        ax1.set_facecolor('#F0F0F0')
        ax1.grid(True)

        figure.tight_layout()
        canvas.draw()

    def month_wise_productname_based(self, df, figure, canvas):
        figure.clear()
```

```python
        env_df = df.loc[df['Product Name'] == 'Staple envelope']
        stp_df = df.loc[df['Product Name'] == 'Staples']
        eas_df = df.loc[df['Product Name'] == 'Easy-staple paper']
        ave_df = df.loc[df['Product Name'] == 'Avery Non-Stick Binders']
        rem_df = df.loc[df['Product Name'] == 'Staple remover']

        env_monthly_sales = env_df['Sales'].resample('M').sum()
        env_monthly_sales = env_monthly_sales.round(2)

        stp_monthly_sales = stp_df['Sales'].resample('M').sum()
        stp_monthly_sales = stp_monthly_sales.round(2)

        eas_monthly_sales = eas_df['Sales'].resample('M').sum()
        eas_monthly_sales = eas_monthly_sales.round(2)

        ave_monthly_sales = ave_df['Sales'].resample('M').sum()
        ave_monthly_sales = ave_monthly_sales.round(2)

        rem_monthly_sales = ave_df['Sales'].resample('M').sum()
        rem_monthly_sales = rem_monthly_sales.round(2)

        ax1 = figure.add_subplot(1, 1, 1)
        ax1.plot(env_monthly_sales.index.to_numpy(), env_monthly_sales.values,
                color="red", marker='o', linestyle='-', label="Staple envelope")
        ax1.plot(stp_monthly_sales.index.to_numpy(), stp_monthly_sales.values,
                color="blue", marker='o', linestyle='-', label="Staples")
        ax1.plot(eas_monthly_sales.index.to_numpy(), eas_monthly_sales.values,
                color="green", marker='o', linestyle='-', label="Easy-staple paper")
        ax1.plot(ave_monthly_sales.index.to_numpy(), ave_monthly_sales.values,
                color="cyan", marker='o', linestyle='-', label="Avery Non-Stick Binders")
        ax1.plot(rem_monthly_sales.index.to_numpy(), rem_monthly_sales.values,
                color="black", marker='o', linestyle='-', label="Staple remover")

        ax1.set_title("Product Name-Based Monthly Sales", fontsize=12)
        ax1.legend(facecolor='#E6E6FA', edgecolor='black')
        ax1.set_xlabel("Date")
        ax1.set_ylabel("Sales")
        ax1.set_facecolor('#F0F0F0')
        ax1.grid(True)

        figure.tight_layout()
        canvas.draw()

    def month_wise_subcategory_based(self, df, figure, canvas):
        figure.clear()

        bin_df = df.loc[df['Sub-Category'] == 'Binders']
        pap_df = df.loc[df['Sub-Category'] == 'Paper']
        pho_df = df.loc[df['Sub-Category'] == 'Phones']
        sto_df = df.loc[df['Sub-Category'] == 'Storage']
        fur_df = df.loc[df['Sub-Category'] == 'Furnishings']

        bin_monthly_sales = bin_df['Sales'].resample('M').sum()
        bin_monthly_sales = bin_monthly_sales.round(2)

        pap_monthly_sales = pap_df['Sales'].resample('M').sum()
        pap_monthly_sales = pap_monthly_sales.round(2)

        pho_monthly_sales = pho_df['Sales'].resample('M').sum()
        pho_monthly_sales = pho_monthly_sales.round(2)

        sto_monthly_sales = sto_df['Sales'].resample('M').sum()
        sto_monthly_sales = sto_monthly_sales.round(2)
```

```python
        fur_monthly_sales = fur_df['Sales'].resample('M').sum()
        fur_monthly_sales = fur_monthly_sales.round(2)

        ax1 = figure.add_subplot(1, 1, 1)
        ax1.plot(bin_monthly_sales.index.to_numpy(), bin_monthly_sales.values,
                color="red", marker='o', linestyle='-', label="Binders")
        ax1.plot(pap_monthly_sales.index.to_numpy(), pap_monthly_sales.values,
                color="blue", marker='o', linestyle='-', label="Paper")
        ax1.plot(pho_monthly_sales.index.to_numpy(), pho_monthly_sales.values,
                color="green", marker='o', linestyle='-', label="Phones")
        ax1.plot(sto_monthly_sales.index.to_numpy(), sto_monthly_sales.values,
                color="black", marker='o', linestyle='-', label="Storage")
        ax1.plot(fur_monthly_sales.index.to_numpy(), fur_monthly_sales.values,
                color="cyan", marker='o', linestyle='-', label="Furnishings")

        ax1.set_title("Sub-Category-Based Monthly Sales", fontsize=12)
        ax1.legend(facecolor='#E6E6FA', edgecolor='black')
        ax1.set_xlabel("Date")
        ax1.set_ylabel("Sales")
        ax1.set_facecolor('#F0F0F0')
        ax1.grid(True)

        figure.tight_layout()
        canvas.draw()

    def plot_month_wise_subcategory_based(self, df):
        win = tk.Toplevel()
        form3 = Form3(win)
        self.month_wise_subcategory_based(df, form3.figure1, form3.canvas1)

    def plot_month_wise_productname_based(self, df):
        win = tk.Toplevel()
        form3 = Form3(win)
        self.month_wise_productname_based(df, form3.figure1, form3.canvas1)

    def plot_month_wise_shipmode_based(self, df):
        win = tk.Toplevel()
        form3 = Form3(win)
        self.month_wise_shipmode_based(df, form3.figure1, form3.canvas1)

    def plot_month_wise_city_based(self, df):
        win = tk.Toplevel()
        form3 = Form3(win)
        self.month_wise_city_based(df, form3.figure1, form3.canvas1)

    def plot_month_wise_region_based(self, df):
        win = tk.Toplevel()
        form3 = Form3(win)
        self.month_wise_region_based(df, form3.figure1, form3.canvas1)

    def plot_month_wise_category_based(self, df):
        win = tk.Toplevel()
        form3 = Form3(win)
        self.month_wise_category_based(df, form3.figure1, form3.canvas1)

    def plot_month_wise_segment_based(self, df):
        win = tk.Toplevel()
        form3 = Form3(win)
        self.month_wise_segment_based(df, form3.figure1, form3.canvas1)

    def binds_month_wise(self, window, df, data_mean, data_ewm):
        window.month_wise.entryconfigure("Sales Quarter 1 and 2 Year 2018",
            command = lambda:self.plot_month_wise(df, "Sales", 2018, "Quarter", "Jan-March",
"April-June"))
```

```python
        window.month_wise.entryconfigure("Sales Quarter 3 and 4 Year 2018",
            command = lambda:self.plot_month_wise(df, "Sales", 2018, "Quarter", "July-Sept",
"Oct-Dec"))

        window.month_wise.entryconfigure("Sales Quarter 1 and 2 Year 2017",
            command = lambda:self.plot_month_wise(df, "Sales", 2017, "Quarter", "Jan-March",
"April-June"))

        window.month_wise.entryconfigure("Sales Quarter 3 and 4 Year 2017",
            command = lambda:self.plot_month_wise(df, "Sales", 2017, "Quarter", "July-Sept",
"Oct-Dec"))

        window.month_wise.entryconfigure("Sales Quarter 1 and 2 Year 2016",
            command = lambda:self.plot_month_wise(df, "Sales", 2016, "Quarter", "Jan-March",
"April-June"))

        window.month_wise.entryconfigure("Sales Quarter 3 and 4 Year 2016",
            command = lambda:self.plot_month_wise(df, "Sales", 2016, "Quarter", "July-Sept",
"Oct-Dec"))

        window.month_wise.entryconfigure("Sales Quarter 1 and 2 Year 2015",
            command = lambda:self.plot_month_wise(df, "Sales", 2015, "Quarter", "Jan-March",
"April-June"))

        window.month_wise.entryconfigure("Sales Quarter 3 and 4 Year 2015",
            command = lambda:self.plot_month_wise(df, "Sales", 2015, "Quarter", "July-Sept",
"Oct-Dec"))

        window.month_wise.entryconfigure("Sales Month 1 and 2 Year 2018",
            command = lambda:self.plot_month_wise(df, "Sales", 2018, "Month", "January",
"February"))

        window.month_wise.entryconfigure("Sales Month 3 and 4 Year 2017",
            command = lambda:self.plot_month_wise(df, "Sales", 2017, "Month", "March",
"April"))

        window.month_wise.entryconfigure("Sales Month 5 and 6 Year 2016",
            command = lambda:self.plot_month_wise(df, "Sales", 2016, "Month", "May", "June"))

        window.month_wise.entryconfigure("Sales Month 7 and 8 Year 2015",
            command = lambda:self.plot_month_wise(df, "Sales", 2015, "Month", "July",
"August"))

        window.month_wise.entryconfigure("Month-Wise Sales Mean and EWM",
            command = lambda:self.plot_month_wise_mean_ewm(data_mean, data_ewm))

        window.month_wise.entryconfigure("Sales by Month",
            command = lambda:self.plot_month_wise_by_month(data_mean, "Sales by Month"))

        window.month_wise.entryconfigure("Region-Based Monthly Sales",
            command = lambda:self.plot_month_wise_region_based(df))

        window.month_wise.entryconfigure("Category-Based Monthly Quantities",
            command = lambda:self.plot_month_wise_category_based(df))

        window.month_wise.entryconfigure("Segment-Based Monthly Sales",
            command = lambda:self.plot_month_wise_segment_based(df))

        window.month_wise.entryconfigure("City-Based Monthly Sales",
            command = lambda:self.plot_month_wise_city_based(df))

        window.month_wise.entryconfigure("Ship Mode-Based Monthly Sales",
            command = lambda:self.plot_month_wise_shipmode_based(df))
```

```
        window.month_wise.entryconfigure("Product Name-Based Monthly Sales",
            command = lambda:self.plot_month_wise_productname_based(df))

        window.month_wise.entryconfigure("Sub-Category-Based Monthly Sales",
            command = lambda:self.plot_month_wise_subcategory_based(df))

    def choose_month_wise(self, df, data_mean, data_ewm,
            data_norm, chosen, figure1, canvas1, figure2, canvas2):
        if chosen == "Sales Quarter 1 and 2 Year 2018":
            self.line_plot_month_wise(df, "Sales", 2018,
                "Quarter", "Jan-March", "April-June", figure1, canvas1)

        if chosen == "Sales Quarter 3 and 4 Year 2018":
            self.line_plot_month_wise(df, "Sales", 2018,
                "Quarter", "July-Sept", "Oct-Dec", figure2, canvas2)

        if chosen == "Sales Quarter 1 and 2 Year 2017":
            self.line_plot_month_wise(df, "Sales", 2017,
                "Quarter", "Jan-March", "April-June", figure1, canvas1)

        if chosen == "Sales Quarter 3 and 4 Year 2017":
            self.line_plot_month_wise(df, "Sales", 2017,
                "Quarter", "July-Sept", "Oct-Dec", figure2, canvas2)

        if chosen == "Sales Quarter 1 and 2 Year 2016":
            self.line_plot_month_wise(df, "Sales", 2016,
                "Quarter", "Jan-March", "April-June", figure1, canvas1)

        if chosen == "Sales Quarter 3 and 4 Year 2016":
            self.line_plot_month_wise(df, "Sales", 2016,
                "Quarter", "July-Sept", "Oct-Dec", figure2, canvas2)

        if chosen == "Sales Quarter 1 and 2 Year 2015":
            self.line_plot_month_wise(df, "Sales", 2015,
                "Quarter", "Jan-March", "April-June", figure1, canvas1)

        if chosen == "Sales Quarter 3 and 4 Year 2015":
            self.line_plot_month_wise(df, "Sales", 2015,
                "Quarter", "July-Sept", "Oct-Dec", figure2, canvas2)

        if chosen == "Month-Wise Sales Mean and EWM":
            self.line_plot_data_mean_ewm(data_mean, data_ewm, figure1, canvas1, "YEAR",
"SALES")

        if chosen == "Sales by Month":
            self.sns_plot_month(data_mean, "Sales by Month", figure2, canvas2)

        if chosen == "Region-Based Monthly Sales":
            self.month_wise_region_based(df, figure1, canvas1)

        if chosen == "Category-Based Monthly Quantities":
            self.month_wise_category_based(df, figure2, canvas2)

        if chosen == "Segment-Based Monthly Sales":
            self.month_wise_segment_based(df, figure1, canvas1)

        if chosen == "City-Based Monthly Sales":
            self.month_wise_city_based(df, figure2, canvas2)

        if chosen == "Ship Mode-Based Monthly Sales":
            self.month_wise_shipmode_based(df, figure1, canvas1)

        if chosen == "Product Name-Based Monthly Sales":
```

```python
            self.month_wise_productname_based(df, figure2, canvas2)

        if chosen == "Sub-Category-Based Monthly Sales":
            self.month_wise_subcategory_based(df, figure1, canvas1)

    def plot_rfm_distribution(self, df, var1, title=""):
        win = tk.Toplevel()
        form3 = Form3(win)
        win.title(title)
        self.plot_piechart(df, var1, form3.figure1, form3.canvas1, "Case Distribution of " +
var1)

    def plot_grouped_rfm_distribution(self, df, var1="", var2="", title1="", label=""):
        win = tk.Toplevel()
        form3 = Form3(win)
        win.title("Distribution of " + var2 + " by " + var1)
        sum_by_cat = df.groupby(var1)[var2].sum()
        self.plot_piechart_group(sum_by_cat, form3.figure1, form3.canvas1, title1, label)

    def month_wise_rfm_based(self, df, figure, canvas):
        figure.clear()

        top_df = df.loc[df['Customer Segment'] == 'Top Customer']
        high_df = df.loc[df['Customer Segment'] == 'High Value Customer']
        med_df = df.loc[df['Customer Segment'] == 'Medium Value Customer']
        low_df = df.loc[df['Customer Segment'] == 'Low Value Customer']
        lost_df = df.loc[df['Customer Segment'] == 'Lost Customer']

        top_monthly_sales = top_df['Sales'].resample('M').sum()
        top_monthly_sales = top_monthly_sales.round(2)

        high_monthly_sales = high_df['Sales'].resample('M').sum()
        high_monthly_sales = high_monthly_sales.round(2)

        med_monthly_sales = med_df['Sales'].resample('M').sum()
        med_monthly_sales = med_monthly_sales.round(2)

        low_monthly_sales = low_df['Sales'].resample('M').sum()
        low_monthly_sales = low_monthly_sales.round(2)

        lost_monthly_sales = lost_df['Sales'].resample('M').sum()
        lost_monthly_sales = lost_monthly_sales.round(2)

        ax1 = figure.add_subplot(1, 1, 1)
        ax1.plot(top_monthly_sales.index.to_numpy(), top_monthly_sales.values,
                color="red", marker='o', linestyle='-', label="Top Customer")
        ax1.plot(high_monthly_sales.index.to_numpy(), high_monthly_sales.values,
                color="blue", marker='o', linestyle='-', label="High Value Customer")
        ax1.plot(med_monthly_sales.index.to_numpy(), med_monthly_sales.values,
                color="green", marker='o', linestyle='-', label="Medium Value Customer")
        ax1.plot(low_monthly_sales.index.to_numpy(), low_monthly_sales.values,
                color="black", marker='o', linestyle='-', label="Low Value Customer")
        ax1.plot(lost_monthly_sales.index.to_numpy(), lost_monthly_sales.values,
                color="orange", marker='o', linestyle='-', label="Lost Customer")

        ax1.set_title("RFM-Based Monthly Sales", fontsize=12)
        ax1.legend(facecolor='#E6E6FA', edgecolor='black')
        ax1.set_xlabel("Date")
        ax1.set_ylabel("Sales")
        ax1.set_facecolor('#F0F0F0')
        ax1.grid(True)

        figure.tight_layout()
        canvas.draw()
```

```python
    def plot_month_wise_rfm_based(self, df):
        win = tk.Toplevel()
        form3 = Form3(win)
        self.month_wise_rfm_based(df, form3.figure1, form3.canvas1)

    def binds_rfm_distribution(self, window, df):
        window.rfm_analysis.entryconfigure("Customer Segment",
            command = lambda:self.plot_rfm_distribution(df, "Customer Segment",
                "The Case Distribution of Customer Segment"))

        window.rfm_analysis.entryconfigure("Sales by Customer Segment",
            command = lambda:self.plot_grouped_rfm_distribution(df, "Customer Segment",
                "Sales", "Sales Distribution by Customer Segment"))

        window.rfm_analysis.entryconfigure("Customer Segment by Year and Quarter",
            command = lambda:self.plot_categorized_distribution(df, "Year", "Customer
Segment",
                "Quarter", "Customer Segment",
                "The Case Distribution of Customer Segment by Year",
                "The Case Distribution of Customer Segment by Quarter"))

        window.rfm_analysis.entryconfigure("Customer Segment by Day and Month",
            command = lambda:self.plot_categorized_distribution(df, "Day", "Customer Segment",
                "Month", "Customer Segment",
                "The Case Distribution of Customer Segment by Day",
                "The Case Distribution of Customer Segment by Month"))

        window.rfm_analysis.entryconfigure("Customer Segment by Segment and Sub-Category",
            command = lambda:self.plot_categorized_distribution(df, "Segment", "Customer
Segment",
                "Sub-Category", "Customer Segment",
                "The Case Distribution of Customer Segment by Segment",
                "The Case Distribution of Customer Segment by Sub-Category"))

        window.rfm_analysis.entryconfigure("Customer Segment by Region and State",
            command = lambda:self.plot_categorized_distribution(df, "Region", "Customer
Segment",
                "State", "Customer Segment",
                "The Case Distribution of Customer Segment by Region",
                "The Case Distribution of Customer Segment by State"))

        window.rfm_analysis.entryconfigure("RFM-Based Monthly Sales",
            command = lambda:self.plot_month_wise_rfm_based(df))

    def choose_rfm_distribution(self, df, chosen, figure1, canvas1, figure2, canvas2):
        if chosen == "Customer Segment":
            self.plot_piechart(df, chosen, figure1, canvas1,
                "Case Distribution of " + chosen)

        if chosen == "Sales by Customer Segment":
            sum_by_cat = df.groupby("Customer Segment")["Sales"].sum()
            self.plot_piechart_group(sum_by_cat, figure2, canvas2, chosen)

        if chosen == "Customer Segment by Year and Quarter":
            self.dist_one_vs_another_plot(df, "Year", "Customer Segment",
                figure1, canvas1, "Customer Segment by Year")
            self.dist_one_vs_another_plot(df, "Quarter", "Customer Segment",
                figure2, canvas2, "Customer Segment by Quarter")

        if chosen == "Customer Segment by Day and Month":
            self.dist_one_vs_another_plot(df, "Day", "Customer Segment",
                figure1, canvas1, "Customer Segment by Day")
            self.dist_one_vs_another_plot(df, "Month", "Customer Segment",
```

```python
            figure2, canvas2, "Customer Segment by Month")

        if chosen == "Customer Segment by Segment and Sub-Category":
            self.dist_one_vs_another_plot(df, "Segment", "Customer Segment",
                figure1, canvas1, "Customer Segment by Segment")
            self.dist_one_vs_another_plot(df, "Sub-Category", "Customer Segment",
                figure2, canvas2, "Customer Segment by Sub-Category")

        if chosen == "Customer Segment by Region and State":
            self.dist_one_vs_another_plot(df, "Region", "Customer Segment",
                figure1, canvas1, "Customer Segment by Region")
            self.dist_one_vs_another_plot(df, "State", "Customer Segment",
                figure2, canvas2, "Customer Segment by State")

        if chosen == "RFM-Based Monthly Sales":
            self.month_wise_rfm_based(df, figure1, canvas1)

    def rf_importance(self, X, y, figure, canvas):
        result_rf = self.obj_data.feat_importance_rf(X, y)
        figure.clear()
        ax1 = figure.add_subplot(1,1,1)
        sns.set_color_codes("pastel")
        ax=sns.barplot(x = 'Values',y = 'Features', data=result_rf, color="orange", ax=ax1)
        ax1.set_title('Random Forest Features Importance', fontweight ="bold",fontsize=14)

        ax1.set_xlabel('Features Importance',  fontsize=10)
        ax1.set_ylabel('Feature Labels',  fontsize=10)
        # Set font for tick labels
        ax1.tick_params(axis='both', which='major', labelsize=10)
        ax1.tick_params(axis='both', which='minor', labelsize=10)
        ax1.set_facecolor('#F0F0F0')
        ax1.grid(True)
        figure.tight_layout()
        canvas.draw()

    def plot_rf_importance(self, X, y):
        win = tk.Toplevel()
        form3 = Form3(win)
        win.title("Random Forest Feature Importance")
        self.rf_importance(X, y, form3.figure1, form3.canvas1)

    def et_importance(self, X, y, figure, canvas):
        result_rf = self.obj_data.feat_importance_et(X, y)
        figure.clear()
        ax1 = figure.add_subplot(1,1,1)
        sns.set_color_codes("pastel")
        ax=sns.barplot(x = 'Values',y = 'Features', data=result_rf, color="Red", ax=ax1)
        ax1.set_title('Extra Trees Features Importance', fontweight ="bold",fontsize=14)

        ax1.set_xlabel('Features Importance',  fontsize=10)
        ax1.set_ylabel('Feature Labels',  fontsize=10)
        # Set font for tick labels
        ax1.tick_params(axis='both', which='major', labelsize=10)
        ax1.tick_params(axis='both', which='minor', labelsize=10)
        ax1.set_facecolor('#F0F0F0')
        ax1.grid(True)
        figure.tight_layout()
        canvas.draw()

    def plot_et_importance(self, X, y):
        win = tk.Toplevel()
        form3 = Form3(win)
        win.title("Extra Trees Feature Importance")
        self.et_importance(X, y, form3.figure1, form3.canvas1)
```

```python
def rfe_importance(self, X, y, figure, canvas):
    result_lg = self.obj_data.feat_importance_rfe(X, y)
    figure.clear()
    ax1 = figure.add_subplot(1,1,1)
    sns.set_color_codes("pastel")
    ax=sns.barplot(x = 'Ranking',y = 'Features', data=result_lg, color="green", ax=ax1)
    ax1.set_title('RFE Features Importance', fontweight ="bold",fontsize=14)

    ax1.set_xlabel('Features Importance',  fontsize=10)
    ax1.set_ylabel('Feature Labels',  fontsize=10)
    # Set font for tick labels
    ax1.tick_params(axis='both', which='major', labelsize=10)
    ax1.tick_params(axis='both', which='minor', labelsize=10)
    ax1.set_facecolor('#F0F0F0')
    ax1.grid(True)
    figure.tight_layout()
    canvas.draw()

def plot_rfe_importance(self, X, y):
    win = tk.Toplevel()
    form3 = Form3(win)
    win.title("RFE Feature Importance")
    self.rfe_importance(X, y, form3.figure1, form3.canvas1)

def corr_coeffs(self, df, figure, canvas):
    figure.clear()
    ax = figure.add_subplot(1,1,1)

    #correlation coefficient of every column with Summary column
    all_corr = df.corr().abs()['Churn'].sort_values(ascending = False)

    # Filters correlations greater than 0.01
    filtered_corr = all_corr[all_corr > 0.01]

    # Define a custom color palette (replace with your preferred colors)
    custom_palette = sns.color_palette("Set1", len(filtered_corr))
    filtered_corr.plot(kind='barh', ax=ax, color=custom_palette)
    ax.set_title("Correlation Coefficient of Features with Churn (Threshold > 0.01)",
fontsize = 9)
    ax.set_ylabel("Coefficient")
    ax.set_facecolor('#F0F0F0')

    # Set font for tick labels
    ax.tick_params(axis='both', which='major', labelsize=10)
    ax.tick_params(axis='both', which='minor', labelsize=10)

    ax.grid(True)
    figure.tight_layout()
    canvas.draw()

def plot_corr_coeffs(self, df):
    win = tk.Toplevel()
    form3 = Form3(win)
    win.title("Correlation Coefficients")
    self.corr_coeffs(df, form3.figure1, form3.canvas1)

def corr_mat(self, df, figure, canvas):
    figure.clear()
    ax = figure.add_subplot(1,1,1)
    categorical_columns = df.select_dtypes(include=['object', 'category']).columns
    df_removed = df.drop(columns=categorical_columns)
    corrdata = df_removed.corr()
```

```python
        annot_kws = {"size": 8, "color":"black"}
        # Filter correlations greater than 0.01
        mask = abs(corrdata) > 0.01
        filtered_corr = corrdata[mask]

        # Drops features that don't meet the threshold
        filtered_corr = filtered_corr.dropna(axis=0, how='all')
        filtered_corr = filtered_corr.dropna(axis=1, how='all')

        sns.heatmap(filtered_corr, ax = ax, lw=1, annot=True, cmap="Set1", annot_kws=annot_kws)
        ax.set_title('Correlation Matrix (Threshold > 0.01)', fontweight="bold", fontsize=12)

        # Set font for x and y labels
        ax.set_xlabel('Features', fontweight="bold", fontsize=12)
        ax.set_ylabel('Features', fontweight="bold", fontsize=12)

        # Set font for tick labels
        ax.tick_params(axis='both', which='major', labelsize=8)
        ax.tick_params(axis='both', which='minor', labelsize=8)

        figure.tight_layout()
        canvas.draw()

    def plot_corr_mat(self, df):
        win = tk.Toplevel()
        form3 = Form3(win)
        win.title("Correlation Matrix")
        self.corr_mat(df, form3.figure1, form3.canvas1)

    def binds_feat_importance(self, window, df, X, y):
        window.feat_eng.entryconfigure("Correlation Matrix",
            command = lambda:self.plot_corr_mat(df))

        window.feat_eng.entryconfigure("Correlation Coefficients",
            command = lambda:self.plot_corr_coeffs(df))

        window.feat_eng.entryconfigure("Random Forest Feature Importance",
            command = lambda:self.plot_rf_importance(X, y))

        window.feat_eng.entryconfigure("Extra Trees Feature Importance",
            command = lambda:self.plot_et_importance(X, y))

        window.feat_eng.entryconfigure("RFE Feature Importance",
            command = lambda:self.plot_rfe_importance(X, y))

    def scatter_train_test_regression(self, ytrain, ytest, predictions_train,
predictions_test, figure, canvas, label):
        # Visualizes the training set results in a scatter plot
        figure.clear()
        ax1 = figure.add_subplot(2, 1, 1)
        ax1.scatter(x=ytrain, y=predictions_train, color='red', label='Training Data')
        ax1.set_title('The actual versus predicted (Training set): ' + label,
fontweight='bold', fontsize=10)
        ax1.set_xlabel('Actual Train Set', fontsize=8)
        ax1.set_ylabel('Predicted Train Set', fontsize=8)
        ax1.plot([ytrain.min(), ytrain.max()], [ytrain.min(), ytrain.max()], 'b--',
linewidth=2, label='Perfect Prediction')
        ax1.grid(True)
        ax1.set_facecolor('#F0F0F0')
        ax1.legend(facecolor='#E6E6FA', edgecolor='black')

        ax2 = figure.add_subplot(2, 1, 2)
        ax2.scatter(x=ytest, y=predictions_test, color='red', label='Test Data')
```

```python
        ax2.set_title('The actual versus predicted (Test set): ' + label, fontweight='bold',
fontsize=10)
        ax2.set_xlabel('Actual Test Set', fontsize=8)
        ax2.set_ylabel('Predicted Test Set', fontsize=8)
        ax2.plot([ytest.min(), ytest.max()], [ytest.min(), ytest.max()], 'b--', linewidth=2,
label='Perfect Prediction')
        ax2.grid(True)
        ax2.set_facecolor('#F0F0F0')
        ax2.legend(facecolor='#E6E6FA', edgecolor='black')

        figure.tight_layout()
        canvas.draw()

    def lineplot_train_test_regression(self, ytrain, ytest, yval, yfinal,
            predictions_train, predictions_test, predictions_val, all_pred, figure, canvas,
label):
        figure.clear()
        ax1 = figure.add_subplot(4, 1, 1)
        ax1.plot(ytrain.index.to_numpy(), ytrain.to_numpy(), color="blue", linewidth=2,
linestyle="-", label='Actual')
        ax1.plot(ytrain.index.to_numpy(), predictions_train, color="red", linewidth=2,
linestyle="-", label='Predicted')
        ax1.set_title('Actual and Predicted Training Set: ' + label, fontsize=10)
        ax1.set_xlabel('Date', fontsize=8)
        ax1.set_ylabel("Sales", fontsize=8)
        ax1.legend(prop={'size': 8},facecolor='#E6E6FA', edgecolor='black')
        ax1.grid(True)
        ax1.set_facecolor('#F0F0F0')
        # Set font for tick labels
        ax1.tick_params(axis='both', which='major', labelsize=8)
        ax1.tick_params(axis='both', which='minor', labelsize=8)

        ax2 = figure.add_subplot(4, 1, 2)
        ax2.plot(ytest.index.to_numpy(), ytest.to_numpy(), color="blue", linewidth=2,
linestyle="-", label='Actual')
        ax2.plot(ytest.index.to_numpy(), predictions_test, color="red", linewidth=2,
linestyle="-", label='Predicted')
        ax2.set_title('Actual and Predicted Test Set: ' + label, fontsize=10)
        ax2.set_xlabel('Date', fontsize=8)
        ax2.set_ylabel("Sales", fontsize=8)
        ax2.legend(prop={'size': 8}, facecolor='#E6E6FA', edgecolor='black')
        ax2.grid(True)
        ax2.set_facecolor('#F0F0F0')
        # Set font for tick labels
        ax2.tick_params(axis='both', which='major', labelsize=8)
        ax2.tick_params(axis='both', which='minor', labelsize=8)

        ax3 = figure.add_subplot(4, 1, 3)
        ax3.plot(yval.index.to_numpy(), yval.to_numpy(), color="blue", linewidth=2,
linestyle="-", label='Actual')
        ax3.plot(yval.index.to_numpy(), predictions_val, color="red", linewidth=2, linestyle="-
", label='Predicted')
        ax3.set_title('Actual and Predicted Validation Set (90 days forecasting) ' + label,
fontsize=8)
        ax3.set_xlabel('Date', fontsize=8)
        ax3.set_ylabel("Sales", fontsize=8)
        ax3.legend(prop={'size': 8}, facecolor='#E6E6FA', edgecolor='black')
        ax3.grid(True)
        ax3.set_facecolor('#F0F0F0')
        # Set font for tick labels
        ax3.tick_params(axis='both', which='major', labelsize=8)
        ax3.tick_params(axis='both', which='minor', labelsize=8)

        ax4 = figure.add_subplot(4, 1, 4)
```

```python
        ax4.plot(yfinal.index.to_numpy(), yfinal.to_numpy(), color="blue", linewidth=2,
linestyle="-", label='Actual')
        ax4.plot(yfinal.index.to_numpy(), all_pred, color="red", linewidth=2, linestyle="-",
label='Predicted')
        ax4.set_title('Actual and Predicted All Set ' + label, fontsize=8)
        ax4.set_xlabel('Date', fontsize=8)
        ax4.set_ylabel("Adj Close", fontsize=8)
        ax4.legend(prop={'size': 8}, facecolor='#E6E6FA', edgecolor='black')
        ax4.grid(True)
        ax4.set_facecolor('#F0F0F0')
        # Set font for tick labels
        ax4.tick_params(axis='both', which='major', labelsize=8)
        ax4.tick_params(axis='both', which='minor', labelsize=8)

        figure.tight_layout()
        canvas.draw()

    def choose_plot_regression(self, chosen, X_final_reg, X_train_reg,
            X_test_reg, X_val_reg, y_final_reg, y_train_reg, y_test_reg, y_val_reg,
            figure1, canvas1, figure2, canvas2):
        if chosen == "Linear Regression":
            best_lin_reg = self.obj_reg.linear_regression(X_train_reg, y_train_reg)
            predictions_test, predictions_train, predictions_val, all_pred =
self.obj_reg.perform_regression(best_lin_reg, X_final_reg, y_final_reg,
            X_train_reg, y_train_reg, X_test_reg, y_test_reg, X_val_reg, y_val_reg, chosen)

            self.scatter_train_test_regression(y_train_reg, y_test_reg,
                predictions_train, predictions_test, figure1, canvas1, chosen)

            self.lineplot_train_test_regression(y_train_reg,
                y_test_reg, y_val_reg, y_final_reg, predictions_train, predictions_test,
predictions_val, all_pred,
                figure2, canvas2, chosen)

        if chosen == "RF Regression":
            best_rf_reg = self.obj_reg.rf_regression(X_train_reg, y_train_reg)
            predictions_test, predictions_train, predictions_val, all_pred =
self.obj_reg.perform_regression(best_rf_reg, X_final_reg, y_final_reg,
            X_train_reg, y_train_reg, X_test_reg, y_test_reg, X_val_reg, y_val_reg, chosen)

            self.scatter_train_test_regression(y_train_reg, y_test_reg,
                predictions_train, predictions_test, figure1, canvas1, chosen)

            self.lineplot_train_test_regression(y_train_reg,
                y_test_reg, y_val_reg, y_final_reg, predictions_train, predictions_test,
predictions_val, all_pred,
                figure2, canvas2, chosen)

        if chosen == "Decision Trees Regression":
            best_dt_reg = self.obj_reg.dt_regression(X_train_reg, y_train_reg)
            predictions_test, predictions_train, predictions_val, all_pred =
self.obj_reg.perform_regression(best_dt_reg, X_final_reg, y_final_reg,
            X_train_reg, y_train_reg, X_test_reg, y_test_reg, X_val_reg, y_val_reg, chosen)

            self.scatter_train_test_regression(y_train_reg, y_test_reg,
                predictions_train, predictions_test, figure1, canvas1, chosen)

            self.lineplot_train_test_regression(y_train_reg,
                y_test_reg, y_val_reg, y_final_reg, predictions_train, predictions_test,
predictions_val, all_pred,
                figure2, canvas2, chosen)

        if chosen == "Gradient Boosting Regression":
            best_gb_reg = self.obj_reg.gb_regression(X_train_reg, y_train_reg)
```

```python
            predictions_test, predictions_train, predictions_val, all_pred = 
self.obj_reg.perform_regression(best_gb_reg, X_final_reg, y_final_reg,
                X_train_reg, y_train_reg, X_test_reg, y_test_reg, X_val_reg, y_val_reg, chosen)

            self.scatter_train_test_regression(y_train_reg, y_test_reg,
                predictions_train, predictions_test, figure1, canvas1, chosen)

            self.lineplot_train_test_regression(y_train_reg,
                y_test_reg, y_val_reg, y_final_reg, predictions_train, predictions_test,
predictions_val, all_pred,
                figure2, canvas2, chosen)

        if chosen == "XGB Regression":
            best_xgb_reg = self.obj_reg.xgb_regression(X_train_reg, y_train_reg)
            predictions_test, predictions_train, predictions_val, all_pred = 
self.obj_reg.perform_regression(best_xgb_reg, X_final_reg, y_final_reg,
                X_train_reg, y_train_reg, X_test_reg, y_test_reg, X_val_reg, y_val_reg, chosen)

            self.scatter_train_test_regression(y_train_reg, y_test_reg,
                predictions_train, predictions_test, figure1, canvas1, chosen)

            self.lineplot_train_test_regression(y_train_reg,
                y_test_reg, y_val_reg, y_final_reg, predictions_train, predictions_test,
predictions_val, all_pred,
                figure2, canvas2, chosen)

        if chosen == "MLP Regression":
            best_mlp_reg = self.obj_reg.mlp_regression(X_train_reg, y_train_reg)
            predictions_test, predictions_train, predictions_val, all_pred = 
self.obj_reg.perform_regression(best_mlp_reg, X_final_reg, y_final_reg,
                X_train_reg, y_train_reg, X_test_reg, y_test_reg, X_val_reg, y_val_reg, chosen)

            self.scatter_train_test_regression(y_train_reg, y_test_reg,
                predictions_train, predictions_test, figure1, canvas1, chosen)

            self.lineplot_train_test_regression(y_train_reg,
                y_test_reg, y_val_reg, y_final_reg, predictions_train, predictions_test,
predictions_val, all_pred,
                figure2, canvas2, chosen)

        if chosen == "Lasso Regression":
            best_lasso_reg = self.obj_reg.lasso_regression(X_train_reg, y_train_reg)
            predictions_test, predictions_train, predictions_val, all_pred = 
self.obj_reg.perform_regression(best_lasso_reg, X_final_reg, y_final_reg,
                X_train_reg, y_train_reg, X_test_reg, y_test_reg, X_val_reg, y_val_reg, chosen)

            self.scatter_train_test_regression(y_train_reg, y_test_reg,
                predictions_train, predictions_test, figure1, canvas1, chosen)

            self.lineplot_train_test_regression(y_train_reg,
                y_test_reg, y_val_reg, y_final_reg, predictions_train, predictions_test,
predictions_val, all_pred,
                figure2, canvas2, chosen)

        if chosen == "Ridge Regression":
            best_ridge_reg = self.obj_reg.ridge_regression(X_train_reg, y_train_reg)
            predictions_test, predictions_train, predictions_val, all_pred = 
self.obj_reg.perform_regression(best_ridge_reg, X_final_reg, y_final_reg,
                X_train_reg, y_train_reg, X_test_reg, y_test_reg, X_val_reg, y_val_reg, chosen)

            self.scatter_train_test_regression(y_train_reg, y_test_reg,
                predictions_train, predictions_test, figure1, canvas1, chosen)

            self.lineplot_train_test_regression(y_train_reg,
```

```python
            y_test_reg, y_val_reg, y_final_reg, predictions_train, predictions_test,
predictions_val, all_pred,
            figure2, canvas2, chosen)

    if chosen == "AdaBoost Regression":
        best_ada_reg = self.obj_reg.adaboost_regression(X_train_reg, y_train_reg)
        predictions_test, predictions_train, predictions_val, all_pred =
self.obj_reg.perform_regression(best_ada_reg, X_final_reg, y_final_reg,
            X_train_reg, y_train_reg, X_test_reg, y_test_reg, X_val_reg, y_val_reg, chosen)

        self.scatter_train_test_regression(y_train_reg, y_test_reg,
            predictions_train, predictions_test, figure1, canvas1, chosen)

        self.lineplot_train_test_regression(y_train_reg,
            y_test_reg, y_val_reg, y_final_reg, predictions_train, predictions_test,
predictions_val, all_pred,
            figure2, canvas2, chosen)

    if chosen == "KNN Regression":
        best_knn_reg = self.obj_reg.knn_regression(X_train_reg, y_train_reg)
        predictions_test, predictions_train, predictions_val, all_pred =
self.obj_reg.perform_regression(best_knn_reg, X_final_reg, y_final_reg,
            X_train_reg, y_train_reg, X_test_reg, y_test_reg, X_val_reg, y_val_reg, chosen)

        self.scatter_train_test_regression(y_train_reg, y_test_reg,
            predictions_train, predictions_test, figure1, canvas1, chosen)

        self.lineplot_train_test_regression(y_train_reg,
            y_test_reg, y_val_reg, y_final_reg, predictions_train, predictions_test,
predictions_val, all_pred,
            figure2, canvas2, chosen)

def plot_cm_roc(self, model, X_test, y_test, ypred, name, figure, canvas):
    figure.clear()

    #Plots confusion matrix
    ax1 = figure.add_subplot(2,1,1)
    cm = confusion_matrix(y_test, ypred, )
    sns.heatmap(cm, annot=True, linewidth=2, linecolor='black', fmt='g', cmap="cool",
annot_kws={"size": 14}, ax=ax1)
    ax1.set_title('Confusion Matrix' + " of " + name, fontsize=12)
    ax1.set_xlabel('Y predict', fontsize=10)
    ax1.set_ylabel('Y test', fontsize=10)
    ax1.xaxis.set_ticklabels(['Churn = 1', 'Churn = 0'], fontsize=10)
    ax1.yaxis.set_ticklabels(['Churn = 1', 'Churn = 0'], fontsize=10)
    ax1.set_facecolor('#F0F0F0')

    #Plots ROC
    ax2 = figure.add_subplot(2,1,2)
    Y_pred_prob = model.predict_proba(X_test)
    Y_pred_prob = Y_pred_prob[:, 1]

    fpr, tpr, thresholds = roc_curve(y_test, Y_pred_prob)
    ax2.plot([0,1],[0,1], color='navy', linestyle='--', linewidth=3, label='Random Guess')
    ax2.plot(fpr,tpr, color='red', linewidth=3, label='ROC Curve')
    ax2.set_xlabel('False Positive Rate', fontsize=10)
    ax2.set_ylabel('True Positive Rate', fontsize=10)
    ax2.set_title('ROC Curve of ' + name , fontsize=12)
    ax2.grid(True)
    ax2.legend(facecolor='#E6E6FA', edgecolor='black')
    ax2.set_facecolor('#F0F0F0')

    figure.tight_layout()
    canvas.draw()
```

```python
#Plots true values versus predicted values diagram and learning curve
def plot_real_pred_val_learning_curve(self, model, X_train, y_train, X_test, y_test,
ypred, name, figure, canvas):
    figure.clear()

    #Plots true values versus predicted values diagram
    ax1 = figure.add_subplot(2,1,1)
    acc=accuracy_score(y_test, ypred)
    ax1.scatter(range(len(ypred)),ypred,color="blue", lw=2,label="Predicted")
    ax1.scatter(range(len(y_test)),
        y_test, color="red", label="Actual")
    ax1.set_title("Predicted Values vs True Values of " + name, fontsize=12)
    ax1.set_xlabel("Accuracy: " + str(round((acc*100),3)) + "%")
    ax1.legend(facecolor='#E6E6FA', edgecolor='black')
    ax1.grid(True, alpha=0.75, lw=1, ls='-.')
    ax1.set_facecolor('#F0F0F0')

    #Plots learning curve
    train_sizes=np.linspace(.1, 1.0, 5)
    train_sizes, train_scores, test_scores, fit_times, _ = learning_curve(model,
        X_train, y_train, cv=None, n_jobs=None, train_sizes=train_sizes, return_times=True)
    train_scores_mean = np.mean(train_scores, axis=1)
    train_scores_std = np.std(train_scores, axis=1)
    test_scores_mean = np.mean(test_scores, axis=1)
    test_scores_std = np.std(test_scores, axis=1)

    ax2 = figure.add_subplot(2,1,2)
    ax2.fill_between(train_sizes, train_scores_mean - train_scores_std,
        train_scores_mean + train_scores_std, alpha=0.1, color="r")
    ax2.fill_between(train_sizes, test_scores_mean - test_scores_std,
        test_scores_mean + test_scores_std, alpha=0.1, color="g")
    ax2.plot(train_sizes, train_scores_mean, 'o-',
        color="b", label="Training score")
    ax2.plot(train_sizes, test_scores_mean, 'o-',
        color="r", label="Cross-validation score")
    ax2.legend(loc="best", facecolor='#E6E6FA', edgecolor='black')
    ax2.set_title("Learning curve of " + name, fontsize=12)
    ax2.set_xlabel("fit_times")
    ax2.set_ylabel("Score")
    ax2.grid(True, alpha=0.75, lw=1, ls='-.')
    ax2.set_facecolor('#F0F0F0')

    figure.tight_layout()
    canvas.draw()

def choose_plot_ML(self, root, chosen, X_train, X_test, y_train, y_test, figure1, canvas1,
figure2, canvas2):
    if chosen == "Logistic Regression":
        best_model, y_pred = self.obj_ml.implement_LR(chosen, X_train, X_test, y_train,
y_test)

        #Plots confusion matrix and ROC
        self.plot_cm_roc(best_model, X_test, y_test, y_pred, chosen, figure1, canvas1)

        #Plots true values versus predicted values diagram and learning curve
        self.plot_real_pred_val_learning_curve(best_model, X_train, y_train,
            X_test, y_test, y_pred, chosen, figure2, canvas2)

        #Shows table of result
        df_lr = self.obj_data.read_dataset("results_LR.csv")
        self.shows_table(root, df_lr, 350, 750, "Y_test and Y_pred of Logistic
Regression")
```

```python
        if chosen == "Random Forest":
            best_model, y_pred = self.obj_ml.implement_RF(chosen, X_train, X_test, y_train,
y_test)

            #Plots confusion matrix and ROC
            self.plot_cm_roc(best_model, X_test, y_test, y_pred, chosen, figure1, canvas1)

            #Plots true values versus predicted values diagram and learning curve
            self.plot_real_pred_val_learning_curve(best_model, X_train, y_train,
                X_test, y_test, y_pred, chosen, figure2, canvas2)

            #Shows table of result
            df_rf = self.obj_data.read_dataset("results_RF.csv")
            self.shows_table(root, df_rf, 350, 750, "Y_test and Y_pred of Random Forest")

        if chosen == "K-Nearest Neighbors":
            best_model, y_pred = self.obj_ml.implement_KNN(chosen, X_train, X_test, y_train,
y_test)

            #Plots confusion matrix and ROC
            self.plot_cm_roc(best_model, X_test, y_test, y_pred, chosen, figure1, canvas1)

            #Plots true values versus predicted values diagram and learning curve
            self.plot_real_pred_val_learning_curve(best_model, X_train, y_train,
                X_test, y_test, y_pred, chosen, figure2, canvas2)

            #Shows table of result
            df_knn = self.obj_data.read_dataset("results_KNN.csv")
            self.shows_table(root, df_knn, 350, 750, "Y_test and Y_pred of KNN")

        if chosen == "Decision Trees":
            best_model, y_pred = self.obj_ml.implement_DT(chosen, X_train, X_test, y_train,
y_test)

            #Plots confusion matrix and ROC
            self.plot_cm_roc(best_model, X_test, y_test, y_pred, chosen, figure1, canvas1)

            #Plots true values versus predicted values diagram and learning curve
            self.plot_real_pred_val_learning_curve(best_model, X_train, y_train,
                X_test, y_test, y_pred, chosen, figure2, canvas2)

            #Shows table of result
            df_dt = self.obj_data.read_dataset("results_DT.csv")
            self.shows_table(root, df_dt, 350, 750, "Y_test and Y_pred of Decision Trees")

        if chosen == "Gradient Boosting":
            best_model, y_pred = self.obj_ml.implement_GB(chosen, X_train, X_test, y_train,
y_test)

            #Plots confusion matrix and ROC
            self.plot_cm_roc(best_model, X_test, y_test, y_pred, chosen, figure1, canvas1)

            #Plots true values versus predicted values diagram and learning curve
            self.plot_real_pred_val_learning_curve(best_model, X_train, y_train,
                X_test, y_test, y_pred, chosen, figure2, canvas2)

            #Shows table of result
            df_gb = self.obj_data.read_dataset("results_GB.csv")
            self.shows_table(root, df_gb, 350, 750, "Y_test and Y_pred of Gradient Boosting")

        if chosen == "Extreme Gradient Boosting":
            best_model, y_pred = self.obj_ml.implement_XGB(chosen, X_train, X_test, y_train,
y_test)
```

```python
        #Plots confusion matrix and ROC
        self.plot_cm_roc(best_model, X_test, y_test, y_pred, chosen, figure1, canvas1)

        #Plots true values versus predicted values diagram and learning curve
        self.plot_real_pred_val_learning_curve(best_model, X_train, y_train,
            X_test, y_test, y_pred, chosen, figure2, canvas2)

        #Shows table of result
        df_xgb = self.obj_data.read_dataset("results_XGB.csv")
        self.shows_table(root, df_xgb, 350, 750, "Y_test and Y_pred of Extreme Gradient
Boosting")

    if chosen == "Multi-Layer Perceptron":
        best_model, y_pred = self.obj_ml.implement_MLP(chosen, X_train, X_test, y_train,
y_test)

        #Plots confusion matrix and ROC
        self.plot_cm_roc(best_model, X_test, y_test, y_pred, chosen, figure1, canvas1)

        #Plots true values versus predicted values diagram and learning curve
        self.plot_real_pred_val_learning_curve(best_model, X_train, y_train,
            X_test, y_test, y_pred, chosen, figure2, canvas2)

        #Shows table of result
        df_mlp = self.obj_data.read_dataset("results_MLP.csv")
        self.shows_table(root, df_mlp, 350, 750, "Y_test and Y_pred of Multi-Layer
Perceptron")

    if chosen == "Support Vector Classifier":
        best_model, y_pred = self.obj_ml.implement_SVC(chosen, X_train, X_test, y_train,
y_test)

        #Plots confusion matrix and ROC
        self.plot_cm_roc(best_model, X_test, y_test, y_pred, chosen, figure1, canvas1)

        #Plots true values versus predicted values diagram and learning curve
        self.plot_real_pred_val_learning_curve(best_model, X_train, y_train,
            X_test, y_test, y_pred, chosen, figure2, canvas2)

        #Shows table of result
        df_svc = self.obj_data.read_dataset("results_SVC.csv")
        self.shows_table(root, df_svc, 350, 750, "Y_test and Y_pred of Support Vector
Classifier")

    if chosen == "AdaBoost":
        best_model, y_pred = self.obj_ml.implement_ADA(chosen, X_train, X_test, y_train,
y_test)

        #Plots confusion matrix and ROC
        self.plot_cm_roc(best_model, X_test, y_test, y_pred, chosen, figure1, canvas1)

        #Plots true values versus predicted values diagram and learning curve
        self.plot_real_pred_val_learning_curve(best_model, X_train, y_train,
            X_test, y_test, y_pred, chosen, figure2, canvas2)

        #Shows table of result
        df_ada = self.obj_data.read_dataset("results_ADA.csv")
        self.shows_table(root, df_ada, 350, 750, "Y_test and Y_pred of AdaBoost
Classifier")
```

Bibliography

Vivian Siahaan and Rismon Hasiholan Sianipar. *TKINTER, DATA SCIENCE, AND MACHINE LEARNING*. North Sumatera: Balige Publishing, 2023.

Vivian Siahaan and Rismon Hasiholan Sianipar. *DATA VISUALIZATION, TIME-SERIES FORECASTING, AND PREDICTION USING MACHINE LEARNING WITH TKINTER*. North Sumatera: Balige Publishing, 2023.

Vivian Siahaan and Rismon Hasiholan Sianipar. *TIME-SERIES WEATHER FORECASTING AND PREDICTION USING MACHINE LEARNING WITH TKINTER*. North Sumatera: Balige Publishing, 2023.

9 798862 262933